Inclusive Pedagogy for English Language Learners

A Handbook of Research-Informed Practices

Inclusive Pedagogy for English Language Learners

A Handbook of Research-Informed Practices

Edited by

Lorrie Stoops Verplaetse
Southern Connecticut State University
New Haven

Naomi Migliacci
Southern Connecticut State University
New Haven

LEA Lawrence Erlbaum Associates
Taylor & Francis Group

New York   London

Lawrence Erlbaum Associates
Taylor & Francis Group
270 Madison Avenue
New York, NY 10016

Lawrence Erlbaum Associates
Taylor & Francis Group
2 Park Square
Milton Park, Abingdon
Oxon OX14 4RN

© 2008 by Taylor & Francis Group, LLC
Lawrence Erlbaum Associates is an imprint of Taylor & Francis Group, an Informa business

Printed in the United States of America on acid-free paper
10 9 8 7 6 5 4 3 2 1

International Standard Book Number-13: 978-0-8058-5720-7 (Softcover) 978-0-8058-5719-1 (Hardcover)

Library of Congress Cataloging-in-Publication Data

Verplaetse, Lorrie Stoops.
   Inclusive pedagogy for English language learners : a handbook of research-informed practices / Lorrie Stoops Verplaetse and Naomi Migliacci.
       p. cm.
   Includes bibliographical references and index.
   ISBN-13: 978-0-8058-5720-7 (alk. paper) 1. English language--Study and teaching (Elementary)--Foreign speakers. 2. English language--Study and teaching (Secondary)--Foreign speakers. 3. Language and languages--Study and teaching. I. Migliacci, Naomi. II. Title.

PE1128.A2V47 2008
372.65'21--dc22   2007017994

Visit the Taylor & Francis Web site at
http://www.taylorandfrancis.com

Contents

Preface   ix

Acknowledgments   xiii

I: In the Elementary Classroom

Chapter 1
  Inclusive Pedagogy: An Introduction   3
  LORRIE STOOPS VERPLAETSE AND NAOMI MIGLIACCI

Chapter 2
  A Scaffolded Approach to Learning to Write   15
  MARIA ESTELA BRISK, DEBORAH A. HORAN, AND ELIZABETH MACDONALD

Chapter 3
  Transforming Standard Practices to Serve the Social and Academic Learning
  of English Language Learners   33
  JERRI WILLETT, RUTH HARMAN, ANDREA HOGAN, MARIA EUGENIA LOZANO,
  AND JOANNE RUBECK

Chapter 4
  Pedagogical Thinking and Teacher Talk in a First-Grade ELL Classroom   55
  JANE YEDLIN

Chapter 5
  Integrating Test Tasks into Everyday Classroom Activities:
  A Coach's Report on Collaborative Action Research Teams   79
  ROBERT C. PARKER

II: In the Secondary Classroom

Chapter 6
  The Development of Teacher Expertise to Work with Adolescent
  English Learners: A Model and a Few Priorities   103
  AÍDA WALQUI

Chapter 7
  Making Mainstream Content Comprehensible Through Sheltered Instruction 127
  LORRIE STOOPS VERPLAETSE AND NAOMI MIGLIACCI

Chapter 8
  Developing Academic Language Through an Abundance of Interaction 167
  LORRIE STOOPS VERPLAETSE

Chapter 9
  Through and Beyond High School: Academic Challenges and
  Opportunities for College-Bound Immigrant Youth   181
  LINDA HARKLAU

III: School and Community Collaboration

Chapter 10
  Community-Based Organizations: Partnerships for Student Success   197
  ANTHONY J. COLÓN

Chapter 11
  High School and University Partnerships: The Strengths and
  Challenges for ELLs   211
  NAOMI MIGLIACCI

Chapter 12
  Activist Organization and Parental Engagement in Philadelphia's Chinatown 225
  DEBORAH WEI

IV: School and District Reform

Chapter 13
  Successful Schooling for ELLs: Principles for Building Responsive
  Learning Environments   245
  MARIA COADY, EDMUND T. HAMANN, MARGARET HARRINGTON,
  MARIA PACHECO, SAMBOEN PHO, AND JANE YEDLIN

Chapter 14
  Bilingual Education for All Students: Still Standing After All These Years 257
  TOMÁS Z. MIRANDA

Chapter 15
    Is It Language, or Is It Special Needs? Appropriately Diagnosing
    English Language Learners Having Achievement Difficulties   277
    GEORGE P. DE GEORGE

Chapter 16
    Meeting the Needs of ELLs: Acknowledging the Schism Between
    ESL/Bilingual and Mainstream Teachers and Illustrating That
    Problem's Remedy   305
    EDMUND T. HAMANN

Chapter 17
    Inclusive Pedagogy in a Mandate-Driven Climate   317
    NAOMI MIGLIACCI AND LORRIE STOOPS VERPLAETSE

About the Authors   343

Index   347

Preface

The purpose of this volume is to provide current and future educators and educational leaders sound recommendations concerning research-informed best practices for English language learners (ELLs) integrated into the K–12 public school system. We have consulted leading researchers, teacher educators, and expert practitioners who have contributed their recommendations to this volume.

By the year 2030, it is conservatively projected that 40% of all public school children will be English language learners (Thomas & Collier, 2002). For those of us working in educational consulting and teacher education, it has become most apparent that educators are eager for information about how to best work with this growing student population. Current state and federal mandates require that educators link their practices to sound research results. This book will help educators define, select, and defend realistic educational practices that include and serve well their English language learning student populations.

Our Audience

Our targeted audience is current and future educational leaders. By the term *educational leaders* we mean current and future educational administrators and any educators who have a keen interest in school reform, whether at the classroom, school, or district level. We anticipate that the book will be useful in educational leadership programs, particularly the foundation courses and courses dealing with issues of diversity and discussions of how best to serve all students. Reviewer response to the book, however, has indicated that the book is also of value to all educators, staff developers, policy makers, parents, and community groups: to anyone interested in the successful education of linguistically and culturally diverse students. We assume that the audience does have experience in teaching and therefore suggest to those who may choose to use the book for preservice teacher preparation that they accompany the chapters with appropriate explanations of pedagogical concepts where necessary. Although a basic understanding of educational practices is assumed as a prerequisite for this text, a critical and distinctive feature of this volume is that no prerequisites in applied linguistics or second language development are required to understand the material in this book.

Currently, many education courses and their textbooks address the topic of educating linguistic minority students as one of a number of topics to be covered in a course. The topic is often covered in a single text chapter or as an add on to the semester's course. Given the growing number of ELL students, the topic is too complex and too important to address in such a brief fashion. This text covers the topic broadly yet thoroughly.

Although the book is primarily descriptive, not quantitative, it contains the rigorous element of reported research. However, this research is written in comprehensible terminology. Unlike the traditional applied linguistic research paper—which contains a literature review, methodology section, research findings and discussion, with a possible brief section on applied implications—the chapters for this volume are quite the opposite of this. The major portion of each chapter consists of a thorough discussion of the specific recommended practices, followed by a description of the research that supports these recommended practices. The research description is brief, written in laypersons' terminology, and stripped of the register particular to applied linguistics, with an accompanying bibliography, so that readers who wish to read about the research in technical detail have access to those publications.

Features

The volume comprises four sections:

    I. In the Elementary Classroom
    II. In the Secondary Classroom
   III. School and Community Collaboration
   IV. School and District Reform

A unique feature of the book is the variety of voices represented. You will find a combination of reporting styles ranging from scholarly writings by university-based teams to first-person writings of a classroom observer to recorded interviews with the editors. We've intentionally honored the voices of the writers by allowing the style used in the development of each chapter to stand on its own.

In an introduction, the coeditors provide the rationale for the book and clarify a number of popular myths regarding the education of linguistic minority students, thus providing a sound common framework for the ensuing chapters. They also provide a short glossary of terms and commonly used acronyms.

Section I, "In the Elementary Classroom," contains four chapters focusing on educational practices that engage all learners, to include the English language learners, with special attention to literacy development.

- In Chapter 2, Maria Brisk and coauthors describe how one urban collaborative group of K–5 teachers and researchers joined together to implement teaching strategies that target uncovered writing and language needs. A rhetorical approach that supports the planning of writing, modeling authentic writing procedures, and peer dialogue is detailed.
- In Chapter 3, Jerri Willett and coauthors focus on the productive use of routines in the heterogeneous classroom, recognizing the importance of routines for a variety of purposes, including providing opportunities for academic learning, language development, and socialization. The chapter follows two teachers' efforts as they work to make existing classroom routines more productive for the ELLs in their classrooms.

- In Chapter 4, Jane Yedlin identifies and describes instructional strategies used by skillful teachers to facilitate ELLs' listening comprehension, speaking abilities, and literacy development. Using transcripts of teacher talk and samples of student writing, she illustrates the effective strategies in practice.
- In Chapter 5, Bob Parker describes how three collaborative action research (CAR) teams experimented with integrating the use of the test tasks, formats, and procedures of the New York City and New York State mandated tests into everyday classroom activities. The chapter details the results of the project and gives other educators ideas on how to use CAR teams in the elementary grades as well as specific examples on how to align curriculum with required assessments and instructional practices for English language learners.

Section II, "In the Secondary Classroom," addresses the unique challenges facing teachers and adolescent language learners mainstreamed in content classroom.

- In Chapter 6, Aída Walqui identifies 10 priorities to consider when designing instruction for secondary immigrant students. She then proposes a model of teachers' understanding, which can serve as a guide for those planning professional development.
- In Chapter 7, Lorrie Verplaetse and Naomi Migliacci discuss sheltered instruction as a means to make complex academic content comprehensible to language learning students who do not yet have the English language proficiency needed to make sense of classroom talk and written text produced in English. In this chapter, they share many curriculum modifications that have been developed by mainstream content teachers in the field who have been trained in sheltered instruction practices.
- In Chapter 8, Lorrie Verplaetse emphasizes the importance of student interaction—oral and written—for content learning, student's personal development, and academic language development. The chapter outlines six strategies to provide an abundance of opportunities for students to interact with the content, with the teacher, and with each other.
- In Chapter 9, Linda Harklau provides specific recommendations for preparing multilingual students for college entry and college-level work, based on a compilation of her own research and related studies.

Section III, "School and Community Collaboration," provides insight into what schools might and must do to create the types of community linkages necessary if schools are to genuinely reflect the communities where they live and serve.

- In Chapter 10, an interview with then vice president of the Center for Community Educational Excellence and the National Council of LaRaza Anthony Colón explores the importance of establishing real connections between schools and the community based organizations that serve the community.
- In Chapter 11, Naomi Migliacci focuses on the factors that contributed to the successful link between a university and a high school and provides ideas for how other schools can collaborate with institutes of higher education. In addition, the chapter looks at practices related to including ELLs in themed academies and factors that contribute to their success as they relate to the link between the high school and the university.
- In Chapter 12, an interview with the School District of Philadelphia's lead academic coach for Asian Pacific American Studies, Deborah Wei, discusses how schools can

more effectively create successful and meaningful linkages with the communities in which their students live.

Section IV, "School and District Reform," explores the question of what entire schools and systems must do to educate and graduate all of their students, recognizing that the English language learning student population is not just the fastest growing student population of students but also is a population of students that has the potential to provide unique learning opportunities to mainstream students.

- In Chapter 13, we reprint a chapter from the Educational Alliance at Brown University's recently published handbook, "Claiming Opportunities," which outlines nine principles for building responsive learning environments in the design of successful schooling for English language learners.
- In Chapter 14, Tomás Miranda provides a discussion of bilingual education and its benefits for all students at a time when bilingual education is under attack. Following a discussion of six principles for effective practice, the chapter presents four practical program models that reflect these principles.
- In Chapter 15, George de George presents a detailed discussion concerning how to diagnose appropriately whether English language learners, who are experiencing achievement difficulties, are suffering from special needs or are simply exhibiting signs of stages of language development. In this chapter, he provides a guide of recommended questions for the student and the student's teachers and family.
- In Chapter 16, through the study of two school districts in two sections of the United States, each of which was facing an exceptionally rapid growth of ELLs, Edmund Hamann discusses how the mainstream teachers and the bilingual and English as a second language teachers became disenfranchised from each other and how the systems successfully worked to bridge this schism. The result was that the schools' reconciliation strategies led to all educators collaborating on behalf of the ELLs.

Finally, in a closing chapter, Migliacci and Verplaetse synthesize the recommendations of the previous chapters, identifying common themes. They also discuss how these best inclusive pedagogical practices can be accomplished in the current climate of high-stakes testing and legislative mandates, leading us to a new set of myths to consider.

Acknowledgments

The ongoing preparation of this collection is an excellent example of the importance of collaboration and interaction to reach authentic goals. So many people have been involved in its development, and we are grateful to each and every one. First of all, we wish to acknowledge and thank the chapter contributors, whose insights bring such richness to this volume. Second, we want to acknowledge and thank all the educators who allowed us into their schools and classrooms for the purpose of future learning. It takes a courageous person to open up his or her classrooms to the scrutiny of research; we are most indebted to each of you.

We also thank our reviewers: those who anonymously screened an earlier version and Nancy L. Commins and Denise Wolk for their thorough reviews of the full manuscript and subsequent helpful comments and revision suggestions. Moreover, our most sincere gratitude goes to Naomi Silverman of Lawrence Erlbaum for her constant support, insight, and gentle guidance throughout this arduous process; we are deeply indebted.

Partial funding for preparation of this volume has been provided by a Training for All Teachers grant through the U.S. Department of Education, Office of English Language Acquisition, #T195B010094. We are most grateful to our Training for All Teachers graduate assistants: Carola Osses, Jennifer O'Brien, Kathleen Doyle, and Talina Tapia for their excellent work in all phases of this project.

In addition, we each have our own group of folks we would like to thank.

From Lorrie: I want to thank Bob and Marilyn Stoops, who gave me at an early age a deep love for learning and a value for hard, honest labor. They continue to be so supportive of my work, for which I am most grateful. I also want to thank Christopher Verplaetse, my son, who is such a wonderful listener: I so often appreciate his thoughtful feedback. And a special thanks to my friends and colleagues Terese, Carol, Elena, and Dan, who have listened to far too many tedious discussions as I wrestled with the nitty-gritty process of putting this book together. Last, to my dear Emily, who has faithfully, though at times impatiently, stayed at my side as I worked seemingly endlessly on this project: I promise to take you out for many more walks now that this task is complete.

From Naomi: I want to thank my family, educators all, especially Hector and Helen Migliacci, as well as siblings Mimi, Rachel, Hector B., and Nick, who continue to spur me on to action in educational issues and to fight for justice for those who might otherwise go unheard. I appreciate all our passionate conversations on how to create meaningful educational environments and for all the ideas you have given me. I want to thank all my friends who have heard the detailed progress of this book and have been so supportive of me throughout this process. You are so appreciated. I wish to thank my colleague, Lorrie, for her insight, support, and guidance. Special thanks to Aria and Bear, who have managed to leave pawprints on all my documents. Finally, thanks to Misha, my faithful friend, who in addition to *sit* and *stay* has learned *wait* when I'm in the middle of writing, and somehow understands that when I sit at the computer, it just means a very, very long nap. Good dog.

Reference

Thomas, W.P., & Collier, V.P. (2002). A national study of school effectiveness for language minority students' long-term academic achievement, Final report: Project 1.1. Santa Cruz: University of California, Center for Research on Education, Diversity, and Excellence.

I: In the Elementary Classroom

Editor's Introduction

Although this section addresses elementary classroom instruction, it is not just for classroom teachers. The changes that are needed in the elementary classrooms to successfully educate our English language learners (ELLs) must be understood and supported by administrators, staff developers, student service personnel, policy makers, and teacher educators.

A false popular assumption about elementary education and ELLs is that little children are like sponges and can pick up English quickly, with little effort. Mistakenly, it is assumed that ELL children can rapidly assimilate into the classroom practices. But let us consider this idea for a moment.

Native-English-speaking children have been hearing English for five years and speaking English for three years prior to arriving at school. By the time they arrive at school they have a full repertoire of the English grammar system and its sound system. Depending on the use of language in their homes, they also have an arsenal of vocabulary; some possess a large school vocabulary; others have a smaller school vocabulary. Some students may come to the classroom speaking a dialect of English, such as inner-city dialects, black English vernacular, or a unique rural dialect. But all of the English-speaking students, unique dialect or not, can listen to a teacher give a direction or read a story, and they can understand that direction or story because they understand English.

The goal of the first three years of U.S. schooling is to introduce children to literacy and numeracy. Children learn to read and write, to express their thoughts in predictable, organized ways, and to reason and calculate with numbers. The primary tool they and their teachers use to attain these learning goals is the English language. English is the medium of instruction. Teachers talk in English, read books in English, explain manipulatives in English, provide corrective feedback in English, question in English, and explore the sounds of letters with English words.

Enter the ELL children who do not yet possess facility in English. Though they are working to attain an understanding of the English language, they are missing fundamentally important lessons about literacy and numeracy, lost to them because of their inability to comprehend the medium of instruction. Though they pick up their conversational skills in English within the first two years, many predictably fall behind in their fundamental literacy skills and the development of academic language skills. This problem

1

escalates by the fourth grade, when the use of literacy becomes a primary learning tool for other school content. As the ELLs are learning early levels of English, the native-English-speaking students are not stagnant in their growth of English vocabulary, literacy, and numeracy. Their language abilities and academic skills are steadily developing. So, for the ELL students to ever catch up with their classmates, they must develop their English and academic skills at a rate even faster than their native-English-speaking peers.

Section I contains stories about a variety of elementary teachers who have made a conscious attempt to address the reading and writing skills of English language learners. It is important to notice how the different authors come to the topic from different perspectives—teachers, teacher trainers, and teacher coaches—and how these authors vary in their approach to their own work, to their profession, and to the students.

In Chapter 2, Brisk, Horan, and MacDonald introduce us to fifth-grade mainstream teachers who make use of a particular writing curriculum titled "The Rhetorical Approach." These teachers are observed inserting scaffolding sidesteps into this approach that are specifically designed to meet the unique needs of the ELLs in the classroom.

In Chapter 3, Willett, Harman, Hogan, Lozano, and Rubeck describe how two teachers, using the school's second- and fifth-grade buddy reading routine, create a combined curriculum that resulted in increased literacy skills and improved behavior around bothersome issues at both grade levels. Key features of this curriculum include ample opportunities for social interaction, interweaving of social worlds and academic worlds, use of everyday routines to scaffold an integrated and purposeful unit, use of authentic texts and audiences, and the explicit teaching of genre and language features within a meaningful context.

In Chapter 4, we delight in Yedlin's detailed description of a highly engaged and engaging kindergarten English as a second language (ESL) teacher, who has a historically significant success rate with her pupils. We learn from Yedlin's observations how an effective teacher makes language come alive for ELLs at varying levels and how she refuses to water down language but instead enriches language experiences with authentic, varied vocabulary accompanied by gestures and visuals to ensure comprehensibility.

Finally, in Chapter 5, Parker describes the everyday classroom activities of elementary teachers in New York City who, through the use of collaborative action research, explore how to infuse test-taking tasks into the everyday classroom curriculum. This chapter brings new meaning to the idea of *teaching to the test,* for it shows how effectively teachers can indeed align curriculum with required state-mandated assessments and instructional practices for ELLs.

It is worthy of note that in three of the four chapters, the teachers make their discoveries about effective ELL pedagogy while engaged in ongoing professional development. In all three cases, the nature of the professional development allowed the teachers to analyze their own current practices and, through collaborative inquiry, to explore how they might reform their practices to better meet the needs of their ELL students.

CHAPTER 1

Inclusive Pedagogy: An Introduction

LORRIE STOOPS VERPLAETSE AND NAOMI MIGLIACCI

This collection was born out of three events, each of which occurred within weeks of each other. The first was the spring 2003 research symposium sponsored by the Annenberg Institute for School Reform and the Education Alliance and the Northeast and Islands Regional Laboratory at Brown University, at which researchers and educators from throughout the country gathered to discuss how U.S. school systems might best serve English language learners (ELLs). One overriding lesson emerged during this symposium: Researchers speak to each other through publications and professional conferences, but far too frequently their messages are not translated into accessible language and disseminated to the practicing teacher and educational administrator. As one educator stated at the symposium, "Speak to me in language that I can understand."

The second event occurred during a 13-week study circle for K–12 administrators on "Educating our ELLs," sponsored by Southern Connecticut State University's Training for All Teachers program, funded by a U.S. Department of Education Title VII grant. At that time, Lorrie Verplaetse, the director of the program, was asked by one of the participants what journal he might read to gain ongoing insight into how to best educate English language learners. She was unable to make a recommendation, as most of the substantive publications on this topic that she could think of speak to an audience educated in applied linguistics.

The third event occurred during a "Training for All Teachers Program" teacher training workshop, at which a staff developer asked if we trainers could identify what specific research supports each of the instructional strategies we were recommending. She needed this information for a state report required by the federal government to ensure that their educational practices were supported by scientifically based research.

In each case, educators were asking for recommendations of what practices better serve English language learning students. They also wanted clear linkages to research as to why these practices are recommended. They wanted the *whats* and *whys* to be explained in nontechnical language so that the information could be understood by educators outside of the field of applied linguistics. That is the purpose of this volume: to recommend the best research-informed practices for English language learners so that schools might educate all their students successfully.

Who Is the English Language Learner?

One of the reasons that learning about effective inclusive pedagogy is so complicated is because the definition of an English language learner is so varied. An ELL student may be a recent arrival from another country, with little to no English ability. This recent arrival may be well educated and literate in another language. On the other hand, this new arrival may be completely illiterate or may have a first language that does not have a written form or may be a child of war, having experienced years of interrupted schooling.

Other ELL students may have been born in the United States to parents who speak a language other than English. These ELL children would have been introduced to English on the street and in television and may have a range of English spoken skills by the time they enter kindergarten. Some of these ELL students may sound like they have strong conversational skills, because as young children they have an ear for the sound of new languages. But their oral fluency may be deceptive as to the actual proficiency levels of English they may possess. Still other ELL students in the third grade and on may possess enough oral conversational skills that teachers might not even recognize them as ELL students, yet they may still need attention to develop the literacy skills and academic language skills needed to succeed in grade 4 and beyond.

Some ELL students have learning disabilities. Others are academically gifted. But they all have one thing in common: They need to develop the academic English skills necessary to succeed in U.S. public schools.

Numbers Tell It All

Early 2006 reports from the U.S. Department of Education, Office of English Language Acquisition (http://www.ed.gov/about/offices/list/oela/index.html), claim that the enrollment of limited English proficient students over the 10 years from 1993–94 to 2003–04 has increased 65.06%. Here are the numbers: In the 2003–04 school year, the total student population in grades K–12 was 49,619,117, with a growth of 9.19% in total student population over the last 10 years. In the same year, the number of English language learners enrolled was 5,014,437, representing that 65.06% growth over those 10 years. California, Arizona, Texas, Florida, Illinois, and New York have the highest numbers of ELLs, with more than 100,000 in each of those states; however, more than twice as many of the states mentioned have a high density of ELLs enrolled in their schools with more than 10% of the population comprising limited English proficient students. Over the past three years 19 states have reported a more than 50% increase in their ELL enrollments. This growth is expected to double over the next 20 years. In a conservative estimate reported by U.S. secretary of education Margaret Spellings (Spellings, 2005) ELLs will represent one out of every four students by 2025. Researchers (Thomas & Collier, 2002) in the field also claiming a conservative estimate project that 40% of all U.S. public school children by 2030 will be ELLs. As of this writing, the U.S. Department of Education claims that approximately one in nine students across the United States is an English language learner. More importantly, though, the growth over the last 10 years has occurred in states that have not traditionally served large populations of ELLs, mostly across the Midwest and southern states. This means that teachers have not been prepared to teach ELLs and that schools and districts are scrambling to meet the needs of these students with little or no training.

There is great diversity among the ELLs enrolled in U.S. schools. Of the more than five million students classified as limited English proficient (LEP), more than 72% are Spanish speaking. Diversity among these students is great as is the diversity among the over 27% who come from Africa, Asia, Eastern Europe, Russia, and other countries. However, about one million drop out of school yearly, with Hispanic students four times more likely to quit. About half of all minority students do not finish high school. Data from the 2000 census revealed that of all minority subgroups, the students least likely to finish high school were immigrant students, failing at a rate of 66% (Garcia, 1994, 1998). According to the U.S. government, these students will earn $260,000 less over their lifetime and will pay $60,000 less in taxes. Every year this means $192 billion in lost wages, lost taxes, and lost productivity (Spellings, 2005).

It is no wonder, however, that ELLs are dropping out of school in such disproportionate numbers to their English-speaking, mainstream counterparts. As mentioned, ELLs are placed in classrooms all day long with teachers who do not know how to raise the academic achievement of these students. A survey of teachers in the 1999–00 school year (U.S. Department of Education, 2002) found that of the 2,984,981 teachers in the United States, 41.2% had LEP students in their classrooms. Of course, this number has increased since the time of the survey by approximately 20%. Of the teachers with LEP students in their classrooms 12.5% had eight or more hours of training over the previous three years on how to teach ELLs. The survey shows states that have experienced the sudden growth mentioned previously with only about 1 or 2% of teachers with training in how to work with ELLs. Recently, a few states require current teachers or preservice teachers to take a course or some training on working with this population. This can mean a 3- or 1.5-credit college course or a one-day teacher in-service during scheduled professional development time. Much of the training or professional development is not ongoing and sustained in a meaningful way to meet the needs of the growing and diversified ELL population.

Other chapters in this book also provide demographic data report numbers somewhat different from those reported in this chapter because of differences in the sources cited. But despite the variance in the numbers, the trends are consistent and quite clear. These numbers and trends reveal that linguistic minority students are the fastest growing student population. They are the population with the highest drop-out rate. And most teachers, administrators, and student service personnel are not sufficiently trained in how to best work with English language learners.

Common Misconceptions Clarified

Most people untrained in issues of second-language development operate with a set of common misconceptions about English language learners. In the field, we commonly speak about the *myths* related to English as a second language (ESL) and second-language learning. Several authors have written about these myths. Two, in particular, well worth reading are (1) Barry McLaughlin's (1992) *Myths and Misconceptions about Second Language Learning: What Every Teacher Needs to Unlearn*; and (2) TESOL, Inc.'s "Myths about Second Language Learning," on page 3 of their book *ESL Standards for Pre-K–12 Students* (1997). In this chapter section, having synthesized, extracted, and expanded the most salient of the misconceptions discussed in the two aforementioned texts, we present a discussion around four myths in an attempt to clarify some of these commonly misunderstood ideas, thus providing the readers of the book a common underlying framework.

Myth #1: Once an English language learner has gained a fluent oral ability, that student has learned enough English to successfully manage in mainstream classes.

Discussion   It is commonly believed that children are like little sponges when it comes to language learning: They pick up a second language easily if we simply immerse them in the target language environment. We see that within one to two years, children seem to be relatively fluent in their new language—or so it seems. Actually, what we are observing at this point is that children have a powerful ability to pick up the sounds of a new language, and they have the ability, in one to two years, to attain an oral fluency of the language skills needed for basic, interpersonal, social communications. Having a simple conversation about topics that children generally talk about (narratives, primarily), we would be fooled into thinking that the child has acquired the new language quite fluently. Thanks to the work of Jim Cummins (1981, 1984) we now realize that the acquisition of *basic, interpersonal communication skills*—commonly known as BICS—is one type of language ability. However, the language skills needed to function in an academic setting—CALP, for *cognitive academic language proficiency*—are quite different. CALP language requires a larger vocabulary, the ability to process long, embedded clauses (relative and subordinate), and the significant use of extensive nominalizations (Schleppegrell, 2004). To attain proficiency in academic language skills (CALP) takes anywhere from 5 to 10 years, depending on how much CALP a speaker has developed in his or her first language (Hakuta, Butler & Witt, 2000; Thomas & Collier, 2002).

Cummins has moved beyond the BICS and CALP terminology in his writings, as have others in the field. In current writings you will see more often references made to *conversational skills* and *academic language*. But we have intentionally chosen to retain the use of this terminology in this book for two reasons. First, the use of BICS and CALP persists in the world of ELL educational practitioners. Second, the understanding of the difference between BICS (i.e., conversational skills) and CALP (i.e., academic language proficiency) is of critical importance to understanding the academic performance of ELL students.

ELL students may sound as if they are English fluent in their oral speech within two years' time, but this is deceptive. They need minimally five years and often as much as 10 years to fully develop the language proficiency they need to operate in an academic setting on par with their native English-speaking classmates. Given this length of time, it becomes apparent that the entire school must own the responsibility of continued language development for our second-language-learning students.

Myth #2: English immersion is good for ELL students, because the more English they have (and the less they use their first language), the sooner they will learn English.

Discussion   *The more, the better* seems to be a reasonable, logical expectation. However, when it comes to second-language learning for school-age students who need to be learning language while also learning content, this seemingly logical proposition is false. In fact, ELL students who are allowed to develop and maintain their first language, especially if they are allowed to learn literacy through their first language, are the students with the greatest chance to succeed academically (August & Shanahan, 2006; Brisk & Harrington, 2000; Cummins, 1991). The students who are introduced to English, while simultaneously learning content and language arts in their home language, are the students most likely to reach and exceed the 50% (average) performance mark when scored with their native English-speaking classmates (Thomas & Collier, 2002). During the first year or two of this type of bilingual instruction, the new English language learner may seem to be acquiring English slightly slower than those children who are immersed in English only. But the long-term results resoundingly show that the students developing both languages develop the stronger literacy skills in both languages. Conversely, those in the English-only environment have significantly weaker chances to develop their literacy skills in either language (Thomas & Collier, 2002).

Teachers will often talk about the grade 4 wall, which ELL children hit and cannot climb over. These ELL children may seem to be developing during grades 1–3 (when they are learning to read and operating primarily in an oral-based classroom), but when they arrive in grade 4 (when they are reading to learn), they suddenly sink rapidly. That is because the children in grades 1–3 might be getting by on their oral development (those BICS abilities), but when it comes time to use CALP skills to learn content, if they have not had the time to develop those academic language skills sufficiently they hit a brick wall. Developing their CALP skills in their home language provides a most important foundation on which to develop CALP skills in other languages. If there is any way possible for children to develop and maintain language proficiency in the first language, it will reap benefits down the road when they are developing their academic language abilities in their new language, English (Brisk & Harrington, 2000, Commins & Miramontes, 2005; Faltis & Hudelson, 1998).

Myth #3: Teachers need to know the home language of an ELL, in order to teach that student.

Discussion   Whenever we tell strangers that we teach English as a second language, the most frequent response is to ask us what other languages we speak. It is assumed that to teach English to students who do not speak English, the teacher must be able to converse with the students in another language. In fact, ESL teachers do not need to know the native language of their students. In many cases, that would be impossible, for it is not uncommon for ESL teachers to have 10 to 50 languages represented by the children in their classes. An ESL teacher uses English to teach ESL. But the English she uses is a very controlled English, and it is an English filled with extralinguistic clues: pictures, gestures, realia, exaggerated tones. This highly controlled use of the language allows the learner to hear messages that are comprehensible to that individual learner at that learner's level of language proficiency. This level is described by Stephen Krashen (1982) as "i + 1." A good ESL teacher learns to deliver messages at different levels of language ability, so that each language learner is hearing comprehensible messages just slightly beyond that learner's current proficiency level.

This news should be good news to most educators, because it empowers classroom teachers into realizing that they do not need to know Spanish or Swahili or Urdu to speak with an ELL student in the classroom. Rather, through the use of highly controlled language and the use of an abundance of extralinguistic clues, teachers can find ways to interact with their ELL students. And as you will read about in the first two sections of this book, teachers can find ways to engage their ELL students in the content—through English—without significantly watering down the curriculum.

Myth #4: Many of our grandparents or great-grandparents came to the United States speaking a language other than English, and they made out fine without special schooling programs.

Discussion   In a sense, this myth makes the claim, My grandparents did it without any special favors. Why are schools making such a fuss now, trying to accommodate linguistic minority children? Our response to this claim must take two directions. The first is directed to the claim that our grandparents did it without any special favors. Did they? In many cases, our immigrant grandparents did not finish high school, nor did they fully learn English. But they were able to obtain a job or a business that allowed them to provide for their families (TESOL, 1997). These jobs did not require the level of English and literacy that most of today's jobs require. And in many cases, these jobs did not require a high school diploma. Furthermore, there were many ways our immigrant grandparents were able to build knowledge through the use of their first language, including formal schooling in that language, community newspapers, and religious groupings, for example (Commins, N.L., 2006, personal communication). Another consideration is whether or not immigrant grandparents were from cultures or family groups that practiced literacy practices in their homes. If they did, they were able to readily transfer those literacy skills to their new language (Brisk, 1998). The current picture of immigration, schooling, and business hiring is quite different from that of our grandparents' time. Now, most jobs require a certain level of English literacy and, minimally, a high school diploma. Furthermore, many of the current waves of immigrants come from cultures and homes that engage in more oral- than literacy-based practices. Consequently, they will not have the natural CALP abilities from their first language to transfer into their new language. Because of these differences, immigrants from two generations ago might have gotten by economically better without having to acquire as much English as today's immigrants need to do (Brisk, 1998; Portes & Zhou, 1993).

Our second response to this myth is that schools are exercising so much energy toward addressing the educational needs of ELLs for a number of reasons. First, as just discussed, current socioeconomic needs require adults in today's American society to have English literacy skills and, most often, minimally a high school diploma if they are to hold a decent job. Second, as the numbers show in an earlier section of this chapter, U.S. public schools are currently not graduating immigrant children at a satisfactory rate; in fact, they are failing at this task. Third, the U.S. federal case, *Lau v. Nichols*, 1974, dictates that all children must have the same access to education. And to expect children who do not speak English to have access to education delivered through the English language is unrealistic. Therefore, schools must make reasonable accommodations for ELL children so that they do have the same opportunities to learn the school content.

It is our hope that educators find this discussion concerning the common misconceptions both relieving and empowering. The discussion is relieving in the sense that they now realize why the success numbers for ELLs may be as dismal as they have been and in the sense of understanding why ELL students may not have performed as well as educators had hoped in the past. It is empowering in the sense that educators now have an understanding of the responsibility with which they are faced. To summarize, the common foundations covered in this discussion of four myths are as follows:

- Basic, interpersonal language skills (BICS) are learned in one to two years.
- Cognitive academic language proficiency (CALP) requires minimally 5 to 10 years to develop.
- Allowing students to use their first language in the development of their second language is very important, especially for the development of literacy.
- Teachers can teach ESL without knowledge of the students' first language, provided they use highly controlled language and many visual supports.
- Earlier generations of U.S. immigrants had access to jobs that did not require as much education and as much literacy ability.

- Schools now make accommodations for ELL students because current jobs require greater education and literacy skills, schools are failing over half of the immigration student population, and federal law decrees reasonable accommodations for ELL students.

SLA Theory and Learning Theory

When undertaking the task of educating language-learning students, it is beneficial to have some sense of second-language-learning theory. This section demonstrates that language-learning theory and traditional-learning theory have much in common. If we were to reduce second-language acquisition (SLA) theory into its most distilled form, a graphic representation of this most concise version of *SLA theory in a nutshell* might look like the visual in Figure 1.1. This figure illustrates four main ingredients required for second-language acquisition. The first ingredient is naturally endowed to each human—a language acquisition device (LAD)—which allows humans to naturally acquire languages. Notice that the plural form of *language* is used here because at least 60% of the humans on Earth are naturally bilingual or polylingual. Linguists debate over the exact epistemological nature of language and language acquisition—how language actually resides in the brain—but there is general agreement that humans are naturally endowed to acquire or learn languages (Chomsky, 1968, 1975; Gass & Selinker, 2001; Jackendoff, 1994; Pinker, 1994).

The next ingredient crucial to language acquisition is comprehensible input. The brain can only acquire language if it receives language input. Many linguists argue that input must be understandable, comprehensible; it cannot be just a constant stream of sound. Still other linguists argue that the input must be not only understandable but also meaningful to the receiver; that is, the language must be both understood and have meaning to the hearer (Gass, 1997; Krashen, 1985).

The third ingredient is the opportunity to produce output, the opportunity to engage with others and to practice language. Language learners acquire a receptive and productive proficiency; if language users are to be an integral part of a community, they must be not only receptive but also productive in their language use. To become productive, they need the opportunities to practice their language in purposeful, meaningful ways (Hall, 1993; Swain, 1985, 1995).

The final, fourth ingredient is a safe yet interactionally stimulating environment. We would argue that if a language learner receives comprehensible input and is encouraged to produce output in purposeful, meaningful ways, then this learner's environment is already safe and interactionally stimulating. However, we include a safe environment to this list of ingredients because language learners may be forced to produce language before they are

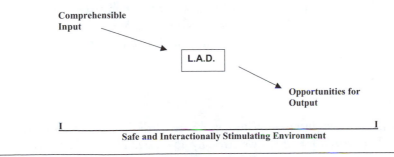

Figure 1.1 SLA theory in a nutshell: Four main ingredients.

SLA Theory	Learning Theory
• Our natural ability to develop language	• Our natural ability to think and learn
• Comprehensible input	• Content material must be understandable
• Opportunities to interact	• Opportunities to engage with content, peers, and teacher
• Safe and interactionally stimulating environment	• Cognitively stimulating and challenging environment

Figure 1.2 SLA theory and learning theory similarities.

ready to do so. Or a language learner may be made to feel as an outsider in the classroom or in social situations. In both of these cases, the language learner would not be in a safe, secure environment. We also include an interactionally stimulating environment as part of this fourth ingredient because as the language learner gains in proficiency, far too often that learner is not sufficiently encouraged to produce frequent, extended language. In this case, the language learner would not be in an interactionally stimulating environment.

The casual reader of articles on language learning and linguistics may be aware that in the field a debate exists as to the nature of language knowledge. Linguists differ in their opinions about whether certain aspects of language are biologically acquired or are learned in a traditional manner. Nevertheless, these four main ingredients fit into either side of the theory debate.

Interestingly, if we took the many theories of traditional learning and attempted to distill these theories into their most essential components, we would once again find four main ingredients, as illustrated in Figure 1.2. What this figure shows is that a human learner of any content matter has the naturally endowed ability to learn, needs comprehensible content as input, needs opportunities to engage with that content—and with others about that content, as some would argue—and needs a cognitively stimulating and challenging environment.

So the public school ELL student faced with learning academic content, while also acquiring the language of the school, essentially needs four main ingredients.

- The naturally endowed ability to learn (humans get this one for free)
- Language input and course content that is comprehensible, understandable
- The opportunity to engage with that content and to interact with others and with the teacher about that content
- A safe, cognitively, and interactionally stimulating environment

This distillation of ingredients presents for us, then, our challenge and our main goals as educators of English language learners. For students who are just learning the language medium of the school, we must determine how to make course content comprehensible and how to create opportunities for students to engage with the content and with others. Additionally, we must be ever sensitive to creating both a safe yet cognitively and interactionally stimulating environment. With these three goals as our compass points, we can modify our classroom practices and can redesign and reform schools to create responsive and inclusive educational environments.

Inclusive Pedagogy

We have chosen the term *inclusive pedagogy* for our title because it so aptly describes the instructional approach for which we strongly advocate. We first heard the term as it relates to English language learners in Schecter and Cummins' (2003) edited volume titled

Multilingual Education in Practice: Using Diversity as a Resource in the chapter written by Schecter, Solomon, and Kittmer. Inclusive pedagogy approaches linguistic diversity from the perspective that language is a resource, in contrast to two other orientations that often shape educational approaches: language as a problem and language as a right (Ruiz, 1988).

As Cummins and Schecter write:

> The language-as-resource orientation appeals to us for two reasons: it is more inclusive than either of the other two orientations, and it incorporates the other two in various respects. It is inclusive insofar as it highlights the interests of the entire society rather than those of particular minority groups and, in so doing, transcends the "us versus them" mentality that characterizes much of the debate in this area. It incorporates many aspects of the other orientations, since solving language problems and eliminating discrimination on the basis of language can be viewed as strategies that will result in the better use of society's human resources (p. 5).

A teacher, a school, or a school district practicing inclusive pedagogy welcomes their linguistic minority students to the learning experience because of their beliefs in the following tenets as described by Chow and Cummins (2003, p. 33):

- They see "students' home languages and cultures as potential resources for learning."
- They believe strongly "in the importance of parental involvement in children's education."
- They share "a commitment to connecting with individual children on a personal level as well as at an instructional level."
- They know and value that students are "exposed to literacy experiences and practices in their first languages outside the school in addition to their English literacy experiences in school."
- They intuitively know that "literacy acquisition belongs as much to the affective realm as to the cognitive realm."

Such practice, which treats language and linguistic minority students as resources, goes far beyond celebrating diversity. Such practice goes far beyond school welcome signs in a variety of languages or specially designated international days and multicultural festivals. The practitioner of inclusive pedagogy values the learner and the cultural and linguistic background this learner brings to the classroom, actively engages each learner with challenging content—despite the language barriers situated between learner and instructor—and sees each student as an individual who desires to learn and to be positively affirmed in the challenging learning process.

It is our sincere hope that this volume will assist those teachers, schools, and districts who are seeking to practice inclusive pedagogy.

Alphabet Soup: ESOL, TESOL, TOEFL

The study of English language learners seems to have an unusually large number of acronyms associated with it. These acronyms are confusing to anyone unfamiliar with the discipline. Following is a list of the most common acronyms and their definitions, with the hopes that this list will bring some clarity to the reader new to this topic.

Ways to refer to the language learner:

- ELL: English language learner (probably the most common term used now)
- LEP: limited English proficient
- NNS: nonnative speaker (often used in studies to that compare talk of native speakers to nonnative speakers)

Ways to refer to the language being learned:

- ESL: English as a second language (even if it may be the learner's third or fourth language; used when the English is being learned in an English-speaking country, that is, by immigrants).
- ESOL: English to speakers of other languages (ESL and ESOL have no substantial difference in meaning; the difference in their use seems to be a regional difference only.)
- EFL: English as a foreign language (used when English is being studied in a country that does not normally speak English; for example, a French high school student in France may study EFL.)

Other acronyms associated with this topic:

- TESOL: Teaching English to speakers of other languages (refers to the teacher training program for ESL teachers)
- TOEFL: Test of English as a Foreign Language (the name of the internationally recognized EFL test that students outside of the United States and other English-speaking countries take to show their competency in oral and written English)

References

August, D., & Shanahan, T. (2006). Developing literacy in second-language learners: Report of the national literacy panel on language-minority children and youth, executive summary. Mahwah, NJ: Lawrence Erlbaum. Retrieved June, 2006 from http://www.cal.org/natl-lit-panel/reports/Executive_Summary.pdf.

Brisk, M. E. (1998). *Bilingual education: From compensatory to quality schooling.* Mahwah, NJ: Lawrence Erlbaum.

Brisk, M. E., & Harrington, M. M. (2000). *Literacy and bilingualism: A handbook for ALL teachers.* Mahwah, NJ: Lawrence Erlbaum.

Chomsky, N. (1968). *Language and mind.* New York: Harcourt, Brace & World.

Chomsky, N. (1975). *Reflections on language.* New York: Pantheon.

Chow, P., & Cummins, J. (2003). Valuing multilingual and multicultural approaches to learning. In S. R. Schecter & J. Cummins (Eds.), *Multilingual education in practice: Using diversity as a resource* (pp. 32–61). Portsmouth, NH: Heinemann.

Commins, N. L., & Miramontes, O.B. (2005). *Linguistic diversity and teaching.* Mahwah, NJ: Lawrence Erlbaum.

Cummins, J. (1981, Winter). Empirical and theoretical underpinnings of bilingual education. *Journal of Education, 16–29.*

Cummins, J. (1984). Wanted: A theoretical framework for relating language proficiency to academic achievement among bilingual students. In C. Rivera (Ed.), *Language proficiency and academic achievement* (pp. 2–19). Avon, England: Multilingual Matters, Ltd.

Cummins, J. (1991). Interdependence of first- and second-language proficiency in bilingual children. In E. Bialystok (Ed.), *Language processing in bilingual children* (pp. 70–89). New York: Cambridge University Press.

Faltis, C., & Hudelson, S. (1998). *Bilingual education in elementary and secondary school communities: Towards understanding and caring.* Boston: Allyn and Bacon.

Gass, S. (1997). *Input, interaction and the second language learner.* Mahwah, NJ: Lawrence Erlbaum.

Gass, S., & Selinker, L. (2001). *Second language acquisition: An introductory course* (2nd ed.). Mahwah, NJ: Lawrence Erlbaum.

Hakuta, K., Butler, Y. G., & Witt, D. (2000). How long does it take English learners to attain proficiency? Policy Report 2000-1. Palo Alto, CA: University of California Linguistic Minority Research Institute. Retrieved October, 2004 from http://www.stanford.edu/~hakuta/Docs/HowLong.pdf.

Hall, J. K. (1993). The role of oral practices in the accomplishment of our everyday lives: The socio-cultural dimension of interaction with implications for the learning of another language. *Applied Linguistics, 14,* 145–166.

Jackendoff, R. (1994). *Patterns in the mind.* New York: BasicBooks.

Krashen, S. (1982). *Principles and practices in second language acquisition.* Oxford: Pergamon.

Krashen, S. (1985). *The input hypothesis: Issues and implications.* New York: Longman.

Lau v. Nichols, 414 U.S. 563, 94 S.Ct. 786, 39 L.Ed.2d 1 (1974).

McLaughlin, B. (1992). Myths and misconceptions about second language learning: What every teacher needs to unlearn. Santa Cruz: University of California, Center for Research on Education, Diversity, and Excellence. Retrieved September 9, 2005 from http://www.ncela.gwu.edu/pubs/ncrcdsll/epr5.htm.

Pinker, S. (1994). *The language instinct.* New York: Harper Collins.

Portes, A., & Zhou, M. (1993). The new second generation: Segmented assimilation and its variants. In P.I. Ross (Ed.), *Interminority affairs in the United States: Pluralism at the crossroads* (pp. 74–96). Newbury Park, CA: Sage.

Ruiz, R. (1988). Orientations in language planning. In S. McKay & S. Wong (Eds.), *Language diversity: Problem or resource?* (pp. 3–25). New York: Newbury House.

Schecter, S. R., & Cummins, J. (Eds.). (2003). *Multilingual education in practice: Using diversity as a resource.* Portsmouth, NH: Heinemann.

Schecter, S. R., Solomon, P., & Kittmer, L. (2003). Integrating teacher education in a community-situated school agenda. In S. R. Schecter & J. Cummins (Eds.), *Multilingual education in practice: Using diversity as a resource* (pp. 81–96). Portsmouth, NH: Heinemann.

Schleppegrell, M. J. (2004). *The language of schooling: A functional linguistics perspective.* Mahwau, NJ: Lawrence Erlbaum.

Spellings, M. (2005). U.S. Secretary of Education keynote address. Presented at the Fourth Annual OELA Conference Celebrate Our Rising Stars Summit: From Essential Elements to Effective Practice. Washington, DC, December 1. Available at: http://www.ed.gov/new/speeches/2005/12/12012005.html.

Swain, M. (1985). Communicative competence: Some roles of comprehensible input and comprehensible output in its development. In S. M. Gass & C. G Madden (Eds.), *Input in second language acquisition* (pp. 236–244). Rowley, MA: Newbury House.

Swain, M. (1995). Collaborative dialogue: Its contribution to second language learning. Paper presented at the American Association of Applied Linguistics Conference, Long Beach, CA.

Teachers of English to Speakers of Other Languages, Inc. (TESOL). (1997). *ESL standards for pre-K–12 students.* Alexandria, VA: Author.

Thomas, W. P., & Collier, V. P. (2002). A national study of school effectiveness for language minority students' long-term academic achievement, Final report: Project 1.1. Santa Cruz: University of California, Center for Research on Education, Diversity, and Excellence.

U.S. Department of Education, National Center for Education Statistics. (2002). Schools and staffing survey, 1999–2000: Overview of the data for public, private, public charter, and Bureau of Indian Affairs elementary and secondary schools (NCES 2002-313). Washington, DC.

CHAPTER 2

A Scaffolded Approach to Learning to Write

MARIA ESTELA BRISK, DEBORAH A. HORAN, AND ELIZABETH MACDONALD

Ten K–5 teachers in an urban district with students of a variety of linguistic background organized a collaborative study of inquiry-based practices during one academic year. The teachers, a college professor, and a graduate student met weekly for two months in the fall with the goal of learning more about the language and writing of students learning English. Through discussions of students' work in the context of second language acquisition theory, the teachers gained knowledge and awareness of language and literacy development of bilingual learners.[1] The school is very multilingual, but the instruction is all in English. Having no specialized staff to work with bilingual learners, the teachers, supported by the principal and in partnership with a university, set out to better prepare themselves to work with bilingual learners. Analysis of students' work was followed by six weeks of discussion about practices that would help these students' writing development. Several approaches were discussed and chosen for implementation. One of them, the rhetorical approach, is addressed in detail in this chapter. This approach walks students through the process of planning and executing writing, developing good habits, and improving their products.

The decision to use the rhetorical approach emerged from teachers noticing that the students' writing exhibited similar characteristics. Across the grades, students tended to write *bed-to-bed* stories in which they strung together a list of phrases or simple sentences joined by *then* or *and*. One Vietnamese first grader wrote,

> One morning I woke up and went to brush my tetth and I went outside and, I went in the car my mom stared to Drive.

The story from a fourth-grade Nepali student showed a similar pattern:

> The first day I lots of work. I ate lunch. ran to play soccer outside Then I was tired enugh. Again I went to study. I studied Social Studies, Maths, Nepali, grammer, English and helth ed It was time to have snacks. I ate my snacks. Then I went to class. It was free time. I did my home work.

The students' writing was mostly lists of undeveloped events composed primarily as simple statements. Topic development, which had been among the concerns teachers brought to their meetings, was minimal. Teachers began examining bilingual learners' writing samples assisted by a rubric that included writing traits as well as language features. Consequently, teachers' conversations turned to how issues of language were impacting writing traits, including not only topic development but also voice.

Oral-Like to Written-Like Language

One common pattern across the grades was students writing short paragraphs that mimicked their oral language. As elementary educators, the teachers were very aware that emergent writers typically write as they speak. However, by looking across grades, teachers realized that few K–5 students were moving away from more oral-like forms and into more written-like forms (Gibbons, 2002). Admittedly, at any K–5 grade there could be bilingual learners who ranged in their English language development from preproduction to early fluency, due to their varying lengths of time learning English. However, even bilingual learners with more developed oral language appeared to produce writing with more oral-like characteristics. Sentences tended to be short, ideas or words were repeated, and sentences were chained together by key words. One Spanish fourth grader strung sentences together with *so,* which echoed his speech patterns:

> So we play evey day on the bus. I bering toy's so we can play we have the best time! So I bering 3 action figer's. We mack a lot of nose (underlined for emphasis).

Another common oral pattern was repetition, such as in the writing of one third-grade Chinese student:

> then we was home taking a bath for bed but until bed we play a little bit while when the sun came down I went to bed at 9:00 p.m. with all my family went to bed until morning we went back to school (underlined for emphasis)

Even at the fifth-grade level, teachers noticed bilingual learners relying on oral language in their writing. These students tended to incorporate into their writing: a relatively small range of vocabulary; a more typical subject-verb-object pattern; and relatively fewer dependent clauses and embedded phrases. Evidence of oral language was not the only feature that teachers noticed across grades.

Rosa's Writing and Language: From First Days to Grandma's House

In addition to oral-language patterns, teachers considered language involving text structure, sentence grammar, vocabulary, and spelling. The writing sample of one Guatemalan girl, Rosa, from Liz's fourth-grade class offers examples of both writing and language issues.[2]

Rosa's Writing Sample #1

> My first day in 1st grade was really scary especially if I did not know any English. When I first got in my class I felt scared and strange because I only knew some English words and I did not have any friends. My teacher was Mrs. C...she was very nice. When we staterd to do work I tried to understand but I just understood a little bit. By that time my mom was gone and I felt really sad but I remembered the words that my mother said to me and those words were "don't be afraid you could do it" and that

was what I did. When we went to lunch I already knew a girl that talk Spanish and English so she helped me. That was the only girl I knew and to be honest she was kind of a troublemaker so I had to stay away from her because I did not wanted to get in trouble. By the end of the day I was not that scare. I wanted to tell my whole family of the experience I have just past which was scary and kind of fun.

Aspects of writing in Rosa's sample that teachers discussed included conventions, such as capitalization and punctuation, as well as writing traits, such as voice. Teachers agreed that Rosa's voice did not uniquely surface in this writing sample. In fact, the passage reminded them of similar recounts by other students. Rosa's unique voice was not evident in descriptive phrases that helped readers experience sadness at her mother's leaving. Rosa's sentences were all statements, including her inclusion of her mother's dialogue. As one participant in the teacher group realized, voice was influenced by Rosa's limited knowledge of descriptive vocabulary, including adjectives, adverbs, and descriptive phrases that would have allowed her to make her sadness of her mother leaving more evident.

Teachers also analyzed other aspects of language that surfaced in writing, seeing them as evidence of bilingual learners' attempting new text structures, sentence grammar, vocabulary, and spelling. For example, in terms of text structure, Rosa wrote one extended paragraph in which she narrated her experience but without developing aspects of her day into paragraphs. As many bilingual learners, she struggled with the past tense marker *ed* when she wrote "understanded," "did not wanted," "was not that scare" (scared), and "got past" (passed). The cohesion of her writing was impacted by her understanding of connecting words, such as when she wrote "especially if" instead of "especially because." Her verb choices showed transfer from Spanish, her native language, as when she wrote "talk Spanish" instead of "speak Spanish." Teachers also highlighted what language Rosa could manipulate. For example, she attempted complex sentences, usually beginning with *when*. Through eight weeks of collaborative inquiry, teachers analyzed the language ability and challenges of students representing such native languages as Arabic, Cantonese, Mandarin, Russian, Haitian Creole, Khmer, Albanian, Nepali, and French.

From Inquiry to Practice: The Rhetorical Approach

This analysis and discussion of language samples led to implementation of instructional approaches that could support these students. Liz chose to implement the rhetorical approach (Brisk & Harrington, 2000; de Alvarado, 1984). This approach helps students plan for writing focusing on the context and content of the text. Before engaging in actual writing, students decide on the audience and purpose for writing. They explore the selected topic from whole to parts. Given the purpose, audience, and content, they choose the most suitable type of text, be it a letter, book, or story. With this information in mind, students draft, revise, edit, and publish their texts.

Improvement through the Rhetorical Approach

Several months later, Rosa wrote the following description of her favorite place.

Rosa's Writing Sample #2

I have a lot of favorite places. But one gets most of my attention. That place is my grandma's house. This is my favorite place because when I go there I feel cozy and safe also I get a lot of attention and last but not least I get love. This is my favorite place.

One reason I chose my grandma's house as my favorite place was because I feel cozy and safe there. I like feeling cozy and safe because when you feel that, you feel more comfortable and you also feel relaxed every single moment. This is one thing I really like about my grandma's house. This is why I chose my grandma's house as my favorite place.

Another reason I chose my grandma's house as my favorite place is because I get a lot of attention there. I like that because I feel very important and I like that. Also, I feel special and that makes me feel happy. This is one thing I loves about my grandma's house.

Last but not least the last reason I chose my grandma's house as my favorite place is because I get love there. That's one thing I love about my grandma's house. I like it because I love to be n a place were people love me and care about me. This I think is the most important reason of why I chose my grandmother's house as my favorite place.

For all this reasons is why I chose my grandma's house as my favorite place. My grandma's house rules, it makes my life fullfil every time I go there. This house is the best. This is my favorite place.

Rosa developed ideas into paragraphs with topic sentences. She chose more descriptive words, such as *cozy, safe, comfortable, relaxed, attention,* and *fullfil.* She increased her range of connectors: *but, because, one reason, another reason, also, last but not least,* and *for all this reasons.* Her voice surfaced in sentences such as, "My grandma's house rules, it makes my life fullfil every time I go there." Not only did her voice begin to surface, but topic development also expanded. She still had some grammatical morpheme problems as when she wrote "fulfil" instead of "fulfilled." These are very difficult aspects of language to acquire (Genesee, Paradis, & Crago, 2004). What happened between Rosa's first writing sample and this one?

Implementation of the Rhetorical Approach

The rhetorical approach is one instructional strategy that supports the writing process (Brisk & Harrington, 2000; de Alvarado, 1984). There are eight general steps in the rhetorical approach: (1) explore a general topic; (2) define the purpose and audience; (3) select subtopics; (4) select the genre and appropriate organizational structure; (5) select information; (6) order examples and details, then write a draft; (7) revise and edit; and (8) prepare a final copy. Liz incorporated the rhetorical approach into a social studies unit on immigration. Although she implemented the eight steps, she occasionally interjected additional sidesteps to respond to students' needs. These sidesteps reinforced the effectiveness of the rhetorical approach, as Liz continually allowed students' needs to influence her instruction (Figure 2.1).

Liz and Rosa's Fourth-Grade Classroom

As part of a large urban school district, many of Liz's students were immigrants from such countries as Vietnam, Ghana, Puerto Rico, Colombia, China, and Guatemala. They brought with them different personal and conceptual understandings of immigration, different educational experiences, and different literacy development in their varying heritage languages and in English. They also brought different knowledge of language and literacy. To maximize these bilingual learners' range of language development, Liz increased opportunities to develop their English not only during reading instruction but also during content-area instruction. By integrating writing into her social studies unit, Liz aimed to develop students' content knowledge as well as academic language (Cummins, 2003).

Liz achieved these goals through infusing her social studies unit on immigration with opportunities for listening, speaking, reading, and writing. For example, to help students

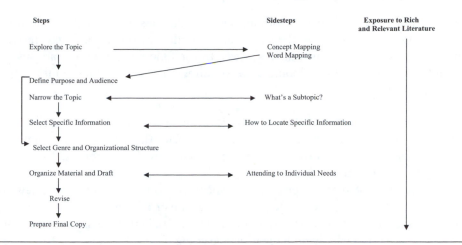

Figure 2.1 Implementation of the rhetorical approach in a fourth-grade classroom

understand immigration historically, Liz enriched the unit with a read aloud of books such as *Letters from Rifka,* a chapter book about a young Eastern European girl immigrating to America at the turn of the 20th century. Read alouds of more challenging texts also exposed students to vocabulary and dialogue that they might not have encountered in their independent reading. Liz incorporated writing into her unit to help students synthesize and convey their overall understanding of immigration. By structuring this writing through the rhetorical approach, she hoped to develop writing and target language needs.

Step 1: Explore a General Topic

The rhetorical approach begins with students' freewriting about a general topic, as a way of activating background knowledge. Sometimes, students are given complete autonomy in topic selection. Other times, the teacher may purposefully direct students to achieve content area goals. Sometimes, this process occurs as a whole class through shared writing. Other times, students freewrite individually.

Liz intentionally focused students on the general topic of immigration to support social studies content. She began the process with a whole-class discussion to reinforce the oral language of students learning English. Then, her fourth graders freewrote individually in their writing journals. This could also have been done in reverse order, with students freewriting first and then discussing orally either in groups or whole class.

During this freewriting, Liz's students were midway through their unit, which covered immigration from the turn of the 20th century to present. Because students had been hearing, reading, and using the term *immigration,* they had developed partial understandings of this concept (Allen, 1999). However, based on their freewriting, Liz noticed significant conceptual gaps for many students. Consequently, she adapted her instruction before proceeding to the next step of the rhetorical approach.

Sidestep 1: Concept and Word Mapping

In response to student needs, Liz led the class through developing a concept map in which they discussed not only what the concept of immigration is but also what it is not. These maps could have been individually created by students; however, Liz realized that her students' ideas would be challenged and expanded through a whole-class discussion. This also provided another opportunity to scaffold language for bilingual learners through building oral language. Liz began with an open-ended question, "What do you think the word *immigration* means?" She then facilitated the discussion through asking students' opinions and by summarizing students' ideas. In the following excerpt from this discussion, students' reveal their developing understandings, as they respond to ideas expressed by their peers.

Terrence: I think it means people that are basically just travelers. People that travel.

Giselle: People that move to a new country or new place that are immigrating it.

Deji: I think it means brought into other countries like terrorists. Never been in country before.

Anna: People want to go to a place. … If somebody had to go do something new and try something new, like a different kind of group or religion.

Giselle: I think it means leaving your homeland to have a better life in another country.

Terrence: … What I'm mostly noticing is people going places. People going from one place to another place.

Jennifer: … It's not when you move from place to place. It's not always immigration because Laura [a classmate] is going to move in three weeks, and she's not going to immigrate.

Liz: What do you think? She says immigration is moving place to place, but others say just because you're moving does not mean you're immigrating.

Giselle: I think if you're moving to another country, then it's immigration, but not if you're going from state to state.

Liz: So moving from country to country is immigration but not state to state?

Jalissa: I think immigrating is like moving from one country to another, but you can also immigrate your own way, like I'm immigrating to Florida...I'm moving to a place not far from here. And I'm going to live somewhere else.

Liz: So what do you guys think? Is Jalissa going to be an immigrant? Is she immigrating to a new place?

Terrence: Depends where you're moving to. Say you're moving where you never been before, and say it's warm not cold. That's kind of like immigrating.

Anna: Not necessarily. Depends on how far you go and how many new things you have to do.

Jalissa: Well, I have been there before. I have been to where I'm gonna live. And I have done lots of things there in the summer, so I would not say I would be an immigrant.

Although Giselle managed to define *immigration,* a number of other students offered different ideas. A common theme in this discussion involved movement. The specific types of movement expressed by individual students reflected personal experiences, either theirs or those of friends. This discussion revealed that students' conceptual understanding was interpreted through their personal experiences. This discussion did not close with a unanimous definition of immigration. However, Liz challenged students in future discussions to continue exploring this concept—what immigration is as well as what it is not. She also encouraged students in making connections between their own lives and those of immigrants they studied in books.

In the following class, students developed a word family map, as shown in Figure 2.2. The purpose of this word family map was to uncover and reinforce root words and morphemes that would help students linguistically unlock the meaning of future words

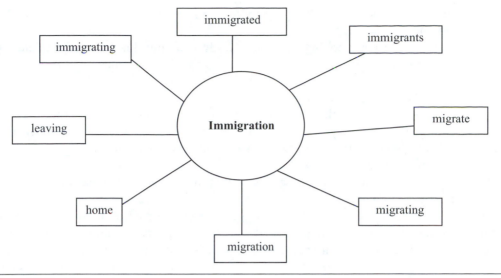

Figure 2.2 Word family map

they encountered. As students shared ideas, other word forms arose, such as *immigrant, immigrating, migrate,* and *immigrated.* One student shared her awareness of language with others when she commented,

> I have two things to say. One is you're using suffixes. When I think of suffixes, seeing up there -ing or -ed. I'm seeing those suffixes because mostly that's what we can come up with and that's the main word…I was also going to say, what does migrate have to do with immigrate? I'm not saying it's wrong, but what's it have to do with it?

This led students to discussing bird migration, which included developing word associations, such as,

> Migrate is a piece of the family because it's a same word but a different personality sort of … different ways of doing it. Like animals instead of people. But immigrate is with people.

While Liz facilitated these student discussions, she also interjected new information, such as describing migrant workers, whose lives would be represented in a future read aloud exercise of *Amelia's Road* (1995). The word map created an opportunity to clarify how these words are used within the context of sentences.

After making and discussing the word family map, students opened their writer's notebooks to write their own sentences containing these words. Volunteers shared some of their sentences:

- We are studying immigration in social studies.
- Rosa immigrated to the United States of America from Colombia.
- Today, you will be immigrating to America.
- I have seen a bird who migrates everywhere.
- I immigrated to America by boat.

Occasionally, Liz drew students' attention to morphemes by asking such open-ended questions as, "What did that -ed do to that word?" To which a student explained, "Turned it into the past tense." These word analyses were important for all students, but especially for bilingual learners who were developing not only concepts but also the word knowledge needed to manipulate language.

Following the concept mapping and word family mapping, Liz returned students to step 2 in the rhetorical approach, which addresses purpose and audience.

Step 2: Define Purpose and Audience

Writers usually consider why they write to a certain audience, as this shapes their written message. Bilingual learners experience an additional challenge. Different cultures have different reasons for writing and different styles depending on audience. Bilingual learners need to be made aware of these differences.

In step two of the rhetorical approach, students discuss both purpose and audience. Instead of assigning an audience or assuming the students were writing primarily to the teacher, Liz allowed her fourth graders to discuss possible people who might want to read what they would write about immigration. After jointly compiling possibilities, the students voted. An overwhelming majority of the class chose Mr. Sullivan, a former student teacher who had been in the class when they began the immigration unit. They wanted "to show him how much we've learned since he left" and "to show him how much progress we made since he teached us since September." Choosing a real audience helped students personalize their purpose for writing. Liz found that many of the students, especially bilingual learners, struggled with finding the words to express their thoughts. With a specific audience, she could push them to clarify their thoughts through prompts, such as "What would Mr. Sullivan want to know you've learned about immigration?"

The class had previously learned that whom they write to impacts how they write. For example, they had discussed letter writing to friends, when they would often assume that the other person would know what they are saying and they can use an informal language register to share their thoughts and feelings. Because the students' purpose was to show Mr. Sullivan what they had learned about an academic topic, Liz pushed them to use more formal, academic language. Instead of narrating or persuading, their primary purpose was informing Mr. Sullivan about certain concepts, events, and history. Having purpose and audience in mind helped later on when they chose the format of the book they wanted to produce. They wanted something nice and impressive.

What specifically would they write about? What was the most appropriate way to present information, given their goal was to demonstrate what they had learned? These questions were addressed in the next two steps of the rhetorical approach in which the students first narrow the topic vertically and then horizontally.

Step 3: Narrow the Topic

After determining the purpose and audience, students narrow the topic by exploring possible subtopics. Brisk and Harrington (2000) refers to this as *narrowing the topic vertically,* or determining the level of generalization. When talking to her class, Liz referred to this as identifying subtopics. Before guiding students in developing subtopics about immigration, she modeled developing subtopics for two familiar topics. First, she offered an example related to science content they had finished studying. Liz explained, "Birds is a topic. Under birds there can be many subtopics. I know this from reading we've done about birds and writing I've done about birds, so one subtopic about birds might be *feathers.* Another subtopic of birds might be *flying.*" Students offered two more subtopics: beaks and habitats. While reiterating the general topic of birds and potential subtopics, the teacher looked for evidence of student understanding and realized another example was needed. For the second example, she chose the Super Bowl, a recent event that had been of great interest to the majority of the class. Students suggested such subtopics as football field, interceptions, singing the national anthem, and teams. These suggestions made Liz aware that the concept of a subtopic was still not clear to most students.

Sidestep 2: What's a Subtopic?
Liz devoted an additional lesson to developing the concept of subtopics through a variety of nonfiction literature as models. First, she showed students a book about bugs that included explicit topics and subtopics, building the connection between reading and writing. At the same time, she asked questions, such as "Based on this title, what do you think the following writing will be about?" During this mini-lesson, she modeled how to create a web with *bugs* written in the middle as the topic and subtopics added as she identified them. In the following excerpt of her mini-lesson, she builds on what the students do know to push them forward in their ability to identify subtopics.

Liz: I wanted to figure out what were the subtopics of this book. So what do you think I had to do to figure it out?
Wee: Read the back.
Jalissa: Read the table of contents.
Liz: The back of book didn't help me in this case. I did look at the table of contents, but guess what? There isn't any in this nonfiction book. So I went ahead and read the book and realized it probably could have had a table of contents. And the first chapter would have been titled introduction because the first page tells me about all types of bugs and what makes a bug a bug or an insect an insect. And as I read on, I realized the second chapter could have been titled ants. Because under this topic of bugs, there was a subtopic of ants. Then I read on more, and I realized that this subtopic was all about dragonflies. So now I'm noticing that I have some kind of chapters here, and they're subtopics of the big topic bugs. Sometimes authors organize them into chapters and put in a table of contents to tell you. But sometimes they don't. But if you're a good reader, you can figure it out even if there is no table of contents.

Following this example, Liz grouped students in pairs, according to common reading levels, and gave them preassigned nonfiction books. As partners, students read the books and then created either a web or bulleted list of the main topic and subtopics. Some of the nonfiction books had titles and subtitles for students needing that explicit guidance. Other students had books that required them to identify the subtopics without having subtitles as clues. Pre-selecting the books took into account different student needs for support during the process. At the end of this partner work, the students reported back to class so that everyone could benefit from a variety of examples.

One pair had read a book on whales and identified subtopics of *how whales breathe* and *singing whales*. Two other students read a book on reptiles with *crocodilians* and *snakes* as subtopics. Another pair read a book on extreme sports with subtopics such as *freestyle motorcross* and *base jumping*. When the class came back together to share the work that they had done in pairs, students appeared to have a better understanding of subtopics.

Leaving the Homeland	The Journey	Settling in a New Place

-Diseases
 	
-Reasons for leaving
  • Poverty
  • War
  • Family
  • Discrimination
  • Natural disasters
  • Famine
	-Diseases
	
	-Ellis Island
	  • stairway of separation
	  • examination
	  • baggage room
	
	-Steerage
	
	-How long did it take?
	
	-Inside the boat
	
	-Traveling on the ocean
	
	-Meeting people on the boat
	
	-Buying tickets
	  • different classes
		-Meeting people
		
		-Finding jobs
		
		-Where did immigrants go?
		
		-Getting a disease in the new place
		
		-Homes
		
		-Schools

Figure 2.3 Immigration subtopics

Back to Step 3 in the Rhetorical Approach

When students returned to step 3 of the rhetorical approach, they were ready to explore subtopics about immigration. Although they exhibited a better understanding of subtopics, Liz scaffolded this process by reminding the class that she had sequenced their immigration unit by presenting the reasons people left their homeland, the journey, and life in America. Next, through a whole-class discussion students developed three major subtopics: leaving the homeland, the journey, and settling in a new place. Liz drew three columns on the board with these headings. The students reexamined their original brainstorming of subtopics, adding any new ideas. As students wrote, Liz circulated the room, scaffolding for some students who seemed stuck by prompting them with questions about the books on immigration that they had read. When the students came back together to share as a group Liz encouraged them to think about what category their subtopic might fall under. For example, steerage would be categorized under the major subtopic of the journey. As students shared their subtopics, Liz would write each one down on a note card and then ask the students to place it in the appropriate column. While categorizing subtopics, students realized that some fell under more than one category. For example, they realized that diseases could be a subtopic of both leaving the homeland and the journey. At the conclusion of the share, the students had categorized all of the subtopics they had currently brainstormed (Figure 2.3).

This activity of categorizing the subtopics was important in organizing the sequence of the class book. It was also a constructive way for students to understand the concept of categorizing. While engaged in the exercise, Liz would write the categorized term on the board while repeatedly defining the word in multiple ways. For example, she would say, "We are categorizing these subtopics," "We are putting these subtopics where they belong," and "We are placing the subtopics in a category with other subtopics that have something in common." Similar to the word family map that the class created with the word immigration, Liz introduced different forms of the word *categorizing* while teaching, such as *category, categorize, categorized,* and *categories.* She always wrote the word on the board, an essential support for second-language learners whose letter–sound discrimination may not yet be proficient and who benefit from the dual input of receiving information in both oral and written forms. It is also important for second-language learners to see the word to reinforce their visually noticing morphemes that are added to or taken from words.

Step 4: Select Information

During the fourth step of the rhetorical approach, students chose the specific information to be covered within each subtopic. Liz had students working on different subtopics of their choosing. Some students worked independently, others in partners, others in triads. Liz encouraged heterogeneous groups in which a second-language learner was paired with a native speaker of English. This provided an authentic context for dialoging and writing about academic topics by using more academic language. This also provided a supportive environment in which emerging speakers of English could take linguistic risks.

Next, Liz provided students with a collection of books and news articles that she had compiled on this topic. She asked students to use their knowledge of tables of contents and glossaries to find out which books would be beneficial in researching their particular topics. During this process, Liz reinforced text structures that reflect expository text, such as tables of contents, glossaries, subtitles, charts, and captions. Liz realized during the process that many of the students were having difficulty locating and synthesizing specific information. As a result, she decided to spend some additional time instructing students on how to conduct research.

Sidestep 3: How to Locate Specific Information

The class had been posing questions about immigration and then reading information to find answers to their questions. This format mirrored that of a nonfiction book, *If Your Name Were Changed at Ellis Island* (1994), which they had been reading together as a class. Chapters of this book posed a question, such as "Why did people leave their homeland?" The following text addressed that question. In a similar format, students turned their subtopics into questions. For bilingual learners, learning to create questions was an essential part of developing sentence grammar in English. Some students needed support formulating a question, but the majority of the class were able to easily transpose their topics into questions. Once the class had their questions written, Liz suggested they try locating information to answer their questions. She modeled this process through asking, "Why did Na leave her homeland?" in reference to a special edition of a local newspaper on immigration. As a think aloud, Liz found answers in the article while taking bulleted notes on chart paper. Students then began this process with their chosen subtopics.

Step 5: Select Genre and Organizational Structure

The next step was to select the genre and appropriate organizational structure, given the students' defined purposes, topic, and audience. The students' purpose was to inform, so they chose an expository text form. Influenced by a science book they had been reading on turtles, they decided to write one class book that included writing by all the students on various subtopics. They could present this book to Mr. Sullivan during their publishing party to show him what they had learned. This text structure required elements of expository text, such as titles, subtitles, glossaries, and a table of contents.

Step 6: Organize Material and Draft

Next, the class discussed how the subtopics should be sequenced. Liz challenged them by asking these questions: "Does this belong here?" and "Would this make more sense later on?" Through this process, students decided which subtopics fit into which categories as well as the order within categories. For example, they decided that in the journey section of the book the topic of buying tickets should come before Ellis Island.

Because they had been working on paragraphing, when they set out to write, they were reminded to include such things as topic and closing sentence. They each wrote at least one paragraph. During this time, Liz conferenced with individual students. She assisted them in filling in any additional information they had overlooked in their initial research and first draft. She also helped students move their notes to paragraphs.

Some students, who were working in groups, further subdivided their topics into smaller categories of information, with each student responsible for writing a different aspect of the overall section. Other students, working together, chose to coauthor their entire section, sitting side by side as they talked through all the content and word choices. Other students worked alone, producing drafts, such as the following.

"Examination"

Examinations was the first stage people went through to Ellis Island. Some where allowed to enter the United Stats right away. And because they did not have diseaes. If they did have diseaes they would be detained that means that they hat to stay until they were healthy. Some people did not stay at Ellis Ilond because of the diseaes they had. And they had to go back to were they came from. But if you didn't have a diseaes you would go to America.

Sidestep 4: Attending to Bilingual Learners' Individual Needs

While conferencing with two more recent arrivals, Liz discovered that they were having difficulty producing writing based on research. Knowing that they both had direct experiences with immigration, Liz suggested that they change their subtopic to *personal stories of immigration.* Their research became interviews with immigrants. Although both students were immigrants, they opted to write about a family member's experience with immigration rather than to share their own. One of the students, Aldo, chose to interview his father, who had emigrated from Africa. The other student, Cecilia, decided to interview her brother, who had left his homeland in South America with his family just a few years earlier. Prior to conducting their interviews, Aldo and Cecilia prepared questions encompassing the class' subtopics: leaving the homeland, the journey, and settling in a new place. Aldo and Cecilia worked together drafting and revising their work. Their final product, titled "Recent Immigrants," was inserted at the end of the class book. This modified assignment not only relieved these students' challenge of finding information for their subtopic, but it also validated their experiences as immigrants. Cecilia contributed the following passage to the class book:

Immigrants come to the United States, but in many different ways. One story of an immigrant happened in my family. The whole story began when my brother came to the United States. HE came to the United States because his parents made him. He did not want to come because he would ruin his career as a doctor. But, it was too dangerous to stay in his homeland. He came in an airplane and landed in an airport. He did not arrive at Ellis Island like most immigrants from the past did. Also, it only took him ten hours to get to the United States. It did not take months or weeks or even days. He even got food on the plane. Now all of these reasons are how you can tell if a person is an immigrant today.

Step 7: Revise

The writing process continued as students individually crafted their drafts through revisions. Because students were at different places of drafting, revising, and editing, the teacher was conferencing with individual students and small groups at different times. During the conference time, the teacher's primary focus was to have students writing well-developed paragraphs. Therefore, she helped students add any additional information or delete or eliminate unnecessary information. During revision, Liz dialogued with students, asking text-level questions, such as "How could this be reorganized or further developed?"

She also guided students in examining language use within sentences. Many bilingual learners demonstrated challenges with sentence structure, such as missing or overused articles, depending on their first language. Other bilingual learners needed support in mastering the use of certain verbs. For example, Spanish speakers struggled with the appropriate use of *do* and *make* because one Spanish verb, *hacer,* carries both meanings in their original language. In terms of grammar, students struggled with writing about events in the past tense and in expressing degrees of meaning through modal auxiliaries: *could, should, might, may, must.* Only after their ideas were developed did students focus on punctuation and spelling.

Step 8: Prepare a Final Copy

Finally, students created a published book, not necessarily a flawless piece of writing but rather one which demonstrated significant though developmentally appropriate editing. Some students, who had finished their section of the publication earlier than others, assisted Liz in typing the book. During a publishing party, they presented the book to Mr. Sullivan. As the following passage illustrates, the students had moved away from the bed-to-bed stories to write about topics of their choice in an interesting and detailed way.

"Reasons People Left Their Homeland"

There were different reasons why people left their homelands at the turn of the 20th century. Some people left their homelands because of poverty and famine. They didn't have enough money or food where they lived. Others left because of natural disasters or catastrophes which included volcanic eruptions. Another reason people left their homeland was because of discrimination in their country. Many people were not allowed to practice their religion as they choose, so they left their country. These are some of the reasons why people left their homeland.

Scaffolding Learning and Teaching

The rhetorical approach walks learners through the writing process, attending to each step in more detail than other process approaches. This process not only helps the students but also orients teachers to the aspects of writing that students have internalized and those that are still a challenge. Bilingual learners' experiences and knowledge about writing vary a great deal. A large number of students tend to be unfamiliar with the expectations of how to carry out writing assignments in American school systems. Presently, the approaches to writing demand a lot from the learner, including creativity; however, most approaches give very little specific direction. For bilingual learners, this may signify a major cultural adjustment, since many school systems around the world use a more prescriptive approach to teaching writing. Even if they experienced a flexible approach in the educational systems in their homelands, these second-language learners need more task and language scaffolding. Such scaffolding frees students to focus more attention on expressing their ideas.

Scaffolding Learning

The rhetorical approach allows teachers to support students explicitly through a series of steps that help develop writing habits. At the same time, this method provides students with opportunities to be creative. Often in the quest to foster creativity, teachers come up short in providing help for students for whom either writing or English or both may be new experiences. Before students can be told with confidence to write independently, they need help in building the necessary elements for second-language literacy: knowledge of content, literacy, and language (Bernhardt, 1991).

In writing, content refers to the topic of any given piece. For young children, this content usually begins with their immediate lives. Consider the examples of two kindergarteners: Enver, an Albanian student, who wrote, "I am driving my car"; and Jing, a Chinese student, who wrote "I love chkn [chicken]." Both sentences were accompanied by detailed drawings. Because these young children perceive the world in relation to themselves, they tend to write simple, one-frame, personal narratives. These expand developmentally over time to involve multiframe drawings accompanied by sentences and eventually to written narratives that are not dependent on drawings and that address issues from perspectives other than their own.

Content in writing also refers to bilingual learners' perceptions of the natural and social world. The content knowledge for science and social studies begins in the cultural *funds of knowledge,* which are first developed within families and communities (Moll & Gonzalez, 1994). This content knowledge expands beginning in the early grades to develop students' conceptual understandings at subsequent grades. In Liz's example, students were developing their knowledge of immigration. This built on students' personal immigration experiences as well as on concepts of family, community, country, and world, all of which had developed progressively through the elementary grades. Depending on their previous schooling, bilingual learners brought varying understandings of this social world into their writings about immigration. Liz built on these funds of knowledge and understandings when she allowed Rosa and Aldo to write personal narratives describing their immigrant experiences.

Through the initial steps of the rhetorical approach, Liz activated and developed bilingual learners' understandings of content. Through brainstorming, students explored what they knew about the topic. They further explored and enriched their understandings of chosen subtopics through further writing, discussion, and research. This content knowledge

Conclusion

As an instructional practice, the rhetorical approach can benefit both first- and second-language learners. For students learning English, this process provides essential support for developing knowledge of language, literacy, and content. The purpose of the rhetorical approach is to develop good habits: good writing habits for students and good teaching habits for teachers scaffolding writing. This approach, which supports the writing process, is broad and flexible enough that teachers can use their own preferred strategies to address the different steps. The development of students' English writing is supported through strategically increasing awareness of the writing process, including topic exploration, establishing purpose and audience, and choosing an appropriate organizational structure. By weaving relevant reading and referring to books through the process, Liz helped students see books as sources and models for their own writing.

The rhetorical approach helped Mary's first-grade students in their initial stages of writing personal narratives, and it helped Liz's fourth graders with more demanding expository pieces. This approach is not a fixed recipe to be followed in the same way as Mary or Liz, but it is a guide to scaffold the essential elements of the writing process. The particular teaching strategies teachers choose to implement in the various steps of the writing process are professional choices based on students' needs. These choices support all students, but especially students learning to write in a second language.

Notes

1. Bilingual and second-language learners for the purpose of this paper are defined as students with a language heritage other than English and who speak English to varying degrees of proficiency.
2. All students' names are culturally appropriate pseudonyms. Liz, the classroom teacher, is one of the coauthors of this chapter.

References

Allen, J. (1999). *Words, words, words: Teaching vocabulary in grades 4–12*. York, ME: Stenhouse Publishers.

Altman, L. J. (1995). *Amelia's road*. New York: Lee & Low Books.

Bernhardt, E. B. (1991). A psycholinguistic perspective on second language literacy. *AILA Review, 8*, 31–44.

Birch, B. M. (2002). *English L2 reading: Getting to the bottom*. Mahwah, NJ: Lawrence Erlbaum Associates.

Brisk, M. E., & Harrington, M. M. (2000). *Literacy and bilingualism: A handbook for all teachers*. Mahwah, NJ: Lawrence Erlbaum Associates.

Brisk, M. E., & Harrington, M. M. (forthcoming). *Literacy and bilingualism: A handbook for all teachers* (2nd ed.). Mahwah, NJ: Lawrence Erlbaum Associates.

Connor, U. (2002). New directions in contrastive rhetoric. *TESOL Quarterly, 36*, 493–510.

Cummins, J. (2003). Reading and the bilingual student: Fact and fiction. In G. G. Garcia (Ed.), *English learners: Reaching the highest level of English literacy* (pp. 2–33). Newark, DE: International Reading Association.

De Alvarado, C. S. (1984). From topic to final paper: A rhetorical approach. *TESOL Newsletter, 2*, 9–10.

Genesee, F., Paradis, J., & Crago, M. B. (2004). *Dual language development and disorders: A handbook on bilingualism & second language learning*. Baltimore: Paul Brooks.

Gibbons, P. (2002). *Scaffolding language, scaffolding learning*. Portsmouth, NH: Heinemann.

Hesse, K. (1992). *Letters from Rifka*. New York: Scholastic.

Hinkel, E. (2002). *Second language writers' text.* Mahwah, NJ: Lawrence Erlbaum Associates.

Johns, A. M. (1997). *Text, role, and context: Developing academic literacies.* Cambridge, England: Cambridge University Press.

Kucer, S. B. (2001). *Dimensions of literacy: A conceptual base for teaching reading and writing in school settings.* Mahwah, NJ: Erlbaum.

Levine, E. (1994). *If your name was changed at Ellis Island.* New York: Scholastic.

Lightbown, P. M., & Spada, N. (2003). *How languages are learned.* Oxford: Oxford University Press.

McLane, K. M. (1986). The writing development of high school second language learners in the context of a holistic English as a second language classroom. Unpublished doctoral dissertation, Boston University.

Moll, L. C., & Gonzalez, N. (1994). Lessons from research with language-minority children. *Journal of Reading Behavior, 26*(4), 439–456.

Raison, G., & Rivalland, J. (1994). *Writing developmental continuum.* Portsmouth, NH: Heinemann.

Solomon, J., & Rhodes, N. (1995). *Conceptualizing academic language.* Washington, DC: National Center for Research on Cultural Diversity and Second Language Learning.

CHAPTER 3

Transforming Standard Practices to Serve the Social and Academic Learning of English Language Learners

JERRI WILLETT, RUTH HARMAN, ANDREA HOGAN,
MARIA EUGENIA LOZANO, AND JOANNE RUBECK

Introduction

Standards-based curriculum and other mandates within the current climate of high-stakes testing and government policies such as the 2001 No Child Left Behind Act have created challenges that many teachers find hard to navigate. The biggest challenge is meeting a variety of learner needs while also meeting the demands of mandated curriculum and instructional techniques and keeping all learners engaged. English language learners (ELL) need extra language support and often have many other needs and resources. Some come to school with strong first-language literacy preparation and content knowledge; some come with needs ranging from special talents to physical, learning, or emotional disabilities; some have already studied English as a foreign language whereas others are hearing or reading English for the first time. Each ELL child is unique, but then so are all members of their new learning communities.

Given the diversity and complexity of each particular heterogeneous class, the idea that there exists a magic best practice is highly unlikely. Rather than taking a best-practice approach, this chapter asks the question, How can teachers transform standard practices to best fit the needs and strengths of their particular learners and to create the best opportunities for their learning? A concomitant question is how can outside experts and administrators work with teachers to enhance and support their professional judgments rather than prescribing best practices? Asking the questions in these ways changes the role of the teacher from one who follows a best practice imposed by outsiders to one who makes professional decisions about teaching based on evidence he or she collects through careful observation and in dialogue with scholars, parents, and colleagues.

Responding to the questions just posed, this chapter focuses on productive use of routine practices in the heterogeneous classroom. As most teachers know, routine practices are essential for the school management of a classroom community, particularly for ELL children for whom the U.S. classroom can be a strange and forbidding place. Well-designed practices are also essential for a variety of other purposes, including providing opportunities for academic learning, language development, socialization, and classroom community development and connecting to children with diverse experiences. Since routine practices are highly variable, they cannot be reproduced in new settings or used in the same setting without giving full attention to the meaning these practices have for particular children across time. Therefore, rather than describing a best practice, this chapter provides a set of principles for teachers, and for those who support them, to evaluate and integrate practices—whether mandated, passed down, or created anew—into their curriculum units as part of their learning communities that evolve over time.

The chapter illustrates how two particular teachers—Joanne Rubeck, a fifth-grade teacher, and Andrea Hogan, a second-grade teacher—grappled with transforming and evaluating the schools' standard practices to better serve instruction and learning. Both teachers work in the same *underperforming* school, as defined by the No Child Left Behind legislation. Joanne and Andrea are teacher–researchers in the Access to Critical Content and English Language Acquisition (ACCELA) Alliance, a partnership between the University of Massachusetts and the Springfield School District that aims to draw on the unique conditions and goals in their particular classrooms when responding to educational reform. The chapter follows these teachers' efforts to draw on powerful principles of learning and their own research when transforming existing classroom routine practices to serve the design and implementation of curriculum units for their heterogeneous classrooms in the context of their inquiry-master's degree program.

Finding Support and Opportunities for Dialogue

This chapter argues that for teachers to truly meet the needs of their students, they need to be in constant dialogue with the research, their professional colleagues and administrators, and the children and their families, but in the end teachers must remain in control of curriculum and instruction for their students. Although there are many ways to find support and opportunities for dialogue, Joanne and Andrea found theirs through the ACCELA Alliance.

ACCELA is a federally funded[1] master's degree in education with licensure in English as a second language (ESL), tailored for teachers in low performing schools. The courses introduce teachers to inquiry, second-language and multicultural theories on literacy and language development, and sociocultural and critical perspectives on classroom interaction. Unlike many forms of teacher inquiry that focus only on teachers' own practices, ACCELA teachers present their findings to and engage in dialogue with school and central office administrators on the implications of their inquiry for school and district policies. During their coursework the teachers, with the help of research assistants, use video recordings of classroom instruction and scanned student and instructional materials to analyze specific classroom interactions, curricular units, or contextual issues, which are discussed in course seminars. Maria Eugenia Lozano and Ruth Harman, doctoral students in the language, literacy, and culture (LLC) program and also authors of this chapter, served as research assistants for Andrea and Joanne during the academic year 2004–05.

Joanne and Andrea in Action

> Through their texts I learned about their concerns about being teased for differ-
> ent reasons: having braces, needing glasses, and being a different race from other
> peers. I learned about their sometimes conflicted sibling and familial relationships,
> bullying tendencies, and fears of older kids who hang around the park picking on
> younger kids.
>
> **Joanne Rubeck**

Joanne wrote this comment when reflecting back on a combined curricular unit she created with Andrea Hogan. Using the school's weekly second-grader and fifth-grader buddy reading[2] to ground the design of their curricular units, Joanne and Andrea developed reading and writing projects that had a shared audience and purpose for both groups. The fifth graders wrote individual picture books to present and share with their younger counterparts; the second graders identified social themes in trade books and then coconstructed multimodal charts with their older buddies. Andrea and Joanne encouraged both groups of students to tap into their personal issues and cultural backgrounds to create and to interpret their community of texts. In March 2005, the two groups came together with members of their families to present their work.

Joanne's quote at the beginning of this section highlighted some of the key points cover in this chapter: First, by tapping into their own social worlds and concerns, children become invested in classroom literacy events and routines (Dyson, 1993; Moll, 1992; Norton, 1997; Solsken, Willett, & Wilson-Keenan, 2000). This is especially important in low-income urban areas where culturally and linguistically diverse students, particularly ELLs, are constructed as at risk by state and district assessments within the current climate of high accountability (Ibrahim, 1999; McNeil, 2000; Olsen, 1997). One of Andrea's students, for example, who prior to the unit had been labeled a behaviorally troubled child adopted a new literate identity in the class as a result of the curricular process. When Andrea tested Abu at the beginning of the year, he appeared to be a nonreader. After completing the group project, Andrea commented about her student, "He just tested as one of my top students leaving second grade. He went from a nonreader to a solid end of the year second grader."

The curricular unit provided a space for the children and teachers to develop meaning-ful and dynamic interconnections with each other and with the texts produced for the final presentation and publication. The remainder of the chapter describes the design and imple-mentation of Joanne and Andrea's coordinated curriculum units in which they embedded the schools' standard and routine practices and the social and academic work produced for the units by the students who were the focus of the teachers' inquiry projects.

One of the key insights that Joanne and Andrea came to was that routine practices must serve social and academic learning. If these practices remain disconnected from the academic curriculum and fail to evolve, they lose their power to serve social and academic learning. When standard practices are integrated into a new curriculum unit, they evolve to meet the new communicative demands of the learning community. Nevertheless, the practices need to remain predictable enough to provide the structure and support needed for English language learners, especially if careful attention is paid to nurturing an inclusive learning community.

The final section in the chapter presents a miniliterature review of the research discussed in the ACCELA courses and drawn on by the teachers to modify standard practices, to create their curriculum units, and to understand the work their students produced. Although the units are very specific to these particular classrooms, they concretely illustrate the following key features outlined in the literature review as essential for teaching culturally and linguistically diverse children successfully:

- Ample opportunities for social interaction and taking up multiple identities
- Interweaving of social worlds, academic worlds, and possible literate futures
- Use of everyday routines to scaffold[3] an integrated and purposeful curricular unit
- Use of authentic contexts, texts, purposes, and audiences
- Explicit teaching of genre and language features within a meaningful context
- Reinforcement of language and content for ELLs through experiential and multimodal activities
- Publication of students' end product to families and larger audiences

Although the specific details presented in this chapter may provide teachers with ideas for their own classrooms and ways to integrate numerous state and district standards and best practices into their curriculum, the major point this chapter highlights is that teachers must draw on their particular students' social and academic needs and interests when planning instruction.

Teaching Content for Language Development

In previous ACCELA courses, Joanne and Andrea already had spent a considerable time analyzing high-stakes genres, student texts, and their own literacy practices. The objective for the fifth course in the program, "Teaching Content for Language Development," was for teachers to understand how to design curriculum that (1) dealt with meaningful and comprehensible content; (2) simultaneously and explicitly attended to the development of both content and language; (3) organized instruction around powerful learning principles and strategies; and (4) met mandated curriculum standards and goals while also respecting and drawing on students' *funds of knowledge*[4] (Moll, Amanti, Neff, and Gonzales, 1992).

The major assignments for this course, taught by Jerri Willett, were to (1) design, implement, and assess a unit for their specific classrooms; (2) conduct case studies of two focal children's engagement with the unit; and (3) present their data to colleagues and school or district administrators, drawing implications for the school and district.

The curriculum design had three parts (Table 3.1). Andrea and Joanne followed Jerri's guidelines in designing their coordinated curricular units: They used principles of backward design[5], incorporated Teaching English to Speakers of Other Languages (TESOL) and

Macro level design of the unit	Enduring understandings and essential questions of unit. Design performance assessments, activities and overall structure according to *Understanding by Design (Wiggins & McTighe, 1998); Sheltered Instruction (Echevarria et al 2000); Scaffolding Reading for ELL (Fitzgerald & Graves, 2004);* Massachusetts State Standards and other professional standards
Content of unit: Meaningful and Comprehensible	Integrates the needs and interests of the students, including the interests of the English language learners (i.e., focus on both content and language objectives; use of pictures and other multimodal texts to support literacy development) Uses teachers' own set of interests and talents to decide what unit to create
Literacy and Language Development	Uses principles of learning and teaching that the teachers have studied in Master's courses in deciding how to teach discrete parts of unit to optimize students' learning

Table 3.1 ACCELA Course Curriculum Design

Massachusetts curriculum standards, and created activities that would support second-language learners through explicit and experiential scaffolding. After a brief description of their school context, this chapter explores how they implemented their project and the texts the students produced.

City and School Context

Gerena Elementary School is in the urban district of Springfield, Massachusetts. The population of Springfield is 156,983, and it is the third largest city in the state (ePodunk, 2005). Latino students make up 48.5% of the school population in the city compared with 11.5% statewide (Massachusetts Department of Education, 2005). Since the elimination of transitional bilingual education in Massachusetts in 2002, mainstream teachers in the city have been under pressure to comply with new state teacher licensure requirements to support ELLS in their mainstream classrooms. Joanne and Andrea, for example, enrolled in the ACCELA program to meet new teaching requirements and to further their understanding of second-language and literacy development. In 2004–05, Gerena served approximately 750 students in grades kindergarten through fifth grade, out of which 68% were Latino, 25% were African American, 7% were White. Ninety-two percent of all students received free or reduced price lunch. In its 2003–04 No Child Left Behind report card the school ranked as one of the lowest performing in Massachusetts Springfield Public Schools, 2004.

Since 1995, Gerena has been training teachers in the *First Steps* approach to literacy and language development instead of implementing a scripted curriculum package for writing development, a common practice in underperforming schools. The First Steps project, developed in Western Australia in 1988 to address the needs of students whose academic and cultural needs were not being met by current school literacy practices, was first introduced into U.S. classrooms in 1995 (*STEPS* Professional Development and Consulting, 2005). Both Joanne and Andrea had been trained to use this approach to instruction.

Joanne's Class Context

Joanne, a young Anglo American, for this study had a mainstream class with 15 Latino and African American students and one Anglo American. Most of the students were placed in this accelerated class because of their high scores on the math portion of the Massachusetts Comprehensive Assessment System (MCAS). Eleven of the students are ELL, ranging in English proficiency from low to high. One of the fifth-grade focal students in this study, Kendria, was a Puerto Rican ELL. Her parents spoke only Spanish at home; Kendria acted as the main translator and interpreter for them in their English transactions. She had one older brother and a younger adopted sister. She was an avid reader and enjoyed peer interaction when writing.

The other fifth-grade focal student of the study, Bernardo, is an 11-year-old Puerto Rican student who lives with his Spanish-speaking mother. He was placed in Joanne's fifth-grade class because of his disruptive behavior in other classes; the hope was that the accelerated students would provide him with positive role models. Before the combined curricular project, Bernardo still had difficulty staying still and relating to his classmates in his new community of learning. When required to take a fifth-grade district wide writing assessment on "Being a good friend" at the beginning of the year, Bernardo produced a string of incoherent sentences about getting good grades, listening to the teacher, and helping people on their math before responding to the prompt (Figure 3.1).

Being a good friend is important because we all need help. I need help sometimes so I can graduate from school and getting a At on my test. And also being to the teacher is being a friend to. So is doing your homework every day is being a friend. Also is reading a book every day. So is sharing is a nice way to be a friend. Helping people on there math is being a friend. For exampl like Tanysha a Sasha they always share whith echother these the best of friend's ever

Being a good friend is important because we all need help

Also is reading a book every day

So is sharing a nice way to be a friend

Figure 3.1 Bernardo's district assessment.

Andrea's Class Context

Andrea, of mixed Italian and American Indian heritage, teaches mainstream second grade. Her class for this study consisted of 17 students, with 5 African American and 12 Latinos. Her four ELL students ranged from very low to high proficiency in English. Out of all her students, eight were behavioral students. Abu, one of the second-grade focal students, was an eight-year-old African American boy living with his mother and his five brothers and sisters. When Andrea tested him on the Dibels Reading Assessment (DRA) at the beginning of the school year, he scored as a high-risk reader. As the year passed, Abu's reading and writing development began to progress, but, as with other children in the classroom, Abu still needed help to manage behavior and social issues. The second focal student, Teresa, was a nine-year-old Latina who was repeating second grade. She spoke primarily Spanish at home and served as interpreter to her mother, who is a monolingual Spanish speaker. At the beginning of the year Teresa scored as a some-risk reader, and by the end of the second grade she scored at grade level.

Joanne and Andrea's Curricular Design

Joanne and Andrea spent the first weeks in Jerri's ACCELA course struggling with the main course assignment. Joanne had difficulty deciding on the social purpose that would shape her curricular unit. After several discussions with other teachers in the course about the authentic contexts they had chosen for their work and after reading about critical literacy[6], she decided the fifth-grade and second-grade weekly meeting would be the ideal audience and context for her children's work. Andrea, whose students were having difficulty relating to one another and to academic material, decided that she needed to focus on the inappropriate behavior before she tackled academic subject matter. After discussing her struggles with both Jerri and Joanne, Andrea carefully selected trade books with themes related to the children's emotional issues (e.g., anger, jealousy, depression). She created a curricular unit that used the fifth graders as facilitators in the children's reading process and understanding of the trade books. For the end presentation, the fifth graders would help the second graders illustrate and describe the main themes in these trade books on large poster boards.

To accomplish the goals of their combined unit, Andrea and Joanne both transformed the routine practices of their classroom (Table 3.2) into meaningful practices that had a particular social purpose and audience. Some of their practices were mandated by school policy (e.g., buddy reading, centers, writing process). Some, such as First Steps (1999) and the minilessons on genre features, were mandated by the school's literacy curriculum. Others, to include asking critical literacy questions, use of scaffolding for ESL learners, and drawing on students' funds of knowledge, were mandated by ACCELA course requirements. Many

Language Arts Routines	
Mini Lessons	Used to present key aspects of the curricular unit
Group Discussion or **Question/ Answer Period**	Used to clarify any difficulties with the concepts presented
Centers	Used to divide students into small working groups to work on: Guided or independent reading or writing projects Hands-on projects Peer or teacher feedback on writing
Buddy Reading	Used to give each student a peer mentor to support reading aloud

Table 3.2 Language Arts Routines at Gerena

of their practices, such as class discussion, Q&A, and teaching comprehension strategies, were passed down from colleagues, professional development, or former teachers. Whatever the source of their routine practices, Joanne and Andrea transformed them to accomplish the academic and social goals for their unit.

Joanne's Curricular Unit on Literary Narratives

The academic purpose of Joanne's curricular unit was to foster an enduring understanding of the linguistic and stylistic features of literary narratives (i.e., children's novels). The social purpose of her unit was to encourage students to use their own issues and knowledge of their second-grade buddies to create a picture book with use of the generic features of literary narratives (e.g., imagery, dialogue, action verbs). In terms of teaching strategies, Joanne wanted to develop a permeable curriculum that allowed her students to use their own funds of knowledge as inroads to academic literacy and as a crossroad between home and school (Dyson, 1993, p. 133). Using the standard routines, Joanne led minilectures on key aspects of fiction writing, facilitated group discussion on literature the class was reading and writing, and scaffolded the students' understanding through hands-on projects and peer interaction and feedback time. Through her careful design and transformation of the normal routines of the fifth-grade reading block, Joanne was able to teach both discrete aspects of fiction reading and writing and also to contextualize her teaching within the larger purpose and goal of the unit (Table 3.3).

Minilessons

Over the course of the two months, Joanne conducted a series of minilectures (e.g., effective openers, imagery or similes, dialogue, conjunctions, character development). In each minilecture she talked about key aspects of fiction but also tapped into the students' own knowledge and creation of literary texts. In this way she interwove the children's own background knowledge of literature and their own interest into her explicit teaching of genre. She also afforded them literate identities as fiction writers and critics from early on in the unit (Hawkins, 2005; Norton, 1997; Toohey, 2000). Joanne provided the students with a "writer's toolbox" folder where they gathered all their toolbox sheets on literary devices discussed in the minilectures. When writing up their own narratives for the picture books, Joanne encouraged the students to check in their toolboxes for inspiration on how to create their own literary pieces. When checking students' understanding of conjunctions or other grammatical features in minilessons or group discussion, Joanne consistently used

Purpose of Unit: Understand how to shape narratives for a particular audience and social purpose Title: Picture Book Narrative Writing				
Writing Process	**Sense of Audience**	**Reading Process**	**Minilessons**	**Scaffolding**
Free write on "What bothers me?"	Sharing of what bothers me with 5th grade peers	Independent and guided reading of *Felita* (Mohr, 1979)	Effective openers	Group discussion and individual work sheets on favorite openers
	Sharing with 2nd grade to share about bothersome issues	Independent and guided reading of *Maniac Magee* (Spinelli, 1990)	Imagery through Similes	Drawing of mind pictures of similes; jigsaw puzzles
Narrative plan of book	Interview of 2nd grade buddy about books and issues	Independent reading of choice of other novels (i.e., *Tuck Everlasting*, Babbit 1975 ; *Charlotte's Web*, White 1999)	Dialogue	Collective picture-book making (with direct speech and description)
First draft of book			Show/ tell	Group analysis of excerpts from *Maniac Magee* and student selected texts
Second draft of book	Peer and teacher feedback on 1st and 2nd draft	Independent analysis and model reading of picture books (i.e., *The Empty Pot*, Demi, 1990)	Conjunctions	Use of new conjunctions in writing up description of What bothers me?
Final published copy	Giving and reading aloud of book to 2nd graders		Character Development	Group discussion on Spinelli and his use of characters
End Product : Picture Book				

Table 3.3 Joanne's Curricular Unit

examples from the literary books they were reading and writing in class. For example, when modeling the use of conjunctions in literature, Joanne used the class's common knowledge of the novel *Roll of Thunder, Hear My Cry* (Taylor, 1979) to link the linguistic features with a literary context.

Joanne: Not only did the Wallaces pollute the well water…What is something else they did? Who can raise their hands?
Miguel: They wanted to kill Hammer.
Joanne: Okay.
Bernardo: Jump Hammer.
Joanne: Good.
Joanne (*writing up the sentence on board, "Not only did the Wallaces pollute the water but they also jumped Hammer") Do you see I am lifting one thing that happened and then adding something even more intense?*

Scaffolding Activities

In their daily centers, Joanne had the students do hands-on activities to reinforce their understanding of the key elements of fiction (Figure 3.2). The students also assembled jigsaw

Kendria's mind picture of her favorite simile: The sunset was as colorful as a rainbow.

For ELL students, linking picture to concept helps content and language comprehension.

Figure 3.2 Kendria's simile.

"What happened was that I was at the mall and my brother put live bugs in a bucket, then he dumped them onto my bed." ['Not only are they ugly, but they're also creepy." Kendria draws on the conjunctions that were modeled, graphed, and explained in class]

"I told my mother and he was ground for 2 weeks."

Figure 3.3 Kendria's bothersome issue.

pieces of simile by looking at the meaning and how the jagged edges of paper fit together. Finally, Joanne led guided reading sessions of *Maniac Magee* (Spinelli, 1990) and discussed key concepts and vocabulary.

Sense of Audience

To develop the children's understanding of audience for their own picture books, Joanne began by asking the students to think about issues that bothered them at home or in school. She asked the students to write up a paragraph or two, using the conjunctions they were also learning at the time, about some burning issue for them. Kendria wrote about how her brother had placed a bucket of worms in her bed (Figure 3.3). Joanne then used a minilesson to hold an open forum on bothersome issues for her fifth graders. Kendria talked about brothers and how they can be very jealous of their younger siblings: "My brother thinks I'm spoiled because I get everything I want." When Joanne and Andrea's group met, the second graders and fifth graders shared their list of complaints about school and home. Joanne then had her students work on interview questions for the second graders about their favorite types of fiction and characters. Kendria was matched up with Teresa, who had a new baby sister in the family and was having difficulty dealing with it. Bernardo chose Abu, who had been constructed by both the fifth and second graders as the most difficult student. In a follow-up interview, Bernardo talked about how important writing the book for Abu was because he had helped Abu deal with bullying and behavioral issues: "I thought of the story because I wanted to give Abu confidence and make him feel better about himself and stop getting into trouble," Bernardo said (Arbulu, 2005).

To deepen their understanding of how writers use personal experiences and their own background to write their stories, Joanne read excerpts from books and articles to the children. For example, she read a short article to the children about what had inspired Spinelli (1990) in his writing of *Maniac Magee*. The children talked about their own toolboxes and writing processes, comparing them to what the writers did.

Writing Process

With a heightened sense of audience and a toolbox of literary devices, the children began creating a narrative plan with orientation, initial event, complication, and resolution. They drew pictures to complement each sequence of the narrative. Kendria decided to write about an older brother who becomes very jealous of his younger sister. In a group discussion time, the children then shared their stories and got feedback from their peers and teacher. Kendria worked closely with a friend and used some of her input in her final product.

L: You could write why he doesn't want a little sister.

K: Because he thought that the little sister was getting all the attention and like…you know what I mean.

L: Yeah, he was getting all the attention and…

K: And everyone was cooing at her.

L: Have you thought about this idea like not at the end but as to the middle before he turn around…the day before he (inaudible) the parents will say, "It's not that we are giving them all the attention, it's not that we don't like you, it's just that newborn babies need more attention 'cause they're brand new, not brand new but little and they're like…"

K: I am going to get my pencil.

Publication

Kendria and Bernard created very rich but dramatically different picture books, but both used key generic features of fictional narratives in their stories. Kendria's own problems with her brother and her interviews with her second-grade buddy very much influenced the topic of her text. She used similes, action verbs, and dialogue in a very tight narrative with a clear orientation, complication, resolution, and coda (Figure 3.4).

In Bernardo's case, Abu's difficulties in the second-grade class, which mirrored some of Bernardo's own problems, shaped the type of fiction he chose to write. Bernardo's book, "How Mitchell Made Friends," describes the bullying and angry behavior of the protagonist (Figure 3.5). In the resolution of the narrative, Mitchell realizes that he is alienating his peers, apologizes to them for his behavior, and invites them to a party. Bernardo, who wrote an incoherent paragraph for the district-wide assessment in September of that year (Figure 3.1), wrote a tight narrative with orientation, complication, resolution, and coda.

When Sammy heard all of this commotion made by the adults, Sammy screamed a piercing scream and ran out of the hospital toward the car. By the time Sammy got to the car, he was out of breath. He locked himself in the car, he turned the car radio all the way up. A while later Sammy started to punch and kick the seats and the ceiling of the car. However, it hurt Sammy more than it hurt the car.

Show, not tell: Kendria shows Sammy's jealousy by describing his rabid run to the family car.

Descriptive details: "He locked himself in the car, he turned the car radio all the way up. A while later Sammy started to punch and kick the seats and the ceiling of the car. However, it hurt Sammy more than it hurt the car."

Picture shows Sammy alone in the car.

Figure 3.4 Kendria's storybook.

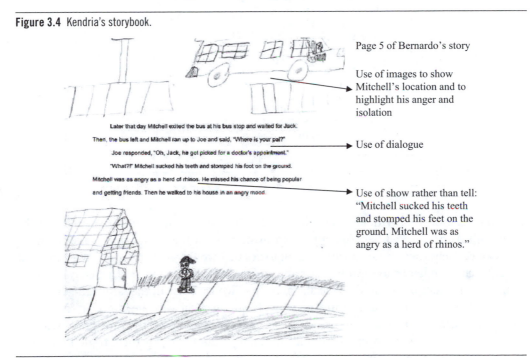

Later that day Mitchell exited the bus at his bus stop and waited for Jack. Then, the bus left and Mitchell ran up to Joe and said, "Where is your pal?" Joe responded, "Oh, Jack, he got picked for a doctor's appointment." "What?!" Mitchell sucked his teeth and stomped his foot on the ground. Mitchell was as angry as a herd of rhinos. He missed his chance of being popular and getting friends. Then he walked to his house in an angry mood.

Page 5 of Bernardo's story

Use of images to show Mitchell's location and to highlight his anger and isolation

Use of dialogue

Use of show rather than tell: "Mitchell sucked his teeth and stomped his feet on the ground. Mitchell was as angry as a herd of rhinos."

Figure 3.5 Bernardo's storybook.

Andrea's Curricular Unit

After having to continually stop her lessons with her second graders to deal with behavior issues among the students, Andrea decided to address the very issues that were impeding her daily teaching through her curriculum content. Therefore, the main purpose of Andrea's curricular unit, "Using Literature to Talk about Social Issues in the Classroom," was to help her students reflect on how their behavior and actions in school affected their

		Purpose of Unit: To express the bothersome issues that affect each individual student Using Literature to Talk about Social Issues in the Classroom		
Writing Process	**Sense of Audience**	**Reading Process**	**Mini Lessons**	**Scaffolding**
Free write on What bothers me	Sharing of what bothers me with classmates			Group discussion Chart writing Individual notebook writing
		Reading of story *Matthew and Tilly* (Jones, 1995)	Finding a theme in a story	Predicting Guessing Retelling the story Role playing
	Sharing with 5th grade about bothersome issues	Independent and guided reading of personalized stories that relate closely to students' lives	Summarizing a story	Collective picture-book making (with direct speech and description)
	Interview with 5th grade buddy about books and issues			
	Presenting the chart to 5th graders	Sharing of the stories written by 5th graders		
End Product: Story Chart				

Table 3.4 Andrea's Curricular Unit

everyday relationships with her, their classmates, and the other teachers. To begin her eight-week unit Andrea asked her students to brainstorm about the things that make them feel sad. Collectively, they came up with a list of issues that would shape the unit. Working with other teachers in her school Andrea was able to find trade books that addressed directly the bothersome issues of her students (e.g., having a newborn baby in the family, dealing with parents' divorce, having a sick family member, laughing at the way they speak). Because the range of reading proficiencies in her class was great, Andrea asked the fifth-grade students to work with their second-grade buddies to identify the theme in their trade books and to create a chart that summarized how feelings changed throughout the story (i.e., beginning, middle, and end). Most of the groups were organized so that the second grader was in charge of the drawings and the fifth grader was in charge of the writing. Table 3.4 summarizes Andrea's unit.

Minilessons and Scaffolding Activities
To provide her students with the skills to identify the theme in their own books, Andrea began her unit by introducing a new story to the class, *Matthew and Tilly* by Rebecca C.

Bernardo (5th grader) and Abu (2nd grader) write a response to their group book. Their worksheet was a cooperative effort, with both Bernardo and Abu taking turns to read the questions. Abu dictated to Bernardo the responses to each of the questions.

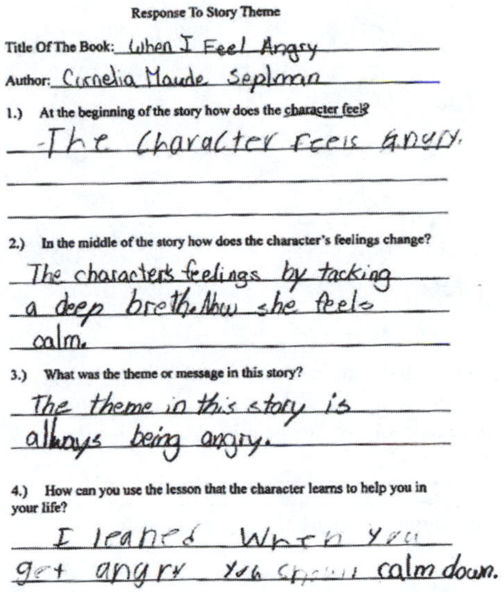

Response To Story Theme

Title Of The Book: When I Feel Angry

Author: Cornelia Maude Seplman

1.) At the beginning of the story how does the character feel?

The Character feels angry.

2.) In the middle of the story how does the character's feelings change?

The characters feelings by tacking a deep breth. Abu she feels calm.

3.) What was the theme or message in this story?

The theme in this story is always being angry.

4.) How can you use the lesson that the character learns to help you in your life?

I leaned When you get angry you should calm down.

Figure 3.6 Abu and Bernardo summarize change of feelings in the story.

Jones. To scaffold this story, students participated in a series of role plays that led to identification of key elements in a story. After each dramatization, Andrea asked her students to retell the story in their own words, to give a reason why the characters reacted in that particular way to the situation, and to talk about how they might have solved the situation in a different way. The sharing of ideas started as an oral activity, but it always ended as a written one either in their unit journals or in worksheets to be completed by the students (Figure 3.6). After writing in their journals and worksheets, students returned to the rug area to share what they wrote.

Sense of Audience

The second graders were told from the beginning that they were going to coconstruct charts with their buddies to summarize the trade books they were reading together and that these charts would be shared at a public presentation. Knowing that their families would be present, the children were engaged in all stages of the unit. They took particular care in their work as they identified the theme and lessons of the trade books. The class focused on how to identify characters' feelings through pictures and how pictures and dialogue do not say the same thing. The class brainstormed lists and role played possible scenarios about what could happen between people to make feelings change. They learned not only that these changes were an important way that authors engaged readers but also that authors developed themes with which their readers could identify. With the help of their fifth-grade buddies, both Abu and Teresa were able to articulate the conflict and resolution of the stories and to recognize their own experiences in the actions and words of the characters. Abu and Bernardo's understandings are illustrated in their theme chart (Figure 3.7).

Presentation

As part of their curriculum units, Joanne and Andrea organized a public sharing of the students' books and charts with parents from both grades in March 2005. The fifth graders

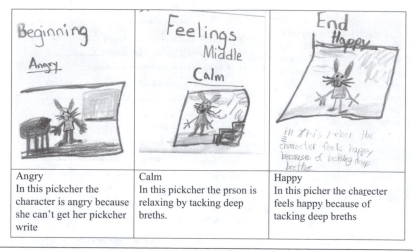

Beginning Angry	Feelings Middle Calm	End Happy
Angry In this pickcher the character is angry because she can't get her pickcher write	Calm In this pickcher the prson is relaxing by tacking deep breths.	Happy In this picher the character feels happy because of tacking deep breths

Figure 3.7 Abu and Bernardo's chart of anger as a theme.

Figure 3.8 Abu and Bernardo present their chart.

sent out invitations and completed the final drafts of their stories with pictures for each page and with a cover title page. Andrea noted,

> When I called Abu's mother to invite her to the celebration, she said curtly that she was busy and couldn't talk. I had called so many times before—always about Abu's behavior. But when I told her how well Abu was doing and that I was inviting her to a celebration, her tone quickly changed.

On the day of the celebration, the second graders presented their charts to their proud parents (Figure 3.8), including Abu's mother, the teachers, and even members of the press (Arbulu, 2005).

Figure 3.9 Kendria read her storybook to Teresa.

Then the fifth graders surprised the second graders with their gifts: a bound copy of the original stories they created for their buddies. In some of the books the illustrations were left uncolored so their buddies could finish them (Figure 3.9).

Reflections on Joanne's and Andrea's Coordinated Units

For Joanne's fifth-grade curricular unit, Kendria and Bernardo were able to write very carefully crafted texts by the end of Joanne's unit. They tapped into the available designs (New London Group, 1996) offered to them by Joanne's carefully planned curricular unit and transformed them to create texts for their own social purposes. In a follow-up interview about the book he wrote, Bernardo told Ruth that he felt writing the picture book was very important: He had helped Abu to understand how to behave in class. Joanne, in reflecting on Bernardo's behavior in class after his role modeling and support of Abu in the buddy project, felt that her own understanding of Bernardo had deepened as a result of the project and had helped her to interact with him differently:

> Although Bernardo saw his role as helping his "troublesome" buddy with his behavior issues, his writing was a reflection of his own concerns and needs. By understanding his motivations, I have been able to adjust my own teaching style to meet his needs. I have had many successes in directing his behaviors toward more positive ends and have observed a significant change in how he acts to make friends. He has become a great support in the classroom.

Kendria, in a follow-up interview, explained that writing from the perspective of an older sibling helped her to understand the emotional pain an older sibling can feel toward a younger more favored sister.

Likewise, in Andrea's second-grade class, Abu's behavior and academic performance changed dramatically after his bonding with Bernardo through the creation of their chart. Andrea explains,

> Once our buddy day started, Abu's behavior started to slowly change. He was the one who always kicked chairs, threw pencils, tipped desks, anything to disrupt and get attention. He is one who also connected his story [trade book] to his own behavior. Now he tries really hard to do the right thing, sometimes I can see him thinking before he acts and even when he does make the wrong choice he realizes it. I'm proud to report that Abu has gone from a nonreader to a solid second-grade reader.

Essentially, Andrea and Joanne modified standard practices to take into account a wider variety of social and academic purposes; both teachers felt they had a much greater understanding of children's needs, resources, and investments after the project. By using the routine practices in innovative ways, the teachers were able to create a cross-grade dynamic learning community within the school. The teachers and children were able to assume a wider variety of literate and social identities and to connect to each other in multiple and dynamic ways (Comber, Thomson, & Wells, 2001; Dyson, 1993; Gutiérrez & Larson, 1995; Norton, 1997).

Reflecting on their curricular project, Andrea felt very grateful for the opportunity to "take the chance and teach something that was outside of the required curriculum." By exploring their children's use of their own social worlds to make sense of the academic, both teachers felt they had gained more access into their children's private worlds and adapted their teaching process as a result (Freire & Macedo, 1987; Luke & Freebody, 1997). Andrea felt that the unit helped her to grow as a teacher and her students to adopt more literate and academic identities:

> I truly believe this unit has helped me as a teacher and also the students. This has opened their eyes to a whole new world. I am so proud of all my students.

Research on This Praxis

A combined multiliteracy and critical literacy perspective (Freire & Macedo, 1987; Luke & Freebody, 1997; Luke, 2000; Kress, 2000; New London Group, 1996) has informed this study's exploration of teachers' and students' literacy practices. First, in institutionalized school contexts, if children are able to perform successfully in the multiple academic registers and contexts of schooling (Bourdieu, 1991; New London Group, 1996; Schleppegrell, 2004), they will have access to richer facilities and resources in their academic life (e.g., gifted and talented programs, after-school honors programs) (Darling-Hammond, 1995; Olsen, 1997). The elementary school classroom is a pivotal site where children are first slotted into particular identities as low- or high-risk learners, terminology taken from the nationally used literacy assessment tool, "Dynamic Indicators of Basic Early Literacy Skills. (DIBELS, 2007). Children of color from low economic urban areas are constructed more frequently as high-risk readers than middle-class white students (Gee, 1999; Wohlstetter & Malloy, 2001).

Working within a system that often marginalizes lower socioeconomic students from a very early age, urban public school teachers need to facilitate their students' access to multiple academic registers and also to incorporate the students' funds of knowledge into their curriculum design. To develop generic competence (Partridge, 2004, p. 7), students need to learn more than the textual features and categories of fixed genres (Bhatia, 1993;

Kress, 2000; Partridge, 2004). Indeed, they need to recognize that genres are both structured and dynamic: The specific audience and context of a text directly influence its generic structure. By creating texts for authentic purposes with audiences larger than their own immediate teacher or classmates, students begin to understand the functional and meaningful interconnections of text and context (Christie & Martin, 1997; First Steps, 1999; Tower, 2003). At the same time, teachers also need to teach students how to identify the specific generic features that tend to recur across similar text types (e.g., abstract nouns, logical connectors, relational verbs in expository texts) (Halliday, 1994; Kamberelis, 1999, Kern, 2000; Schleppegrell, 2004).

By understanding that genre is a plastic entity that changes according to its audience and context but that also has certain typical conventions, students begin to manipulate academic genres for their own academic and social purposes. It is by playing the loose rules of the game that genre participants can manipulate and redesign them (Bhatia, 1993; Kress, 2000). Teachers must encourage students to draw on available resources that both scaffold their understanding of a specific genre and encourage them to creatively transform them. In the language arts block, students can be taught to enact or to resist generic conventions depending on the academic register and context.

The teaching of genre for ELLs and all culturally and linguistically diverse students, therefore, entails the use of authentic contexts, the scaffolding of generic features of texts (e.g., minilessons, modeling, discussion, hands-on projects) and the production and publication of a text that is socially meaningful to the student (Christie & Martin, 1997; First Steps, 1999). For ELL students—who often need explicit scaffolding of text structure, reinforcement of content through multimodal representation, validation of their own cultural backgrounds, and a purpose for the reading or writing of a text—the approach described in this chapter fosters their language and content comprehension in mainstream classes (Moll, et al., 1992; Partridge, 2004; Peregoy & Boyle, 2000). Everyday classroom routine practices provide an ideal space for this development of academic learning, language development, socialization, and classroom community development.

Research specifically focused on language and academic routine practices in socialization (Boggs, 1985; Floriani, 1994; Gutiérrez & Larson, 1995; Gutiérrez, Baquedano-Lopez, & Turner, 1997; Heath, 1983; Kong & Pearson, 2003; Schieffelin & Ochs, 1986; Solsken, Willett, & Wilson-Keenan, 2000; Toohey, 2000; Vasquez, Pease-Alvarez, & Shannon, 1994; Willett, 1995, Willett, Solsken, & Wilson-Keenan,1999; Wilson-Keenan, Willett, & Solsken, 2001) suggests that routine practices in the home, community, and school are important for language and academic socialization. Productive routine practices change gradually in response to evolving needs of the participants and in support of academic growth. Routine practices help get daily work done efficiently, but they do much more. They construct habits, knowledge, identities, and relationships that will reverberate throughout a child's development and will provide essential scaffolding for learning and investment in important goals. Moreover, routine practices are never merely imposed on children but are jointly constructed according to the meanings these practices have for them. Children often pick up and use routine practices for their own purposes and play bidding for friendship, practicing important skills and identities, and gaining attention from their parents and teachers. Research also shows a sinister side to routine practices—they can contribute to inequitable educational outcomes, no matter how well intentioned the original purpose for the practice. To counteract these possible inequities, understanding home or children's play routines can help teachers design classroom practices that better meet the needs of children while providing them with opportunities to perform a wider variety of identities and competencies.

Joanne and Andrea's coordinated units were created in the context of a community of teacher researchers (Cochran-Smith & Lytle, 1999; Kamler & Comber, 2004; Lieberman & Miller, 2001). Through reflective dialogue with their data, state and professional standards, the research literature, and their colleagues, they were able to modify their routine practices to better support students' academic learning, to connect to their immediate social worlds, and to help them visualize their literate futures (Luke & Freebody, 2000). Research on teachers' professional development suggests that teachers who critically and systematically examine their classroom practices, the academic and social development of their students, and the nature of classroom interaction and student work are generally more effective in supporting student learning and advancing their own professional development (Cochran-Smith & Lytle, 1993; Darling-Hammond, 2000; Newmann, King, & Youngs, 2000; Weinbaum, Allen, & Blythe, 2004).

Conclusion

This chapter focused on constructing rich and productive literacy events with children in linguistically and culturally diverse classrooms, illustrated through the classrooms of Andrea and Joanne. Their units highlighted the importance of teachers having the freedom, space, time, and support to make professional decisions about the best way to guide the learning of their particular students. It is impossible to imagine generic scripted curriculum or teacher-proof materials, strategies, or routine practices capable of connecting as well with particular children. Joanne and Andrea not only exercised their professional judgment; they also took up their professional responsibility to critically and systematically examine their classroom practices, the academic and social development of their students, and the nature of classroom interaction and the support it provides. Joanne and Andrea used a variety of materials and pedagogical strategies from their colleagues; commercial sources, mandated materials, and curriculum guides; professional books and workshops; university classes; and state and professional standards, but their use of these materials was ultimately shaped by the academic and social needs of their particular students, which they learned about through participant observation and other methods of data collection. As Hargreaves (2000, p. 168) warned, "Failure of teachers to engage in systematic and sustained inquiry will result in deprofessionalization forces wresting control of curricular and pedagogical practices from teachers." Teachers who lose control of these practices will not well serve English language learners, who are, by definition, nonstandard. They are counting on their teachers to reach their hearts and minds in ways that no outside expert, packaged curriculum, or mandated practice could ever do.

Notes

1. ACCELA is funded by Title III No Child Left Behind: National Professional Development; by Title VII Career Ladder and by Title II Teacher Quality.
2. Buddy Reading is a common practice in cross-age reading programs in multiethnic, multilingual inner-city schools. In this practice, students from higher grades read regularly with students in lower grades (Whang, Samway, & Pippitt, 1995).

3. Scaffolding is a pedagogical practice that provides students with support to accomplish a task or to develop understanding. Gradually, support is withdrawn, and responsibility for performance is shifted to the learner. What counts as support depends on the specific learner, but many strategies and techniques can serve as scaffolding, including graphic organizers, explicit instruction, use of examples, breaking down tasks into steps, providing hints, using multiple modalities, asking questions, giving demonstrations, telling stories, activity structure, and team work. Principles for effective scaffolding include activating prior knowledge, providing authentic and meaningful contexts and activities, engaging in collaborative interaction, giving choices to enable active construction of meaning and ownership of task, and providing multiple perspectives, illustrations, examples, and clarifications.

4. *Funds of knowledge* refers to the bodies of knowledge, ways of thinking, practical skills, and everyday practices and interactions available to children in their households and communities. Drawing on children's funds of knowledge as a basis for curriculum units and frames of reference is an important way to support academic learning.

5. *Backward design* is a method of curriculum design with three phases: (1) Identify desired results, which should be worthy of and requiring of understanding; (2) determine acceptable evidence of understanding and performance and what kinds of assessments will provide this evidence; and (3) plan learning experiences and instructions that will develop desired understandings.

6. Critical literacy involves developing an awareness of the ideological nature of texts and their ability to position readers. It also involves learning how to develop the ability to construct powerful texts for particular social purposes. Teachers often help students develop awareness by working with texts that are meaningful to students or that have direct consequences for them or those they care about. Students are taught to ask important questions about texts, such as, What is the text saying about the world and from what point of view? How does the text attempt to persuade readers to take up its viewpoint? Who benefits from the views being expressed and what are the consequences for those who do not benefit? What assumptions does the text make about its readers? Should the reader accept or resist what is being promoted?

References

Arbulu, N. (2005, April 10). Buddy system bonds pupils. *The Springfield Republican*.

Babbitt, N. (1975). *Tuck Everlasting*. New York: Farrar, Straus & Giroux.

STEPS Professional Development and Consulting. (2005). Banks Street College report on First Steps. Retrieved May 21, 2005, from http://www.stepspd.org/research/research.asp?section=Research&inner=1.

Bhatia, V. K. (1993). *Analyzing genre: Language use in professional settings*. London: Longman.

Boggs, S. (1985). *Speaking, relating and learning: A study of Hawaiian children at home and at school*. Norwood, NJ: Ablex.

Bourdieu, P. (1991). *Language and symbolic power*. Cambridge, MA: Harvard University Press.

Christie, F., & Martin, J. R. (1997). *Genre and social institutions: Social processes in the workplace and school*. London: Casssell Academic.

Cochran-Smith, M., & Lytle, S. (1993). *Inside/outside: Teacher research and knowledge*. New York: Teachers' College Press.

Cochran-Smith, M., & Lytle, S. (1999). Relationships of knowledge and practice: Teacher learning in communities. *Review of Research in Education, 24*, 249–305.

Comber, B., Thomson, P., & Wells, M. (2001). Critical literacy finds a "place": Writing and social action in a low-income Australian grade 2/3 classroom. *Elementary School Journal, 101*(4), 451–464.

Darling-Hammond, L. (1995). Policy for restructuring. In A. Lieberman (Ed.), *The work of restructuring schools: Building from the ground up* (pp. 157–176). New York: Teachers College Press.

Darling-Hammond, L. (2000). Teacher quality and student achievement: A review of state policy evidence. *Education Policy Analysis Archives, 8*(1). Retrieved from http://olam.ed.asu.edu/epaa/v8n1/.

DIBELS. (2007). DIBELS data system description. Retrieved April 30, 2007 from http://dibels.uoregon.edu/data/DIBELS_Data_System_Desc.pdf

Dyson, A. (1993). *Social worlds of children learning to write in an urban primary school.* New York: Teachers College Press.

Echevarria, J., Vogt, M., & Short, D.J. (2000). *Making content comprehensive for English language learners.* Needham Heights, MA: Allyn and Bacon.

First Steps (1999). *Writing resource book.* Portsmouth, NH: Heinemann.

Fitzgerald, J., & Graves, M. F. (2004). *Scaffolding reading experiences for English-language learners.* Norwood, MA: Christopher-Gordon Publishers.

Floriani, A. (1994) Negotiating what counts: Roles and relationships, texts and contexts, content and meaning. *Linguistics and Education, 5,* 241–274.

Freire, P., & Macedo, D. (1987). *Literacy: Reading the word and the world.* South Hadley, MA: Bergin and Garvey.

Gee, J. (1996). *Social linguistics and literacy: Ideology in discourses.* London: Taylor & Francis.

Gee, J. (1999). Critical issues: Reading and the new literacy studies: Reframing the National Academy of Science report on reading. *Journal of Literacy Research, 31*(3), 355–374.

Gutiérrez, K., & Larson, J. (1995). Language borders: Recitation as hegemonic discourse. *International Journal of Education, 31,* 22–36.

Gutiérrez, K., Rymes, B., & Larson, J. (1995). Script, counterscript, and underlife in the classroom: James Brown versus *Brown v. Board of Education. Harvard Educational Review, 65,* 445–471.

Gutiérrez, K., Baquedano-Lopez, P., & Turner, M. (1997). Putting language back into language arts: When the radical middle meets the third space. *Language Arts, 74*(5), 368–378.

Halliday, M. A. K. (1994). *An introduction to functional grammar.* London: Edward Arnold.

Hargreaves, A. (2000). Four ages of professionalism and professional learning. *Teachers and Teaching: History and Practice, 6*(2), 151–182.

Hawkins, M. (2005). Becoming a student: Identity work and academic literacies in early schooling. *TESOL Quarterly, 39*(1), 59–82.

Heath, S. (1983). *Ways with words: Language, life and work in communities and classrooms.* New York: Cambridge University Press.

Ibrahim, A. (1999). Becoming black: Rap and hip-hop, race, gender identity, and the political of ESL. *TESOL Quarterly, 33*(3), 349–368.

Jones, R. C., & Peck, B. (Illustrator). (1995). *Matthew and Tilly.* East Rutherford, NJ: Penguin Putnam Books for Young Readers.

Kamberelis, G. (1999). Genre development and learning: Children writing stories, science reports and poems. *Research in the Teaching of English, 33*(4), 403–460.

Kamler, B., & Comber, B. (2004). Getting out of deficit: Pedagogies of reconnection. *Teaching Education, 15*(3), 293–310.

Kern, R. (2000). *Literacy and language teaching.* Oxford: Oxford Press.

Kong, A., & Pearson, P. D. (2003). The road to participation: The construction oral literacy practice in a learning community of linguistically diverse learners. *Research in the Teaching of English, 38*(1), 85–124.

Kress, G. (2000). Genre and the changing contexts for English language arts. *Language Arts, 6*(6), 461–469.

Lieberman, A., & Miller, L. (Eds.) (2001). *Teachers caught in the action: Professional development that matters.* New York: Teachers College Press.

Luke, A. (2000). Critical literacy in Australia: A matter of context and standpoint. *Journal of Adolescent & Adult Literacy, 43*(5), 448–461.

Luke, A., & Freebody, P. (1997). The social practices of reading. In S. Muspratt, A. Luke, & P. Freebody (Eds.), *Constructing critical literacies: Teaching and learning textual practice* (pp. 1–18). St Leonards, New South Wales: Allen & Unwin.

Luke, A., & Freebody, P. (2000). *Literate futures: Report of the literacy review for Queensland state schools.* Brisbane: Queensland Government Printer.

McNeil, L. (2000). *The contradictions of school reform.* New York: Routledge.

Moll, L., Amanti, C., Neff, D., & Gonzales, N. (1992). Funds for knowledge for teaching: Using a qualitative approach to connect homes and classrooms. *Theory into Practice, 31*(4), 132–141.

Mohr, N. (1979). *Felita.* New York: Puffin Books.

New London Group (1996). A pedagogy of multiliteracies: Designing social features. *Harvard Educational Review, 66*(1), 60–92.

Newmann, F. M., King, M. B., & Youngs, P. (2000). *Professional development to build organizational capacity in low achieving schools: Promising strategies and future challenges.* Madison: Center on Organization and Restructuring of Schools, University of Wisconsin-Madison.

Norton, B. (1997). Language, identity, and the ownership of English. *TESOL Quarterly, 31*(3), 409–428.

Olsen, L. (1997). *Made in America.* New York: New Press.

Partridge, B. (2004). *Genre and the language learning classroom.* Ann Arbor: University of Michigan Press.

Peregoy, S., & Boyle, O. (2000). English learners reading English: What we know, what we need to know. *Theory into Practice, 39*(4), 237–247.

Schleppegrell, M. J. (2004). *The language of schooling: A functional linguistics perspective.* Mahwah, NJ: Erlbaum.

Solsken, J., Willett, J., & Wilson-Keenan, J. (2000). Cultivating hybrid tests in multicultural classrooms: Promise and challenge. *Research in the Teaching of English, 35,* 179–211.

Spinelli, J. (1990). *Maniac Magee.* New York: Little Brown and Company.

ePodunk (2005). Springfield, Massachusetts: Springfield community profile. Retrieved May 21, 2005, from http://www.epodunk.com/cgi-bin/genInfo.php?locIndex=3146.

Springfield Public Schools (2004). School report card – Gerena. Retrieved April 30, 2007 from http://www.sps.springfield.ma.us/websites/NCLB03-04/Gerena.htm

Taylor, M. (1979). *Roll of thunder, hear my cry.* New York: Puffin Company.

Toohey, K. (2000). Learning English at school: Identity, social relations and classroom practice. Clevedon, England: Multilingual Matters.

Tower, C. (2003). Genre development and elementary students' informational writing: A review of the literature. *Reading Research and Instruction, 42*(4), 14–39.

Vasquez, O. A., Pease-Alvarez, L., & Shannon, S. M. (1994). *Pushing boundaries.* New York: Cambridge University Press.

Weinbaum, A., Allen, D., & Blythe, T. (2004). *Teaching as inquiry: Asking hard questions to improve practice and student learning.* New York: Teachers College Press.

Whang, G., Samway, K. D., & Pippitt, M. (1995). Buddy reading: Cross-age tutoring in a multicultural school. Portsmouth, NH: Heineman.

White, E. B. (1999). *Charlotte's web.* New York: HarperCollins.

Wiggins, G., & McTighe, J. (1998). *Understanding by design.* Alexandria, VA: Association for Supervision and Curriculum Development.

Willett, J. (1995) Becoming first graders in an L2: An ethnographic study of L2 socialization. *TESOL Quarterly, 29*(3), 473–503.

Willett, J., Solsken, J., & Wilson-Keenan, J. (1999). The (im)possibilities of constructing multicultural practices in research and pedagogy. *Linguistics and Education, 10*(2), 165–218.

Wilson-Keenan, J., Willett, J., & Solsken, J. (2001). Families as curriculum partners in an urban elementary inclusion classroom: In J. Murphy & P. Byrd (Eds.), *Understanding the courses we teach: Local perspectives on English language teaching* (pp. 92–114). Ann Arbor: University of Michigan Press.

Wohlstetter, P., & Malloy, C. (2001). Organizing for literacy achievement: Using school governance to improve classroom practice. *Education and Urban Society, 34*(1), 42–65.

CHAPTER 4

Pedagogical Thinking and Teacher Talk in a First-Grade ELL Classroom

JANE YEDLIN

I think my children [ESL students] can do exactly what the … [English proficient] children can do. However, there are ways I help them that are different … I'm committed to them. I'm connected to them. I like them.

**(Excerpt from interview with Eileen Romano[1],
grade 1 English as a second language teacher)**

Teachers and administrators recommended Eileen Romano's first-grade English as a second language (ESL) classroom to me as an ideal site for a study of teacher language and English language learner (ELL) literacy instruction. They praised her teaching, her students' writing, and the relatively large proportion of her students who go on to do well in regular education classrooms. Mrs. Romano teaches in a high-poverty, urban New England school district with a large immigrant population. She is an elementary-certified and ESL-endorsed teacher with many years of experience, a master's degree in literacy, and the respect of her colleagues.

After my first few visits to Mrs. Romano's classroom, I was convinced that this monolingual, European American teacher was someone from whom I, and others, could learn a great deal. For her part Mrs. Romano welcomed me into her self-contained ESL classroom. She told me that she enjoyed the opportunity to talk about her teaching and her students. During the year that I spent observing, videotaping, collecting writing samples, participating in, inquiring about, and reflecting on life and language in Room 202, I came to understand that at the heart of Mrs. Romano's practice was her determination that all of her 23 students could and would be included. This chapter reports on the pedagogical thoughts that Mrs. Romano shared with me as we watched some of the teacher-in-front-of-the-class writing lessons I had videotaped in her classroom. Other dimensions of the study are reported elsewhere.

There's a Lot Going On in First Grade

Mrs. Romano's account[2] of her job—teaching first-grade ELLs in an urban elementary school—conveyed the challenge and complexity of her work, her enthusiasm, and her sense of urgency about how much her ELLs need to learn at this important grade level.

> First grade is packed! … We have goals to meet, we have things to do by the end of the year. … From September to June they do so much growing … especially [ELL students] … There's a lot going on all at the same time, reading and learning [basic vocabulary, and word formation]. "This is your nose," and "These are your ears," and "You say one nose and two ears," things like that that a two year old has learned [in his language]. But they're learning all of that [at the same time] they're learning the sounds of the letters and how to read. … The kids have to learn … not only [conversational] English … but [also] the language of rubrics, the language for assessment, the language for school, the language for what's expected of them when they get to second grade. They need to know these things. They need to know Dolch words, they need to know beginning sounds, ending sounds, middle sounds. It's a lot … and with all that it's packed with, it comes with that much in reward because it's just amazing … !

Mrs. Romano explained that in her ESL classroom she helped children learn English literacy skills and oral English concurrently, whereas in regular education classrooms, reading instruction builds on English proficient children's oral language competence and culturally influenced background knowledge. Mrs. Romano once mused that in a "suburban, middle-class first grade" classroom of English-speaking children from literate homes, much of the foundation for reading in English has already been laid, and "a child just learns to read."

Mrs. Romano saw her students as having academic needs, but she did not stigmatize those needs as deficits, although she knew that many teachers did. "It's not like a hindrance to have them in your class. It's not like you can say, 'Oh my goodness! This kid doesn't know any letters of the alphabet.'"

Her approach to teaching ELLs involved saturating the environment with oral and written language in a variety of forms and drawing children's attention to the language in use: "You simply immerse them in what they need, the language, the alphabets, the stories, … hearing people speak to each other, hearing stories read on tape. And you read stories and other children read stories, talking all day long."

She described some of the differences between her class and a mainstream first-grade class in her own school:

> We might read books at lower levels for a longer period of time, and we might still be learning the alphabet in January and February. … I'm getting children in May right from Peru. So, I have [new] children all the time. … I'm always doing alphabet work [with someone] every single day. Basic A, B, C work. There are children at that level all through the year in my room, and that's … [a] difference.

I asked Mrs. Romano about her expectations for her ELL students' achievement in an educational climate that emphasizes challenging standards, high expectations, and accountability.

> I think my children can do exactly what the other children can do. However, there are ways I help them that are different. I spend … more time with [oral] language, a lot more time reading books. … [ELL students need] to hear language. … Every minute I can–I … play little games with language. [For example to draw attention

to prepositions of location when we come across one,] I have to show them: "above," "beyond," "below," "behind." [They get familiar with the sounds of English by listening to] books, just to hear [the] music [of language], … they need a lot more of that … and I try to make it as pleasurable an experience as I can.

One of the challenges that Mrs. Romano faced in her classroom was the heterogeneity of her students. Mrs. Romano's classroom was similar to many urban ESL classrooms in the diversity of students' primary languages: Spanish, Russian, Creole, Chinese, Laotian, Khmer, and a Mayan language. During the year of the study, they ranged from non-English-speaking newcomers, who had never attended school, to children who were born in the United States and had attended full-day, ESL kindergarten. The educational levels of the children's parents also varied from a mother who was a teacher in China to a few parents who seemed not to be literate in their home languages. Some children had family members who spoke English and had literacy skills in English, whereas others did not. A number of students were the younger siblings of Mrs. Romano's former students. Student heterogeneity increased during the school year as some class members moved away and newcomers took their places.

When asked about her strategies for including newcomers and students with little English proficiency in classroom life, Mrs. Romano told me,

I often will pick … children with the very limited English … to do little jobs for me, to see how much they are learning, like, "Carlos, take this paper to Miss Carol." At the beginning they have no clue what I'm talking about, but they catch on … other children will say, "Miss Carol … " and start saying it in Spanish. … I'll look [Carlos] in the eyes … [and repeat], "Miss Carol," and hand him the paper [and he'll give it to my assistant]. So then I'll follow with that a couple of times during the week, I'll do the same thing. "Take the paper to Miss Carol." Or … "Would you shut the door?" The first time, they don't know what I mean, so I get up and show them. I shut the door. And tomorrow I'll ask them again, "Would you shut the door?" So they learn those commands. … I try to choose [beginners] to do those kinds of things.

Mrs. Romano explained to me that she made increasingly complex linguistic demands of students as they understood more. "I'll [give a] one-step … [instruction to a beginner] whereas [a more advanced student] can handle [multiple-step directions]. 'Could you take this paper to Mr. Carter and, on the way out, shut the door?' I wouldn't [say] that to [a beginner]."

Although Mrs. Romano reported simplifying language for the benefit of beginners, she firmly believed that beginning ELLs also benefited from hearing and observing the linguistically more complex interactions between their teacher and more advanced classmates. "All the kids hear what's happening. … They're all there learning together."

Mrs. Romano explained that the wide range of language proficiencies in the group was one of the reasons for the many reiterations and restatements observed in her speech in the classroom videotapes. For example, during a recorded December writing lesson, Mrs. Romano told the children that "good writing has details." Then she provided the class with an explanation of what she meant by details: "Details tell more about your topic." Next, she supplied and elicited several topic-specific examples of appropriate details: "If you write about your mom, what details can you tell me about your mom? What does she like to do? What do you do together? What makes her smile? Tell me more about your mom."

Finally, she explained some reasons for including details: "Details make the reader more interested." When Mrs. Romano and I watched this lesson together on videotape, she told me that she had introduced and explained the somewhat abstract word *details* in several previous lessons and had given examples from different topics and contexts.

> This [lesson that we just watched] wasn't even an introduction [to the concept of details], but [I still] I went through all those steps. I think you still have to do that every time. Because there's the child who might not ... [have heard or been ready to understand before] ... maybe they weren't there when you talked about details [before]. So, especially when you're teaching them, it has to be reinforced, reiterated, revisited, and all those things again and again and again.

When I asked Mrs. Romano how she determined when such reiteration was necessary, she told me that her information came from attentively watching children's behavior, listening to their language, and reading what they wrote.

> When I observe them [and read their writing], it influences my teaching ... you're constantly going back and reexamining. ... I...know a particular child needs to work with past tense. She's not getting the past tense. She doesn't pronounce it when she reads it, and when she writes it, she doesn't...[use past tense forms]. So, I might do a little lesson on past tense, like "You played at the park," and things like that. Past tense is hard for second-language learners. ... It takes a while.

Mrs. Romano reported tuning her speech in response to children's comprehension levels. She characterized the nature of her tuning for beginners as the use of shorter utterances, the use of actions, and contextual cues to make the language comprehensible, as well as providing children with repeated exposures to the same and similar messages.

We Don't Water Down Language

Although Mrs. Romano used many strategies to facilitate her students' understandings, she identified one type of simplification that she refused to employ. She was adamant that, when reading books to children, substitution of simpler words into the original text was unacceptable: "I don't use fake words for real words. I use real language."

Mrs. Romano was surprised to hear from her own son that his teacher, in a suburban, mainstream kindergarten, had substituted the word *nails* for the word *talons* when reading aloud a book about birds of prey. This was a book that her son knew well from repeated readings at home.

> I was interested that she [the suburban kindergarten teacher] did that because I don't even do that in ... [my] second language classroom. ... I think that you lose the flavor of the book. Not only that, you lose such an experience. There are children who will grab onto that word and they'll be able to tell someone, "Oh, that bird has talons. It's a bird of prey." I use those words with the kids in the classroom.

Mrs. Romano articulated the difference between the lexical reductionism of her son's teacher and her own lexical elaboration.

> I read that book [to my students]. I read *talons* and I say, "Talons. Do we know what the talons are?" And I use the hands. I do this a lot ... I'm showing them the talons, and my fingers are all crunched up like talons. Immediately, they know what talons are. ... I say, "Talons are the nails on the bird's feet. They are what the bird uses to kill his prey." Then you get into, "What is prey?" It just goes on, [but] ... , I don't change it.

My classroom observations of read-alouds in Mrs. Romano's classroom indicated that she was proud of providing her ESL class, children with full access to the standard curriculum, to its vocabulary and to the author's words.

Mrs. Romano asserted that in her classroom, "We speak the same language as the other classrooms. [We use words like] *author, illustrator,* [and] *text*. We don't water down language [just] because these are second language learners." She told me that in her first years of teaching ELLs, there was a separate ESL literacy curriculum and mimeographed materials for English language learners in the district. She remembered feeling that she and her students were excluded from the books, from the "real stuff." Since that time Mrs. Romano has become a strong advocate for equal access to the curriculum for ELLs and their teachers. She is quick to remind the observer that her ESL class differs from the mainstream first-grade classroom down the hall, only in that "there are ways I help them that are different."

Providing students with equal access to class participation was also important to Mrs. Romano. Watching herself call on children during the videotaped lessons, she was very pleased with what she saw as her equitable distribution of turns.

> I picked a variety [of children]. … I know that some of them … may [not] understand. I don't stay away from someone like Joel… [although] I know I …[might not] under-stand his speech because he [is] not clear all the time. I give him an opportunity to speak. And you have to.

Mrs. Romano acknowledged both the awkwardness that can result when the teacher cannot understand a student's answer and the temptation to avoid embarrassment by not calling on the hard-to-understand students. However, she was adamant that it was unacceptable to avoid such students. She reported wryly that other students could usually understand their classmates' English and interpret for her.

"How Do You Teach ESL If You Don't Speak Any Other Language?"

I noticed that unlike some teachers, who enforced English-only policies in their class-rooms, Mrs. Romano seemed to fully accept and take for granted children's use of their home languages. When I asked her about it, she was outspoken in her belief that an English-only policy would be unreasonable and counterproductive. She told me that she intentionally seated new students near others who spoke the same language for support and for company.

> You have children who come in December and can't say hello in English, and what are you going to say [to them]? "You mustn't speak your language?" I think that's terrible! That's just mean. … I know other teachers who do it. How are you going to learn if you're sitting there and you can't say [or understand] anything? I don't make an issue of it.

The year following this study, Mrs. Romano enrolled in a community college Spanish class. She told me that her major motivation was to be able to communicate better with Spanish-speaking parents: "One of the obstacles is that I don't speak the language [they speak] at home, so it's hard for me to connect with the parents." Although she told me that knowing Spanish would be helpful in the classroom too, Mrs. Romano did not feel that bilingualism was a necessary prerequisite for good ESL teaching.

Daily Routines and Modeling

Mrs. Romano described herself as acutely aware of the different levels in her classroom, always trying to maintain progress without leaving the least proficient students behind. She talked to me about her responsibility for the beginners in her class. This issue came up as we watched videotaped modeled writing lessons from the spring; Mrs. Romano commented, "… You might think I've already [talked about] capitals and periods, but I have to do it every day till June because, [for] one or two children, it hasn't sunk in yet—[children] who weren't there developmentally. You wonder who catches what and who doesn't. That's why you have to model … all the time." She gave the following example:

> Rene [a recent arrival from Central America] is just words right now, one word, one word. He isn't real sentence-y yet, so he's probably not listening to [my talk about] capitals and periods. Or if he is listening, he has no use for that now. But when he does [listen], if I don't say it anymore it won't become part of his structure when he writes. It sounds so ridiculously redundant, but you can't package it and put it away.

I asked Mrs. Romano what she felt she needed to do for the most recent arrivals and those who had not attended kindergarten here. She talked about how ELLs learn through social participation in routine classroom activities as well as through direct, finely tuned instruction in basic vocabulary.

> You need to immerse [the beginners] in the classroom and just let them be there. … Let them live in the routine and see what's happening. In the beginning, I don't think you … exclude them from any activity, for instance journal writing because they can't write or reading because they can't read. I think they need to be included in all things. I think you just need to let them go through the stages that they will go through, mimicking, modeling behavior of the other students. … But for the most part, they need to be involved in the classroom daily activities. I think that it is very important that they see how the classroom works and operates, that they hear what's going on. It's amazing … week by week … you can see progress.

Mrs. Romano spoke about how more advanced students served as models, helping to make language comprehensible and participation possible for others.

> Eventually they get the language. You use a lot of the same things every day. … We tally the boys and girls every day. We read the word wall every day. We count the days in the month every day. We count how many days we've been in school every day. We sing the alphabet every day with the sounds and without the sounds. We read the schedule every day. There are things that are repeated over and over and over.

Given the opportunity to participate in such a language-rich learning environment, Mrs. Romano found that most children grew in comprehension and in the ability to participate: "It just happens. They just get it eventually." As an observer, I pointed out that Mrs. Romano helped it happen by skillfully directing children's participation in the daily routines. Although beginners might be given the job of accompanying a song about red, green, and blue cars by holding up the appropriately colored cutouts on cue, more proficient students would follow the words to the song with a pointer on the large song chart.

In addition to social participation in routines and whole-group instruction, Mrs. Romano stipulated that for newcomers and the least English proficient, "There [also] needs to be some [individual or small-group] instruction … where you're taking them alone and work-ing with them on letters and vocabulary words, simple picture words like *mom* and *dad*."

Mrs. Romano made a point of telling me that such individual or small-group instruction was made possible by the help she got from her competent assistant teacher, Miss Carol. Mrs. Romano told me that she would observe how beginning-level students behaved during certain large-group activities, like story reading. From their behavior she determined whether they were at a level to benefit from the activities or whether their time could be better spent with the teacher's aide in direct instruction.

> [When] I'm reading a story … some of them will be attentive, will listen and hear the language, the flow of it, and sit still even though they're not understanding exactly. But they're getting a lot of other things, intonation … some … words. … I do a lot of physical stuff, a lot of expression, a lot of pointing and miming kinds of things when I'm explaining words and language. But the ones who are really itchy [restless] and … [distracting] the other kids, I'll have the assistant take them aside and work with them on something else, colors or numbers—something where they can be a little more productive in that time.

Another strategy of Mrs. Romano's was to distribute active roles and tasks, so beginners could participate, for example, in the morning routines on the rug or in doing errands and chores.

> I often try to involve them in situations where they can be successful, like pointing to the alphabet when we sing the alphabet [song], or I often let the children point to the song [pictures and lyrics] as we sing. Sometimes, before they're ready for the one-to-one correspondence, they just point along. Even though I know that they're not going to get each word, I'll guide the [pointer] with them as they go. … Then … they learn the words one at a time. I include them. That's very important. There are a lot of things they can do. They can write the number of the date on the calendar. … They count. If the day is the second, we put the two cents in the pocket chart. For money, they can count out the pennies. … I can't use the same child every day so I try to spread it around.

Similarly, Mrs. Romano believed that being part of a literacy community where they were expected to engage in the same activities as their more advanced classmates fostered the English literacy development of beginning students. She cited, as an example, a little girl from her current (2001–02) class:

> When she first started she couldn't say a word of English. … She went through a period where she … would fool around because she wasn't understanding … during that period, I had the assistant work with her, and then I talked with the mother to tell her to pay attention. She is now writing in the journal, words that go with pictures. In the beginning it was just scribbling and pictures, but now they're words that actually connect to the pictures.

> We all do a book log every day. They read ten books and they have to write down five of the ones they read, the titles and authors … and at the beginning on her book log, she was just scribbling letters all the way through. She knew that words needed to go there, but she didn't know what words. She didn't know it was titles and authors. She [didn't know what] to extract from the book. She was just scribbling capital letters, lower case letters, nonsense, just letters. But she knew that it was writing, which I accepted. Then we showed her that you have to [copy] the author and the title. [I don't know] whether

or not she's understanding what we mean by author and title, but she now has grasped what parts to take off the cover of the book. Now she is writing titles and authors. ... She's probably [only] reading a couple of them ... but she's already following the pattern. She's made progress in that area.

Mrs. Romano's belief that ELLs could learn through participation was very far from a sink-or-swim approach to immersion. This belief was enacted by her scaffolding of class activities and her structuring of participant roles. Moreover, Mrs. Romano's understanding of language and literacy development allowed her to recognize and appropriately support children's incremental progress toward instructional goals.

Getting and Directing Students' Attention: "Grab Their Ears, Invite Their Involvement"

As we watched the videotaped lessons together, Mrs. Romano pointed out various strategies she used to capture, direct, and focus students' attention and to engage them. This was not an easy task in a classroom of 23 active first graders, many of whom understood relatively little of the English stream of speech. Mrs. Romano called my attention to variations in her voice, volume, and intonation, her postures, positions, and gestures. Once, when the group in front of her on the rug seemed very noisy and unsettled, Mrs. Romano crouched down very close to the children, looked straight at them, and whispered instructions. She explained it to me:

> That posture just kind of brings them all forward. It focuses them on me. They hear my voice. They have to be quiet to hear my voice. I just think it is a more warming, a more inviting way to get their attention.

We noted her use of phrases such as, "Who's ready to listen?" "Everybody look at me now" to signal students to pay special attention. She directed visual attention explicitly by saying, "We're looking at the chart now" and "We're looking here at the green writing. I'm touching it with my finger."

Mrs. Romano told me that she often used the power of names to engage children who seemed not to be paying attention or perhaps not comprehending. "To gather one child's attention, I'll say, 'Oh, remember, Sasha, when we talked about ... .' I'll use our past experiences to gather them close, to make them feel more involved."

As we watched the videotapes, Mrs. Romano was gratified to observe many signs of children's engagement. For my part, I was impressed that Mrs. Romano did not simply think of attention as something children would automatically "pay." The various phrases and metaphors she used in the discussion—such as "gather ... attention," "gather them close," "grab their ear," "bring ... them all forward," and "a more warming ... inviting way to get their attention" reflected her view of attention as multisensory, affective, and something the teacher elicits and cultivates.

Building Vocabulary and Academic Language

Mrs. Romano began some writing lessons by reviewing criteria for good writing. In one such lesson introduction she asked the class, "When we write topics or sentences or stories, how do you know ... it's good?" I asked why she didn't simply say, "When we write, how do you know ... it's good?" She explained that her redundancy (e.g., *topics, sentences, stories*) was extremely deliberate. She was casting a wide net for children whose prior knowledge included any or all of the terms she used. Mrs. Romano tried to provide this multilevel class with talk that offered everyone something to grab onto from the stream of speech.

> This might be how I catch … different children. If I just said, "When you do writing … ," some of them might not know what I'm talking about. But [some] can grab onto the word "sentences." A few might say, "Oh, I know sentences". … The lower children probably focus on "sentences" … some [other] children probably focus on [the word] "topic." They know what that means, to develop a topic, to pick a topic … others, like David, [might focus on the word] "stories."

In the videotaped lessons, we watched Mrs. Romano use a variety of strategies to build comprehension. Frequently she made reference to prior learnings and experiences when explaining something new: "I try to use different words and phrases that I know they understand, or something that maybe we've said before. I focus in on my language and what I'm saying."

Another way that Mrs. Romano promoted comprehension was through the use of concrete and tangible props as scaffolding devices. This was most striking in a story-writing lesson where she used cutouts to illuminate and differentiate the somewhat abstract notions of character and setting.

> I thought that if they drew and cut out the character and setting separately and then had to paste them [individually] onto a board, [the distinct concepts of character and setting] became more tangible … I had one [set of cut outs] to show them. … I had a model, which always helps, especially with ESL children.

Similarly, in the story-writing lesson a piece of paper that had been prefolded into three columns conveyed tangibly the story structure concepts of beginning, middle, and end. The columns provided a concrete structural scaffold for children's writing.

A language input strategy that Mrs. Romano noticed herself using in the videotaped lessons was the repetition of conceptually important words and phrases. This was very noticeable in one of the class's early writing assignments. Watching herself initiate a prewriting brainstorming session on the topic "My favorite place," Mrs. Romano observed, "I kept saying it over and over and over. … Think about [your] favorite place, [your] favorite place … What's [your] favorite place? Who can think about a favorite place? … So [the phrase 'favorite place'] just going in and in and in."

Following the brainstorming of children's favorite places (e.g., *beach, park, my cousin's house*, numerous fast food restaurants, *Puerto Rico*) and Mrs. Romano's modeling of her own favorite place composition, she prepared the children to write their own pieces by repeating and pointing to the topic sentence, "My favorite place is … " by modeling the sentence structure orally and making sure students could map each of the spoken words onto its written form: "This is early in the [school] year … so I keep saying it over and over because I want them to start [with the sentence] 'My favorite place is_____'. … As I say 'favorite place,' I'm pointing to [the written words]."

Mrs. Romano had many strategies for teaching new vocabulary, including paraphrasing, defining, giving examples, sometimes drawing or pantomiming, and often discussing or negotiating meaning. An interesting discussion occurred as Mrs. Romano composed her favorite place story about lying in her hammock with her young son, Danny. David, a highly verbal student in the class, responded to the teacher's story by exclaiming in an exaggerated, high-pitched voice, "Oh, isn't that romantic!" After watching that segment of the videotape,

Mrs. Romano described and explained to me her negotiation of the meaning of romantic with David.

> And I said, "It could be [romantic], but not with my son." I'm not stern, but I'm not light about it either. "It's not romantic because it's my son." And I say what it is. "It's relaxing and comfortable, like how you might snuggle with your mom. It's not at all romantic!" I tell him clearly that [the] word [romantic] isn't used to describe a mother and son.

As we watch the videotaped favorite place lesson, Mrs. Romano relived her own and the children's excitement of coconstructing the meaning of *hammock,* a new English word that, for many of the children, referenced a culturally familiar object. Mrs. Romano described the step-by-step construction of meaning:

> I said, "My favorite place is my hammock." … Immediately, I wrote and spelled the word [aloud] and then, "What is it," they ask. And I say, "Let me draw you a picture." So … I draw a picture and explain it. I probably figured I could show them more easily than explaining it. And as I draw it, you can see their faces light up as they connect … a lot of them know [what a hammock is] once I drew a picture. And also in my description, there's a lot of language involved. You have to put it "in between" the two trees, and I draw with my marker "in between" the two trees. And they're riveted … they didn't know the word. Look at all their faces. And I explain that it's kind of like "a bed in between trees." And then Andre connects. "Oh, I know … what you do on that. You lie on it." And then I said, "Yes you do." And Andre says, "My cousin has one of those in Puerto Rico." And I say, "Does he?" And I get all excited about it. And I add more language. " … It's so relaxing."

Many of the verbal interactions we watched between Mrs. Romano and the children aimed to clarify meanings and to elicit more precise, more correct, or more academic language from them. We discussed this while watching the favorite place lesson, in which Andre continued to air his knowledge of hammocks. Mrs. Romano interpreted,

> Andre's saying, "Some of them are brown, some of them are white." I say, "Yes, they come in different colors. You're right." So, I say back what he said in a different way, a more sophisticated way. But, yet, I'm saying exactly what he says and saying, "You're right." I'm validating his point. And I try to do that often. They're offering information and that's important. And it lends itself to great explanations of language or just reiterating the language in a different way.

As mentioned previously, Mrs. Romano believed strongly that children should be exposed to and taught authentic vocabulary and academic language. She pointed out her strategies for doing this in numerous points during the lessons: "I try to give the language that I read in professional books and the terms that I hear at workshops. I try to give them that … so that as they move through the grades, they've heard this [metalinguistic] language."

Mrs. Romano usually accomplished her teaching of academic language and her use of metalinguistic terms through a combination of familiar examples from prior shared experiences, elaboration, restatement, and explicit definition. These teaching strategies were evident in the videotaped discussion of the attributes of good writing. Mrs. Romano told me,

> I review the [concept of] *topic* again. "You write about one thing." And I give an example, "My mom." "I like my mom. My mom is nice." … And then I say I want more than that. I want detail. I explain again what *details* are. "*Details* means to tell more

about something," and then I give examples of those details. "My mom ... "—three examples of things your mom might like to do. And then I go back and reexplain what details are. I say again, "Details means to tell more about."

We watched on tape as Mrs. Romano prepared to read aloud a story she'd read to them before: *Alfie Gives a Hand* (Hughes, 1985). Mrs. Romano told them, "This time we're going to focus on the characters." Then she elaborated the meaning of *focus* and *characters* by paraphrasing her utterance using more familiar words: "We're going to pay attention to who the people in the story are." She explained her pattern of language use to me:

> I use ... the terminology ... [like *focus* or *characters*]. They know I'll say a big word, and then I'll explain it right after that. And I don't think I've ever told them that. Now that I've explained this big word, they just know it from hearing it ... they know how I do it.

Later in the December favorite place lesson Mrs. Romano provided yet another opportunity for students to apply and process metalinguistic concepts and vocabulary. After writing about her own favorite place, her hammock, Mrs. Romano asked the students to evaluate her writing according to the rubric for good writing.

> I asked, "Do I have details in my writing?" And someone said, "Yes, you have colors ... colors are details," because I used different colored markers. And I say " ... Yes, colors are details, but, well that's not the detail I'm talking about ... Did I tell you why I like my favorite place? Did I tell you what I do there? Did I tell you how it makes me feel?"

Likewise, in the lesson on story writing Mrs. Romano first discussed concepts of story elements and story structure.

> [I talked to them] about the elements of the story and I talked about characters, setting, problem, and solution. And I wrote down what those words were and then I explained [them] to the children and wrote down the definitions. ... [Then] I put those elements in the order in which they appeared in the story; beginning, middle, end. And I explained that, most often, the beginning introduces the reader to the characters and the setting and sometimes the problem, although sometimes the problem can come in the middle ...

Then Mrs. Romano went back and applied the concepts of story elements and story structure to the familiar *Alfie Gives a Hand* (Hughes, 1987), the story they'd read and discussed several times. She elaborated on the terms to remind students of their meanings and used familiar examples from the story. Later in the lesson, when she wrote her own model story about a trip to the beach, Mrs. Romano used the same terms and elaborated their meanings yet again.

Mrs. Romano told me that she looks for and takes advantage of opportunities to teach academic vocabulary across the curriculum. She pointed out an example of how she taught math vocabulary using the story-writing paper that had been folded into three columns for writing the beginning, middle, and end of the story. "I say, 'OK, now remember, the paper is in three parts, three equal parts. It's thirds,' I say. 'It's in thirds, three equal parts.' So, naturally I'm explaining fractions."

Mrs. Romano took evident pride in having taught first-grade ELLs academic words like *thirds* and *equal parts* during a writing lesson. This pride reflected her conviction that one of the most important things she could do for children was to provide them with access to vocabulary.

As we watched a moment of laughter in one of the taped lessons, Mrs. Romano said that she had noticed humor sometimes emerged from attempts to disambiguate language. Children's smiles and laughter at times provided her with feedback on whether children understood. She told me that she often used humor to create a pleasant atmosphere, adding that humor could also clarify meaning and facilitate comprehension.

> I told the kids, "Julianne said her favorite place was her house." But when she said it, she said "my house." So, when I'm writing it [on the chart paper] I'm saying, "Julianne's favorite place is my house. Oops! No, it's not my house. It's her house." And I just happened to say that. It can be very confusing, but I explained it a little bit, and the children who understood what I said or got a feel or a little glimpse of humor out of that are gaining the language.

Mrs. Romano's insights illuminated, for me, the multiple roles of humor in her classroom: cognitive as well as affective.

Issues of Grammar and Syntax

Making decisions about whether, when, and how to address children's grammatical and syntactical errors—and when to ignore them—was something that Mrs. Romano reported doing constantly. She told me that often she addressed grammatical errors by paraphrasing what the child said in a corrected form or by using a corrected form in her response to the child. "[If what the child says is] … grammatically incorrect, I can just answer back grammatically. … I restate it … without saying, 'That's wrong; you say it this way.' I just answer it back in the correct form."

Children's responses to Mrs. Romano's paraphrasing varied, she said, often according to their level of English proficiency, with beginners less likely to be aware of the correction.

> … Most often … when they restate it, they restate it the way … [I] said it because they know … what I'm doing without me telling them … because they live with me all the time. But not everyone [notices the restatement or] restates it correctly … [it] depend[s] on where they are in their [language development] stage.

Several considerations influenced Mrs. Romano's responses to children's grammatical and syntactic errors. As we watched tapes of the two writing lessons, Mrs. Romano mentioned the following considerations: the child's proficiency level, the relationship between the error and the lesson focus, the time available, error type, error frequency, affective issues, and whether failure to remodel would tacitly provide other children with poor quality input.

Mrs. Romano reported that she was most likely to correct or remodel when the grammatical or syntactic error was in written form, particularly in a story that the author would repeatedly read individually and to the class audience. She was careful to mention that she differentiated between grammatical errors, which she tended to refer to as *language*, and phonetically accurate misspellings, which she viewed as signs of phonetic competence. In the April story-writing lesson several children read their stories aloud to the group, and Mrs. Romano reread some stories aloud as well.

> Oh, Jaime read … "and my team win the game" … I try to attend to the language [grammar] right away. The spelling is not as important to me but the language [is]. I think the language is more important because I want them to hear it said correctly. And you notice that when I read it, although it said "go," I read "went," and although it

said "win," I think I read "won." And then I explained it to him. I said, "Here it should be 'went' and it should be 'won.'"

Mrs. Romano sometimes, but not always, explained to children the reason for her grammatical remodeling. Moreover, her grammatical explanations varied in their depth. We watched a videotaped writing conference in which Mrs. Romano reminded Martin of the reason for revisions previously made to his story: "Now see, [we changed 'play' to] 'played' because we already did it." After watching the interaction on tape, Mrs. Romano explained to me, "I am talking about past tense, and I'm reteaching what I talked about before when I was editing."

One of the most memorable corrections I remember was not caught on videotape but was noted in my field notes from early in the school year. Beatriz had written, "Me and Alma go to the park after school." Mrs. Romano asked Beatriz to write instead, "Alma and I … " Her explanation was that it is more polite to put the other person first, and "the English language likes it better" if you write "Alma and I" at the beginning of the sentence. When I recounted the remembered incident to Mrs. Romano, she laughed and responded that it would have been be fruitless to enter into an explanation of subject and object pronouns with Beatriz. She added sheepishly that "English likes it better" was a phrase of last resort when she did not want to say that something was incorrect.

At times, Mrs. Romano opted not to remodel or change children's language. During the "What's your favorite place?" brainstorming I watched her pause and briefly consider what to do when Harry volunteered, "the snow." Mrs. Romano responded, "Harry's favorite place is 'in the snow,'" and wrote the phrase "in the snow" on the chart. When Matilde volunteered "ice skating" as a favorite place, Mrs. Romano paused again and looked thoughtful before writing on the chart. After we watched the taped episode together, I asked Mrs. Romano what her considerations were when Matilde said "ice skating."

> I do that a lot. I was thinking, "A place. Ice skating is not a place. The ice skating rink is a place or the ice rink is a place. But I didn't want to change it, I think, because I wanted to [write] what she said. I don't remember what happened at the next stage. But maybe later, when they were writing their stories, I might have asked her to explain the rink or [I might have] … explain[ed] to her that the rink is a place.

It was evident to me that Mrs. Romano's decisions about correction were complex ones that she took quite seriously, weighing the consequences of different responses. She wished to show respect for children's emerging English skills and their communicative intent, while at the same time she wanted to give them the corrective feedback they would require to achieve at increasingly higher levels of proficiency and formal correctness.

Feedback and Responsiveness

Mrs. Romano explained that her reluctance to paraphrase or correct the form of Harry's or Matilde's favorite place responses reflected her effort to balance corrective feedback with children's sense of ownership of their ideas. Throughout the viewing of the taped lessons, Mrs. Romano proudly pointed out the positive feedback she gave to children. During the favorite place brainstorming, after several children had named fast-food-chain restaurants as their favorite places, Oscar, a quiet child identified as having special needs, raised his hand and softly volunteered, "the beach." Mrs. Romano's response to Oscar was "Oh, the beach! Wow, you thought of that." Oscar beamed. Mrs. Romano told me that after listing the many fast-food restaurants that children named as their favorite places, she was genuinely thrilled to have a different kind of favorite place named. Moreover, she explained, it was her goal to give warm, positive, and enthusiastic feedback as often as possible. As she watched the tape, Mrs. Romano was pleased to see the quality of her interactions with the children. "[I was] … making it so important … watch their faces. And I've done it to each one of them. 'Oh, Fantasy Land [a local amusement park]. I didn't think of that. That's a great place!' Just to give them points, make [their contribution] special and worthy."

Mrs. Romano told me that she tried to find authentic ways to respond positively to children's contributions and answers, even when they were not completely appropriate or correct. "I validate what they say … like if we're doing *p* words and you say *apple*, I say, 'Apple begins with *a*.' You do hear the *p*, but it's in the middle not the beginning."

She explained her reasons:

> It's important to make mention [of children's comments]. [It's important for them] to know that what they said was heard. … They're thinking on topic. They're thinking about what we're doing. They're offering information, and that's important … it lends itself to great explanations of language or just reiterating the language in a different way.

When Mrs. Romano was composing her favorite place journal entry, she said, "My favorite place is in my hammock. I like my hammock because … " One of the children completed her sentence, calling out, "It's very comfortable."

> When he said, "It's comfortable," I responded with amazement, [exclaiming], "How did you know?" instead of "Yeah, you're right." I'm not flat [in affect]. I'm committed to them. I'm connected to them. I like them, and [watching the videotaped lessons] I can see why they like me.

When Andre read the beginning of his story to the group, Mrs. Romano responded with interest and curiosity about what would happen next. After watching this on tape she interpreted their interaction for me, explaining that her intention had been both to show interest and to scaffold the next part of the story.

> His story begins, "One summer day, I went inside a building," or something like that. And I make the comment, "I wonder what will happen inside that building," using a dramatic voice and letting him know that his story is leading me to think about what might come next and also maybe encouraging him to think [himself] about what might come next.

Mrs. Romano told me that in her interactions with children as they composed and revised, she asked them many responsive questions based on what they said or wrote. If a child said, "I played a game," Mrs. Romano told me she would ask, "What game did you play?" Or if a child wrote, "My mom is nice," Mrs. Romano responded by saying, "You told me here that your mom is nice. Now tell me about some of the nice things about your mom. What does she do with you? What nice things does she do for you?"

Mrs. Romano explained that she asked such questions to show responsive interest in the child's topic as well as to elicit the kinds of details that would make children's writing longer, more informative, more individual, and more interesting.

Modeling Writing Strategies: "When We Write, We Think"

In her lessons Mrs. Romano modeled and identified writing and thinking strategies. She told her students on several occasions, "When we write, we think," and she tried to demonstrate this as well.

> I show them … I'm thinking now. I want them to see me thinking as a writer and see my eyes go up, just kind of in a thinking mode, and let them know that before you write, you need to think a little bit about what you're going to say … and I even say [out loud], "That's how I'm going to start it." Kind of like I'm thinking it through. So, I want them to see the process.

Mrs. Romano also used one child's real or hypothetical strategy use as a model for others. In the December favorite place lesson, David was the first child picked by Mrs. Romano to leave the rug and go to his seat to start writing. As he headed for his seat, Mrs. Romano talked to the group about the strategies David might use to spell the words he wanted to write. "He might look in his binder for words. He might listen to the sounds of the letters. He might look up at the word wall or at a chart and find the word he needs." As we watched this on videotape, Mrs. Romano explained her purpose to me: "I'm telling them what they can [all] do when they're going to write. What kinds of things they can do to help them [selves] to write. So, I'm helping them know that resources are out there and which resources there are."

Mrs. Romano told me that she was "always on the lookout" for opportunities to teach different writing strategies. One of the composing strategies that Mrs. Romano often modeled was frequent rereading of the work in progress. We watched on tape as she composed and reread her favorite place piece to the class. As she reread it, she spontaneously saw an opportunity to demonstrate strategies for adding words using a caret (∧) to mark the insertion point.

> I had written, "I like to lie in my hammock with [my son] Danny." But when I read it [aloud], I added, "and talk." Then I said to the children, "I do like to do that. Let me get rid of my period and add that. 'I like to lie in my hammock with Dan ∧and talk.' So, it's never too late to add [if you] think of something else."

From the day I first watched Mrs. Romano teach the favorite place lesson, I was curious about her seemingly idiosyncratic choice of her hammock as a topic to write about. I finally got my chance to ask her about it during the interview. Mrs. Romano explained that she had deliberated the choice of a topic that would be understandable enough to serve as a model yet unique enough that children would not copy it or follow it too closely. She wanted a topic that would provide some support but not too much. She hoped that her somewhat inimitable topic would promote children's independence and originality. She told me,

> I decided to write about my hammock [to show that] everyone's favorite place isn't the same. Also, when … I explained why it was my favorite place, it goes … into my personal experience … to show that writing can be based on personal experience and doesn't need to be like anyone else's. In fact, you want it to be your own. Mine was nothing like any of theirs … often at this age and at this ability … they'll be influenced by others very quickly and very easily.

Once again I was impressed by how much reflection and analysis went into Mrs. Romano's talk and into the scaffolding she designed to support and challenge children's writing.

Talk That Teaches Phonemic Awareness, Spelling, and Letter Recognition

As we watched the videotaped lessons, Mrs. Romano called my attention to some of the strategies she used to teach phonemic awareness, spelling, and letter recognition. Frequently, when writing on chart paper in front of the group, she asked the children for help spelling words. Where words or word parts were phonetically transparent, she pronounced them phoneme by phoneme and had the children help her by identifying the corresponding letters.

> I used the word *comfortable*. It was a new word … then I said, "Help me spell it," and I sounded the letters out. I make each sound, and children who know it name the letter and I write it. That's helpful to the children who are learning how to spell and also the ones who are just learning the [names of] letters or what the sounds of the letters are.

Where words or word parts were not phonetically transparent, Mrs. Romano supplied the difficult parts such as the silent *e* in *comfortable*: "When I come to the last letter I say that … 'I have spelled this word [comfortable] before and I know that there's a silent … 'and all I say is 'silent,' and they say 'e.'"

Mrs. Romano pointed out that she frequently elicited verbal participation by beginning a familiar phrase or sentence and then pausing, signaling the children to complete the phrase. "I just kind of lead them, and then I stop and they fill in the blank." Mrs. Romano told me that when children were able to fill in the blank, they demonstrated language learning and felt more of a sense of participation and accomplishment than when they simply listened.

Mrs. Romano told me that it was important for the children to realize that spelling a long word such as *comfortable* was a great accomplishment, and it was also important that they understand and remember the phonemic segmentation strategy used. As children gained experience with words and letters she expected them to be increasingly able to segment words and represent the sounds with letters for themselves.

Mrs. Romano told me that she "agreed to disagree" with mainstream colleagues over some issues in the teaching of writing. One such area of disagreement was how to respond when children asked her how to spell a word they wanted to write.

> I often will spell for my children early on. I've had this discussion with other teachers and they will never spell [words for children]. I remember having a discussion about that and saying, "Well, I feel like at home as a parent if my child asked me to spell something [I would tell him]. One teacher said to me, "Well maybe you're confusing your job as a mother and your job as a teacher." And I said, "Well maybe I am, but they don't have mothers who can spell … for them in English" … There is a certain stage where I think that child needs it (the spelling of a word) to come quickly, [not to] have to struggle for it. Then after I've spelled it for them or after I've shown it to them on the word wall and they can find it there. You need to show them. It's just like [when I direct a child to do something for the first time. When I say,] "Take this paper to the trash." Am I not going to show that child where the trash is? I think I need to at least show the child the first time where the trash is and then the second and third time, expect the child to be able to take the paper to the trash.

Mrs. Romano expanded on how ELLs progress toward more independence in spelling by giving the example of a new arrival:

> … A child who just came [to the United States] … asked [me] how to spell *I like*. Even the fact that he can ask that is unbelievable. So, I simply write, "I like Fantasy Land"

on the paper and say, "That's how you spell it." ... I won't continually spell that for ... months because, after the first time, maybe the second, the child should be able to find *like* on the word wall. Maybe *Fantasy Land* ... should be written on a chart somewhere or maybe in that child's personal dictionary.

Despite some pressure from her colleagues and literacy experts to leave children to invent their own spellings, Mrs. Romano became convinced that this was not a productive approach with beginning ELLs. The cognitive work of expressing ideas in English and representing them in graphemes was overwhelming to children who were unfamiliar with the lexicon and sound system of English. She saw spelling as requiring appropriately tuned input, like other aspects of language. Over the years she had provided increasing spelling support and more explicit strategy instruction to her students and was convinced that student writing had improved in length and quality as a result.

Heterogeneity: Strategies That Meet the Needs of Advanced Students

During the year of my fieldwork, David was one of the most English proficient, literate, and outspoken children in Mrs. Romano's class. Mrs. Romano viewed David as both a resource and a responsibility. She was aware and somewhat troubled by the fact that she called on him more often than she called on other children. She explained to me that this was because his responses often served as models for other children and helped them to understand what she expected.

> There are times when I choose [David] to answer because I know he will direct them. ... He's where I want them to be, and I need that answer then [for the rest of the class]. You can use this heterogeneity to your benefit. I enjoy it. It's obviously a huge challenge.

Mrs. Romano also felt a responsibility to provide David and other advanced students with all that they needed to maintain their own progress. I asked Mrs. Romano to talk specifically about the writing development of the most advanced children—those like David who would be exited from ESL at the end of the school year and would be mainstreamed for second grade.

> The ones who are mainstreamed are always reading on grade level because that's the criteria that they need to meet. ... Writing is very different. They tend to read [at a] more advanced [level] than they write. Children in general tend to struggle more with the writing. It is harder, [but]...[I also suspect] ... that has a lot to do with the [relative lack of] opportunities. ... I think that writing is something that they need more of, more opportunity. ...
>
> As a teacher, personally, I find that every year I'm learning more and trying different things. And then I try something and say, "Well, I like what I did last year better." So you're always learning ... what you want to do to spark that writing higher ... obviously, [their] language is not perfect. They don't have the King's English.

I asked Mrs. Romano to elaborate on the ways in which even the more advanced children's writing fell short of what she called the *King's English*. She identified subject–verb agreement (e.g., "My brothers likes" instead of "My brothers like"), preposition use (e.g., "In vacation" instead of "On vacation"), adjective–noun order, and failure to use the past tense as common writing problems even for those whose reading was close to grade level.

Mrs. Romano explained that she tried to challenge all her students, but especially the most advanced, to write at greater length and in more detail.

> I try to tell [them] to tell me more … to expand. I want more information, more detail. … So, the ones who I'm exiting … they can't just write, "I like this book … ." I would say, "This is incomplete. … " I tell them things like, "You need to connect it to your life or connect it to another story or recommend it to someone. Tell somebody why you liked this book, why they should read the book." So, those kinds of things are being asked of those [more advanced] children.

Once again, Mrs. Romano identified ways in which her observation and assessment of children's proficiencies influenced her to tune her instruction and her talk to the multiple levels in her classroom.

Shrinking the Task

When the tape of the story lesson ended, Mrs. Romano and I talked about what a big undertaking it had been for the first-grade ELLs to write such long and well-constructed stories. Mrs. Romano analyzed her scaffolding of the story-writing task that made it manageable.

> I've shrunken the task. I've taken the story, I've broken it down into elements [character, setting, and problem], and then I've broken the story into three parts [beginning, middle, and end] and placed those elements in each part. … I've made it doable without being overwhelming … if I [had just] asked them to write a story, they wouldn't be able to do it.

Watching the story-writing lessons, Mrs. Romano was pleased to observe how effectively how she had shrunken the task. Her analysis conveyed imagery that is central to her conception of the role of an effective ESL teacher, one who helps children reach meaningful goals by strategically breaking down complex tasks into clear elements and sequential steps to make it doable.

Reflections: Making Connections to the Research

This chapter highlights Mrs. Eileen Romano's commentary on taped lessons and perspectives on the relationships between her students' English language development and the facilitative characteristics of her talk and her pedagogy. Mrs. Romano exemplifies what Kohl (2002, p. 146) describes as the teacher who reflects on how her language is "being heard and understood." This perspective provides a window through which to view this experienced ESL teacher's understandings about second-language pedagogy, This study of a skillful ESL teacher contributes to the knowledge base called for by Wong-Fillmore and Snow (2000, p. 7), who avow the importance of investigating what effective teachers know about language and how they use their knowledge to "design the classroom language environment so as to optimize language and literacy learning of ELLs."

The following section briefly reviews bodies of literature on language acquisition and supportive classroom environments for ELLs, focusing on aspects most relevant to Mrs. Romano's account of her pedagogy.

Mrs. Romano's account reflects a social interactionist theoretical perspective, whereby adults, through their verbal interactions with children, shape language and literacy development (Snow, 1983). Models of literate language provided by teachers may be internalized and used by students as they think, speak, and write (Vygotsky, 1978) through a process of guided apprenticeship, whereby learners observe and assist an expert in performance of a task. The expert guides the participation of the learners who become increasingly able to take responsibility (Rogoff, 1990).

Linguistic Interaction

Mrs. Romano's practice is aligned with Long's (1980) research demonstrating the importance of interaction between second-language learners and more proficient speakers who adjust their language from moment to moment to facilitate learners' comprehension. Skillful ESL teachers like Mrs. Romano not only simplify language for learners (Kliefgen, 1985) but also facilitate learners' language production by creating verbal scaffolds and participation structures that support and extend language performance beyond what learners are able to produce independently (Chaudron, 1988; Ellis, 1994). Goldenberg (1993) and Ellis (1994) suggest that participation in such collaborative discourse extends and develops second-language learners' communicative competence.

Furthermore, mothers' and second-language teachers' speech has been described as containing a high frequency of semantically contingent utterances, which incorporate words used by the previous speaker, and utterances that extend, expand, or paraphrase child–learner utterances, resulting in longer, more grammatical, more explicit, or more polite utterances (Chaudron, 1988; Ellis, 1984, 1985; Ochs & Schieffelin, 1984, 1986; Snow & Ferguson, 1977). These expanded or paraphrased utterances may be viewed as providing the child with well-structured linguistic input on a meaningful topic or, alternatively, as negative evidence (Sokolov & Snow, 1994) of how not to say something. For example, the child utterance "Daddy goed" might be paraphrased and expanded as "Yes, Daddy to work."

Another type of semantically contingent response employed by Mrs. Romano is the clarifying question, which may be asked to elicit information needed by the listener or to prompt production of a more complete, correct, or informative utterance (Heath, 1992; Pan & Snow, 1996). For example, in response to the learner utterance, "We played," the teacher might ask, "What did you play?"

The finding that intensive verbal interaction and semantic contingency are not features of adult–child exchanges in all cultures (Ochs & Scheffelin, 1984) has led to questions about whether these are, in fact, critical to language acquisition. Snow (1994) hypothesizes that although responsiveness may be one of the ways children are provided with the linguistic data they need, another source of linguistic data may be children's observation of and participation in repetitive and predictable texts and routines. Mrs. Romano provides children with verbal interaction, semantic contingency and responsiveness, as well as repetitive routines and predictable texts.

Language Input

Studies of child-directed speech (CDS) (Pine, 1994) and studies of talk directed to second-language learners (Wesche, 1994) have demonstrated that such talk differs from talk to adults and to more proficient speakers in various ways. Principal among these differences are stylistic characteristics observed in Mrs. Romano's talk and described by her grammatical simplification, limitation of vocabulary, repetitiveness, redundancy, and explanatory elaboration thought to facilitate comprehension (Chaudron, 1988; Ellis, 1985, 1994; Snow, 1995).

Wong-Fillmore (1982) argues that though teacher talk to second-language learners must be simple enough to serve as linguistic input for second-language acquisition, it must also be

complex enough to convey subject matter and to build vocabulary and background knowledge. Of course, fine tuning teacher talk is difficult in the ESL grade-level classroom like
Mrs. Romano's where children are placed by age but may vary greatly in prior knowledge
and English proficiency level. Nonetheless, Mrs. Romano tries conscientiously to provide
appropriately leveled input and to teach subject matter to children at all levels. Ellis (1985)
and Long (1985) emphasize the importance of finely tuned teacher talk that is responsive to
students' increasing proficiency levels.

Vygotsky's (1978) notion of the zone of proximal development (ZPD) is also relevant to
this study and to the discussion of linguistic simplification. The zone of proximal development can be understood as the distance between what a learner can produce or comprehend
independently and what that same learner can accomplish or comprehend with appropriate
assistance. Linguistic simplification, elaboration relating new words and concepts to familiar examples, and scaffolding learner discourse through collaboration are ways the teacher
can facilitate children's accomplishment of linguistic tasks that they could not perform
alone. The ZPD can also be conceptualized as the child's next developmental step—the
next level of difficulty slightly above the child's independent level of capability. Pinnell and
McCarrier (1993, p. 152) suggest a similar idea when she advises teachers to teach to the
"edge of children's development." A related notion is Krashen and Terrell's (1983, p. 32)
hypothesis that language acquisition occurs when the learner manages to comprehend the
gist of a message that contains linguistic features somewhat above his current competency.

Schmidt's (1990) and Ellis's (1993) research suggest that when teachers explicitly point
out grammatical features, students are more likely to notice these forms in the input they
receive. This noticing, in turn, may enhance the value of the input for language acquisition. Moreover, Doughty's (1991) findings support the instructional efficacy of a concurrent
classroom focus on meaning-oriented communication and attention to language form.

Yedlin's (2001) analysis of Mrs. Romano's talk to first-grade ELLs during writing instruction found that teacher talk was characterized by fine tuning of input, explicit attention to
linguistic form, and collaborative and other verbal strategies that might enable children
with a range of language proficiencies to accomplish literacy tasks that would otherwise be
beyond them.

Academic Discourse

The research on input and interaction reviewed in this chapter focuses primarily on the
acquisition of syntax and the development of what Cummins (1981) calls *basic interpersonal
communication skills* (BICS), which refers principally to the ability to participate in face-to-
face verbal communication that is routine and formulaic or is based in a shared context containing concrete referents to support meaning. Studies by Cummins (1981), Snow, Cancino,
DeTemple, and Schley (1991), and Skutenabb-Kangas and Toukomaa (1976) bear witness
to the fact that proficiency in BICS is not in itself a strong predictor of children's academic
success. School achievement depends on cognitive academic language proficiency (CALP)
(Cummins, 1981), which is the ability to understand and produce syntactically and semantically explicit discourse in the relative absence of immediate contextual and interpersonal
cues (Cummins, 2001).

A related notion associated with successful literacy attainment is *extended discourse*, the
term used by Snow, Dickinson, and Tabors (2001, p. 2) to identify oral discourse that poses
some of the same challenges as reading and writing. This is described as talk that "requires
participants to develop understandings beyond the here and now and that requires the

use of several utterances or turns to build a linguistic structure, such as in explanations, narratives and pretend" (ibid.).

Other descriptions of academic discourse make mention of specialized vocabulary (Corson, 1997; Snow et al., 1991; Spanos, Rhodes, Dale, and Crandall, 1988), certain language functions and grammatical structures (Chamot & O'Malley, 1987, 1994; Coehlo, 1982; Halliday, 1989), and discussions about thinking (i.e., metacognitive) and about language (i.e., metalinguistic).

It is widely recommended that preschool and primary-grade teachers of ELLs develop children's academic or extended discourse abilities by providing academic language input and by facilitating opportunities for children to participate in academic discourse. However, Bartolomé (1998) and Delpit (1995) point out that not all classrooms do provide children with such opportunities.

Linguistically diverse learners have been shown to benefit from explicit skills instruction (Wong-Fillmore, 1985), demonstration of how to do assigned work and clear statements of learning goals (Tikunoff, 1983), instruction in learning strategies (Chamot, et al., 1992) and teaching of metacognitive skills including self-monitoring and evaluation of outcomes (Dianda & Flaherty, 1995). Supportive teachers of second-language learners are theorized to discuss word meaning and syntax and to draw attention to features of the written code (Snow, Burns, & Griffin, 1998).

Moreover, the increasing focus on literacy standards for K–12 students at state and national levels means that teacher talk during writing instruction is increasingly likely to include explicit metalinguistic discussion of concepts such as the characteristics of good writing, writing strategies, and criteria for evaluation (New Standards Primary Literacy Committeee, 1999).

Given the acknowledged importance of academic discourse, and the studies that document its absence in some classrooms serving minority children (Bartolomé, 1998; Delpit, 1995; Reyes, 1992), this study has investigated what academic discourse might look like in the first-grade ESL classroom of an exemplary teacher.

Notes

1. Pseudonym.
2. Elicited during interviews and conversations.

References

Bartolomé, L. I. (1998). *The misteaching of academic discourses: The politics of language in the classroom*. Boulder, CO: Westview Press.

Chamot, A., & O'Malley, M. (1987). The cognitive academic language learning approach: A bridge to the mainstream. *TESOL Quarterly, 21*(2), 227–249.

Chamot, A., & O'Malley, M. (1994). *The CALLA Handbook*. Reading, MA: Addison Wesley.

Chamot, A., Dale, M., O'Malley, M., & Spanos, G. (1992). Learning and problem solving strategies of ESL students. *Bilingual Research Journal, 16*(3 & 4), 1–34.

Chaudron, C. (1988). *Second language classrooms: Research on teaching and learning*. Cambridge, England: Cambridge University Press.

Coehlo, E. (1982). Language across the curriculum. *TESL Talk, 13*, 56–70.

Corson, D. (1997). The learning and use of academic English words. *Language Learning 47*(4), 671–718.

Cummins, J. (1981). The role of primary language development in promoting educational success for language minority students. In California State Department of Education (Ed.), *Schooling and language minority students: A theoretical framework* (pp. 3–49). Los Angeles: Evaluation, Dissemination and Assessment Center, California State University.

Cummins, J. (2001). *Language, power, and pedagogy.* Clevedon, England: Multilingual Matters.

Delpit, L. (1995). *Other people's children: Cultural conflict in the classroom.* New York: New Press.

Dianda, M., & Flaherty, J. (1995). *Effects of success for all on the reading achievement of first graders in California bilingual programs.* Los Alamitos, CA: Southwest Regional Educational Laboratory.

Doughty, C. (1991). Second language instruction does make a difference: Evidence from an empirical study of SL relativisation. *Studies in second language acquisition, 13*(4), 431–469.

Ellis, R. (1984). *Classroom second language development.* Oxford: Pergammon.

Ellis, R (1985). Teacher-pupil interaction in second language development. In S. Gass & C. Madden (Eds.), *Input and second language acquisition* (pp. 377–393). Rowley, MA: Newbury House.

Ellis, R. (1993). Second language acquisition and the structural syllabus. *TESOL Quarterly, 27,* 91–113.

Ellis, R. (1994). *The study of second language acquisition.* Oxford: Oxford University Press.

Fillmore, L. W., & Snow, C.E. (2000). *What teachers need to know about language.* Washington, DC: Center for Applied Linguistics.

Gatbonton, E. (1999). Investigating experienced ESL teachers' pedagogical knowledge. *Modern Language Journal, 83*(1), 35–49.

Goldenberg, C. (1993). Instructional conversations: Promoting comprehension through discussion. *Reading Teacher, 46*(4), 316–326.

Halliday, M. (1989). Some grammatical problems in scientific English. Paper presented to the Society of Pakistani English Language Teachers, Karachi, Pakistan.

Hoggard, L. S. (1996). Critical attributes of classroom culture for literacy development of English language learners. Doctoral dissertation, University of California, Los Angeles.

Hughes, S. (1985). *Alfie gives a hand.* NY: Mulberry Books.

Kliefgen, J. (1985). Skilled variation in a kindergarten teacher's use of foreigner talk. In S. Gass & C. Madden (Eds.), *Input in second language acquisition* (pp. 59–68). New York: Newbury House.

Kohl, H. (2002). Topsy-turvies: Teacher talk and student talk. In L. Delpit & J. Kilgour Dowdy (Eds.), *The skin that we speak: Thoughts on language and culture in the classroom* (pp. 145–163). New York: New Press.

Krashen, S. & Terrell, T. (1983). *The natural approach: Language acquisition in the classroom.* Hayward, CA: Alemany Press.

Long, M. (1980). Input, interaction, and second language acquisition. Unpublished doctoral thesis, University of California, Los Angeles.

Long, M. (1985). Input and second language acquisition theory. In S. Gass & C. Madden (Eds.), *Input and second language acquisition* (pp. 377–393). Rowley, MA: Newbury House.

New Standards Primary Literacy Committee. (1999). *Reading and writing grade by grade: Primary literacy standards for kindergarten through third grade.* Pittsburgh: National Center on Education and the Economy.

Ochs, E., & Scheffelin, B. (1984). Language acquisition and socialization: Three developmental stories and their implications. In R. Schweder & R. LeVine (Eds.), *Culture Theory: Essays on mind, self, and emotion.* (pp. 276–323). Cambridge, U.K.: Cambridge University Press.

Ochs, E., & Scheffelin, B. (Eds.). (1986). *Language socialization across cultures.* New York: Cambridge University Press.

Pan, B.A., & Snow, C.E. (1996). *Functions of requests for clarification in parent-child interaction.* Paper presented at the Fifth International Pragmatics Conference. Mexico City, July 4–9, 1996.

Pine, J. (1994). *The language of primary caregivers.* In C. Gallaway & B. Richards (Eds.), *Input and interaction in language acquisition* (pp. 15–37). Cambridge, England: Cambridge University Press.

Pinnell, G., & McCarrier, A. (1993). Interactive writing: A transition tool for assisting children in learning to read and write. In E. Hiebert & B. Taylor (Eds.), *Getting reading right from the start: Effective early literacy interventions* (pp. 149–171). Boston: Allyn & Bacon.

Reyes, M. (1992). Challenging venerable assumptions: Literacy instruction for linguistically different students. *Harvard Educational Review, 62*(4), 427–446.

Rogoff, B. (1990). *Apprenticeship in thinking.* New York: Oxford University Press.

Schmidt, R. (1990). The role of consciousness in second language learning. *Applied Linguistics, 11,* 129–158.

Skutenabb-Kangas, T., & Toukomaa, P. (1976). Teaching migrant children's mother tongue and the language of the host country in the context of the sociocultural situation of the migrant family. Helsinki: The Finnish National Commission for UNESCO.

Snow, C. E. (1983). Literacy and language: Relationships during the pre-school years. *Harvard Educational Review, 53,* 165–189.

Snow, C. E. (1994). Beginning from baby talk: Twenty years of research on input and interaction. In C. Gallaway & B. Richards (Eds.), *Input and interaction in language acquisition* (pp. 3–12). Cambridge, England: Cambridge University Press.

Snow, C. E. (1995). Issues in the study of input: Fine-tuning, universality, individual and developmental differences, and necessary causes. In B. MacWhinney & P. Fletcher (Eds.), *Handbook of child language* (pp. 180–194). Oxford: Blackwell.

Snow, C. E., Burns, M. S., & Griffin, S. (Eds.). (1998). *Preventing reading failure in young children.* Washington, DC: National Academy Press.

Snow, C. E., & Fergusen, C. (Eds.). (1977). *Talking to children: Language input and acquisition.* Cambridge, England: Cambridge University Press.

Snow, C. E., Cancino, H., DeTemple, J., & Schley, S. (1991). Giving formal definitions: A linguistic or a metalinguistic skill? In E. Bialystok (Ed.), *Language processing and language awareness by bilingual children.* New York: Cambridge University Press.

Snow, C., Dickinson, D., and Tabors, P. (2001). *Language development in the preschool years.* In D. Dickinson & P. Tabors (Eds.), *Beginning literacy with language* (pp. 1–27). Baltimore: Paul Brookes Publishers.

Sokolov, J. L., & Snow, C. E. (1994). The changing role of negative evidence in theories of language development. In C. Gallaway & B. Richards (Eds.), *Input and interaction in language acquisition.* (pp. 38–53). Cambridge, England: Cambridge University Press.

Spanos, G., Rhodes, N., Dale, T., & Crandall, J. (1988). Linguistic features of mathematical problem solving. In R. R. Cocking & J. P. Mestre (Eds.), *Linguistic and cultural influences on mathematics learning* (pp. 221–240). Hillsdale, NJ: Erlbaum.

Tikunoff, W. J. (1983). *An emerging description of successful bilingual instruction: Executive summary of SBIF study.* San Francisco: Far West Lab for Educational Research.

Vygotsky, L. S. (1978). *Mind in society: The development of higher psychological processes.* Cambridge, MA: Harvard University Press.

Wesche, M. B. (1994). Input and interaction in second language acquisition. In C. Gallaway & B. Richards (Eds.), *Input and interaction in language acquisition* (pp. 219–248). Cambridge, England: Cambridge University Press.

Wong-Fillmore, L. (1982). Instructional language as linguistic input: Second language learning in classrooms. In L. C. Wilkinson (Ed.), *Communicating in the classroom* (pp. 283–297). New York: Academic Press.

Wong-Fillmore, L. (1985). When does teacher talk work as input? In S. Gass & C. Madden (Eds.), *Input in second language acquisition* (pp. 17–50). New York: Newbury House.

Yedlin, J. (2001). Development of an instrument for the analysis of teacher talk to young second language learners during literacy instruction. Qualifying paper, Harvard Graduate School of Education, Cambridge, MA.

CHAPTER 5

Integrating Test Tasks into Everyday Classroom Activities: A Coach's Report on Collaborative Action Research Teams

ROBERT C. PARKER

Introduction

This chapter is a description of how I coached seven across-schools collaborative action research (CAR) teams that were experimenting with integrating the use of the test tasks, formats, and procedures of the New York State mandated tests into everyday classroom activities. The chapter also includes the products produced by the teams and findings of the action research activities of the CAR teams. All the CAR teams mentioned in this description emphasized the implementation of effective practices for supporting English language learners (ELLs) as they worked toward meeting the performance and content standards of the New York Public Schools. The chapter also includes a description of how I changed my method of teacher-inquiry coaching to be more clinical in nature as I sought to support the teachers as their coach.

The examinations on which the seven CAR teams focused were the fourth-grade English Language Arts exam and the high-school-level English Regents. To determine if this inquiry focus was a valid one, the teams developed baseline performance assessment activities to analyze student control of the language and test-taking skills necessary for successful performance on the target tests. The teams' members developed these diagnostic assessments based on an analysis of a variety of resources about the target tests as well. Finally, the test tasks were infused into literacy and content-area lessons in both languages of the students, predominately Spanish and English.

To scaffold learning, the team members developed a variety of teaching and learning tools. Again, they continuously collected evidence of student growth toward control of the target skills (i.e., they used the diagnostic assessments as formative assessments) and used team meetings to evaluate the students' writing, note-taking, and listening skills with a common scoring guide. A unique aspect of this CAR activity was that the targeted test tasks were integrated into the lower grades, starting in first grade, not just into the grade in which the test was to be given. In other words, the mandated tests for fourth grade were examined by first- through fourth-grade teachers and the test tasks were infused into the curriculum at all grade levels. Two of the teams were based in single schools, but the third team was made up of members from several elementary schools.

What Is Collaborative Action Research?

Collaborative action research is a process in which voluntary school teams systematically examine their own classroom practices to see if these practices are effectively assisting all their students in meeting the predetermined performance standards of the school system. It is a looping process and can be used for any of the following:

- Identifying problematic learning or assessment situations
- Reviewing student performance data
- Studying relevant literature from the field
- Identifying and field testing classroom strategies
- Revising and refining the use of target strategies based on the level of student success in the classroom
- Reflecting and discussing with colleagues about the effect of the changes
- Documenting the process
- Sharing the findings of the action research activity with other teachers

The focus is always on making learning and teaching changes based on student performance and need. However, Sagor (2000, p. 3) informs that "the primary reason for engaging in action research is to assist the 'actor' in improving and/or refining his or her actions."

Background Information

This section describes my coaching background to illustrate the evolution of the approach taken with the CAR teams. Additionally, this section outlines the responsibilities of a coach and the process by which I worked with the CAR teams.

In the early 1980s I was hired as a freelance consultant to implement a sequence of biweekly sessions on communicative competencies for managers in a surgical instruments company in the Boston, Massachusetts, area. The main concern of the human resource officer who hired me was that department managers lacked effective presentation, discussion facilitation, and writing skills. Consequently, work orders were often misunderstood by employees, and on-the-floor work teams spent a great deal of time trying to clarify expectations expressed in memos and announcements. Many members of the work teams were nonnative speakers of English, and this added to the miscommunication.

My first task was to interview managers and work teams to establish a clear view of the issues and to observe the on-the-floor work teams attempting to implement work orders and other directives. I was fascinated with the activities of the work teams. The self-managing teams followed a meeting protocol that effectively dealt with the usual interpersonal issues of group decision making while identifying and solving problems. My interest in the self-managing teams led me to the theories of Kurt Lewin, an American psychologist. In the 1940s Lewin promulgated a theory of inquiry that included a looping process made up of analyzing a problem, planning how to deal with the issue, implementing the plan (i.e., the action taken), and evaluating the results of the implementation of the plan. To me, this sounded similar to the seven steps of problem solving I had learned about in undergraduate social psychology and discourse analysis courses. However, to better understand how to apply my knowledge I became a member of the American Society for Training and Development and participated in workshops and seminars about self-actualizing teams, job-embedded staff development, and facilitating study and focus groups.[1]

At the beginning of the 1990s, as a member of the Education Alliance at Brown University, I coordinated the activities of the New England Superintendents Leadership Council. One of my responsibilities was to coach system-wide focus or problem-solving teams that focused on the educational issues of bilingual student enrollments. Each team was composed of teachers, counselors, students, and a community member and was chaired by the superintendent.

All these experiences and growing expertise as a team coach supported me in facilitating the implementation of numerous school-based study groups whose members field tested in their classrooms the practices and strategies being studied in the team meetings. I also facilitated several focus groups that used the problem-solving protocol I learned about in college and from the work teams at the surgical instruments company.[2] Soon I was providing "coach the coaches" training in several New England school districts since it was economically more feasible for a school system to develop the coaching skills of teacher leaders and administrators than to continuously hire outside consultants to act as coaches.

By the early 1990s I had made the connection between the team coaching I was providing and collaborative action research. I studied some of the literature and found Richard Sagor (1992) especially informative. I was soon coaching and training district coaches to coach CAR teams in Connecticut, Maine, New Hampshire, and Vermont.

All of these experiences led me to identify a set of tasks and roles and responsibilities of a performance or process coach of CAR teams that assisted administrators who hired me as a CAR coach to understand how I would coach a team or teams in their school or schools. The following outlines the responsibilities of a coach.

Responsibilities for Coaches of Teacher Inquiry Teams or Action Research Teams

- Attends team meetings at least twice a month or based on an arrangement with the school
- Elicits and guides professional conversations around student work and instructional practice
- Mediates between team members and the administration
- Guides teams as it identifies areas of focus; keeps them focused on the inquiry question
- Assists the team members in identifying strategies to use to deal with their issue or focus; acts as a resource and guide but does not tell the team what to do—members make that decision through consensus
- Gradually increases team authority and self-management as its members' knowledge and competence grow
- Acts as a critical friend to the whole team or to individual members who request in-class coaching
- Provides technical assistance to team members as they document and reflect about their work
- Facilitates and maintains a respectful climate during meetings for all participants
- Facilitates the collection and organization of the team documentation and the impact on the changes in participants' instructional practices

I also developed a set of guiding questions for team members as they began the CAR process, which are outlined in the next section.

Guiding Questions for Teacher Inquiry and Action Research Teams

- What is our question, issue, interest or concern?
- If we are exploring an issue or problem, is this a real problem or a symptom of a problem?
- What performance data do we have to determine or confirm that this is an issue worth exploring? Will we and others benefit from an exploration?
- Why is this question, issue, or problem of importance to our school? How does it align with the standards, expectations, and goals of the superintendent? How will our school or classrooms be different when we finish our inquiry? How will student performance be better?
- How will each of us explore our inquiry question relative to our grade or proficiency level?
- What's our plan—how will we proceed? How many meetings will we have each month? How will we communicate with each other?
- How will we decide which practice or strategy to study and experiment with in our classrooms? What criteria or rationale will we use to make this decision?
- What do we mean by *best practice* and *recommended practice*?
- How will we study and plan for experimenting in class? Will we try out our changes or strategies with all students or a cohort?
- How will we collect performance data to show impact of the changes on our students?
- How will we document our meetings; our data, literature review, and analysis; our in-class planning, changes, and results; our findings; our reflections?
- How will we share our findings with other teachers in the school and in other schools?
- How will we work with our coach? What protocols will we use?
- How will we keep focused and sustain our efforts?

During the 1998–99 school year, the Educational Alliance at Brown University, in collaboration with the New York City Board of Education, implemented a CAR activity in 13 schools. I coached five of these CAR teams. Many of the teachers involved in this activity were also members of the across-school districts activity, described in the next section. To make the activity even more complex, the activity was also aligned with a federally funded performance assessment activity named Project Performance Assessment Collecting Evidence (PACE). The project provided training and process coaching for teachers to develop and experiment with performance assessment as a practice for collecting evidence of student progress toward meeting state-mandated language arts content standards. The activity was funded for three school years between 1999 and 2003. Consequently, the participants in the across-schools project focused on using performance assessment scoring guides as a strategy for collecting evidence of student growth during the across-schools CAR activity.

Activities, Products Developed, and Findings of the Across-Grade and Across-Schools Collaborative Action Research (CAR)

The following section provides details on the CAR teams I worked with on across-grade and across-schools collaborative.

Description

Seven separate CAR teams situated in elementary, intermediate, and high schools explored the impact of integrating the use of the test tasks, formats, and procedures of City and State Department of Education mandated tests into literacy and content-area lessons rather than drill and practice them just before the testing period. This chapter is concerned only with what the elementary teams did.

All the schools had significant ELL enrollments, many who were recent immigrants, and in classrooms with Spanish-speaking students, teachers used both Spanish and English for instruction. The majority of the students in these schools received free lunch. All the teachers involved in the activity were credentialed as bilingual, English as a second language (ESL), and content teachers.

Issues and Concerns

The seven teams decided to experiment with this same instructional practice after attending a CAR kick-off meeting sponsored by the New York City Board of Education in collaboration with the Education Alliance at Brown University in fall 2000. During this meeting, team members discovered they shared a common concern or issue.

Team members found that a majority of their students were not ready for successful performance on the tests that were mandated by the city and New York State departments of education. Students were not good writers of expository paragraphs and compositions. They were not good interpreters of writing prompts, at taking notes during read-aloud activities (an important task in all the target tests), at using the notes or at using a semantic or graphic organizer to plan an extended writing response, and at quickly revising and editing written responses in on-demand situations. In addition, their writing was full of structural errors in both languages.

Applied Research

During the kick-off meeting and later during the initial team meetings in their schools, team members reviewed several articles about activities that promote student learning and strategies for test preparation. A few meta-analysis reports were especially helpful in the development of a theoretical construct for their action research activities. Team members decided that the practice of integrating test tasks into classroom instruction and of using the experience to diagnose need and determine growth of skill was a reliable practice based on the "evidence that making events contiguous when teaching, assigning, evaluating, and remediating performance of tasks enhances the academic achievement of students in kindergarten, elementary, secondary, college and adult learning classrooms. Moreover, academic achievement was improved in a wide range of content areas" (Friedman & Fisher, 1998, p. 52). Through sharing, discussion, and reflections, the teams came to an agreement on the learning principles that were fundamental to their inquiry and action activities.

1. Students internalize and induce competencies over a long development period when the competencies are continuously reentered in authentic learning tasks.
2. Applying the competencies in learning–performance tasks in other contexts than in test-practice materials and with released test items is a more authentic experience that leads to the ability to succeed in on-demand testing experiences.
3. Continuous assessment allows or encourages teachers to diagnose—as well as document growth of competencies—student needs. This diagnosis mechanism

tends to identify other linguistic (in this case, the second-language acquisition needs), language learning, and prior knowledge needs as well; that is, infusion of test tasks into classroom activities indirectly impacts or builds outcomes and objectives of other syllabus areas.

4. The practice of infusing test tasks encourages teachers to align their instruction with student need; that is, instruction tends to become more student-performance-data driven.

5. The target practice supports students in developing and applying learning protocols and procedural knowledge or operational skills that are useful in lifelong learning and on-the-job situations in real life.

6. The practice has an affective impact because it provides opportunities to talk about and to demonstrate how to do well on mandated tests; that is, it helps students connect the value of learning strategies with test requirements.

7. The practice creates a context wherein traditional test-prep activities become real and useful to students. How to take test strategies and tips can be integrated into the analysis and application of directions and prompts provided to students as they apply the test protocols.

As the teams began to study the literature, several members of the teams were concerned that most of the research reports studied were not conducted with bilingual and ESL students. Thus, would the findings of these reports be applicable to their students? I suggested that the teams organize their action research activity around attempting to discover if the research finding expressed in Friedman and Fisher (1998) is applicable to native-language students who are learning to learn with English.

Inquiry Question

After several meetings in their own schools, and the CAR coach passing information from one team to another, the teams agreed to explore this general inquiry question:

Will integrating testing formats and tasks into everyday instruction raise bilingual students' communicative competencies necessary for successful performance on city and state mandated tests?[3] Will it benefit students if this practice is implemented in the first grade or in lower English proficiency levels in upper elementary, middle, and high school grades?

Teams or individual team members crafted the general inquiry question to align with the cognitive and curriculum needs of specific grades. For example,

- Grade 1: Will training and guiding students in taking and transcribing notes develop the listening and procedural knowledge competencies students will need for mandated tests?
- Grades 2 and 3: Will assisting students in maintaining a response log help them in developing the writing competencies necessary for success with short responses on the mandated tests?
- Grade 4 and intermediate grades: If students are trained in using graphic organizers and are provided with ample opportunities to practice on-demand extended written responses, will this have a positive impact on their performance on the English Language Arts test and English Regents?

Action Plan, Strategic Plan

Team members engaged in a series of activities according to an Action Plan they developed with their CAR coach. First, the teachers interviewed other teachers in their respective schools about the feasibility of the activities. They also reviewed student written work as well as any test data available on their students. The idea was to collect evidence that their concerns for their students' performance was warranted and that the inquiry question the teachers had chosen was worth exploring. Second, each team analyzed the relevant mandated tests to identify the language tasks within them. They developed a skill set that a student would need to complete the task. Third, team members reviewed several professional books and articles on effective instructional practices. From their review of this literature, the teams decided on their instructional strategies. They agreed that an effective strategy would be composed of a series of steps. These are outlined in the next section.

The Elements of the Practice

All team members integrated the test tasks—identified in learning principle 2 as previously defined—into content lessons. Elementary grade teachers integrated the test tasks into ESL classes, math, social studies, and science lessons. Since all the elementary teachers were expected to use balanced literacy or writing workshop during literacy development, they did not attempt to integrate test tasks into literacy lessons. However, all the teachers used written response activities to accomplish the objective. No monolingual content teachers served as members of the target CAR teams.

Using a Protocol   The instructional practice followed the sequence or protocol of the targeted tests. Teachers analyzed the tests and created the following list, which outlines the tasks students needed to do to perform on the tests.

- Students listen to or read a selection with which they are not acquainted, usually a nonfiction text.
- Students organize the content of the selection on a graphic organizer or take notes.
- Students participate in oral and written comprehension activities about the selection—the students' specific comprehension skill and strategy needs are identified from various assessment data.
- Students generate, based on a prompt, short written responses, which are usually two- to three-sentence-paragraph definitions or focused descriptions.
- Students generate extended written responses based on a prompt; across the school year, students practice writing 2-4 paragraph reflective, persuasive, summary, chronological, process, biographical, and literary analysis and evaluation compositions.

In math lessons, students were asked to write a sequence of sentences that described how they solved a computation or word problem or explained why they solved a problem in the manner they used.

Periodically students analyzed samples of tests to learn test-taking strategies such as how to interpret visual clues and written prompts, how to quickly plan a written response, and how to monitor completion of the prompt steps.

Scaffolding Strategies   Teachers used a common set of scaffolds to mediate student learning. Depending on the students' ages as well as communicative competency levels or language proficiency, teachers used a variety of scaffolding strategies to assist students in completing the sequence outlined in the previous section. Following are the strategies teachers agreed to use.

- Written response spirals up from complete sentences, sets of logical-order sentences, paragraphs, and multiple-paragraph writing.
- Visuals and descriptions—in both languages, whichever is appropriate—are provided to establish comprehension.
- Teachers model the protocols and use think-aloud strategies to help students become familiar with testing protocols.
- Teachers provide completed or partially completed samples of completed work that represent their expectations.
- Teachers always provide students with copies of the scoring guides they use to evaluate student performance.
- Teachers always conference with students or continuously guide students as they work through the performance tasks.
- Teachers provide charts or copies of the content of a task; for example, the elements of a paragraph or reading for information strategies are articulated on charts and referred to—and reviewed—continuously during class activities.

Collecting Evidence   Teachers collected evidence of positive impact on student performance. They used a variety of performance assessment strategies including scoring guides that include primary trait inventories and performance rubrics; student self-evaluation; and performance portfolios to collect evidence of student growth. Teams of teachers in a school used common inventories and rubrics and met periodically to validate their scoring guides, especially the performance rubrics, to establish consistency of purpose across the grades and English proficiency levels. To determine if this inquiry focus and the target treatments were effective, the teams developed baseline performance assessment activities to analyze student control of the language and test-taking skills necessary for successful performance on the target tests. The teams developed these diagnostic assessments based on an analysis of a variety of resources about the target tests. Then, the test tasks were infused into literacy and content-area lessons in the students' two languages. For scaffolded learning, the team members developed a variety of teaching and learning tools. Again, they continuously collected evidence of student growth toward control of the target skills (i.e., they used the diagnostic assessments as formative assessments) and used team meetings to evaluate the students' writing, note-taking, and listening skills with a common scoring guide. A unique aspect of this CAR activity was that the targeted test tasks were integrated into lower-grade and proficiency classes, not just into the grade or level classrooms that matched the mandated tests.

The primary trait inventory represented a specific type of composition or paragraph. The scoring guide was always shared with the students, and teachers demonstrated how to use the scoring guide as a plan for writing. Sometimes the scoring guide was adapted for younger students, but key procedural vocabulary was kept as is. Thus, the inventory of the scoring guide became the syllabus for the integration of the test tasks into instruction. The goal—not always easy to meet—was to devote every other team meeting to analysis and evaluation of student work with a common scoring guide.

When initially practicing the individual tasks of the test-taking sequence (e.g., listening to or reading a selection, taking notes, completing an organizer, generating a written response, editing the response), teachers asked students to work in collaborative groups.

Group members practiced the target task and used the teacher-provided scoring guide to evaluate their work (i.e., their written product). However, once the group members became comfortable or relatively proficient in using the target task, individual students were expected to complete the task by themselves in future assignments. The teacher then evaluated individual student work and reviewed the written product with the student based on the scoring guide she or he used to evaluate the student's work. A majority of the teachers in this study also required students to periodically self-evaluate their work based on the scoring guide. And during teacher–student conferences, students evaluated their own work based on the inventory of traits on the scoring guide.

How Teams Adapted the Plan for Their Schools

This section includes a plan for how elementary CAR teams adapted the strategies for their purposes. One team wrote the following objective with an outline for how they would accomplish their objective.

Objective: *Establish protocol for infusing test tasks, formats, strategies, and procedures into classroom activities.*

1. Use nonfiction selections for interactive read aloud (e.g., *Scholastic First Discovery Book Series*—science topics with pictures; *Scholastic Reader Newspapers*; check library for materials with sufficient illustrations; use sections of social studies and science textbooks and chapter books).
2. Use this language development procedure (combines guided reading and language experience).
   - Ask comprehension and open-ended questions during interactive read aloud.
   - Continuously ask students to describe (analyze) what they are learning (i.e., response is more complex than oral retell).
   - Have students do an oral retell of key elements of the narrative; use brainstorming and round-robin strategies.
   - Record the key elements of the narrative the students' words on a flip chart or easel paper as a set of logical-order sentences.
   - Use sentence extender activity to demonstrate how to create more sophisticated sentences.
   - Record the sentence extenders on the easel paper.
   - Demonstrate editing of sentences.
   - Guide students through a choral reading of the edited sentences.
   - Have students write their own versions of a set of logical-order sentences (i.e., summarize or paraphrase the nonfiction narrative).
   - Eventually, have students write summary paragraphs and paraphrases of the target story.
   - Have low-proficiency students draw a sequence of pictures representing the narrative and write a sentence for each picture in the sequence.
3. Use the primary-trait inventory and rubric developed by the team.
4. Collect student samples; align the samples with the rubric.
5. Meet with other team members to complete a standards-setting activity based on everyone's set of student samples. Team meetings can focus on the development of the inventory and rubric while teachers conduct the procedure and train students in participating in the procedure and collect student writing samples.

Team Language Focus

- First-grade teacher conducts this in English.
- Second-grade teacher conducts in both languages.
- Third-grade teacher eventually conducts the main steps as an on-demand assessment activity, after students get used to the procedure; that is, his or her activities replicate the New York State fourth-grade English Language Arts testing conditions.
- Fourth-grade teacher conducts this in Spanish. (The rubric and inventory need to be adapted for use with Spanish speakers and writers.)
- Reading specialist conducts it in English during Project Read activities.
- ESL specialist follows the protocol in ESL activities.

Selected Findings from the Action Research Process

The following insights are gleaned from the study. These insights are what led me to reconsider how I coach teams.

With regard to scoring-guide development, it took a considerable amount of time to bring teachers to an agreement on what the levels of performance criteria—the rubric—really meant. As the coach, I needed to assist with the development of the scoring guides and to work and rework the rubrics so that they could be used effectively to gather data on student performance.

Team meetings required a meeting protocol. All teams comprised 10 to 12 members plus the facilitator and coach. This meant that teams needed to develop and follow a meeting protocol to allow all participants to be heard and to prevent a few dominant personalities from taking over the meetings. The development of meeting protocols and agendas to follow, as well as team-building activities, were part of the coaching responsibilities.

Participants did not always use the terminology of instruction and learning in the same way. This led to confusion when discussing student work and analyzing test tasks to identify skill sets. Time was also wasted in defining terms. To facilitate this situation, I developed charts comprising key definitions and lexicons for such educational terms as *skill, learning strategy, scaffolding,* and *obligatory language.* Glossaries from several resources were shared across the teams.

In this way, I became more directive as a coach, even while letting teams develop their strategies and styles. To effectively evaluate student performance and to examine if the strategies are successful, teams needed some uniformity and information common to all.

Materials and Tools Developed to Implement the Action Part of the Process

The definition of the *action* part of the process of action research comes from Anna Uhl Chamot (Chamot & O'Malley, 1994). One of the actions of the teacher teams was to develop scoring guides to assist them in assessing student performance.

Selected Scoring Guides   After analyzing the various mandated examinations, notably the New York State fourth- and eighth-grade English Language Arts tests and the English Regents, as well as student work samples, the teams developed various scoring guides for collecting evidence of performance growth. The primary trait inventories for the scoring guides were used as curriculum frameworks for planning lessons or for remediating student work. They were especially helpful in planning minilessons about language structures, usage rules, spelling and punctuation conventions, and writing strategies. All teachers on all the teams stressed the use of the writing process steps. However, each teacher emphasized language and learning objectives appropriate for his or her grade level or the students' proficiency level, but all the team members used the same assessment administration process and set of performance rubrics. This facilitated evaluation of student work by teams and the discussions about the quality of student work. It also facilitated discussion and comprehension of the teachers when all the teams came together at the end of each school year to share their experiences.

Thus, there was flexibility in how test-infusion tasks were implemented so that they aligned with the language needs and cognitive development levels of the students. But the implementation process was systematic, and the performance evaluation criteria were standardized across the grade and school levels.

The example shown in Table 5.1 is of a scoring guide for an oral retell for the beginner or newly arrived ESL student. Students were asked to retell a sequence without support from a teacher or peer. Teachers used the rubric to indicate the level of performance the student had achieved on the trait or skill.

Teachers also developed frameworks for writing. Teachers used these frameworks during instructional time while modeling the process of writing through write-aloud and think-aloud activities. Tables 5.2 and 5.3 are examples of frameworks teachers used for writing paragraphs.

Teachers also developed and used the following rubrics to assist in scoring student work. (See Tables 5.4 to 5.10).

Strategic Learning Strategies   Teachers on the CAR teams identified the following strategic learning strategies with examples for how these should be carried out.

- Thoughts and actions that assist learning tasks
- Ways to understand, remember, and recall information
- Ways to practice skill efficiently

In other words, teachers expected certain learning behaviors of their students. The following list of examples is what teachers hoped their students would do to help them learn content material. Teachers used this list to generate minilessons in their classrooms.

Examples of Expected Learning Behaviors

- Students generate and follow a strategic plan for completing a project or extended-learning assignment.
- Students maintain an electronic portfolio.
- Students use reading strategies relevant to content and purpose of assignments and classroom activities.
- Students use read for information strategies: skim, survey, jot down and take notes in their own words, reference, underline key points, make notes in the margin that make connections.
- Students use textbook-reading strategies (e.g., SPQ3R).
- Students use graphic organizers and semantic webs.
- Students use and interpret scoring guides to plan how to complete assignments and to prepare writing assignments.
- Students take notes during listening and reading experiences.
- Students transcribe notes into their own words.
- Students use learning management strategies (e.g., organize and update notebooks, learning logs, response journals).

- Students collaborate with other learners or join cooperative learning groups to prepare for tests.
- Students conference with a teacher or peer.
- Students use predictions and prepractice activities.
- Students outline reading materials based on class notes.
- Students use think-aloud strategy—conduct internal dialogues.
- Students use metacognitive strategies: describe how they are completing or have completed assignments; self-monitor; self-evaluate quality and quantity of effort and product.
- Students practice test-taking strategies such as responding to prompts for extended writing.
- Students use "wh" questions to review and recall reading and lectures or presentations.
- Students use study guides.
- Students jot down ideas on 3 × 5 cards or in a notebook when reviewing content or preparing for a test.

Evidence That the Practice Was Effective

The CAR teams that participated in this activity collected test data as well as maintained student performance portfolios to show the positive impact of their action research treatment and experimentation. The effect on the students' writing skills was especially apparent with significant increase in their ability to write a wide range of short and extended written-response genres, such as retell, summary, definition, descriptive paragraphs, and reflective, persuasive, and critical lens essays.

An interesting, unexpected performance effect of this activity was the success of the target students on other mandated district tests. For example, students who developed the aforementioned competencies starting in the first and second grade performed higher than expected on the third-grade multiple-choice reading examination; elementary and high school students who practiced these competencies in their first- and second-language classes performed higher than expected on the Language Assessment Battery (LAB), required for exit from direct second-language development services.

Collaborative Analysis of Student Learning Teachers who experimented with the practice of collaborative analysis of student learning documented growth of individual students by saving student work (e.g., samples of note taking, organization of information, written responses, conferencing) and by using the scoring guides to evaluate student work in individual student performance portfolios. Teachers in a school came together regularly to evaluate this student work as a team, using the common scoring guides developed by the teachers based on their initial analysis of the mandated tests, language-development standards, and second-language development needs of their students.

Teachers documented growth around individual student use of a variety of skill areas.

- Test-taking strategies
- Comprehension of main ideas of listen-to and reading selections
- Specific writing formats and genres
- Specific sentence elements such as subject–verb agreement and use of adjectives and transitional words, as well as the use of inflectional endings (i.e., word forms)
- Conventions of punctuation and spelling in both languages
- Note-taking skills; the transcription of notes; the use of notes for writing compositions

Table 5.1 Oral retell—beginner/newcomer ESL

Name	Date

ORAL RETELL – BEGINNER/NEWCOMER ESL
Performance Inventory
When student is asked to complete the task *without* support.

Primary Trait/Behavior	Performance Level
1. Retells an *Informational Narrative* with no coaching or visual clues	1 2 3 4
2. Retells the narrative sequence in logical order	1 2 3 4
3. Includes in the retelling the main points or ideas	1 2 3 4
4. Identifies story details from memory accurately	1 2 3 4

Performance Rubric

LEVEL	CONTROL OF TRAIT OR SKILL
1 Pre-production Stage	Not enough language product to evaluate. Demonstrates little or no use of target trait, behavior or skill. Demonstrates minimal L_2 proficiency. Requires continuous, direct instructional support and scaffolding as well as comprehension prompts.
2 Emergent/ Early Production/ Low Functional Stage	Performance is characterized by many errors. Demonstrates limited use of target trait, behavior, or skill. Demonstrates an emerging communicative proficiency or control in L_2. Requires direct instructional support and scaffolding as well as comprehension prompts.
3 Development/ Speech Emergence/ High Function Stage (Still Dependent)	Performance is characterized by several errors. Demonstrates limited use of target trait, behavior, or skill. Demonstrates a developing communicative proficiency or control in L_2. Still requires direct instructional support and scaffolding and comprehension prompts.
4 Early Oral Fluent/ Developing Stage	Performance is characterized by some errors. Demonstrates adequate or the beginning of automatic use of target trait, behavior, or skill. Continues to demonstrates a developing communicative proficiency or control in L_2. Occasionally requires direct instructional support and scaffolding and comprehension prompts.

Comments/Observations

- Procedural knowledge (e.g., use of graphic organizers, writing process steps, attending to tasks, planning to write, extended revision and editing)
- Metacognitive skills (e.g., self-evaluation and strategic planning by students)

That is, teachers documented individual student growth in specific learning areas, comprehension, test-taking strategies, language analysis, and writing competencies.

Table 5.2 Paragraph framework

> **Paragraph Framework for a Stand-Alone Paragraph**
>
> A. Introductory or Topic Sentence: States main point or purpose; might restate composition prompt question as a statement.
> B. Body Sentences/Supporting-Detail Sentences: Support the opening statement or topic sentence with details, ideas, or concepts; can interpret or define the opening statement.
>   Sentence
>   Sentence
>   Sentence
>   Etc.
> C. Concluding Sentence: Bring closure or draw conclusion that is linked to introductory or topic sentence

Table 5.3 Composition framework

> **Framework for a Multiple Paragraph Composition**
>
> A. Introductory Paragraph: Begins broadly and narrows to a main point or idea: states the purpose of the composition; may be a restate of the composition prompt or question provided in an essay test.
>   If the composition is an essay, this is the place where the argument or thesis is stated before arguing about it in the body of the composition. An essay does not merely inform. It takes a stand. "What do I want the reader to understand? Feel? Do?"
> B. Body or Argument of the composition: Made up of one or more paragraphs that clarify and expand upon the main point of the composition.
>   Paragraph
>   Paragraph
>   Etc.
>   The final sentence of each of the body paragraphs is called the "Transitional Sentence" and must link the information in its paragraph with the next paragraph.
>   If the composition is an essay, the writer offers a defense and development of the thesis or point of view that was introduced in the Introductory Paragraph.
> C. Concluding Paragraph: Ends the composition with a "winding up" or makes a final "connection" to the purpose stated in the Introductory Paragraph.
>   If the composition is an essay, the writer draws the final connection to the main point or thesis in the Introductory Paragraph.

Impact on Teachers as Learners   Impact on team members was apparent after a few months of meetings. For example, teams exhibited the following behaviors.

- Use of a variety assessment tasks—not just informal checklists—for diagnostic and achievement purposes
- Continuous revision of native language and ESL syllabi to more closely align with skills necessary for performance on mandated tests as well as to align with state and city content standards

Table 5.4 Performance inventory for notebook

Keeping a Content Area Note Book						
Name						
Date						
Teacher						
Grade						

Performance Inventory

Trait/Behavior	Performance Level					
1. I label my notebook with the name of the specific subject.	1	2	3	4	5	6
2. I complete a school heading on each entry.	1	2	3	4	5	6
3. I include the teaching point of every lesson in my notebook.	1	2	3	4	5	6
4. I include any classroom notes that my teacher may present or give me.	1	2	3	4	5	6
5. I keep my handwriting neat and readable.	1	2	3	4	5	6
6. I obtain a parent signature in my notebook when requested by my teacher.	1	2	3	4	5	6

Table 5.5 On-demand performance rubric

Performance Rubric	
On-demand Performance: When student is expected to apply trait or behavior without support or mediation	
Level 1	Does not use target trait or behavior
Level 2	Limited ability to perform: use of trait is rarely appropriate
Level 3	Moderate ability to perform: inconsistent use of trait or behavior
Level 4	Adequate ability to perform: indications of a growing control of the target trait or behavior; more appropriate use of behavior than not
Level 5	Automatic ability to perform: few misuses of the trait or behavior; meets expectation (standard)
Level 6	Fluent ability to perform: consistently meets expectation (standard)

- Collaboration on curriculum articulation among native language, ESL, and standards curriculum teachers
- Experimentation with integration of test tasks into instruction that led to more reflective collaboration among teachers
- Greatly improved quality of discussion during team meetings (e.g., discussion focused on joint problem solving, analysis of student learning, sharing of knowledge and resources, collaborative teaching, critical-friendly activities)

Impact on Test Performance   Although it was too early to see a direct relationship of the use of the practice with student performance on the targeted mandated tests and the existence

Table 5.6 Performance inventory for note taking

Performance Task: Take notes based on an oral sample and transcribe the notes		
Primary Trait	**Performance Scale**	
Note Taking is characterized by…		
1. Listens with intent and purpose.	1 2 3 4 5 6	
2. Writes main points or ideas.	1 2 3 4 5 6	
3. Writes most important subordinating details.	1 2 3 4 5 6	
4. Records helpful or important examples.	1 2 3 4 5 6	
5. Writes or indicates key words.	1 2 3 4 5 6	
6. Uses an organizer or mental map.	1 2 3 4 5 6	
7. Uses symbols, arrows, etc.	1 2 3 4 5 6	
Note Transcribing is characterized by…		
8. Rewrites notes in own words.	1 2 3 4 5 6	
9. Uses colors or sub-titles to re-organize or better organize notes.	1 2 3 4 5 6	
10. Summarizes most important information.	1 2 3 4 5 6	
or		
Connects notes to text or outside reading about the target topic.		
Oral samples could be based on audio tapes, a tape of radio news, weather or talk show broadcast, a tape of a portion of a fiction or non-fiction narrative, a read aloud, an in-class presentation, or a lecture.		

of the teams was disbanded in future years due to a reduction in funds, informal analysis shows growth in area of English language arts and the examinations that show proficiency in reading and writing specifically. For example, during the 2000–01 school year, one third-grade teacher identified students she expected to perform at levels 1, 2, 3, and 4 on the mandated reading examination. To target the skills students needed to raise their academic achievement, the teacher articulated on wall charts the elements of effective listening, note taking while listening, using organizers to plan writing assignments, writing summary paragraphs, and writing compare–contrast essays. She used these charts as her primary trait inventory and a five-level performance rubric for evaluating student work in these five performance tasks. She applied these tasks to social studies, mathematics, and balanced literacy lessons in both Spanish and English. Her students outperformed students in the other three third-grade classrooms in her school on the 2001 administration of the mandated reading examination. A majority of those designated she had designated as level-1 performers actually performed at levels 2 and 3; a majority of those expected to perform at 2 actually performed at level 3, and three out of four students designated as level-3 performers actually performed at level 4 on the performance rubric.

Another teacher taught her fourth-grade dual-language students how to take notes during listening experiences. They applied these strategies during read-aloud activities that were

Table 5.7 Performance inventory for multiple-paragraph response

Performance Task: Listens to an oral sample and writes a multiple paragraph response about the topic/theme of the sample based on a writing prompt.

PERFORMANCE INVENTORY

Primary Traits	Performance Scale					
1. Uses standard multiple paragraph framework:	1	2	3	4	5	6
1.1 Introductory paragraph that states main point or purpose; re-states prompt question	1	2	3	4	5	6
1.2 Body paragraph(s) that support, clarify or expand upon opening statement Ends with a "transitional sentence."	1	2	3	4	5	6
1.3 Concluding paragraph that naturally brings closure to theme or stated purpose.	1	2	3	4	5	6
2. Uses these sentence elements:	1	2	3	4	5	6
2.1 simple sentences that include a subject and predicate	1	2	3	4	5	6
2.2 compound sentences that include a subject and predicate	1	2	3	4	5	6
2.3 verb phrases	1	2	3	4	5	6
2.4 prepositional phrases	1	2	3	4	5	6
2.5 uses transitional-connecting words	1	2	3	4	5	6
3. Punctuation: Sentences start with a capital letter.	1	2	3	4	5	6
4. Punctuation: Sentences end with a period.	1	2	3	4	5	6
5. Spelling: All the words are spelled correctly.	1	2	3	4	5	6
6. Writing/printing is neat and readable.	1	2	3	4	5	6

conducted in two languages. Student work was collected and evaluated with a scoring guide. She conferred with the students about their performance on the scoring guide. She provided ample extended written-response activities, emphasizing several expository writing genres. Students used scoring guides as a self-monitor for their work and as a guide for conferencing with the teacher. Her students outperformed the other two fourth grades—a Spanish bilingual fourth grade and mainstream fourth grade—in her school on the state-mandated fourth-grade English language arts test.

Another example illustrates the progress of a first-grade student whose teacher participated in the across-schools CAR project. Karen was enrolled in Ms. Rivera's first-grade bilingual classroom. Ms. Rivera has been a bilingual teacher at CES35X[4] for 15 years. When she started infusing some of the fourth-grade test tasks into instructional activities during November, Karen's oral English was at the intermediate ESL level as determined by an ESL textbook placement test. Her oral comprehension and memory skills were quite advanced for a second-year ESL student. She was usually able to orally retell main points of a listen-to selection with key words and to draw a picture about a favorite moment in a story and was beginning to develop her ability to participate in classroom discussions about read-aloud stories when provided with visual and oral prompts. However, consistent with second-

Table 5.8 Performance rubric for completing the task without support

<table>
<tr><td colspan="2">PERFORMANCE EVALUATION RUBRIC
When student is asked to complete the task without support</td></tr>
<tr><th>LEVEL</th><th>CONTROL of TRAIT OR SKILL</th></tr>
<tr><td>1
Readiness/
Instrumental Stage</td><td>Not enough language product to evaluate. Demonstrates little or no use of trait or skill, and minimal L_2 proficiency. Requires continuous, direct instructional support and comprehension prompts.</td></tr>
<tr><td>2
Emerging/
Low Functional Stage</td><td>Performance is characterized by many errors. Demonstrates minimal use of target skill or trait, and emergent L_2 proficiency. Requires direct instructional support and comprehension prompts.</td></tr>
<tr><td>3
Upper Emergent/
High Functional Stage</td><td>Performance is characterized by several errors. Demonstrates limited use of target skill or trait, and developing L_2 proficiency. Requires direct instructional support and comprehension prompts.</td></tr>
<tr><td>4
Early Fluent/
Developing Stage</td><td>Performance is characterized by some errors. Demonstrates adequate use of target skill or trait, and developing L_2 proficiency. Occasionally requires direct instructional support and comprehension prompts.</td></tr>
<tr><td>5
Fluent/
Automatic Stage</td><td>Performance is characterized by few errors. Demonstrates automatic use of target skill or trait, and a synthesis control of L_2 proficiency. Occasionally requires direct instructional support and comprehension prompts.</td></tr>
<tr><td>6
Fluent/
Authentic Stage</td><td>Performance is characterized by minimal errors and compares favorably with same-age speakers of target language. Demonstrates consistent use of target skill or trait with authentic L_2 proficiency. Rarely requires direct support.</td></tr>
</table>

language acquisition, Karen's ability to retell nonfiction selections was limited, as was her ability to write phrases or sentences in written-response activities. She required considerable support and practice writing more than one-sentence responses or providing more detail, organizing ideas and events, using appropriate formats, and using English punctuation and usage conventions. By April, after consistent and continuous practice in listening with intent, organizing content on simple graphic organizers and with drawings, producing a variety of paragraph written responses after analyzing a writing prompt, and revising and editing the responses—all tasks included in the fourth-grade state ELA test—Karen demonstrated considerable growth in writing and other skill areas. As Ms. Rivera commented,

After a few months of using this practice I was able to document that Karen's oral and written recall included more information and was more accurate. Karen increasingly was less interested in retelling with illustrations and more interested in retelling in writing. She was able to write sentences that included more information or ideas, and

Table 5.9 Performance inventory for multiple paragraph response based on writing prompt

Performance Task: Reads a selection and writes a multiple paragraph response about the topic/theme of the sample based on a writing prompt.

PERFORMANCE INVENTORY

Primary Traits	Performance Scale					
Content:						
1. Responded to elements in the prompt.	1	2	3	4	5	6
2. Appears to understand content information.	1	2	3	4	5	6
3. Appears to understand key concepts.	1	2	3	4	5	6
4. Uses nomenclature/key vocabulary of topic.	1	2	3	4	5	6
5. Expresses self in complete thoughts.	1	2	3	4	5	6
Format:						
6. Uses standard multiple paragraph framework:	1	2	3	4	5	6
6.1 Introductory paragraph that states main point or purpose; re-states prompt question	1	2	3	4	5	6
6.2 Body paragraph(s) that support, clarify or expand upon opening statement Ends with a "transitional sentence."	1	2	3	4	5	6
6.3 Concluding paragraph that naturally brings closure to theme or stated purpose.	1	2	3	4	5	6
Structures:						
7. Uses these sentence elements:						
7.1 sentences include a complete subject and predicate	1	2	3	4	5	6
7.2 Appropriate grammatical structures	1	2	3	4	5	6
7.4 Variety of transitional-connecting words	1	2	3	4	5	6
Conventions:						
8. Punctuation:						
8.1 Sentences start with a capital letter.	1	2	3	4	5	6
8.2 Sentences end with a period or question mark.	1	2	3	4	5	6
9. Spelling: All the words are spelled correctly.	1	2	3	4	5	6
10. Writing/printing is neat and readable.	1	2	3	4	5	6

the details were appropriate to the main ideas in her sentences. Her vocabulary grew as well. In the future I will not wait for oral fluency before I introduce writing activities in a child's second language. I have discovered how writing impacts listening, reading, and speaking. Although I wasn't able to collect the evidence, Karen's mother reported that there was also a positive growth in her first language, Serbian.

A sample of Karen's writing in early November reveals her level of writing proficiency. After participating in a read-aloud activity that reinforced comprehension with visuals, students were asked to retell the narrative in writing, similar to an on-demand writing prompt of a test in which the writer does not receive mediation in completing the assignment from

Table 5.10 Evaluation rubric

Planning Composition Emphasis (for infusing test tasks into lessons and units)	
Short Written Response	**Extended Written Response** Multiple Paragraphs

1. Time and Logical Order:
    1.1 Retell: chronological and
        logical order set of sentences
    1.2 Retell: synopsis of plot;
        sequence of events
2. Summary:
    2.1 based on story or narrative
        elements or based on *wh*
        questions
    2.2 paraphrase; précis
3. Definition
4. Description of attributes and
    elements
5. Explanation
6. Value judgment with
    justification
7. Reflection
8. Analysis
9. Paragraph Format
    9.1 Introductory or Topic
        Sentence
    9.2 Body Sentences support
        topic sentence with details
        and examples
    9.3 Concluding Sentence brings
        closure or draws conclusion.
10. Organizers: matrices, charts,
    tables, Venn Diagrams, flow
    charts, story boards, concept
    webs
11. Options: paragraphs of
    persuasion, comparison,
    contrast, cause and effect
	1. Scenario (based on WH framework)
	2. Reports:
	    2.1 Research Report
	    2.2 Book Report
	    2.3 Inquiry Report
	3. Reflective Essay
	4. Persuasive Essay
	5. Narrative: story and
	    informational account
	6. Development Frameworks:
	    6.1 Cause-effect
	    6.2 Compare-contrast
	    6.3 Problem-solution
	    6.4 "Critical Lens" – relate a quote
	         or moral to previously read
	         texts
	    6.5 "Text to Self" – relate a moral
	         in a story to one's life
	    6.6 "Text to Text" – relate how
	         several texts deal with a
	         concept or argument or strand
	         of ideas or experiences
	    6.7 Literary analysis based on
	         narrative elements
	7. Composition Format
	    7.1 Introductory Paragraph:
	         purpose or statement of
	         argument/thesis
	    7.2 Body or Argument of Composition:
	         clarify and expand
	    7.3 Concluding Paragraph:
	         "winding up" or makes "final
	         connection."

Language Elements/Structures / Functions Emphasized	**Writing Mechanics/Conventions Stressed**
Each team will identify these items based on an analysis of student work.	Each team will identify these items based on an analysis of student work.

the teacher or another student. The title of the read-aloud science book was *Way Out in the Desert*. Karen's printing was messy with numerous smudges and changes. All the writing was pushed against the left edge of the paper without a margin. Karen wrote,

Way out desert

Way out in desert Lived a mother hone tood and his one baby hone tood.

A sample of Karen's writing in early April from a similar on-demand writing prompt shows that Karen was starting to use the paragraph format and was writing full-idea sentences. She also followed directions by placing a title in the center and by providing the appropriate headings (Figure 5.1).

CES35X

Karen_____

Class 1-108   *18, of may 2001*

When is morning or evening the dolphin leaps. When the sun is going down. The dolphin eat silver fish. The young dolphin swim beesde her mother. When the dolphin are swiming they tuch their flipperss. The mother call her baby by wiselling The dolphin has bick. Dolphin has blowhole the kiler whale don't find the dolphin. The dolphin don't find the mother. The dolphin going back to his mother bicess the killer whale is coming.

Ms. Rivera articulated her goals in the following way: *Participating in the Action Research project will provide me an opportunity to analyze the 4th grade ELA test (and the second and third grade tests also) so that I can look at the skill areas I need to introduce to my children—to begin to prepare them now at their level. I would like to build upon the strategies needed to score well on the exams well in advance. And these are language development skills they need now, in both languages, and will be developed by my emphasizing the test tasks in my first grade.*

Figure 5.1 Diving dolphin.

Conclusion

In sum, the CAR teams successfully documented student growth in language proficiency as they worked toward achieving the tasks that would be required of them on state- and city-mandated tests. Teachers analyzed the tests for the tasks required and infused them into their lessons. By using a protocol to consistently integrate strategies that would help students learn the language and succeed on the tests and by using rubrics and scoring guides that outlined the academic behaviors required of the students to do well, the teachers were able to show across all schools and teams evidence of increased student performance.

To do this, however, I had to change my coaching style to be more directive and focused on the task of infusing the test tasks. I also had to create and develop many of the tools while getting teacher input from each site. Though this was time consuming, it made for more effective teams and stronger evidence of student achievement.

Notes

1. At this time I developed a better understanding of the concept of teacher inquiry in the classroom (Strickland, 1988).
2. Helpful during this professional growth was Griffen (1983).
3. During the three years of this activity, team members were especially concerned about student performance on such tests as the first- and second-grade Early Performance Assessment in Language Arts, the third-grade CTB/McGraw-Hill, the fourth-grade English Language Arts, the eight-grade English Language Arts instruments, and the New York State English Regents.
4. CES35X is a neighborhood school that is predominately Spanish bilingual. Karen's mother had heard from a neighbor that several of the teachers were very good teachers who taught in English as well as Spanish; consequently, she enrolled Karen there. There were no Serbian bilingual classes in the district.

References

Chamot, A., & O'Malley, J. (1994). *The Calla handbook: Implementing the cognitive academic language learning approach.* Boston: Addison-Wesley.

Friedman, M. I., & Fisher, S. P. (1998). *Handbook on effective instructional strategies.* Columbia, SC: Institute for Evidence-Based Decision-Making in Education.

Sagor, R. (1992). *How to conduct collaborative action research.* Alexandria, VA: Association for Supervision and Curriculum Development.

Sagor, R. (2000). *Guiding school improvement with action research.* Alexandria, VA: Association for Supervision and Curriculum Development.

Strickland, D. S. (1988). The teacher as research: Toward the extended professional. *Language Arts* 65(8), 754–765.

Ticunoff, W. J., & Mergendoller, J. W. (1983). Inquiry as a means to professional growth: The teacher as researcher. In Griffen, G. A. (Ed.), *Staff Development: Eighty-Second Yearbook of the National Society for the Study of Education* (pp. 210–227). Chicago: University of Chicago Press.

II: In the Secondary Classroom

Editor's Introduction

Just as in Section I, although Section II addresses secondary classroom instruction, this section is not just for classroom teachers. The changes that are needed to successfully educate English language learners (ELLs) in the middle and high school classrooms must be understood and supported by administrators, staff developers, student service personnel, policy makers, and teacher educators.

Middle and high school ELL students bring to their education experiences a unique combination of benefits and challenges. One of the greatest challenges is the immediacy of their needs: the immediacy to engage in the course content and the immediacy to attain the language skills needed to take part in that course engagement. Unlike elementary school students, who might be able to get by with some preliminary early social language skills, secondary students face course requirements that demand a level of academic language proficiency. As discussed in Chapter 1, the development of this academic language proficiency can take from 5 to 10 years.

To expect the ELL student to engage in course content—as it is most often currently taught—without the necessary language tools is unreasonable. To expect the ELL student to develop the academic language skills needed to engage in that course content in a short period of time is equally unreasonable. To hold adolescent students back, or to immerse them in courses with insufficient compensatory support, or to place them in less challenging courses due to their language proficiency levels is unfair to the students. At the age of adolescence, their minds are cognitively developed; they need cognitive stimulation. The only barrier that prevents such students from engaging with the content is the medium of teaching: the use of the English language.

One of the greatest benefits accompanying adolescent ELL students is that such students have a fully developed cognitive foundation. If they are not children of war, or of extreme poverty, or in rural areas lacking secondary education, they have been to school and have learned literacy, numeracy, and traditional school content in their own language. In fact, many times, immigrant students are ahead of their U.S. classmates in certain course content. For these students, the turnaround time can be somewhat shorter than the upper limits of the predicted 5 to 10 years. They already have the cognitive foundation and the course background from which to approach their new academic experiences. We have learned that those knowledge bases can be reasonably transferred into the new education experiences. Within two years, they can develop enough conversational English to allow them to understand much of what is being said in the high school classroom and to participate in beginning ways. Their productive skills will still be developing, and it will predictably take several more years for them to write and speak with the academic fluency expected of high school students, but they will not be altogether lost.

But the critical key to whether secondary ELL students gain access into the course content is how well content teachers learn to make their cognitively challenging course materials comprehensible to ELLs, despite the heavy use of English language as the medium of instruction. Section II presents a variety of strategies practiced by middle and secondary teachers who have made a conscious attempt to meet the needs of their ELL students. Notice that throughout these four chapters there are common, consistent suggestions on how to make the content comprehensible, how to increase the students' opportunities to engage with the content, and how to maintain high levels of expectation for students, even when teacher and students are faced with language barriers between them.

In Chapter 6, Walqui outlines 10 priorities to consider when designing instruction for immigrant students. These priorities, accompanied by illustrative student quotes, outline in detail ways teachers can alter current traditional instructional models to provide access and engagement for their language learning students. She ends the chapter with a discussion about the nature of professional development, presenting a model of ongoing teacher development.

In Chapter 7, Verplaetse and Migliacci address the challenge of making course content comprehensible by describing instructional strategies that are part of a national movement called *sheltered instruction*. The strategies discussed are illustrated by examples of actual work from teachers who have been involved in professional development training with the chapter authors over the past five years.

In Chapter 8, Verplaetse discusses how to develop academic language through an abundance of interaction by describing instructional strategies that promote oral and written interaction. Critically missing from the ELL student's secondary experience is the opportunity to talk in extended sentences about academic ideas and to write extended texts for this same purpose. Students must have these opportunities if they are to develop the academic language skills necessary for high school and college success.

Finally, in Chapter 9, Harklau writes about a topic seldom discussed in the literature on linguistic minority students: planning for the college-bound ELL student. In this chapter, she explores the academic challenges and opportunities facing ELL students and outlines steps schools can take to counter the systemic barriers currently in place for ELL students with college aspirations.

As in Section I, it is worthy of note that in three of the four chapters, the authors make reference to the importance of professional development. Walqui dedicates a significant portion of her chapter to conceptualizing what the ideal professional development model would look like. Verplaetse makes extensive use of examples from teachers who have taken part in their federally funded teacher training activities. And in the fourth chapter, though not explicitly speaking to teacher training opportunities, Harklau closes by identifying further readings educators may pursue on the topic of preparing multilingual students for college.

CHAPTER 6

The Development of Teacher Expertise to Work with Adolescent English Learners: A Model and a Few Priorities

AÍDA WALQUI

The presence of adolescent English language learners (ELLs) in American schools has increased dramatically in the last decade and a half. Recent studies indicate that in the year 2000, ELLs in middle and high schools comprised 5.3 percent of all students nationwide, with wide variation across states: California, 11.9%; Illinois, 5.4%; Colorado, 4.4%; and North Carolina, 2.9%. As a whole, these students are underperforming and are dropping out of school in larger proportions than their native English-speaking peers. Most English learners in schools are not recent arrivals to the American school system. In fact, 57% of ELLs in middle and high schools were born in this country, have exclusively attended American schools, and represent the second or third generation of immigrants to the United States (Batalova & Fix, 2005).

The failure of schools to meet the needs of ELLs is directly linked to degrees of teacher expertise, for it is widely recognized that teachers play the most crucial role in the success or failure of their students (Darling-Hammond, 2000; Goldhaber, Brewer, & Anderson, 1999; Goldhaber, 2002). To accelerate the academic performance of all students, and in particular that of students for whom English is a new language, it is necessary for teachers to receive appropriate preparation and professional development that will enable them to create quality opportunities for English learners to develop their potential (Barron & Menken, 2002; National Educational Research Policy and Priorities Board, 1999; August & Hakuta, 1997).

English learners are students with tremendous potential. However, unless we have quality teaching in their classes, their potential will not be realized. This chapter takes a look inside effective classrooms for adolescent English learners and through a sociocultural lens analyzes how instruction is orchestrated and enacted to engage students in work that ripens their potential. Though the focus here is on middle and high schools, the ideas presented are equally applicable to the education of second-language learners in elementary schools. Data used throughout derive from work conducted for the last decade[2] studying how ELLs—and their teachers—learn under optimal conditions. They include observations, audio- and videotaped classes, and interviews with students, parents, teachers, and administrators conducted to get a fuller picture of the impact pedagogical arrangements can have on the education of English language learners.

From this process I derived a set of 10 priorities to help teachers evaluate and improve the quality of instruction in their classrooms. Although some teachers do apply these priorities when designing and delivering instruction in classes that have English language learners, they have not always reflected on what these priorities are, nor have they systematized them as the base that undergirds their pedagogical approach. Because instruction remains frustrating for many students, not just for those learning English and content simultaneously, it is appropriate to highlight these priorities. Furthermore, those most affected by teaching and learning are seldom asked for their suggestions. Students' voices are typically absent from discussions of the quality of their schooling, yet students have valid information that can guide our critiques and plans. Thus, I included the voices of immigrant students—quotes taken from my interviews—to develop the priorities and to guide this discussion.

How each teacher articulates and implements these priorities greatly depends on the teacher's own characteristics, the characteristics of the students, local circumstances, and other relevant aspects of the context. There is no single approach applicable to every student or in every teaching situation. Varied approaches and instantiations are needed, depending on the local context (Shulman & Associates, 1995).

Ten Priorities to Guide Instruction Design for Immigrant Students

(1) Use the classroom culture to develop a community of learners to which all students belong.

> High school is hard for me because my English is so limited. Sometimes it is hard for me to do things because of my English. There are times when I feel a lot of pressure because I want to say something, but I don't know how to say it. There are many times when the teacher is asking questions, I know the answer, but I'm afraid that people might laugh at me. I know I just need to be a little patient with myself.

10th-grade student from Mexico, two years in the United States, interview in Spanish

> To me, the big issue is that we need more teachers who care about us, who treat us as human beings, who greet us and want to help us. Too many teachers don't really care. They are just doing their job, coming to school and going home.

9th-grade student from the Philippines, three years in the United States

In effective classrooms, teachers and students engage in the coconstruction of a culture that values the strengths of each person and respects their interests, abilities, languages, and dialects. Within these classrooms all participants in the class, including the teacher, move among the roles of expert, researcher, learner, and teacher, supporting themselves and others. Immigrant teenagers bring a variety of experiences to the classroom that, if correctly tapped, can serve as a springboard to new explorations that can enrich everyone's experience. As Bialystok and Hakuta (1994, p. 203) note, "The exciting challenge for teachers and learners of a second language is to construct a context for creative and meaningful discourse by taking full advantage of the rich, personal, cultural, and linguistic backgrounds of the participants."

The voices of the students quoted at the beginning of this section illustrate what happens when this culture does not exist; students feel insecure, ashamed, and unwelcome. The establishment of a respectful, nourishing, and challenging culture with high expectations for everyone is a sine qua non for the success of English learners. Also necessary is the understanding that in a classroom with a warm, accepting climate, it is not embarrassing to admit one's limitations. As Jesús, the struggling reader in Ferreiro, Pellicer, Rodríguez, Silva, & Vernon (1991, p. 8) admitted, as he volunteered to continue the read-aloud in class: "Yo leo, es que yo no sé leer bien...para enseñarme [I read...I do not know how to read well... so that I can teach myself]." Jesús understood that in his class it is acceptable to confess one's inability to read well. He also knows (i.e., he has been taught) that one learns to read by reading. If Jesús wanted the opportunity to practice, he deserved to have that opportunity. The other students in the classroom were attentive and patient, even though Jesús's reading was not very clear, because they understood that their attention would help him become a better reader. They understood this because they had been explicitly taught that their support of peers was an important norm that characterized the classroom.

Lave & Wenger's (1991) concept of *peripheral legitimate participation* is relevant to the notion of community building and learning in a classroom. When English language learners join a class in English, the teacher represents the community of practice of which the students want to become members: people who are knowledgeable about the subject matter and proficient in English. These students are peripheral to the central activity they are being apprenticed into, but for their education to be successful, they must be treated as legitimate participants in the activity and the target community. That is, although they are all newcomers to the language and many of them to American schools, they need to be treated from the beginning as the central participants they will become. To become competent, they need to be considered as such. If a new student is greeted by a teacher who seems to convey his or her belief that education in English will be very hard, or unattainable for them, students are delegitimized by the teacher. In turn, they will take on oppositional behaviors and will reject schooling. This is one of the reasons why so many English learners drop out of school.

Although expectations for all learners need to be high, it should also be understood that all students will not progress at the same pace or in the same ways but will move differentially toward the attainment of common goals supported by collective norms and practices. As a student confessed to me when I visited International High School (IHS), one of the premier schools for English learners in the country,

> Teachers at IHS really care about how we treat other students. They tell us to understand them, especially if they don't have a high level in English. We always support them, talk to them so that they do not feel so lonely because we also passed through those things. When you are away from home the first thing that worries you is how other people are going to treat you. Here in this school everybody makes me feel comfortable, not like in other schools where they make you feel like you are the worst thing in the world.... .

Angela Pérez, video interview, April 2002

(2) Foster teaching that promotes students' conceptual and academic development.

> Why did I leave school? In most classes they give you lists of words to memorize and worksheets to complete. You see students in regular classes reading interesting books. Not us. Teachers say: When you learn English you will be able to read. But that didn't happen the three years I spent in school.

17-year-old from El Salvador

> When I entered the regular English classes, I found they were much more difficult than the ESL classes. It made me feel that I didn't walk, but jumped from the ESL to regular classes. I had to study very hard to recover the gap. I wish schools can have a better ESL program so the transition is easier.

Mainstreamed student from Vietnam

Effective English as a second language (ESL) classes, even at beginning levels, can focus on themes and can develop skills that are relevant for teenagers and for their studies in mainstream academic classes. Students are not helped if what they study is trivial or is presented to them atomistically. Instead, teachers can discuss similarities and differences in families around the world, even in the first week of class. In this way they can help students develop vocabulary that will prove useful in other classes later on, such as *structure, nuclear, extended, role,* and *responsibility.* Likewise, if the teacher presents a minilecture and shows students how to take notes—for example, by helping them draw the family tree of a student she or he has just described—they can learn academic skills (e.g., note taking) that can be transferred to other contexts. Immigrant students need to learn not only new content but also the language and discourse associated with each discipline. Such explicit teaching prepares immigrant students for the genre-specific language associated with the discipline of their content classes.

Effective teaching prepares students for high-quality academic work by focusing their attention on key processes and ideas and by engaging them in interactive tasks in which they can practice using these processes and concepts. ESL and subject-matter teachers need to know what linguistic and cognitive demands they are preparing their students for and develop the necessary linguistic, cognitive, and academic proficiencies. Content-area teachers need to determine what knowledge in their field is crucial and what is not. It is not uncommon to hear secondary school teachers say they teach a specific point because the program calls for it or because it is the next point in the curriculum. Because of an overreliance on curricula and textbooks, teachers are sometimes more focused on getting through them by the end of the semester or year, or on not skipping some part of them, than they are on what students are learning or need to learn (see, e.g., Ball & Rundquist, 1993).

One of the most serious challenges subject-matter teachers face in their teaching is how to use mainstream texts with their second-language learners or what kind of disciplinary language to use in their lectures and directions. One solution to the problems has been to use simplified texts—oral or written—but this solution does not work because it does not really prepare students for mainstream courses. Instead, what teachers need to consider is how they can keep the difficulty of the text constant while graduating the assistance they provide specific groups of students to access its content by using adequate scaffolding. Appropriate scaffolding enables students to participate in activities that are beyond their current level of ability to understand on their own. To achieve this, rather than simplifying a text, teachers

should amplify and enrich the linguistic and extralinguistic context that enables stu
work with new concepts and relationships packaged in new language. With this an
tion, students will not just get one opportunity to understand the new concepts but will be
able to construct their understanding on the basis of multiple cues (Walqui, 2003, p. 111).
Gibbons (2003) calls this practice the building of *linguistic abundancy*.

*(3) Use students' experiential background as a point of departure and an anchor
in the exploration of new ideas.*

> Now that I am learning English I feel that Spanish is the most helpful way I can learn
> my second language because you are always comparing how you say things in your
> first and your new language. … That is why this linguistics project is so useful, com-
> paring how children learn their first language and how I am learning English now.
> Also, it is good that our school likes us to use our native languages. If I was in a school
> where teachers would not let me use my Spanish I would be feeling so bad because I
> think it is a right to use your own language when you are learning in a second lan-
> guage to learn new things, I wouldn't be happy there … I would be trying to find an
> international high school.

Colombian student, 16 years old

> Why was I sent to the office? There is this new girl in class, and I was helping her
> because she does not understand a thing that goes on. I thought I did not, either,
> but when Carmen asked me for help I realized I did, and I was explaining to her in
> Spanish, and the teacher got mad. She said, "Don't you know I do not understand
> Spanish?" And I answered, "So? Carmen needs help." But I got a referral.

15-year-old from Mexico, 28 months in the United States

Immigrant adolescents know a great deal about the world, and this knowledge can provide
the basis for understanding new concepts in a new language. However, the knowledge they
already have is often overlooked because of the misconception that students who have
studied elsewhere or have not had previous formal schooling are tabulae rasae on which
knowledge needs to be imprinted. The tendency to see immigrant students as blank slates
derives in part from their minority status: Because they hold a subordinated and less prestigious position in society, they are not perceived as possessing valuable knowledge.

Another reason that teachers do not tap into students' prior knowledge during instruction is the traditional transmission model of teaching, which assumes that it is the teacher's
role to pass on important knowledge to students, whom it is assumed lack it.

Students will learn new concepts and language only when these are firmly built on
previous knowledge and understanding. Tharp and Gallimore (1988, p. 108) define comprehension as involving "the weaving of new information into existing mental structures." As
students realize that their everyday knowledge is not only valued in class but is also desired,
a sense of trust and competence is achieved that promotes further development. This does
not come easily at first. Some students have been socialized into lecture and recitation
approaches to teaching, and they expect teachers' monologues to tell them what lessons
are about. However, after engaging in activities that involve predicting, inferring based on
prior knowledge, and supporting conclusions with evidence, they realize that they can learn
actively and that working in this way is fun and stimulating.

Table 6.1 Compare and contrast matrix

	Our School	*Esmeralda's School*
Different groups of students visible in the school (use the names they are given by other students)		
What are some of the characteristics that make them stand out as different from other groups?		
How are the different groups of students valued by the adults in the school?		
How are they perceived by their peers?		

If understanding involves weaving new information into preexisting structures of meaning, then teachers must help English learners see connections through a variety of activities. In preparation for reading a selection from Esmeralda Santiago's (1994) *When I was Puerto Rican*, a teacher may invite students to work in groups and to jot down what they know about their school in the first column of the compare-and-contrast matrix (Table 6.1), which serves as a way of organizing the retrieval of students' prior knowledge in advance of new work.

The teacher explains what kind of information she or he expects in each cell and then reminds students to only jot down words and phrases in the organizer, not to write complete sentences. Students work in groups of four filling in the chart. As they collaboratively discuss what may be appropriate information, their thoughts are focused on their school, its many student groups, and the different evaluation they receive from adults and peers. Then the teacher distributes the selection from the book where the author narrates her first experience in a middle school in New York City, when she was sent to the lowest-tracked class, section 8-23. Because students have activated their prior knowledge about school hierarchies, they will now have a conceptual basis that will serve as a bridge to the understanding of the Santiago selection.

The use of advance organizers serves several purposes: It promotes schema building before a topic is introduced; it focuses learners' attention on important aspects of the information to come; and, if the diagram is used for note-taking purposes, it alleviates students' anguish by letting them know beforehand what information they should be able to understand and take notes on. Students in general, and English learners in particular, need to be able to process information from the top down (i.e., to have general knowledge of the broad picture before studying the details) as well as from the bottom up (i.e., vocabulary, syntax, and rhetorical devices to understand the language). Furthermore, by viewing the skeleton of a passage in advance, students' apprehension is lowered, helping them tolerate ambiguity and encouraging them to be willing and accurate guessers. Rubin (1975) argues that these are some of the most important qualities of a good language learner.

The effective teaching of second-language learners also involves Vygotsky's (1978) concept that "the only 'good' learning is that which is in advance of development." The zone of proximal development (ZPD), that area of potential growth the learner may enter if given the right kind of support. In this process, social interaction is essential. Bruner (1986) extends this notion with the concept of *interactional scaffolding:* instruction that enables students to take risks safely and to extend their abilities with the help of their teachers and peers. Scaffolds are used as support mechanisms to allow English learners to handle tasks involving language that is too complex for them to understand or produce. Without such support, students might not succeed. Scaffolds are temporary; that is, as the teacher observes that students are capable of understanding and producing language on their own, responsibility is gradually handed over to them. *Kidwatching,* to use Goodman's (1978) apt expression, implies that the teacher carefully monitors each learner's growing understanding and developing academic skills, providing scaffolds and challenges as the need arises. Rather than simplified tasks or language, English language learners require amplification and enrichment of the linguistic and extralinguistic context. With this type of instruction they do not have just one opportunity to come to terms with the concepts to be learned but instead may construct their understanding on the basis of multiple clues and perspectives encountered in a variety of class activities.

A strength that adolescent teenagers bring to this country is age-appropriate communicative competence in their own languages. This knowledge can be helpful at times for the negotiation of classroom concepts that may be inaccessible otherwise. Let us imagine, for example, a student from Russia who has lived in the United States for several years and has consequently developed the ability to understand most of what goes on in his science class. A recently arrived student from Russia has joined his class. Occasional interactions in Russian between these two students can be beneficial for the newcomer when his efforts to make sense of concepts and processes in English are met with failure. If the teacher treats these interactions in Russian as productive, while at the same time scaffolding her or his instruction for the new student enough so that he can—besides using his native language—also participate in English tasks, the teacher will be validating the importance of the student's prior knowledge and enhancing his opportunities to construct new understandings in a supportive climate. As Angela Pérez's previous quote illustrates, this is not only good pedagogy; it is also a human right.

At times, as Pérez reveals, a teacher may become suspicious of students having brief interactions in class in a language the teacher cannot understand and may interpret these interactions as rebellious behavior. Understanding that students scaffold for each other through these exchanges in their native language can help teachers to put similar incidents in perspective. The incident illustrates how helping the newcomer helped the more experienced student to realize that she understands more about the subject than she would have previously given herself credit for.

(4) Focus teaching and learning on substantive ideas that are organized cyclically.

> I used to get very upset because I couldn't understand everything the teacher said. I just stopped listening. But Ms. Long always gives us the main points before she explains or we read, and then a few days later she touches on the same topics but with different materials. Now I know if I am patient, I can understand everything that is important.

> **10th-grade student from Brazil, two and a half years in the United States**

> I love the themes in our ESL book because you read about the same problems in many different stories, and you understand them better every time. I think all classes should be in themes.

> **Polish student, in the second year in an American school**

Working effectively with English learners requires that teachers select from the many themes that compose a subject area the ones central to the discipline. Schwab (1964) calls these themes *substantive* and connects them to the syntactic structures of a field, which include the canons of evidence and proof that are shared by subject matter communities. These key concepts form the basis of the curriculum taught. They should not be organized in a linear progression of items, but rather the curriculum should be based on the cyclical reintroduction of concepts at progressively higher levels of complexity and interrelatedness. Cyclical organization of subject matter leads to a natural growth in the understanding of ideas and to gradual correction of misunderstandings. The concern for immediate comprehension, an assumption of linear curricula, negates what we know about learning. As Gardner (1989, p. 158), speaking of education in general, says,

> First of all, when you are trying to present new materials, you cannot expect them to be grasped immediately. (If they are, in fact, the understanding had probably been present all along.) One must approach the issues in many different ways over a significant period of time if there is to be any hope of assimilation.

As we develop the academic skills of immigrant students, we also need to inform them about this cyclical aspect of the learning process to help ease their frustration over not mastering new content and skills immediately. Furthermore, if teachers carefully choose the key concepts to be explored in class, these will serve to generate future understanding as students progress in their schooling and in English.

(5) Contextualize new ideas and tasks.

> When I first read the poem "Rayford's Song" I did not really understand it. I knew it presented a painful situation for a student but did not completely understand why. Then the teacher asked us to prepare a Mind Mirror in our groups of four showing what was going on in Rayford's mind by using two quotes, two phrases we created, two symbols, and two drawings. Discussing how to draw the picture of the boy's mind, how to select good quotes, and how to draw relevant pictures helped me understand how cruel his teacher was. Rayford only spoke one time, but he spoke very well.

> **9th-grade student from Somalia, three years in the United States**

In my chemistry class I can always do well because the teacher first demonstrates an experiment, and then we try a similar one. Then he asks us to write down the procedure and the conclusions in groups of two or four. I can do it. I can even use the new words because I know what they mean.

10th-grade student from Chile, three years in the United States

English language learners often have problems in classes trying to make sense of decontextualized language. This situation is especially acute in the reading of textbooks. Secondary school textbooks are usually linear, dry, and dense, with few illustrations. Embedding the language of textbooks in a meaningful context by using manipulatives, pictures, a few minutes of a film, and other types of realia can make language input comprehensible for students. It is sometimes assumed that contextualization consists of using pictures to help convey ideas, but any sensory environment created to illuminate new information helps to contextualize new language and concepts. Teachers may provide verbal contextualizations by creating analogies based on students' experiences. This, of course, requires that teachers find out about students' backgrounds, as a metaphor or analogy that may work well with English speakers may not clarify meanings for English language learners. In this sense, good teachers of immigrant students continually search for metaphors and analogies that bring complex ideas closer to the students' world experience. With the increasing availability of CD-ROM, the Internet, and other new technologies in schools, it is essential that teachers of immigrant students learn to use them. They are especially suitable for use with immigrant students because the teacher can select and sequence material for particular groups of students that provides a rich textual, visual, and auditory basis for understanding.

(6) Explicitly teach academic strategies, sociocultural expectations, and academic norms.

Because this school is only for immigrant students, we do not know how American high schools work. So, at the beginning of the year, the seniors prepare an orientation week for the ninth graders where they tell us everything about the school, what we have to do, what we cannot do, how to study for classes, how teachers teach, and what they expect from students. It is really nice. I remember when I first came to the States, this was my first school, but there was a Rumanian girl who was a senior, and she could explain things to me in Rumanian. Now I am looking forward to helping a new student or some new students next year.

11th-grade student from Rumania, three years in the United States

What I really love about my ESL teacher is that she explains to us how to organize our thoughts and how to write in school ways. She also teaches us what to do to be good, critical readers. That is so helpful in my other classes, and I know it will be good for life.

10th-grade student from Mexico, two years in the United States

Effective teachers develop students' sense of autonomy through the explicit teaching of strategies, or plans of attack, that enable them to approach academic tasks successfully. The teaching of such metacognitive strategies is a way of scaffolding instruction; the goal is to hand over responsibility to the learner and to automatize the necessary skills. In reading, for example, instruction in strategies such as reciprocal teaching can be very successful in helping students construct their understandings of English texts. In reciprocal teaching

(Brown & Palincsar, 1985; Palincsar, David, & Brown, 1992), a teacher and a group of students take turns leading a dialogue aimed at revealing the meaning of a text. During this dialogue, the assigned teacher, an adult or a student, summarizes the content, asks questions concerning the gist of the reading, clarifies misunderstandings, and predicts future content, all of which involve comprehension—fostering and monitoring strategies. Teachers need to judge if their English learners are ready to engage in reciprocal teaching and scaffold the activity as needed. For example, initial practice in reciprocal teaching may focus on how to summarize a text and ask good questions. From then on, other components can be added.

The discourse of power—the language used in this country to establish and maintain social control—should be taught explicitly to minority students (Delpit, 1995), since it is not acquired automatically. Guidance and modeling can go a long way toward promoting awareness of and facility with this discourse. For example, preferred and accepted ways of talking, writing, and presenting are culture specific. In an exploratory study of the written discourse of several languages, Kaplan (1988) discovered that the way Americans structure their discourse follows a linear, deductive progression in which each paragraph is structured in the "this is what I am going to say—I am saying it now—this is what I said" format. Although British written discourse is also structured linearly, it is inductive, thus giving rise to some British criticism that American writing is boring. Latin writers, on the other hand, and Spanish writers in particular can proceed through many zigzags in which the topic shifts into parallel explorations and then goes back to the main idea. Unless Spanish-speaking writers are explicitly shown these differences in writing styles, they may apply the structures preferred in their native language to English, thus producing writing that appears chaotic to North American teachers and students. However, explicit teaching of the rules of the discourse of schooling is only a first step in the scaffolding of students' performance. In a second stage, students need to become ethnographers, collaboratively studying the reality of this culture and discerning its rules so that they become proficient participants in it.

Subject-matter teachers also need to alert students to the multiple ways experts in the discipline use language for different purposes. The work of Halliday (1994) and his colleagues in Australia (Martin, 1990; Mercer, 2000) using systemic linguistics and a focus on genre has been very productive. Derewianka (1990) suggests a curriculum cycle in which students are introduced to a genre, a text illustrating that genre is read, the purposes and schematic structure of the genre are modeled, then teacher and students together engage in joint construction of a text in the chosen genre, and, finally, students are invited to independently construct a text preparing multiple drafts and working through peer and teacher reviews. Eventually students can undertake the writing of the genre quite independently. Gibbons (2002) adapts that technique to second-language-learner education.

Student awareness of differences, modeling by teachers of preferred situated behaviors, and study by students themselves of differences and preferred behaviors are three steps in the development of learner proficiency and autonomy that need to be included in the education of language-minority students to make them effective in their multiple worlds.

(7) Use tasks that are relevant, meaningful, engaging, and varied.

> If you want me to be honest, the biggest problem here is that we're bored. We spend too much time sitting in classes that are dead, unexciting. Teachers talk to the blackboard, and always lecture, lecture, lecture. It's the same day after day, every day, every period, except when they get mad because somebody complains or does something to wake

us up. It's boring. You can't just sit through that. And sometimes it really is
and that's when you think, Why should I get up to go to school? What am
out of it?

9th-grade student from Mexico, three years in the Unite ...ates

I was very happy when at the beginning of the year the teacher told us we were going to
read novels. She brought us copies of *The Pearl*. I thought, Great! The characters even
seem to be Mexican…but she had us read a word at a time, and if we didn't know it, we
had to look it up in the dictionary, write a couple of sentences using it. It was February,
and we still had not finished the book. I hated the book, I did not understand it, and
who cared about it after such a long time anyway?

10th-grade student from Mexico, two and a half years in American schools

Most classes for immigrant students are monotonous, teacher fronted, and directed to the
whole class; teacher monologues are the rule (Ramírez & Merino, 1990). If students do not
interact with each other, they do not have the opportunity to construct their own understandings, so naturally they often become disengaged. Because immigrant students are usually
well behaved in class, teachers are not always aware that they are bored and are not learning.
Good classes for immigrant students not only provide them with access to important ideas
and skills but also engage them in their own constructive development of understandings.

It should be mandatory for every teacher of immigrant students to shadow a student for a
day at school and to get first-hand knowledge of their usually passive schooling experience.
Most teachers, having experienced school from the students' perspective, would most likely
want to transform their teaching.

*(8) Maximize learners' opportunities to interact while making sense of language and
content through the use of complex and flexible forms of collaboration.*

I learned so much from the world religions project. At first, I thought it would not be
so interesting because I am not especially religious. But as we started our research,
and then exchanged information and viewpoints, I could see there were so many
similarities among such different religions. It is the same way we feel here: We come
from many nations and many languages, we all look different on the surface, but
underneath we are very similar and share a lot. That is why we like to collaborate.
It helps us see all those important things.

High school student from Russia, three years in the United States

I always think that it is better for me to work in small groups because then I am not
afraid to participate. I am basically a very shy person, and if I have to speak in front of
everybody, I rather die. In small groups nobody is afraid, not even to make a mistake.

Middle school student from Cambodia, four years in the United States

Collaboration is essential for second-language learners because to develop language, they
need opportunities to use it in meaningful, purposeful, and enticing interactions (Kagan &
McGroarty, 1993). In the best classes I have observed, rather than having individual
students present to the whole class, teachers use the jigsaw configuration: They regroup
the students who have worked collaboratively on various projects into new formations

to present to other small groups what they have learned. In this way, all students' oral presentations convey new information to a small group. The group may later use this information for other activities such as discussing a problem and solving it jointly and then may write about it individually.

Collaborative work needs to provide every student with substantial and equitable opportunities to participate in open exchange and elaborated discussions. It must move beyond simplistic conceptions that assign superficial roles to second-language learners, such as being the go-getter or the time-keeper for the group (Adger, Kalyanpur, Peterson, & Bridger, 1995). In these collaborative groups, the teacher is no longer the authority figure; rather, students work autonomously, taking responsibility for their own learning.

The teacher provides a task that invites and requires each student's participation and then hands over to the students the responsibility for solving the problem. Though teachers supply the tasks, they do not provide learners with specific questions to be answered but instead encourage them to take a personal perspective on the topics that arise in small-group discussion.

Collaborative tasks do not involve learners in routine procedures but instead present them with problems that have complex solutions with no single right answer or standard set of steps (Cohen, 1994). These tasks should move toward maximal student involvement, in which students choose the theme they will investigate and the focus and strategies for their investigation.

Diverse types of jigsaws are ideal for English learners because they provide them with multiple opportunities to discuss content with different classmates, first as they become experts at one short story and then as they share their expertise with others who read different stories to later engage in discussion of common elements running through the pieces as well as in the appreciation of differences. For example, in a language arts class the theme being studied is the short story, and for the next three periods the teacher will focus on short stories dealing with betrayal. Four excellent stories are chosen, and the questions given beforehand to all students are the same, highlighting key elements common to the four stories. Later on students may compare how the stories differ from each other. In classes where I saw well-constructed interaction, students were challenged, supported, and thoroughly engaged. They participated in quality interactions, where the sustained dialogue built on the participants' ideas, which in turn promoted improved understanding of concepts. As is testament to the level of engagement, students never skipped these classes and always arrived on time. These students learned a great deal about the short story as a genre and about human experience, and they also developed their academic uses of English and strengthened their humanity.

The following quote from a freshman from Colombia who at the time of the interview had been in the United States for two years illustrates how this productive collaboration can also take place in highly heterogeneous academic environments and can create a culture of learning and support at the school.

> I remember a case of a Mexican student who when he came to school he could not speak any English, and he couldn't read or write in his own language. He was at first very afraid people would laugh at him, but with Mr. DeFazio's help and our help, he is progressing very well…because in this school everybody cares about everybody. I know at one point this boy felt like he wanted to die, but here, because we all work with him, he is doing great.

(9) Give students multiple opportunities to extend their understandings and to apply their knowledge.

> I loved the time capsule project. At the beginning of the year Miss Heisler asked us to take a shoebox to school and to put in it cards talking about the important things in our life at the time, our dreams, our fears, our strengths, our weaknesses. We then decorated our boxes, and she said they were going to be buried until the end of the year. So, we all went together to put them away in a room nobody uses. Then, on the last day of school, we went and opened them. It was so interesting to compare how much we had changed in just one school year. … There were things I said then that I do not believe in anymore…that was a great way of showing us how much we grow and learn English.

9th-grade student from Guatemala, two years in the United States

> The United Nations simulation? I loved it! After we read so many different perspectives on the Palestinian situation we can see many different sides, and in the UN discussion we can discuss and try to win new understandings. It is difficult to imagine an easy solution to the problem.

10th-grade student from Romania

One of the goals of learning is to be able to apply acquired knowledge to novel situations. For English learners, these applications reinforce the development of new language, concepts, and academic skills as students actively draw connections between pieces of knowledge and their contexts. Understanding a topic of study involves being able to perform in a variety of cognitively demanding ways (Perkins, 1993).

In one of the schools I visited, the teacher of an ESL class gave students opportunities to engage in substantive interactions where the dialogue built on the participants' ideas to build understanding of concepts. After the class had read a myth using a variety of interactive tasks, the teacher divided the myth into three sections. Groups of students were assigned to write the dialogues they thought might have occurred during a particular moment of the myth. Although these dialogues were developed collaboratively within each group, each student kept his or her own script and used it for the final performance of a drama on that section. Students analyzed, compared, made connections, hypothesized, monitored their understandings, assisted each other, and finally transferred the knowledge they acquired to a new situation, re-presenting a narrative text as a dramatic one.

This teacher's approach did not primarily depend on transmitting knowledge but rather depended on scaffolding her instruction so that her students could perform in complex ways. Learning to explore cause and effect, examining the main components of a myth, and looking for evidence to support an interpretation were all developed and refined over time. The teacher's main purpose was to develop her students' ability to use English in a variety of school contexts beyond her class, which she did by structuring her lessons so that substantive concepts and the language needed to express them could be developed.

The student in the first quote at the beginning of this section has had the opportunity to compare how much a year has meant in terms of personal, academic, and linguistic development. Providing students with similar opportunities to build self-awareness and with the knowledge that progress has occurred in their lives is an effective way of preparing them for life after school.

(10) View authentic assessment as an integral part of teaching and learning.

As I opened my time capsule I remembered that a friend had to translate for me what we had to do. I could not write very much in English, so I completed my cards in Spanish. At the end of the year, everything I wrote in Spanish I can write in English. And what made me happy was to see that my dreams for the year had come true. I can now speak, read, and write in English more or less; of course, I still have a lot to learn, but I also have two more years in the school to do that.

10th-grade student from Mexico, one and a half years in the United States

Boy, was I nervous the day before the presentation of my senior project. I wished I was in ESL II so I could do it in Spanish, but then, talking to my friends who were doing their presentation in Spanish, they were just as nervous as me. So we decided to rehearse together one more time. I felt good because the rehearsal made me realize that I understood the topic of my research better than anybody else and that I could probably answer the questions from the jury. How did it go? Fine, I was nervous at first, but when I started presenting and I looked at my panel and they were smiling, I forgot about my nerves and continued. The whole thing went by fast and well.

12th-grade student from Mexico, three years in the United States

Assessment should be done not only by teachers but also by learners, who assess themselves and each other. Considerable research supports the importance of self-monitoring in the learning of second languages (O'Malley & Chamot, 1989; Oxford, 1990; Rubin & Thompson, 1982). Authentic assessment activities engage second-language learners in self-directed learning, in the construction of knowledge through disciplined inquiry, and in the analysis of the problems they encounter.

For example, correction of pronunciation errors is especially effective when students are put in charge of monitoring their own oral production in English. This can be done by recording, within each collaborative team of students, the individual presentations at the final stage of a jigsaw project. The cassette recordings can then be given to students so that they can listen to their own presentation and can write comments reflecting on it—analyzing their production, pinpointing troublesome areas, and exploring corrective strategies.

Likewise, portfolios of student work can powerfully indicate to students their progress in the acquisition of English and academic dexterity, as the first student quote in this section indicates. This is especially important during the intermediate stages of language development, when students tend to feel that they are not progressing very much. Other experiential assessment practices—such as self-evaluation narratives, the use of rubrics, and the senior project—also hold promise for the education of high school immigrant students.

Teacher assessment of English learners' writing needs to be especially considered. Teachers tend to focus on the most superficial aspects of a student's text (e.g., spelling and verb forms) and miss the important details that should be considered first: Did students address the assignment? Did they present relevant ideas? Were their ideas organized in coherent ways? (Walqui-van Lier & Hernández, 2001). It is linguistic knowledge that tends to be assessed and not the conceptual and general value of learning a second language (Rea-Dickins & Rixon, 1997). An excellent example of this is found in the book *The Spirit Catches You and You Fall Down*, when author Anne Fadiman (1997) presents the tragic misconstructions of interactions between Hmong communities and health workers in the California Central

Valley. Her ethnography includes a glimpse of the evaluation of a student writing gone terribly wrong in the classroom. The teacher had asked her students at Merced's Hoover Junior High to write an incident for an autobiography. May, a Hmong student, wrote,

> On our way to Thailand was something my parent will never forget. It was one of the scariest time of my life, and maybe my parents. We had to walked by feet. Some of family, however, leave their kids behind, kill, or beat them. For example, one of the relative has tried to kill one of his kid, but luckily he didn't died. And manage to come along with the group. Today, he's in America carrying a scar on his forehead.
>
> My parents had to carried me and two of my younger sisters, True and Yer. My mom could only carried me, and my dad could only my sister. True with many other things which they have to carry such as, rices (food), clothing, and blankets for overnight. My parents pay one of the relative to carry Yer. One of my sister who died in Thailand was so tire of walking saying that she can't go on any longer. But she dragged along and made it to Thailand.
>
> There was gun shot going on and soldier were close to every where. If there was a gun shot, we were to look for a place to hide. On our trip to Thailand, there were many gun shots and instead of looking for a place to hide, my parents would dragged our hands or put us on their back and run for their lifes. When it gets too heavy, my parents would tossed some of their stuff away. Some of the things they had throw away are valuable to them, but our lives were more important to them than the stuffs (pp. 154, 155).

"You have had an exciting life!" wrote her teacher at the end of the essay. "Please watch verbs in the past tense. (p. 155)"

Authentic assessment is embedded in everyday practice: How is a given student performing? At what stage is she in the development of her ability to express a sequence of events? Is she ready to take the lead in a reciprocal teaching activity? All of these questions, which teachers ask themselves every minute of their teaching, are assessment activities, and they inform and determine teaching arrangements. It is commonly assumed that classroom assessment is low stakes. Rae-Dickins and Rixon (1997) warn us, though, that in fact it is not necessarily low stakes, because it is often the case that high-stakes decisions are predicated on learners' in-class performance. What did the teacher in Fadiman's (1997) example think of May? She treated her simply as a language producer that needed to be corrected, not a person with valuable ideas and terrible experiences from which she, and everybody else in the classroom, could grow intellectually and academically. All good assessment, then, provides learners with opportunities to learn and helps teachers know their students, value them, and determine what and how to teach them next.

The Development of Teacher Expertise: A Model

How can all teachers be supported to deliberately plan and implement lessons based on these 10 priorities? To help conceptualize how teachers might develop their expertise, this section discusses what it is that accomplished teachers of ELLs know and are able to do. I use a model of teacher understanding and expertise that I hope will make possible rich and focused conversations about the complexities of teaching linguistically diverse students. As will become clear in the discussion, the knowledge and skills required are not just of a

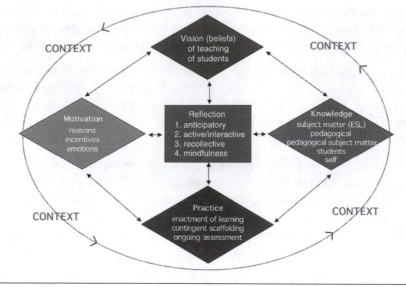

Figure 6.1 The development of teacher understanding

technical nature but include, just as importantly, personal, social, and political aspects of a teacher's professional life and context.

The model (Figure 6.1) depicts two main aspects of teacher understanding and its development:

1. A mapping of the domains that constitute the knowledge, dispositions, emotions, and abilities of accomplished teachers working in specific contexts (the upper part of the diagram)
2. The notion that teacher understanding and expertise are accomplished over an extended, ongoing time continuum, with certain aspects becoming more salient than others at different times (the timeline at the bottom)

Throughout their studies and professional lives, teachers develop in six domains: vision, motivation, knowledge, reflection, practice, and context. But this development does not just occur at the individual level; it is a result of complex interactions with colleagues and with institutions. Beginning with preservice education, the systems in which future teachers study and later practice support this growth or constrain it. It is important, however, to raise a note of caution about the organizing model presented here. By necessity, a diagram such as this one is unidimensional and idealized and as such fails to represent the considerable conceptual and practical overlap between its components. The domains represented are not discrete or neatly separable into categories, nor do they all develop in organized, sequential ways. They constitute an organic model and coexist in mutually supporting relations; thus, they cannot be thought of as existing independently or related to one another in a linear fashion. Nevertheless, it is important to discuss them in abstraction because in this way the organizer can be used to characterize teachers' locations in the process of learning to become accomplished teachers and thus help them plan their development. More importantly, the process can help conceptualize the work of teacher professional growth in a more focused and organic way.

Unpacking the Model

Vision This construct encompasses teachers' ideologies, objectives, and dreams, all of which provide a sense of direction to their students' learning. Accomplished teachers believe in the educability of each and every English learner and seek to ensure equal learning opportunities for all. They also realize that teaching is not a neutral act and that through their teaching they may contribute to maintaining the status quo for their students and their families, or they may help them build a more equitable societal order in the future (Fairclough, 1992). Pennycook (1994), for example, points out that ESL teachers need to become aware of what vision of society they are working toward to develop professionally. Vision includes a clear ultimate goal of (1) optimal instruction; and (2) a vision of students as capable individuals.

Optimal Instruction What are the images teachers have of what is possible in teaching second-language learners? Can they conceive of accelerated, rigorous teaching for all students that takes into consideration the differential starting points and multiple abilities represented in any given class? As Valdés (2001, p. 147) observes, in many English language development classes "Little went on in the classroom that could prepare [students] to develop the kinds of proficiencies they would need to succeed in other classes." Her comments are corroborated by the work of August and Hakuta (1997), Lucas (1997), and Walqui (2000).

Teacher preparation programs and opportunities for ongoing professional growth need to build visions that run counter to these realities, visions that set the goal high and achieve it. They then need to deconstruct the processes that led to these teachers' success so that others have multiple examples of what is possible with English learners and can initially emulate some of these practices to eventually appropriate them by recreating and constructing their own.

Vision of Students as Capable Individuals This may be thought of as short-term vision, focused on developing specific students' potential as learners within the time frame that a teacher works with them (e.g., a semester, an academic year), and long-term vision, which conceptualizes them as future capable actors in the societies of which they form a part. As one conscientious teacher of ELLs said to me (Walqui, 1997, p. 246), exasperated by the video of a colleague whose practices demonstrated that she had an extremely limited vision of her students' capabilities,

> I would suggest that she go somewhere outside the school, where these students are in a social function, or a cultural event, where she is not teaching them anything, so that she can appreciate them, not only as competent, but so that she could see them a little bit more like people. … There is a certain level that you have to respect the students that you are teaching, that you have to see them as viable contributing individuals, that they have a history behind them. … They need to feel that there is something more to them than just this peephole that is coming through their class… .

A decade and a half ago, Goodlad's (1990) national study of teacher education found that a rich vision of what minority students could achieve was lacking in preservice education. In his words, "…The idea of moral imperatives for teachers was virtually foreign in concept and strange in language for most of the future teachers we interviewed. Many were less than convinced that all students can learn; they voiced the view that they should be kind and considerate to all, but they accepted as fact the theory that some simply cannot learn" (p. 264). Fifteen years later, with few exceptions, the situation has worsened in pre-service programs.

Among practicing teachers the situation is equally bad. The MetLife Survey of the American Teacher 2001 (p. 10) concludes that "teachers and principals in schools with more than two-thirds minority students [i.e., with a very high presence of English learners] are less likely than those in schools with one third or fewer minority students to report that all or most of their students will achieve their full academic potential for this year (59% vs. 76%)."

Knowledge This category represents the range of cognitive understandings that inform instruction: (1) general pedagogical knowledge; (2) subject-matter knowledge to include knowledge of how to teach English as a second language and how to embed that knowledge in the teaching of academic content; (3) pedagogical content knowledge; (4) knowledge of students; and (5) teacher self-knowledge.

General pedagogical knowledge (Shulman, 1987) comprises the general corpus of knowledge and skills concerning learning, learners, and the goals and processes of education. Knowledge about how children and teenagers learn, general principles of instruction (such as the importance of setting up collaborative activities that promote substantive interaction in class and the role of wait time), the development of metacognitive skills, and issues on curriculum development belong in this area.

Subject-matter knowledge comprises the teacher's knowledge of what Schwab (1964) calls the substantive and the syntactic structures of the subject area. The substantive structures include main concepts in the field and the paradigms that give structure to the subject and that guide future developments in the area. The syntactic structures of a field include the canons of evidence and proof that are shared by subject-matter communities. In the education of English language learners, for example, subject-matter knowledge includes not only knowledge about the subject being taught (e.g., science) but also knowledge of educational linguistics, sociolinguistics, teaching English as a second language—ESL or English language development—and knowledge of and about other languages if education is to be carried out bilingually. Thirty years after the communicative revolution in language teaching emerged, little has changed in classrooms geared to teach English as a second language or academic content through the medium of English. This failure to address in rigorous ways the conceptual, linguistic, and academic needs of English learners in schools has led Valdés (2001, p. 145) to call classes specifically intended for ELLs "the ESL ghetto." This ghetto is characterized by classes that present atomistic bits and pieces of "artificial-sounding language…or …the somewhat distorted language of subject-matter teachers to use 'simplified' English in order to give students access to the curriculum" (p. 13).

Deep subject-matter knowledge is essential for content-area teachers of ELLs since only a robust understanding of the discipline can help them select central concepts and relationships in the discipline to develop with their students while attending to the explicit teaching of the academic discourse needed.

Pedagogical content knowledge is the knowledge teachers possess about how to teach a specific subject, and themes within that subject, to specific groups of students. It includes access to multiple forms of representations for concepts—the availability of appropriate examples, metaphors, similes, ways of structuring the teaching of a specific concept and its interconnections to make it accessible and to promote the development of deep understandings in students. It also includes knowledge of content and performance standards that must be met, as well as ways of assessing their achievement across individual students. This weaving of new concepts together with ways of presenting them to specific students makes teaching an extremely complex endeavor.

Knowledge of students—their strengths, what they bring to the classroom, and who they are outside of school—is essential for teachers. For example, sometimes teachers correlate the linguistic limitations of second-language learners or the features displayed by second-dialect speakers with academic limitations, and that incorrect correlation leads them to water down their curriculum and to expect little of students. As the students' voices in this chapter show, the fact that they do not know English does not mean they do not know about life, that they have not developed important knowledge that may be tapped into to build complex academic skills.

Knowledge of students has to be based on a cultivated ability to observe and learn about the cultures represented in class. It is generative rather than fixed or stereotypical. For this reason it is important for preservice and in-service teachers to conduct mini-ethnographies of students and their communities in order to learn firsthand who they are, how they are evolving, and what their strengths, struggles, and aspirations are.

Knowledge of self is what teachers develop as they evolve professionally. Being able to see themselves not only in their accomplishments but also in their failures and contradictions enables teachers to grow and improve. Lack of self-knowledge among educators can impede their ability to create optimal learning experiences for immigrant students. It can also help perpetuate the hidden curriculum of schools, which transmits meanings such as: (a) what it means to *be good,* (b) what matters, (c) the value or hierarchy and authority, and (d) the demeaning of learning (Fairclough, 1992).

Practice   This area represents the teachers' skills and strategies for enacting their goals and understandings in practice. Understanding alone is not enough but needs to be combined with the ability to act on it in effective ways. At times we meet teachers who can articulate a coherent grasp of what ought to be happening in a class but who demonstrate a discrepancy between their knowledge and the ability to implement it. It is in the translation of understanding into practice that failure is particularly common. To reduce such failures, support during implementation is needed. Such support should include an extended, coherent, and well-supported period of teacher induction and ongoing learning, where coaching, videotaping, and the deconstruction of practice via iterative sequences of video discussion, planning, and critical implementation can take place.

Motivation   This category is composed of the reasons, incentives, and emotions that give energy and meaning to a teacher's visions, understandings, and practices. It is commonplace in education to say that people who join the teaching profession do so motivated by a desire to change the world. To ensure that this motivation is strengthened in practice, teacher-preparation programs need to prepare their students to work on changing the world within school structures that are sometimes toxic. An example is the time-honored practice of giving the most experienced teachers in a high school their favorite assignments (typically advanced placement classes with fewer students who are better prepared academically) and assigning new teachers (sometimes emergency credentialed, with little or no preparation to teach) the most complex assignments, those that require the most expertise. If experienced teachers helped their new colleagues apprentice into the job, choosing the most challenging assignments, modeling expertise, coaching them, and offering them advice and their pedagogical and emotional support, then most teachers' motivation, knowledge, and vision would be reinforced, which would in turn benefit teaching and learning.

The current climate of high-stakes accountability adds to the complexity of factors that undermine motivation. In California, for example, the Academic Performance Index (API) system has added even more pressures to the teaching force, leading them to such negative practices as teaching to the test, encouraging student absence during official testing time, and, in some dramatic cases, even allowing cheating. As seen, without supportive structures in place at the school, motivation is eroded, and good teaching for English learners is not possible.

Reflection   Reflection in teaching occurs when knowledgeable practitioners try to make sense of their actions in classrooms by engaging in, among other activities, evaluating, planning, remembering, and contemplating, all of which contribute to the understanding of their work in schools. The model of teacher understanding draws on van Manen's (1991) view of four types of reflection in teaching: (1) anticipatory (i.e., planning); (2) active–interactive (i.e., thinking on their feet, as teachers teach and deliberate among alternative actions); (3) recollective (i.e., revisiting past events to learn from them for future applications); and (4) mindfulness (e.g., pedagogical wisdom, the result of having appropriated the right ways of acting in teaching after an extended history of engagement in reflection).

Teachers, and in particular teachers of ELLs, seldom have the opportunity to engage in reflective practice. Professional development geared to develop their expertise needs to offer venues that engage them in collaborative reflection on their practice. For example, teachers need the time to plan lessons together, to reconsider past assignments, and to reformulate or refine them for future applications. Professional-development sessions could help them articulate and make explicit the considerations they engaged in as they taught a class and also could provide them with opportunities to collaboratively examine student work against standards to plan future pedagogical actions. In current work being conducted by WestEd with teachers of second-language adolescents (Walqui & Koelsch, 2006), teachers are videotaped, and the videos are used to invite commentaries and reflections, with highly successful results. These are the kinds of reflective activities that enhance teacher expertise in working with their students.

Context

Do teachers work in collegial environments that enable them to examine with others classroom situations, students' progress, and their own teaching with others? Do they work in schools where teachers close their doors and where little is shared about what really happens in the classroom? Are most conversations in the school opportunities to advance teachers' expertise? Is a collegial context constructed in which teachers can share their ideas and concerns with ease and where they assist each other in the development of understandings about how to work with ELLs? Visions of compelling teaching and optimal visions of students evolve in a particular context, and can either be strengthened or debilitated by that context. In similar fashion, knowledge—in its many forms here discussed—the ability to reflect, to become motivated or demotivated, and to enhance practice are transformed by the environments in which teachers operate. Context embeds dimensions that move from classroom to the school, district, community, state, and federal demands and responsibilities, and it includes the interactions that take place among all these dimensions.

As argued in this chapter, all domains of teacher understanding overlap and reinforce or impede the development of teacher expertise. For example, professional development offerings typically shy away from discussion of the competing visions that different individuals and agencies have for the education of English learners and what needs to be done about it. There is a strong tendency to understand teachers' professional growth as a technical issue, one that is not political in nature (Hargreaves, 1994). However, both in preservice and in-service education, promoting the careful consideration of ethical and political components of teaching is worthwhile. Being always situated in the particular, good professional development—as good teaching—needs to respond to the specific circumstances of teachers' and students' lives. The model presented here is a tool that I hope will enable readers to establish rich conversations about the nature of teacher expertise in the service of linguistically diverse students.

Notes

1. An earlier version of this chapter comes from Walqui (2000). Adapted with permission.
2. A Mellon grant given to the Center for Applied Linguistics made it possible for me to study exemplary instructional approaches for ELLs in secondary schools. I visited nominated middle and high schools to study how teachers orchestrated their teaching in these settings and to interview students, teachers, and administrators. A grant given by the Spencer Foundation in 1997 enabled me to study and propose a model for the development and implementation of teacher knowledge. Finally, a Regional Educational Laboratory grant (2001–05) afforded the opportunity to go back to the schools, to videotape accomplished teachers in action, to study their craft, and to design teacher professional development materials.

References

Adger, C., Kalyanpur, M., Peterson, D., & Bridger, T. (1995). *Engaging students: Thinking, talking, cooperating.* Thousand Oaks, CA: Corwin Press.

August, D., & Hakuta, K. (Eds.). (1997). *Improving schooling for language minority children.* Washington, DC: National Academy Press.

Ball, D., & Rundquist, S. (1993). Collaboration as a context for joining teacher learning with learning about teaching. In D. Cohen, M. McLaughlin, & J. Talbert (Eds.), *Teaching for understanding: Challenges for policy and practice* (pp. 13–42). San Francisco: Josey-Bass.

Batalova, J., & Fix, M. (2005). English language learner adolescents: Demographics and literacy achievements. Washington, DC: Migration Policy Institute.

Barron, V., & Menken, K. (2002). *What are the characteristics of the bilingual education and ESL teacher shortage?* Washington DC: National Clearinghouse for English Language Acquisition and Language Instruction Educational Programs.

Bialystok, E., & Hakuta, K. (1994). *In other words: The science and psychology of second-language acquisition.* New York: Basic Books.

Brown, A., & Palincsar, A. (1985). Reciprocal teaching of comprehension strategies: A natural history of one program for enhancing learning. Technical report 334. Eric Reproduction Service ED 257 046.

Bruner, J. (1986). *Actual minds, possible worlds.* Cambridge, MA: Harvard University Press.

Cohen, E. (1994). Restructuring the classroom: Conditions for productive small groups. *Review of Educational Research, 64,* 1–35.

Darling-Hammond, L. (2000). Teacher quality and student achievement: A review of state policy evidence. *Education Policy Archives, 8.* Available at: http://epaa.asu.edu/epaa/v8n1.

Delpit, L. (1995). *Other people's children: Cultural conflict in the classroom.* NY: The New Press.

Derewianka, B. (1990). *Exploring how texts work.* Victoria, Australia: Primary English Teaching Association.

Fadiman, A. (1997). *The spirit catches you and you fall down*. New York: Farrar Straus and Giroux.

Fairclough, N. (1992). *Critical language awareness*. London: Longman.

Ferreiro, E., Pellicer, A., Rodriguez, B., Silva, A., & Vernon, S. (1991). *Haceres, quehaceres y deshaceres con la lengua escrita en la escuela rural*. Mexico D.F.: Departamento de Investigaciones Educativas del Centro de Investigacion y Estudios Avanzados (Instituto Politecnico Nacional).

Gardner, H. (1989). *To open minds: Chinese clues to the dilemma of contemporary education*. New York: Basic Books.

Gibbons, P. (2002). *Scaffolding language, scaffolding learning*. Portsmouth, NH: Heinemann.

Gibbons, P. (2003). Scaffolding academic language across the curriculum. Presentation at the American Association of Applied Linguistics, Arlington, VA, March 25.

Goldhaber, D., Brewer, D, & Anderson, D. (1999). A three–way error components analysis of educational productivity. *Education Economics*, 7(3), 199–208.

Goldhaber, D. (2002). The mystery of good teaching. *Education Next*, 2(1), 50–55.

Goodlad, J. (1990). *Teachers for our nation's schools*. San Francisco: Jossey Bass.

Goodman, Y. (1978). Kid watching: An alternative to testing. *National Elementary School Principal*, 57, 41–45.

Halliday, M.A. K. (1994). *Introduction to functional grammar, second edition*. London, England: Edward Arnold.

Hargreaves, A. (1994). *Changing teachers, changing times: Teachers' work and culture in the postmodern age*. New York: Teachers College Press.

Kagan, S., & McGroarty, M. (1993). Principles of cooperative learning for language and content gains. In D. D. Holt (Ed.), *Cooperative learning: A response to linguistic and cultural diversity* (pp. 47–66). McHenry, IL: Delta Systems and Center for Applied Linguistics.

Kaplan, R. B. (1988). Contrastive rhetoric and second language learning: Notes toward a theory of contrastive rhetoric. In A. C. Purves (Ed.), *Writing across languages and cultures: Issues in contrastive rhetoric* (pp. 275–304). Beverly Hills, CA: Sage.

Lave, J., & Wenger, E. (1991). *Situated learning: Legitimate peripheral participation*. Cambridge, England: Cambridge University Press.

Lucas, T. (1997). *Into, through, and beyond secondary school: Critical transitions for immigrant youths*. Mc Henry, IL: Delta Systems and Center for Applied Linguistics.

Martin, J. (1990). Literacy in science: Learning to handle literacy as technology. In F. Christie (Ed.), *Literacy for a changing world* (pp. xx–xx). Hawthorn, Australia: ACER.

Mercer, N. (2000). *Words and minds: How we use language to think together*. London: Routledge.

MetLife (2001). The MetLife survey of the American teacher 2001. Key elements of quality schools. Available at: http://www.ced.org/docs/report_survey_american_teacher01.pdf.

National Educational Research Policy & Priorities Board (1999). *Investing in learning: A policy statement with recommendations on research in education by the National Educational Research, Policy, and Priorities Board*. Washington, DC: National Educational Research, Policy, and Priorities Board, U.S. Department of Education.

O'Malley, J. M., & Chamot, A. U. (1989). *Learning strategies in second language acquisition*. Cambridge, England: Cambridge University Press.

Oxford, R. (1990). *Language learning strategies: What every teacher should know*. New York: Newbury Press.

Palincsar, A., David, I., & Brown, A. (1992). Using reciprocal teaching in the classroom: A guide for teachers. Unpublished manuscript. The Brown/Campione Research Group.

Pennycook, A. (1994). *The cultural politics of English as an international language*. London, England: Longman.

Perkins, D. (1993). *An apple for education: Teaching and learning for understanding*. (EdPress Elam Lecture, Rowan College of New Jersey). Glasboro, NJ: EdPress.

Rae-Dickins, P., & Rixon, S. (1997). The assessment of young learners of English as a foreign language. In C. Clapham & D. Corson (Eds.), *Encyclopedia of language and education: Language testing and assessment* (vol. 7) (pp. xx–xx). Dordrecht, The Netherlands: Kluwer Academic Publishers.

Ramirez, J.D., & Merino, B.J. (1990). Classroom talk in English immersion, early exit and late-exit transitional bilingual education programs. In R. Jacobson & C. Faltis (Eds.), *Language distribution issues in bilingual schooling*, pp. 61–103. Clevedon, England: Multilingual Matters.

Rubin, J. (1975). What the "good language learner" can teach us. *TESOL Quarterly*, 9, 41–51.

Rubin, J., & Thompson, L. (1982). *How to be a more successful language learner.* Boston: Heinle & Heinle.

Santiago, E. (1994). *When I was Puerto Rican.* New York: Vintage Books.

Schwab, J.J. (1964). The structure of disciplines: Meanings and significance. In G. W. Ford & L. Pugno (Eds.), *The structure of knowledge and the curriculum.* Chicago, IL: Rand McNally.

Schwab, J. J. (1996). The practical four: Something for curriculum professors to do. In E. R. Hollins (Ed.), *Transforming curriculum for a culturally diverse society* (pp. xx–xx). Mahwah, NJ: L. Erlbaum.

Shulman, L. (1987). Knowledge and teaching: Foundations of the new reform. *Harvard Educational Review. 57,* 114–135.

Shulman, L. S. & Associates (1995). Fostering a community of teachers and learners. Unpublished progress report to the Mellon Foundation.

Tharp, R., & Gallimore, R. (1988). *Rousing minds to life: Teaching, learning, and schooling in social context.* Cambridge, England: Cambridge University Press.

Valdés, G. (2001). *Learning and not learning English: Latino students in American schools.* New York: Teachers College Press.

van Manen, M. (1991). *Researching lived experience.* Albany: State University New York Press.

Vygotsky, L. (1978). *Mind in society.* Cambridge, MA: Harvard University Press.

Walqui, A. (1997). The development of teachers' understanding: Inservice professional growth for teachers of English language learners. Unpublished dissertation. Stanford University School of Education, Stanford, CA.

Walqui, A. (2000). *Access and engagement: Program design and instructional approaches for immigrant students in secondary school.* Washington, DC: Center for Applied Linguistics and Delta Systems Co., Inc.

Walqui, A. (forthcoming). *Scaffolding instruction for English learners: A conceptual framework.*

Walqui, A. (2003). *Conceptual framework: Scaffolding instruction for English learners.* San Francisco, CA: WestEd.

Walqui, A., & Koelsch, N. (2006). *Scaffolding academic uses of English.* San Francisco, CA: WestEd.

Walqui-van Lier, A., & Hernandez, A. (2001). A scaffold for change: Professional development for teachers of English learners. San Diego, CA: San Diego County Office of Education.

CHAPTER 7

Making Mainstream Content Comprehensible Through Sheltered Instruction

LORRIE STOOPS VERPLAETSE AND NAOMI MIGLIACCI

Mainstream middle school and secondary educators with English language learners (ELLs) students integrated into their classrooms are faced with the following three challenges, as discussed in Chapter 1:

1. How to make the course content comprehensible to ELL students in the class who do not understand the language
2. How to engage those students with the content, with their peers, and with the teacher
3. How to provide a safe, yet cognitively and interactionally stimulating environment

Thirty years ago, school systems mistakenly believed that immigrant students needed to be sent to the English as a second language (ESL) classroom or bilingual education classroom until they had adequately developed their English skills. Now educators, armed with the knowledge that it takes 5 to 10 years to develop the second-language skills required to successfully navigate academic language, realize that immigrant students in middle school and high school may sound like they are fluent in basic conversational English but may well still be developing the academic language skills needed to understand oral and written academic texts, to write about academic content, and to hold discussions on academic topics. No longer do mainstream teachers have the luxury of thinking that they are teachers of only a particular discipline. Faced with the challenge of ELLs in the classroom, who range in language proficiency, mainstream content teachers are learning that they are also responsible for the ongoing language development of their students.

Partial funding for this chapter has been provided by a Training for All Teachers Grant through the U.S. Department of Education, Office of English Language Acquisition, #T195B010094. We wish to thank the teachers and teacher candidates whose work is represented in this chapter; we appreciate their willingness to share their practices with others. We are also grateful to our graduate assistants, Carola Osses, Jennifer O'Brien, and Kathleen Doyle for their excellent work in all phases of this project and to Dr. Dan Soneson for his technical assistance.

How, then, do mainstream content teachers make complex academic topics comprehensible to English language learners, when the medium of instruction is the oral language and written language of English? They do so through sheltered instruction. *Sheltered instruction* is a term that first described a manner of teaching content in a classroom composed entirely of English language learners. In a sheltered content class, the teacher is certified in the content discipline (e.g., history, math, health, physics), but the teacher has learned how to deliver the course content in comprehensible ways: through controlled language usage, by simplifying language delivery, and through the use of many visuals, gestures, and realia. In sheltered instruction classrooms, the teacher has two goals: (1) to teach the content; and (2) to guide the language development necessary for students to engage in the content.

Far too often, however, school systems are unable to provide a sheltered classroom for each course; consequently, mainstream teachers most often have language-learning students integrated into their traditional, mainstream classrooms. However, even in this mainstream setting teachers can employ sheltered instructional strategies, thus making the content comprehensible for ELLs, while simultaneously fully engaging the native-speaking English students. This is the sheltered instruction discussed in this chapter.

For the past five years, funded by a U.S. Department of Education Title VII grant, Southern Connecticut State University's Training for All Teachers (TAT) program has been offering professional development training on the topic of sheltered instruction to Connecticut teachers, administrators, and student service personnel. In this training, teachers learn how to make entire lessons comprehensible and how specifically to make written text and classroom talk comprehensible. This is one portion of the sheltered instruction equation: to make content comprehensible. The other main component of sheltered instruction is how to engage students with the content and how to create opportunities for the students to interact with the content, their peers, and their teachers, also covered in the TAT training.

This chapter reviews the instructional strategies recommended to make content comprehensible, addressing whole lessons, written text, and classroom talk. (The following chapter in this book addresses the second portion of the equation: interaction and engagement.) Here are shared samples of teacher-developed materials employing these sheltered strategies. Then research is identified that supports these strategies, making reference to a national movement in sheltered instruction, called the sheltered instruction observation protocol (SIOP) model.

Making Lessons Comprehensible Through Contextualization

Through the work of Jim Cummins (1981, 1984) educators have come to understand the nature of academic language. Almost all schooling is accomplished through the medium of language. Academic language as compared to social, interpersonal language treats the speaker and receiver as if they are distanced from one another; it has been called the *language of strangers*. It is so because it is decontextualized; that is, it assumes a lack of shared history, it limits opportunities for negotiation of meaning, and it uses words rather than visuals to convey most of its meaning.

The following example illustrates this difference between basic, interpersonal language and decontextualized, academic language. Consider the following social, interpersonal language event. Imagine that a person sitting next to you in a class or meeting wants to borrow the book you are currently reading. That person might lean over, point to the book, and say, "Can I see that?" And if you misunderstood him, you might point to your pencil and say, "This?" At which point, the neighbor could respond, "No, that," pointing again to the book. This is a highly contextualized event. The two speakers have a shared history because the event is happening in the here and now. The two speakers also have the realia, the book, and other visuals, such as the use of the pointing gesture. Finally, the two can negotiate meaning if necessary by asking questions of each other at the moment. See how small an amount of language is required to accomplish this task of requesting a particular book: just four small words, "Can I see that?"

Now let us decontextualize this event. Imagine that it is 10 years later, and a classmate or colleague of yours who has moved away gets in touch with you for the first time in 10 years to borrow the same book from you. Imagine that she is writing either an e-mail or a postal letter. No longer do the two of you hold a shared history, so the first thing the writer would have to do is to write a paragraph or two about where she is and how she has been and then recall the time when the two of you had the book in common. Also, the writer does not have the ability to point, nor is the book physically present in the written communication, so there are no visuals to assist the event. The writer would have to compensate for the lack of visuals by clearly describing the book she wishes to borrow. Finally, because the message is written, the sender and receiver have no opportunity to negotiation meaning; therefore, the author of the message must assume that all necessary information is provided in the text. Consider how much more language is required to accomplish the same task of requesting a particular book when the task is decontextualized. And the difference is not just in the amount of language. If we were to study the language of the memo, we would discover that it contains a number of syntactic complexities (e.g., embedded relative clauses, such as "that book we read for Smith's Leadership class") not required in the basic, interpersonal interaction.

Academic lectures and textbooks are classic examples of decontextualized language. So, too, are classroom discussions, though slightly less so, at times. These events are heavily dependent on language to carry the message, which is problematic for English language learner (ELL) students in the mainstream classroom who do not yet have the language necessary to comprehend the event.

This understanding of academic language, however, has empowered educators to understand what must be done to make such academic language events comprehensible; the events need to be contextualized. We contextualize lessons by building background knowledge—thus creating a shared history—by using an extensive amount of visuals, gestures, and realia and by creating opportunities for students to negotiate meaning.

The following section discusses these three instructional strategies, providing illustrative examples of how to implement each.

Building Background Knowledge, Creating a Shared History

Taking time to build the necessary background—thus creating a shared history—is essential for ELLs if they are to understand course content. Elementary school teachers frequently employ this strategy as a prereading activity, but secondary teachers have been less apt to take the class time to create a shared history.

KWL Chart   One classic way to develop background knowledge is to create a *know, want, learn* (KWL) chart. In such a chart, students identify what they think they know (K) about a particular topic. Students can do this in pairs during class, in full class discussion, or at home as a homework assignment. Of course, the more that students engage together about the topic, the more they create a shared history and the fuller that history becomes.

K	W	L
What I think I know....	**What I want to learn.........**	**What I have learned.......**

Figure 7.1 KWL chart.

After students have identified what they know about a topic, they then identify what they want (W) to learn about the topic. Again, students can accomplish this in a variety of ways. Finally, at the end of the learning of event, students then identify what they have learned (L) about the topic. Figure 7.1 illustrates what a typical KWL chart looks like.

Some instructors add a fourth column to create a KWHL chart; the H stands for "how I am going to go about learning" what I want to learn about the topic.

Think–Pair–Share   Another classic way students can build shared background knowledge about a topic is to conduct a think–pair–share exercise. To illustrate this exercise, we turn to a seventh-grade social studies teacher* who developed a sheltered instructional unit on the Declaration of Independence. During the second lesson of this unit, the teacher planned to discuss when and how the colonists declare independence. At the beginning of the lesson, she asked the students to think about "What do you think the Declaration of Independence says?" First they thought about it by themselves. Then they paired up and discussed their thoughts with a partner. Finally, the pairs reported back their thoughts to the full group, as the teacher recorded their ideas on the board.

Making Use of the Cultural Capital in the Room   Teachers who are consciously aware that immigrant students in their classroom represent additional cultural capital (Bourdieu,

---

* This teacher requests to remain anonymous.

1986) make use of this resource during the class time spent to build shared background. For example, when studying volcanoes, some of the students in the classroom may have lived near volcanoes and can share about that experience. As another example, the video *Helping English Learners Succeed: An Overview of the SIOP* (Center for Applied Linguistics, 2002) depicts a classroom teacher preparing to study the reasons the English pilgrims chose to leave their homeland. She first begins the lesson by asking students in the class to identify reasons why they have moved from one place to another.

Taking time to create a shared history is always good instructional technique but is essential when working with English language learners. Oftentimes, this practice is called *activating background knowledge*. For ELLs in the classroom, however, who have their own background knowledge that because of cultural differences may differ distinctively from that of American mainstream students, this activity often creates the shared background knowledge necessary to make the upcoming content comprehensible.

Use of Extensive Amount of Visuals, Gesture, and Realia

The use of visuals is probably the most important strategy that teachers can employ with language learners. We all know the expression, "A picture is worth a thousand words," and it is so true. The more opportunities students have to visualize, the easier they will be able to comprehend.

Effective Use of Visuals   The effective sheltered instructor makes conscious use of visuals that other teachers would not think to use. To illustrate this, consider an eighth-grade health science course in which the class is studying the human skeletal system and ways to care for the skeleton. Helpful visuals that teachers will naturally consider to use are pictures of bones, actual samples of bones, and perhaps samples of x-rays. Imagine that the students are reading a section on cartilage, learning how cartilage is elastic-like when it is young and becomes brittle and as it grows old. The sheltered instructor will additionally think to bring in a piece of elastic to illustrate *elastic-like* and a dried twig to snap when referring to the term *brittle*. Thus, with no additional classroom time, through the teacher's use of such effective visuals the ELL student can also understand along with the English speakers in the class how cartilage is flexible when young and inflexible and easily broken as it ages.

Extensive Use of Hands-On Experiences   Another classic way to make use of realia and visuals is to turn lengthy lectures or lengthy reading assignments into hands-on experiential activities or to precede lengthy reading assignments with a hands-on experience. Therefore, before reading about water displacement theory, students actually design clay boats and determine which boats float and which boats do not float. Then they discuss in pairs or small groups why certain boats float and others sink—thus creating a shared history. Then they are introduced to the topic through lecture or reading. The more the students can work with manipulatives, the more that lessons are not delivered simply through language; consequently, English language learners will receive more chances to be able to make sense of the course content.

The use of visuals and manipulatives are common in the elementary classrooms. Middle schools and high schools use them considerably less often. Nevertheless, their use is essential if a teacher wishes to accommodate the language learning students in the classroom. Moreover, their use enhances the comprehensibility of the content for other students in the classroom whose learning styles may lean to the visual or tactile.

Creating Opportunities to Negotiate Meaning

A third way to contextualize a lesson is to provide ample opportunities for students to negotiate meaning. Unlike reading in isolation, during which the reader cannot check for understanding with the author, the classroom provides the perfect venue for students and teachers to regularly negotiate meaning to ensure that both understand what the other is saying.

Increased Question-and-Answer Opportunities   The most obvious way to increase classroom opportunities for students to negotiate meaning is to increase the number of question and answer opportunities. But we know that what does not work is for the teacher to merely ask, "Are there any questions"—particularly if the pause time after this teacher question is not sufficient enough to signal to the students that they are expected to think on the topic for the moment and that questions are truly welcomed. So the first recommendation in this category is for teachers to provide plenty of opportunities for questions and answers and to be sensitive to the pause time needed after such invitations for questions. Another excellent way to allow for questions and answers is to provide plenty of opportunities for one-on-one interactions as a teacher moves about a classroom, while students are working on projects, or before or after class.

Inquiry-Based Instructional Style, Instructional Conversations   A second way to ensure that students can negotiate meaning is to shift instructional style from lecturing to conducting instructional conversations, or inquiry-based discussions. In such teacher-fronted events the teacher may initiate a discussion by wondering aloud on a topic; however, because the teacher does not lecture and does not evaluate student responses but rather signals only that she or he is listening to the students' ideas by paraphrasing or repeating the students' thoughts or is simply responding with "uh-huh"-type responses, the class discussion becomes driven by the students' ideas, guided by the teacher's effective questioning strategies. Chapter 8 provides details about instructional conversations.

Tickets into or out of the Classroom   Another creative way for students to be given the opportunity to ask questions and for teachers to negotiate meaning is to ask students to produce *tickets* to allow them out of class at the end of class or into the class at the beginning of class. Such tickets can consist of assignments like the following:

List three things you learned in today's class.
List one thing you have learned and one question you are still wondering about.
Identify three ways to care for your skeleton; also, ask any questions you may still have.

Give One, Get One Activity   A fourth strategy to allow students to negotiate meaning is an activity called *give one, get one*. In this activity, after a lesson has occurred or during a lesson, after a particular learning event has occurred, each student is provided a handout, which looks like Figure 7.2.

Students are asked to identify one thing they have learned and one thing they still have questions about. Then they are invited to get up and walk around the room interviewing other students and writing down from each student they meet one thing that student has learned or one question that student still has. They are instructed also to write down the interviewed student's name next to the recorded entry. Students are given 5–10 minutes to get as many additional ideas or questions recorded on their sheet as possible; then they are asked to return to their seats.

Write down one thing that you have learned in this lesson.	Write down one question that you still have about this lesson.
1.	1.
2.	2.
3.	3.
4.	4.
5.	5.
6.	6.
7.	7.
8.	8.
9.	9.
10.	10.

Figure 7.2 Give one, get one.

In full-class discussion, students report on what other students have learned or still are wondering about. They are instructed to identify the other students' ideas by using the students' names, such as, "Tom says that he is still wondering how to best care for a broken bone," or "Susie reported that she now knows how to measure the mass of the item." Through this interaction, students can articulate in their own words what they are learning or still questioning. Students who are hesitant to speak up in full-class discussions will hear their ideas presented to the full class with their names attached; this is a validating experience for quiet students. And teachers can take a temperature of the room to determine what content has indeed been learned by the majority of the class and what content needs further coverage.

Contextualizing lessons is the foundation on which sheltered instruction is designed. Teachers take the mainstream course content and find ways to ensure a shared background; they use an abundance of visuals and hands-on activities; and they provide for plenty of opportunities for students to negotiate meaning. Following are two samples of mainstream lessons that teachers have modified through contextualization so that the lessons are more comprehensible to the integrated ELLs in the classroom.

Lesson 1: DNA, Ninth-Grade Biology Class Using the textbook *Biology: The Living Science* (1998), mainstream students are expected to read about DNA structure and the findings of scientists Chargaff, Franklin, and Watson & Crick. To provide a sense of the language and reading skills required to process the text, a brief excerpt of the chapter is included here.

Chargaff's Rules

In 1950, American biochemist Erwin Chargaff discovered a curious fact about the nucleotides in DNA. Chargaff studied the nucleotide composition of many different samples of DNA, and he found that the amount of each type of nucleotide differed in each sample. However, the amounts also followed a distinct pattern. The amounts of adenine (A) thymine (T) were almost always equal, as were the amounts of cytosine (C) and guanine (G).

This pattern has proven true for the DNA of almost every organism, and it is now known as Chargaff's rules. However, neither Chargaff nor any of his contemporaries had any idea why DNA should follow this pattern (pp. 175, 176).

Recognizing that a number of students in her biology class were English language learners and were at varying language proficiency levels, this high school biology teacher (anonymous by choice) decided she wanted to contextualize this lesson to increase its comprehensibility. She designed the following lesson activity to accomplish this (see Figure 7.3).

In this assignment, the chart becomes a visual display of the same information about the distribution of adenine, thymine, cytosine and guanine. By asking the students to study the chart and by identifying the numeric DNA patterns for the various animals, students are collectively able to build a background of understanding; they are in a sense creating a shared history. And if they are allowed to work in pairs on this assignment, they would be provided the opportunity to negotiate meaning. Through this hands-on experience, shared with other students, the ELL students are much more prepared to attempt to engage with the subsequent written textbook or the classroom discussion—which will be conducted in the medium of academic English. Interestingly, many other non-ELL students will also benefit from this assignment, because it allows the students to engage in the meaning of the content in a variety of ways rather than just through reading a text.

Lesson 2. Colonization of Indochina, High School History Lesson   This lesson comes from a high school history unit titled "Debating the Future of Indochina in 1945: Making Your Case," (Danford, 2002) modified by Immacolata Testa, a high school ESL teacher in the vocational system in Meriden, Connecticut, when this lesson was prepared. Ms. Testa revised the originally designed classroom activities through contextualization to make the dense text and language-heavy activities more accessible to language learning students, as illustrated by Figures 7.4–7.6.

To provide a sense of the language proficiency required to access the dense reading text, a brief section of the reading text is included here. It should be noted, however, that Ms. Testa added simplified summaries in the margins to make the text more accessible to the new English speakers. This instructional strategy is discussed in the next section of this chapter. An excerpt of the reading is shown in Figure 7.4.

In the previous lesson, Ms. Testa had already activated previous background by asking students to identify the key countries on the map, to share what those countries are called by members of the class who are not from the United States, and to share what they already know about those countries. Thus, the class had already begun to create a shared history. As student were asked to read sections of the text, Ms. Testa, assigned them to pairs and had them fill out the T-chart illustrated in Figure 7.5. This T-chart has been partially filled out to assist the ELL learners as they attempt to negotiate the written text. Other T-charts designed for the mainstream students may contain key questions they need to answer or simply may have instructions to write down the main ideas for each of the four sections of the chart. This chart visually organizes the reading material into three clear sections—Indochina, French Occupation, and Japanese Occupation—thus assisting the ELLs by providing

Name: _____   Date: _____

Introduction to DNA Structure: Chargaff's Rules
Homework

In 1950 an American scientist, Erwin Chargaff, discovered an interesting pattern in DNA. None of the scientists at the time had any idea what the results meant, but they believed the results were important. See what you think:

A, T, G, and C represent 4 pieces of the DNA molecule.

Species	%A	%T	%G	%C
Human	20	20	30	30
Chimpanzee	18	18	32	32
Zebra fish	28	28	22	22
Yeast	30	30	20	20
Iguana	19	19	31	31

1. What is the pattern Chargaff discovered?

    _____

2. What do you think this data may suggest? (Hint: check the picture on page 177 of your book if you need help.)

    _____

    _____

3. Add Chargaff and his experiment to your concept map from class.

Figure 7.3 Introduction to DNA structure: Chargraff's Rules. Class: Biology, 9th grade, Unit: DNA.

Modified Text for Beginner and Early Intermediate ELLs

French Occupation

France sent its navy into the waters off Vietnam, and what started out as protection for the missionaries turned into an effort to take over the area completely. By the 1980's, France had conquered Indochina and declared it a colony. This was not unusual for that time; many countries took over other regions and countries without asking the residents what they wanted. For many years, this was just the way things worked, and not many people thought anything of it.

Indochina, however, was never a quiet colony for France. Right from the start, rebel groups were organizing themselves, trying to get France out of their country. With France in charge, Indochina became very poor; schools had to close down and much of the money in the area went to the French government. Vietnam was especially active in resisting French power. Many Vietnamese scholars organized peaceful rebel groups and tried to make their own government to replace the French. Other groups sent representatives to Paris to ask France to grant rights, and by the 1930s, the Vietnamese protesters were getting violent. Some terrorist groups started bombing French buildings and assassinating French officials.

- By 1890, France occupied the area and claimed Indochina as a colony.

- Rebel groups organized to get France out
- France didn't take Vietnamese requests for freedoms and equal rights seriously. Protesters became violent and terrorist groups started bombing French buildings and killing French gov't. employees (officials).

Figure 7.4 Sample of reading text: French occupation of Indochina. Class: History, grades 9–12; Unit: Debating the future of Indochina in 1945; Teacher: Immacolata Testa, Meriden, CT.

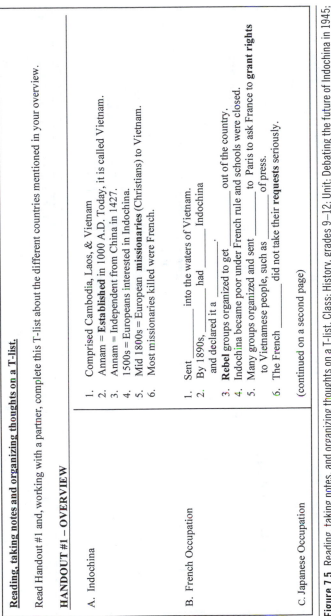

Reading, taking notes and organizing thoughts on a T-list.

Read Handout #1 and, working with a partner, complete this T-list about the different countries mentioned in your overview.

HANDOUT #1 – OVERVIEW

A. Indochina

1. Comprised Cambodia, Laos, & Vietnam
2. Annam = **Established** in 1000 A.D. Today, it is called Vietnam.
3. Annam = Independent from China in 1427.
4. 1500s = Europeans interested in Indochina.
5. Mid 1800s = European **missionaries** (Christians) to Vietnam.
6. Most missionaries killed were French.

B. French Occupation

1. Sent _____ into the waters of Vietnam.
2. By 1890s, _____ had _____ Indochina and declared it a _____.
3. **Rebel** groups organized to get _____ out of the country.
4. Indochina became poor under French rule and schools were closed.
5. Many groups organized and sent _____ to Paris to ask France to **grant rights** to Vietnamese people, such as _____ of press.
6. The French _____ did not take their **requests** seriously.

C. Japanese Occupation

(continued on a second page)

Figure 7.5 Reading, taking notes, and organizing thoughts on a T-list. Class: History, grades 9–12; Unit: Debating the future of Indochina in 1945; Teacher: Immacolata Testa, Meriden, CT.

Lesson 1:

HOMEWORK ASSIGNMENT:

After reading handout #1 (overview), please ponder the following questions (and try to answer them in your notebook):

1) What do you think should happen to Indochina now?

2) Who gets to decide? Does France get the region back since they had it before? Should Vietnam, Laos, and Cambodia just be made independent countries with their own governments?

3) Japan "owned" the region last; and since the U.S. beat Japan, should the U.S. now control the region?

4) China helped Vietnamese rebels set up the government that's now in charge. Should China be in control?

Figure 7.6 Homework assignment: Questions to ponder. Class: History, grades 9–12; Unit: Debating the future of Indochina in 1945; Teacher: Immacolata Testa, Meriden, CT.

the major subtopics of the text. Working in pairs, students were encouraged to negotiate meaning through their own discussions.

Finally, in the homework assignment (Figure 7.6) students were asked to ponder a series of questions. Notice that these are not recall questions that ask students to recall facts from the reading; rather, students were asked to begin to wonder, to opine, about their own ideas. Encouraging students to have their own opinions, to speculate, once more creates a shared history and the opportunity to negotiate meaning as they begin to prepare to take part in an oral debate about the future of Indochina.

The chapter has thus far discussed methods whereby instructors can contextualize entire lessons, thus making the lesson's content more comprehensible to those students who do not have a strong proficiency in the language of the lesson. Three primary strategies have been identified to accomplish this contextualization: (1) creating a shared background; (2) using visuals, realia, and hands-on experiences; and (3) creating opportunities for students to negotiate meaning.

Because course content is delivered via the medium of the English language, two particular aspects of course content delivery are particularly problematic for secondary ELL students: (1) reading academic texts; and (2) listening and understanding academic classroom talk. Therefore, each of these particular challenges is addressed in the next section of the chapter.

Making Written Academic Text Comprehensible

Three important ways to help make text comprehensible already have been discussed: (1) building background knowledge (shared history); (2) increasing the use of visuals and realia to accompany a written text; and (3) providing opportunities for students to negotiate meaning. Three additional instructional strategies to make written academic text comprehensible are (1) use of graphic organizers; (2) use of timelines and summary outlines; and (3) modifying text as access into authentic text.

Graphic Organizers

Graphic organizers are a way of organizing the course content's meaning visually. Traditionally, graphic organizers are used as a postreading tool or a tool to be used concurrently while reading an assignment, and these remain excellent instructional strategies. But the sheltered instructor will make an additional use of graphic organizers by using them as a prereading tool.

For example, consider the following worksheets handed out to tenth-grade ELL history students as a preparation for the next day's reading and discussion on the topic of "Causes for the Dust Bowl," a lesson within a unit on "The Great Depression" designed by Mr. Michael Crotta of New Haven, Connecticut. The first worksheet (Figure 7.7), the simpler of the two, was designed for students possessing beginning levels of ESL proficiency. The latter of the two worksheets (Figure 7.8) was designed for intermediate level proficiency—and for any other students who may wish to have a preview of coming events. Language learning students would have the opportunity to take home the prepared graphic organizers and to use their dictionaries to make sense of a limited text. Though the text is limited, the information students can glean from such limited text, organized as it is visually, will provide ELL students more opportunities for access into the complicated text of the following day's readings and topic discussions.

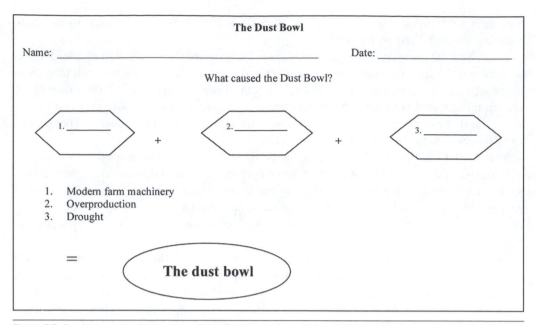

Figure 7.7 Graphic organizer for beginning ELLs: Dust Bowl. Class: History, 10th grade; Unit: Great Depression; Teacher: Michael Crotta, New Haven, CT.

Figure 7.9 is another example of a graphic organizer designed to be used as a prereading and concurrent reading tool to make the text's content comprehensible. This graphic organizer was also created by Mr. Crotta as part of his 10th-grade unit on the Great Depression. This organizer has been partially filled out for intermediate ELL students; it could have been fully filled out for beginning-level ELL students. In preparation for reading, ELL students receive this handout before they attempt to read the text so that they might become familiar with core ideas and language. This will help them determine what they should focus on and search for in the dense reading text.

For beginning ESL students who have little or no knowledge of English, they could be given this same graphic organizer already filled out in simple English. They could work through the text of the graphic organizer to glean the essential information from the reading text.

Timelines and Summary Outlines

Timelines and brief summary outlines are an excellent way of providing to language learning students the essential gist of text. Two examples of such summary outlines can effectively illustrate this. Referring once again to the lesson on the colonization of Indochina, Ms. Testa created the timeline shown in Figure 7.10. Used as a prereading tool, this timeline can help students make sense of long, dense academic text.

Similarly, Figure 7.11 depicts a timeline of the chapters from the novel *The Contender*, designed by Ms. Lorraine Pica, of the Salisbury, Maryland, school system while she was a graduate student and was functioning as an ESL tutor at the town's high school. The student whom she was tutoring had been assigned to a high school literature class, where she sat in the back, did not understand the language, was left alone during class, and was failing the course. Ms. Pica met with the student once a week. She provided her with this timeline as one tool to help make sense of the extended text—written in a new, foreign language from

Name: _____

Date: _____

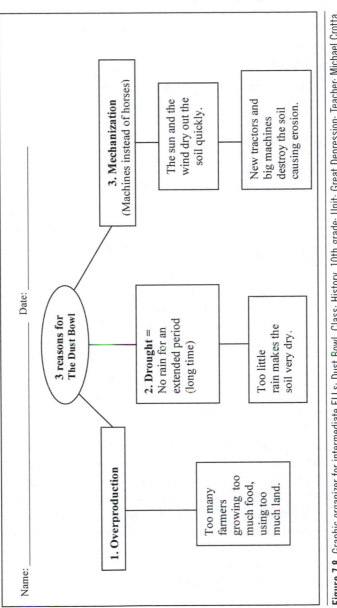

3 reasons for The Dust Bowl

1. Overproduction

Too many farmers growing too much food, using too much land.

2. Drought = No rain for an extended period (long time)

Too little rain makes the soil very dry.

3. Mechanization (Machines instead of horses)

The sun and the wind dry out the soil quickly.

New tractors and big machines destroy the soil causing erosion.

Figure 7.8 Graphic organizer for intermediate ELLs: Dust Bowl. Class: History, 10th grade; Unit: Great Depression; Teacher: Michael Crotta, New Haven, CT.

Lesson 4: President Hoover's Efforts.   **Section 3 reading guide for ESL students**

Name: _____   Date: _____

President Hoover intervened (he tried) four times to help the United States economy during the Depression. As you read pages 656 and 657, please complete the chart below.

President Hoover intervenes in the economy

Action (intervention)	Purpose (reason)
1. Construction projects like the Boulder Dam	
2.	To raise crop prices for farmers
3. Federal Home Loan Bank Act	
4.	Gave emergency money to banks

Figure 7.9 Partially filled-out graphic organizer to accompany reading for intermediate ELLs. Class: History, 10th grade; Unit: Great Depression; Teacher: Michael Crotta, New Haven, CT.

this particular student's perspective. With this tool, and with the help of negotiating meaning in these weekly tutorial sessions, the ELL student was able by the end of the unit to write a very brief paragraph conveying the idea that sometimes she, too, feels like a contender.

Modification of Text

A third way to make dense text accessible to language learning students is to actually modify the text. This is sometimes seen as a controversial suggestion, suggesting that it dumbs down the authentic text. This argument makes sense for the elementary grades, where students must have full, rich access to the authentic text to acquire that language. But at the middle and secondary level, oftentimes a dense text is simply too inaccessible to someone who is just beginning to learn the language. Yet the immediacy for the student to understand the course content is palpable. At these times, it makes sense to offer the student an accommodation that will allow that student access to the course content. If such accommodations are made and materials are modified for ELL students, the recommendation given here is that they be used to supplement the authentic text, not to replace the authentic text.

Margin Summaries or Highlighted Sections   One way to modify text is to offer simplified summaries of paragraphs on the margins of the text. Figure 7.4 provides an illustration of how Ms. Testa simplified the written text by summarizing on the margins. Or a teacher can simply highlight the important sentences in a paragraph and teach the ELL student to selectively try to read first the highlighted sections of the text.

Rewritten Text   Another option is to simply rewrite portions of text. Following is the rewrite of the introduction to *The Invisible Man* by Ralph Ellison as part of an 11th-grade instructional unit modified by Ms. Stevie Randhawa, (Kennedy & Gioia, 2002) a graduate student

TIME LINE OF EVENTS

1000 — Empire of Annam (Vietnam) was established.

1100's — Kingdom of Khmer (Laos & Cambodia) was established.

1427 — Annam (Vietnam) became independent from China.

1500's — Europeans became interested in the area.

1800's — Europeans began converting natives of Indochina.

1890's — France conquered and colonized Indochina.

1930's — Vietnam began protesting against French powers.

1940 — Japan sent troops to Indochina.

1945 — Japan gave control to Bao Dai's Government.

Figure 7.10 Timeline of events: Indochina. Class: History, grades 9–12; Unit: Debating the future of Indochina in 1945; Teacher: Immacolata Testa, Meriden, CT.

TIME LINE OF EVENTS   THE CONTENDER by Robert Lipsyte

Chapter	Event
1	Boy robs store.
2	Alfred goes to Donatelli's gym.
4	Alfred visits Aunt Dorothy & Uncle Wilson.
5	Alfred decides to be a contender.
6	First day training at the gym.
7	Madison Square Garden Boxing match.
8	Alfred says No to Hollis & Major. Will not rob the store with them.
9	Alfred tells Aunt Pearl about boxing.
10	Alfred tired, frustrated.
11	Clubroom party & Coney Island.
12	Alfred almost quits.
13	Custom mouthpiece.
14	Wins first fight.
15	Aunt Pearl shares her girlhood dream.
16	KO's Griffin.
17	Thanksgiving with family.
18	Donatelli wants Alfred to quit.
19	Alfred fights a good fight. (Loses.)
20	Alfred helps James.

Figure 7.11 Chapter timeline of "The Contender." Class: English literature, grades 9–12; Unit: The Contender; Teacher: Lorraine Pica, Salisbury, MD. This figure is reprinted here with permission of *Thresholds in Education Journal*, Northern Illinois University, DeKalb, IL. http:www.cedu.niu.edu/lepf/thresholds

at Southern Connecticut State University. Figure 7.12 shows the introduction to the novel: two paragraphs of beautifully written, dense text. Ms. Randhawa's lesson plans called for a full class period to discuss the meanings within this introduction. Yet she was aware that she had multiple language proficiencies present in the classroom. Consequently, she rewrote the introduction for four levels of language development to include one for ELL students who had significant lapses in their formal education and were developing their first literacy skills while learning English as a new language. These rewrites are shown in Figure 7.13.

Another example of modifying written text is the following work designed by Ms. Mary Johnson for an 11th-grade English literature course covering Shakespeare's *Julius Caesar*. Ms. Johnson provided a simply written two-page summary of Act 1, Scene 1, one page of which is illustrated in Figure 7.14. Notice her intentional use of repeated syntactic patterns to make the sentences more readily comprehensible for the early language learner.

Figure 7.15 illustrates a marvelous set of text modifications for a middle school poetry class discussing Alfred Noyes' "The Highwayman (Hume, 1999)." Ms. Pat McGovern of New Haven, Connecticut, took the textbook pages, one of which contains the poem and the second of which contains an illustration of the highwayman, and wrote short summary statements in the margin, framed out the stanza she wanted the ELL students to be fully aware of, added a small glossary below the text, and labeled important aspects of the illustration. Consider how much more accessible this modified version of the poem is to the language learning students than the original, unmarked version would be. Teachers should keep several copies of modified, marked versions of their school texts for their beginning ELL students so that they, too, may have access to the meaning of the authentic text, which will be discussed in class on any given day.

This section has looked at ways to make dense, written academic text accessible to ELL students who are at early levels of their language proficiency. Strategies to accomplish this include (1) using graphic organizers as prereading tools, sometimes fully filled out for beginning language learners; (2) using timelines and other summary outlines; and (3) actually modifying the written text by highlighting key phrases, summarizing in the margins, or providing rewritten summary gists. Such modified texts are not meant to replace the authentic texts; rather, they are meant as supplementary materials to be used as access into the content of dense texts.

Making Classroom Talk Comprehensible

Classroom talk—whether teacher lectures or classroom discussion—can sound like a stream of unintelligible speech to the language learner. Consider your own experience when exposed to a foreign film without having access to English subtitles. Many of the strategies already mentioned can be helpful in making such talk comprehensible, particularly the use of visuals, ensuring shared background knowledge, and creating extensive opportunities to negotiate meaning and to check for understanding. This section offers several other instructional strategies to assist in making classroom talk comprehensible.

Adjusting Teacher's Speech

Teachers can learn to speak in ways that are better understood by new English language learners. This does not mean that teachers need to speak more slowly or loudly; rather, they need to learn how to pause and repeat important terms and expressions more frequently.

Lesson 1
Handout 1

Name:
Date:

Invisible Man
Prologue Paragraphs 1 and 2

I am an invisible man. No, I am not a spook like those who haunted Edgar Allan Poe; nor am I one of your Hollywood-movie ectoplasms. I am a man of substance, of flesh and bone, fiber and liquids — and I might even be said to possess a mind. I am invisible, understand, simply because people refuse to see me. Like the bodiless heads you see sometimes in circus sideshows, it is as though I have been surrounded by mirrors of hard, distorting glass. When they approach me they see only my surroundings, themselves, or figments of their imagination — indeed, everything and anything except me.

Nor is my invisibility exactly a matter of a biochemical accident of the epidermis. That invisibility to which I refer occurs because of a peculiar disposition of the eyes of those with whom I come in contact. A matter of the construction of the *inner* eyes, those eyes with which they look through their physical eyes upon reality. I am not complaining, nor am I protesting either. It is sometimes advantageous to be unseen, although it is most often rather wearing on the nerves. Then too, you're constantly being bumped against by those of poor vision. Or again, you often doubt if you really exist. You wonder if you aren't simply a phantom in other people's minds. Say, a figure in a nightmare which the sleeper tries with all his strength to destroy. It's when you feel like this that, out of resentment, you begin to bum people back. And, let me confess, you feel that way most of the time. You ache with the need to convince yourself that you do exist in the real world, that you're a part of all the sound and anguish, and you strike out with your fists, you curse and you swear to make them recognize you. And, alas, it's seldom successful.

Ellison, R., Invisible Man, Pearson/Longman., p.32.

Figure 7.12 Prologue to "Invisible Man." Class: Literature/Language Arts, grades 9–Adult; Unit: Invisible Man; Teacher: Parminder Stevie Randhawa, New Haven, CT.

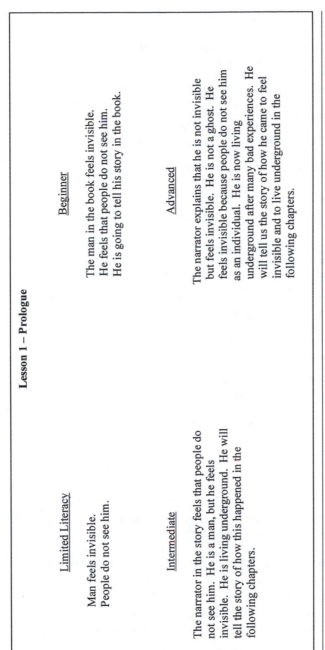

Lesson 1 – Prologue

Limited Literacy

Man feels invisible.
People do not see him.

Intermediate

The narrator in the story feels that people do
not see him. He is a man, but he feels
invisible. He is living underground. He will
tell the story of how this happened in the
following chapters.

Beginner

The man in the book feels invisible.
He feels that people do not see him.
He is going to tell his story in the book.

Advanced

The narrator explains that he is not invisible
but feels invisible. He is not a ghost. He
feels invisible because people do not see him
as an individual. He is now living
underground after many bad experiences. He
will tell us the story of how he came to feel
invisible and to live underground in the
following chapters.

Figure 7.13 Rewritten text to "The Invisible Man" prologue written for 4 levels of language proficiency. Class: English Literature, 11th grade; Unit: Invisible Man; Teacher: Parminder Stevie Randhawa, New Haven, CT.

Act 1, Scene 1:

Caesar has returned to Rome after defeating Pompey.
Pompey used to rule Rome.
Caesar won the war.
Now Caesar rules Rome.

The people of Rome are happy that Caesar won.
The people of Rome are celebrating.
The people of Rome are not working today.
The people of Rome are in the streets to see Caesar.

Flavius and Marullus do not like Caesar.
Flavius and Marullus believe Caesar has too much power.
Flavius and Marullus are angry that the people are not at work.

A carpenter and a cobbler are with a crowd of people.

Marullus asks the carpenter "What is your job?"

The carpenter says, "I am a carpenter."

Marullus is angry at the carpenter.
Marullus is angry because the carpenter is not at work.
Marullus is angry because the carpenter is not in his work clothes.
Marullus asks the cobbler what his job is.

The cobbler does not like Marullus.
The cobbler decides to joke with Marullus.
The cobbler tells Marullus that he is a cobbler.*
(* The word "cobbler" also meant "a clumsy worker.")

Marullus does not like the joke.
Marullus tells the cobbler to be honest with him.

The cobbler tells Marullus that he likes his job.
The cobbler tells Marullus that he mends soles.

Flavius is angry.

(Page 1 of 2)

Figure 7.14 Rewriting of act 1, scene 1 for Shakespeare's "Julius Caesar." Class: English Literature, 11th grade; Unit: The Tragedy of Julius Caesar. Teacher: Mary Johnson, Naugatuck, CT.

Pausing When a teacher pauses after certain phrases, the language learner has the chance to process what is being said. Teachers are encouraged to speak in their natural pace and tone but to make more use of pauses: at the end of sentences and with longer wait times after asking a question. Even while teachers are lecturing, if ELLs are in the room it can be an effective strategy to review important concepts, making use of pauses after each important concept.

Frequent Repetition of Important Terms and Expressions In every discipline, for every topic, some key phrases and expressions contain high frequency and significance. Such phrases should be repeated often. For example, if during an eighth-grade science lesson on three functions of bone tissue students read that bones are the *site of cell making,* the teacher

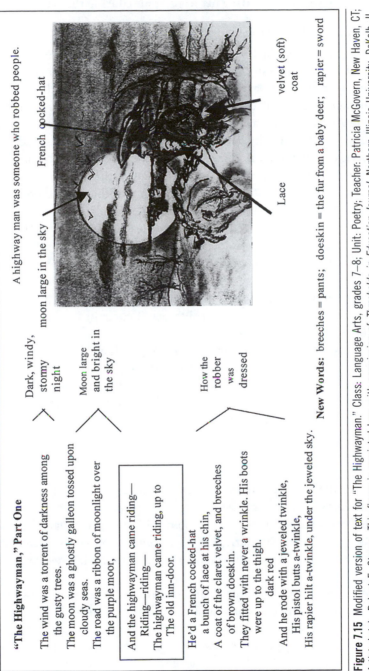

"The Highwayman," Part One

The wind was a torrent of darkness among
the gusty trees.
The moon was a ghostly galleon tossed upon
cloudy seas.
The road was a ribbon of moonlight over
the purple moor,

And the highwayman came riding—
Riding—riding—
The highwayman came riding, up to
The old inn-door.

He'd a French cocked-hat
a bunch of lace at his chin,
A coat of the claret velvet, and breeches
of brown doeskin.
They fitted with never a wrinkle. His boots
were up to the thigh.
dark red
And he rode with a jeweled twinkle,
His pistol butts a-twinkle,
His rapier hilt a-twinkle, under the jeweled sky.

A highwayman was someone who robbed people.

Dark, windy,
stormy
night

Moon large
and bright in
the sky

How the
robber
was
dressed

French cocked-hat

moon large in the sky

Lace

velvet (soft)
coat

New Words: breeches = pants; doeskin = the fur from a baby deer; rapier = sword

Figure 7.15 Modified version of text for "The Highwayman." Class: Language Arts, grades 7–8; Unit: Poetry; Teacher: Patricia McGovern, New Haven, CT; Artist sketch: Robert E. Stoops. This figure is reprinted here with permission of *Thresholds in Education Journal*, Northern Illinois University, DeKalb, IL. http:www.cedu.niu.edu/lepf/thresholds

might recognize that expression as an important one; that is, it would be highly productive for the language learners to be able to understand and produce that expression when trying to explain the functions of bone tissue. Therefore, the teacher would make it a point to repeat that expression frequently during her lectures and during the class discussion.

Use of Listening Guides (Partially or Fully Filled Out)

Just as graphic organizers can be a powerful tool to help make sense of written text, they can also be most helpful in making sense of lectures or class discussions. These and other forms of listening guides can be shared with students before the class discussion or lecture so that ELLs can take time to look up words that are new to them and to come to the lecture or discussion already familiar with terms and concepts about to be discussed.

Figure 7.16 is an example of a listening guide designed by a seventh-grade teacher for a unit on the American Revolution. In this case, the guide is designed as a graphic organizer on the advantages and disadvantages facing both the Continental Army and the British Army. Students are expected to listen and to fill in blanks as they hear them.

Figures 7.17 and 7.18 show two styles of listening guides for a discussion on the "Impact of the Depression on Families," developed by 10th-grade teacher Mr. Crotta. The first listening guide was designed for mainstream students to fill out as they took part in a minilecture and subsequent discussion. The second has main points already entered into the ovals; this graphic organizer was developed for beginning ELL students with low levels of language proficiency. They were encouraged to take the graphic organizer home the night before and take the time to translate the terms so that they could come to the discussion somewhat familiar with this English vocabulary.

The next listening guide, shown in Figure 7.19, was developed by Ms. Testa to help early ELL students make sense of the documentary film *Roots of War* (Vecchione, 1983). Notice that all the statements are true and in chronological order. ELL students could take this tool home the night before the film and try to make sense of the brief, written English text. Then, when back in class, they were asked to view the film while looking at the guide and circling any words they may hear and recognize.

Modeling Language and Use of Word Walls

As streams of unintelligible sound surround the new language learner, any access that learner may have to reminders of important terminology and expressions can help. Therefore, it is most valuable to have word walls in the classroom, with new vocabulary posted and easily seen by students at their desks. Similarly, it is most helpful to provide students with samples of modeled expressions so that ELL students can begin to recognize key expressions.

Word Walls   Word walls are commonly found in elementary classrooms because they are powerful tools for literacy development. But they are also powerful tools for second-language vocabulary development, particularly in classrooms where students are learning language at the same time they are engaged in content through the new, target language. Secondary-content teachers who realize this will make use of word walls in their classroom.

An example of such a wall might come from the eighth-grade health class on the skeletal system. On that word wall would be words like *cartilage, elastic-like, brittle,* and *sites of cell making.* Other terms would be added as the unit progressed. Teachers may choose to illustrate new terms with iconic representations—simply hand drawn or from clip art. The

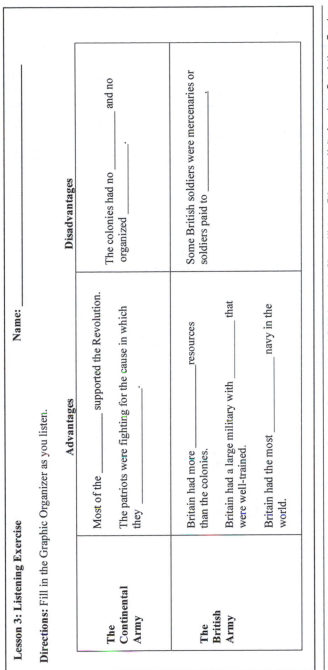

Lesson 3: Listening Exercise　　　　**Name:** _____

Directions: Fill in the Graphic Organizer as you listen.

	Advantages	Disadvantages
The Continental Army	Most of the _____ supported the Revolution. The patriots were fighting for the cause in which they _____.	The colonies had no _____ and no organized _____.
The British Army	Britain had more _____ resources than the colonies. Britain had a large military with _____ that were well-trained. Britain had the most _____ navy in the world.	Some British soldiers were mercenaries or soldiers paid to _____.

Figure 7.16 Listening guide to accompany lecture about the Continental and British armies. Class: History, 7th grade; Unit: American Revolution; Teacher: Anonymous.

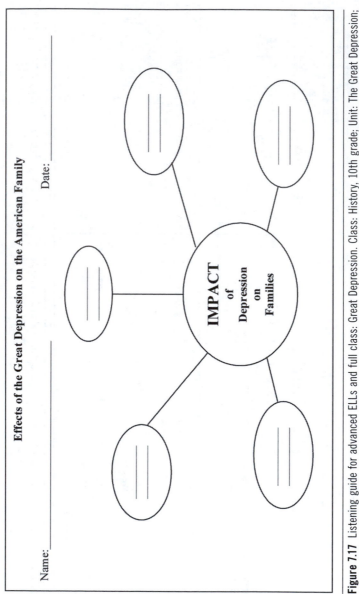

Figure 7.17 Listening guide for advanced ELLs and full class: Great Depression. Class: History, 10th grade; Unit: The Great Depression; Teacher: Michael Crotta, New Haven, CT.

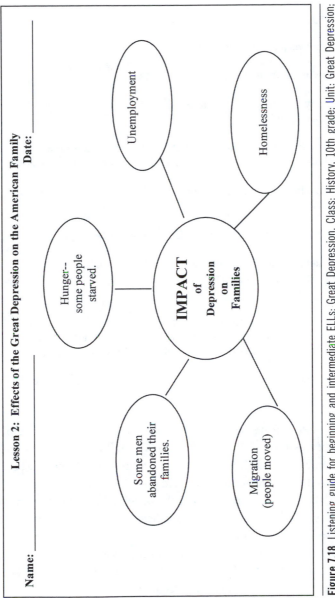

Figure 7.18 Listening guide for beginning and intermediate ELLs: Great Depression. Class: History, 10th grade; Unit: Great Depression; Teacher: Michael Crotta, New Haven, CT.

LISTENING GUIDE on Documentary (Roots of War)

For Pre-Production and Beginner ELLs

DIRECTIONS: As you watch the documentary, "Roots of War", circle any words you hear.

An army of half a million.

Vietnam was an undeclared war.

A war without frontlines or clear objectives.

It was a war with deep roots, deeper than most
Americans knew.

Ho Chi Minh and his followers fought for decades against the
French then against the Americans and their South Vietnamese Ally.

It was the first war Americans opposed in huge numbers, openly and
passionately.

The Vietnam War ended when the Communists took Saigon.

Two and one-half million Americans fought in Vietnam and
58,000 Americans died there.

Figure 7.19 Listening guide to accompany film, "Roots of War," for early ELLs. Class: History, grades 9–12; Unit: Debating the Future of Indochina in 1945; Teacher: Immacolata Testa, Meriden, CT. This figure is reprinted here with permission of *Thresholds in Education Journal*, Northern Illinois University, DeKalb, IL. http:www.cedu.niu.edu/lepf/thresholds

ELL students in the mainstream class will refer to the word wall more frequently than the mainstream teacher can ever imagine.

Modeled Language   Providing samples of modeled language will help ELL students both understand expressions and produce them. The following two examples of modeled language come from Ms. Testa's high school history unit on Indochina. Figure 7.20 depicts a worksheet that students used to glean information from a text followed by small group discussion. Notice that in questions 2 and 3, she provided an example answer so that ELL students can understand how to use the worksheet and can also appreciate some of the language needed to answer the questions. Similarly, in Figure 7.21, which shows a guide designed to accompany a class discussion, Ms. Testa provided sentence starters for the ELL students, such as "I don't like the fact that…" Starters like this help the language learners know how to properly begin statements of agreement and disagreement.

A final example of modeled language comes from a high school English language arts unit on the short film *Cipher in the Snow* (Atkinson, Mizer, & Pearson, 1973). This unit is designed especially to help students learn how to prepare acceptable written responses to state standardized exam questions on literature interpretation. Figure 7.22 shows a handout of questions and expressions to help ELL students know what language is used to discuss understanding, interpretations, connections, or a critical stance. ELL students can use these

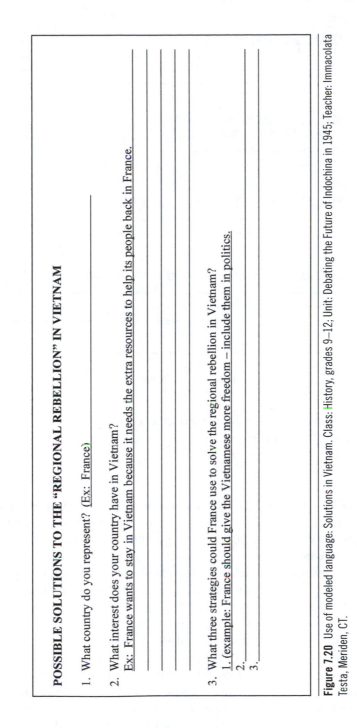

POSSIBLE SOLUTIONS TO THE "REGIONAL REBELLION" IN VIETNAM

1. What country do you represent? (Ex: France)
   _____

2. What interest does your country have in Vietnam?
   Ex: France wants to stay in Vietnam because it needs the extra resources to help its people back in France.
   _____
   _____
   _____
   _____

3. What three strategies could France use to solve the regional rebellion in Vietnam?
   1. (example: France should give the Vietnamese more freedom – include them in politics.
   _____
   2._____
   3._____

Figure 7.20 Use of modeled language: Solutions in Vietnam. Class: History, grades 9–12; Unit: Debating the Future of Indochina in 1945; Teacher: Immacolata Testa, Meriden, CT.

DISCUSSION on PRESENTED PROPOSALS

I.   <u>**What I like**</u> about proposal #1:
            a) I like the fact that _____
            b) _____
            c) _____

II.   <u>**What I don't like**</u> about proposal #1:
            a) I don't like the fact that _____
            b)_____
            c)_____

III.   <u>**What I like and don't like**</u> about proposal #2:
            a)_____
            b)_____
            c)_____

IV.   <u>**What I like and don't like**</u> about my team's proposal:
            a)_____
            b)_____
            c)_____

Figure 7.21 Use of modeled language—for discussion proposals: Vietnam. Class: History, grades 9–12; Unit: Debating the Future of Indochina in 1945; Teacher: Immacolata Testa, Meriden, CT.

expressions and questions to help make sense of class discussions; moreover, these expressions can become part of the student's productive repertoire as the student begins to take part in oral discussions and written assignments.

Framing Main Ideas

A fourth way to make classroom talk more comprehensible is to frame main ideas on the blackboard as classroom lectures or discussions progress. That is, every so often the teacher writes on a designated spot on the board, in telegraphic speech, the main idea of what is being spoken about the moment.

For example, in an eighth-grade science class, the students were observed presenting the findings of their small group science projects. One group was presenting the results of their Pepsi/Coke Taste Test; making use of pictures of Coke and Pepsi and graphs illustrating the survey results. As the group of students continued with their presentation, one of the ELL students tugged on the arm of the researcher and asked, "What are they talking about?" The researcher simply wrote down on this student's notes, "Which tastes better?" This framed the main idea for her, and she was able to follow along from that point on.

There are several explanations for why she was unable to understand this presentation. Perhaps she did not have the cultural background necessary to understand taste tests. Also, she may have missed the first sentence or two of the presentation. It takes language learners several sentences to get used to a new voice and new intonation patterns. Yet in American academic discourse, the first few sentences are used to deliver the main ideas of the ensuing

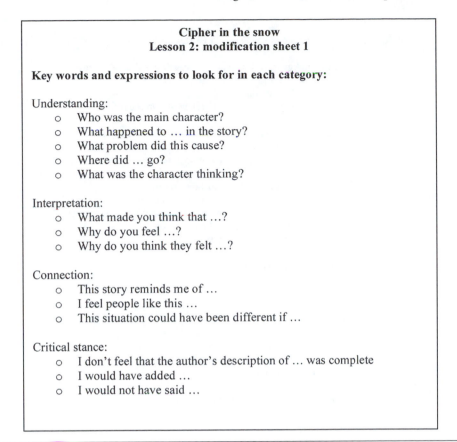

Cipher in the snow
Lesson 2: modification sheet 1

Key words and expressions to look for in each category:

Understanding:
- o   Who was the main character?
- o   What happened to … in the story?
- o   What problem did this cause?
- o   Where did … go?
- o   What was the character thinking?

Interpretation:
- o   What made you think that …?
- o   Why do you feel …?
- o   Why do you think they felt …?

Connection:
- o   This story reminds me of …
- o   I feel people like this …
- o   This situation could have been different if …

Critical stance:
- o   I don't feel that the author's description of … was complete
- o   I would have added …
- o   I would not have said …

Figure 7.22 Use of modeled language: "Cipher in the Snow" exercise. Class: English Literature, grades 9–12; Unit: Poetry; Teacher: Anonymous.

talk. Consequently, ELL students often miss the introductory points of talk. But, by framing the main ideas visually for ELL students, they too can make sense of the essential gist.

An example of how the strategy of framing main ideas can be used in the classroom comes from the seventh-grade history unit on the American Revolution. In this case, each day the teacher wrote the main idea on the board at the beginning of every lesson:

- Lesson 1. How did the Revolutionary War begin?
- Lesson 2. The colonists declare independence!
- Lesson 3. The Continental Army versus the British Army
- Lesson 4. Important battles
- Lesson 5. The end of the war

This section has reviewed instructional strategies to make sense of classroom talk, to include: adjusting teacher speech, using graphic organizers and listening guides, modeling speech and using word walls, and framing main ideas. In an engaged classroom, sometimes classroom talk moves swiftly. The engaging teacher does not want to stall the fast-paced dynamics of an energized classroom. Still, when ELL students are present in the class, the teacher can stop at times for a moment of review and can speak more clearly, making use of pauses and repetitions of important phrases. At that same time, the teacher can take a moment to record the main idea on a specially designated place on the board—a sort

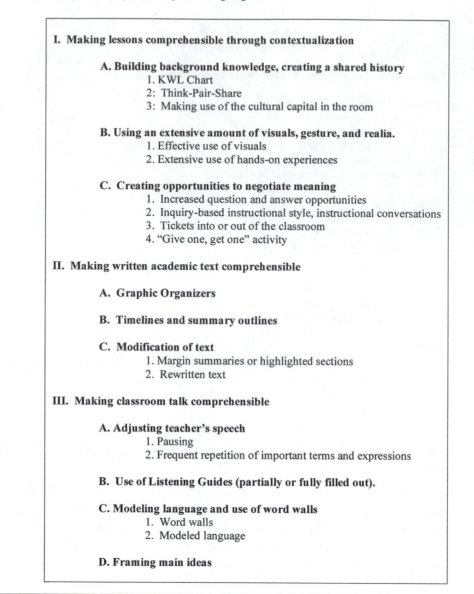

I. **Making lessons comprehensible through contextualization**

    A. **Building background knowledge, creating a shared history**
        1. KWL Chart
        2: Think-Pair-Share
        3: Making use of the cultural capital in the room

    B. **Using an extensive amount of visuals, gesture, and realia.**
        1. Effective use of visuals
        2. Extensive use of hands-on experiences

    C. **Creating opportunities to negotiate meaning**
        1. Increased question and answer opportunities
        2. Inquiry-based instructional style, instructional conversations
        3. Tickets into or out of the classroom
        4. "Give one, get one" activity

II. **Making written academic text comprehensible**

    A. **Graphic Organizers**

    B. **Timelines and summary outlines**

    C. **Modification of text**
        1. Margin summaries or highlighted sections
        2. Rewritten text

III. **Making classroom talk comprehensible**

    A. **Adjusting teacher's speech**
        1. Pausing
        2. Frequent repetition of important terms and expressions

    B. **Use of Listening Guides (partially or fully filled out).**

    C. **Modeling language and use of word walls**
        1. Word walls
        2. Modeled language

    D. **Framing main ideas**

Figure 7.23 Sheltered strategies to make content comprehensible for ELLs.

of headline. Additionally, that same teacher can prepare listening guides for students who may need such assistive tools. With such strategies, the energy of this engaged class can be shared by the language learners in the room.

"Yes, But… ."

A wide variety of strategies have been presented in this chapter to contextualize lessons, to make written text comprehensible, and to make classroom talk comprehensible. A visual summary of these strategies is given in Figure 7.23. Inevitably, in professional development workshops when these sheltered strategies are offered as possible solutions to making content comprehensible to ELLs, teachers are faced with several predictable reactions, described following.

"...But This Is Just Good Instruction"

The first reaction is, "But this is just good instruction; all my students can benefit from this." Truthfully, this comment is heard more frequently from elementary teachers than secondary teachers. The answer to them is this: Yes, the strategies are extremely useful for many of our mainstream students too, particularly any who have any sort of language delay issue. But although these strategies are excellent strategies for all students, for ELL students they are essential. Language learning students, still in the early phases of their new language development, cannot access mainstream content without them.

"...But Who Has the Time?"

A more common comment from secondary teachers is this: "Who has the time?" That is a legitimate concern. Who, indeed, has the time to do any lesson planning, let alone modifying each of those lessons for the ELLs? The response to this concern is complex. First, it is necessary to acknowledge that teachers do not have the time to do what they need to do now as it is. Then, teachers need to be reassured that any little change helps and that even if one accommodation is made in one lesson and the next day another accommodation is tried, the ELL students will receive input that, prior to those accommodations, was absolutely inaccessible to them. As accommodations are made, a teacher's library of sheltered modifications grows from year to year.

But then it is necessary to look at how to find answers outside of the box.

- Summer curriculum grants can be awarded to teachers who wish to take summer time to modify some of their instructional units to provide ELL access.
- Teachers can have mainstream classrooms create graphic organizers as a means of processing course content. Then teachers can take those organizers created by the A students and use them in following years as prereading tools for ELL students.
- Teachers can make use of student community service requirements by requesting more advanced students to create margin summaries or graphic organizers (Fentress, A., 2006, personal communication).
- Teachers can contact local universities that teach content-based ESL courses in their graduate schools and can arrange for graduate students to modify authentic class materials as course assignments.
- Administrators can create physical ways for schools or departments to collect and disseminate locally created materials to all teachers, thereby sharing their work (Commins, N. L., 2006, personal communication).

Collectively, teachers are some of the most creative problem solvers. When they learn that certain tools can facilitate students' learning, they find solutions.

"...But How Is This Fair; Isn't It Cheating?"

We used to worry that giving the main points away in pre-reading exercises or in listening guides would not be fair. Now we realize that we are giving the ELL students course information in short, distilled, gist-like ways, because that is the way that they can make sense of the information embedded in this new, strange language. Consider the following illustration. Imagine that you are in a busy train station in Poland with no knowledge of Polish and have asked the clerk, who speaks no English, for information about connections to Vienna. Imagine that the clerk hands you a five-page booklet filled with various schedules and paragraphs of explanations—in Polish. Now imagine that the same clerk hands you the same booklet but first highlights the section you need to read. Further, he quickly writes out a brief graphic organizer showing you the various ticket options you have. These strategies would help you gain access to the dense amount of information provided in the booklet. Which treatment would you find most helpful?

There is a difference between treating students equally and treating students fairly. Teachers do not question the need to make accommodations for students who are visually impaired and who do not have access to the written word. Similarly, it is necessary to make accommodations for students with hearing impairments, who need access to the oral word. In both cases, students with special needs are not treated equally; they are treated fairly so that they have access to the course content.

English language learners come to the same learning event without access to the meaning of English words and without the ability to parse the long streams of English sound into meaningful units because they are facing a new language. We know that it will take ELL students one to two years to develop their basic, interpersonal spoken language and, on average, an additional three to seven years to fully develop their academic language skills. Reason and social justice would dictate that during that period accommodations must be made to help make the course content comprehensible to them. And if that is not enough, the Supreme Court in the 1974 *Lau vs. Nichols* case determined that "there is no equality of treatment merely by providing students with the same facilities, textbooks, teachers, and curriculum; for students who do not understand English are effectively foreclosed from any meaningful education" (p. 566).

The same arguments for fairness hold true when it comes to assessment. Currently, great outside pressures force educators to measure outcomes through one standardized assessment tool. To accurately measure the learning growth of ELLs, teachers must expect to make accommodations in the testing process as well as in the teaching process: "With the demands being made by state institutions in the name of accountability and productivity, a vital piece of the puzzle has not been considered: test validity…It is an incorrect and erroneous assumption [educators] work under when they consider second language learners to be the same as native English students, except that they 'just need to hurry up and catch up'…Valid testing is all that anyone really wants, and a sense of accountability from the schools…It just seems that the demand for accountability has pushed aside concerns for a valid instrument, and a one-size-fits-all attitude has come to dominate public and political conversations" (Commins & Miramontes, 2005, p. 92). Chapter 17 further discusses the issues of assessment.

"…But I Want to Give the Students the Full Flavor of the Text"

This comment usually comes from language arts teachers who love their language and the written works produced by their favorite authors. Rightfully, they want to share that beauty with their students. When teachers present this argument in workshops or in class, one of us provides them a beautiful poem by Lermontov, written in the Russian Cyrillic alphabet or she recites it to them in Russian. The teacher may enjoy the sound of the strange language, but has that teacher appreciated any of the flavor of the text? Obviously not; the oral text is inaccessible to the listener.

For high school language arts teachers who wish to preserve some of the beauty of the authentic text, but who also want to find ways to convey the gist of the text meaning to the language learning students we recommend the following. For the sake of content comprehension use the techniques of making written text comprehensible but also extract out some small, reasonable quote or series of quotes and ask the ELL students to read through those quotes, thus providing them with brief opportunities to begin to experience the full flavor of the text.

An example of this can be seen in Figure 7.15, which illustrates "The Highwayman," where four lines have been framed:

"And the highwayman came riding—

Riding—riding—

The highwayman came riding, up to

The old inn-door."

Additionally, the teacher who modified the text for William Shakespeare's *Julius Caesar* (Figure 7.14) could similarly have selected several well-known lines from this act and introduced them to the ELL students.

Research that Supports Sheltered Instruction

The purpose of sheltered instruction is to make content comprehensible through a variety of strategies and to engage students in that content through cognitively stimulating interaction with the content, with fellow students, and with the teacher. A task with a purpose as broad and extensive as this presents a myriad of research areas to consider. The following review of the relevant research focuses on two distinct areas that are most likely less well known to educator practitioners: the role of comprehensibility and negotiation of meaning on second-language development and the measured impact of sheltered instruction on student performance.

Role of Comprehensibility and Negotiation of Meaning on Second-Language Development

There exists a large literature over the past 25 years on the topic of comprehensibility negotiation of meaning in second-language development.

Pica's (1994, pp. 500–01) review of negotiation research neatly outlines three conditions that language learners need to learn a language:

1. "Comprehension of message meaning is necessary if learners are to internalize L2 [second language] forms and structures that encode the message … input must be made comprehensible if it is to assist the acquisition process" (see, e.g., Krashen, 1980, 1985; Long, 1980, 1983, 1985a, 1985b).
2. "Learner production of modified output is also necessary for L2 mastery…comprehensible output" (Swain, 1985).
3. "Attention to L2 form is needed as learners attempt to process meaningful input (Long, 1990; Rutherford & Sharwood Smith, 1985; Schmidt, 1990; Sharwood Smith, 1991)" and "…with comprehension seen (particularly by Krashen, 1983, 1985) as the 'entrance requirement' for access to form."

Although it is difficult to precisely capture the particular relevance of comprehensibility to specific linguistic or cognitive aspects of second-language acquisition (SLA), there is little debate over the necessity of comprehensibility of language input for SLA.

In this review of the literature, Pica (1994) highlights several important studies emphasizing that modifying the input can assist in making a message more comprehensible. Three studies in particular reveal that modified language input can increase comprehensibility;

that is, by changing the input, by simplifying the language in some ways, the message becomes increasingly understandable. Studies by Chaudron (1983) and Long (1985a) show that second language learners could comprehend and recall the content of small lectures when the words and sentences in the lectures were modified to include more repetitions, more use of paraphrases, insertions of conjunctions, and enumerators that mark relationships. Pica, Young, and Doughty (1987) followed up with a study looking at interactions composed of one speaker giving directives to a hearer, who had to follow the directions. When the directives were given with modified input to increase comprehensibility—by the use of repetitions, rephrasings, and reduction in syntactic complexity—the hearers were better able to follow directions. These three studies strongly suggest that modified input can increase comprehensibility of message.

The next direction the research took was to explore how negotiations of meaning in interaction enhance the comprehensibility of message meaning. In other words, researchers wanted to see if allowing interlocutors to interact about their understanding would enhance the language learner's comprehension of a message. In the Pica, Young, and Doughty (1987) study, in which interlocutors gave each other directions on a task, under another experimental condition the input was not modified at all; rather, the interlocutors, particularly the language-learning hearer, was encouraged to ask as many questions as needed to ensure comprehension of the message. This condition produced significant improvement on message comprehensibility over the control group and over the condition previously mentioned, where the input directions had been modified and simplified. Interestingly, even language learners who had simply observed these negotiations for meaning and had not taken part in the negotiations benefited from the interactions in that they, too, performed more highly on the direction-following tasks, thus indicating an increased comprehensibility.

The studies mentioned thus far speak to the first condition of what second-language learners need; that is, learners need to have comprehensible input. This input can be made comprehensible through speaker modifications. Additionally, and even more significantly regarding SLA, the input can be made comprehensible through negotiating meaning in interaction.

The last two conditions of what learners need are to create comprehensible output and to attend to L2 form. Both of these aspects of SLA are also significantly affected by negotiation of meaning, as reported in the major review article on the role of input and interaction in SLA by Gass, Mackey, and Pica (1998). According to this review, Holliday (1995) and Linnell (1995) report that as a result of negotiation for meaning, learners modify their output in ways that often produce more target-like language structures. Pica (1994, 1996) show that as a result of negotiations for meaning, learners produced output with a variety of linguistic modifications, all of which are able to provide the language learner with lexical and grammatical information about the target language. Finally, Nobuyoshi and Ellis (1993), LaPierrre (1994), and Donato (1994) all show that adolescent and adult learners' output produced as the result of negotiations for meaning result in short- and possibly long-term restructuring of language forms.

To summarize the literature, in brief language learners need three ingredients to learn language: (1) to receive comprehensible input; (2) to produce comprehensible output; and (3) to attend to L2 forms. Input can be made comprehensible through modifications to the input and through negotiation of meaning. Negotiation of meaning also leads to increased comprehensible output and attention to form.

One cautionary thought regarding this research is this: SLA research most often focuses on minute linguistic segments of language development; therefore, care must be taken when these findings are extrapolated to broader notions of language development.

Measured Impact of Sheltered Instruction on Student Performance

The second body of research reviewed here is the measured impact of sheltered instruction on student performance. Sheltered instruction is a relatively new phenomenon. Much of the research of the last 15 years on sheltered instruction has been conducted by the national Center for Applied Linguistics (CAL) and the Center for Research on Education, Diversity and Excellence (CREDE); this research has delved into what comprises sheltered instruction and how it can be measured. For the past decade, sheltered instruction researchers and program developers—in particular, Echevarria, Vogt, and Short (2000)—have been working on defining and describing this unique methodology.

Before researchers could begin to measure the efficacy of this methodology, they needed to get clarity on what exactly the program consists of, because in the world of practice, the concept of sheltered instruction was realized in a variety of ways. To rectify this, Echevarria, Vogt, and Short developed an observational protocol that allows teachers to analyze their own lesson planning and lesson delivery from a sheltered perspective (see also Short, 2000). This protocol, called the *sheltered instruction observation protocol*, is a checklist consisting of eight elements: preparation, building background, comprehensibility, strategies, interaction, practice and application, lesson delivery, and review and assessment. In nationally conducted seminars educators are trained to understand what recommended behaviors comprise each of the eight elements; they are also trained in how to observe other teachers or videos of their own teaching and to record on the rubric-like checklist which behaviors they are adequately employing. The 2000 text explains in detail the eight aspects of sheltered instruction and how to use the protocol checklist as a guide. The protocol instrument has been subject to considerable statistical scrutiny to ensure its reliability and validity (Echevarria & Short, 2004).

Now that the concept of sheltered instruction has been operationalized by a statistically acceptable measurement device—the SIOP—researchers can begin to measure the efficacy of sheltered instruction on student performance. To date, the SIOP authors have reported on at least two studies of this sort. In one such study, the subsequent writing abilities of two groups of students were compared: One group of students had been taught by teachers trained in the use of the SIOP method; the other group of students had been taught by teachers not trained in SIOP. Short and Echevarria (2004–2005, p. 11) report, citing Echevarria, Short, and Powers (2003), that "our research found that ELLs whose teachers were trained in implementing the SIOP performed significantly better on an academic writing assignment than did a comparison group of ELLs whose teachers had had no exposure to the model." In a second study measuring the impact of SIOP on the performance of students with learning disabilities, it was found that students taught by teachers trained in SIOP methods "made significant improvement in the writing" (Echevarria & Short, 2004, p. 42). There is reason to believe that future studies will similarly confirm the positive impact sheltered instruction will have on ELL student performance, as well as the performance of other students in mainstream classes.

Two cautionary thoughts regarding the SIOP and its national training movement are worth mentioning. The SIOP is a marvelous tool for educating teachers and measuring their behaviors. It has been found however, that after the SIOP training, teachers frequently ask for specifics as to how to explicitly apply the sheltered behaviors to their own practices in their own disciplines. Our federally funded teacher training over the past five years has done considerable work on helping teachers specifically apply the SIOP methodologies to their own teaching. Additionally, anonymous reviewers of an earlier version of this manuscript cautioned that far too often educational leaders are mistaken in believing that once their faculty members have received SIOP training they have received sufficient professional development on ELL issues. These reviewers emphasized that in addition to SIOP training, to service ELL students adequately educators need further professional development in issues of literacy and, as just mentioned, explicit ways to implement sheltered instruction within their own disciplines.

References

Atkinson, K. (Director), Mizer, J. (story writer), & Pearson, C.L. (screenplay writer). (1973). *Cipher in the Snow* [film]. Provo, UT: Brigham Young University Production Company.

Bourdieu, P. (1986). The forms of capital. In J. G. Richardson (Ed.), *Handbook for theory and research for the sociology of education* (pp. 241–258). New York: Greenwood Press.

Center for Applied Linguistics. (2002). Helping English learners succeed: An overview of the SIOP. Video. Washington, DC: Author.

Chaudron, C. (1983). Simplification of input: Topic reinstatements and their effect on L2 learners' recognition and recall. *TESOL Quarterly, 17,* 437–458.

Commins, N. L., & Miramontes, O. B. (2005). *Linguistic diversity and teaching.* Mahwah, NJ: Lawrence Erlbaum.

Cummins, J. (1981, Winter). Empirical and theoretical underpinnings of bilingual education. *Journal of Education, 163,* 16–29.

Cummins, J. (1984). Wanted: A theoretical framework for relating language proficiency to academic achievement among bilingual students. In C. Rivera (Ed.), *Language proficiency and academic achievement* (pp. 2–19). Avon, England: Multilingual Matters, Ltd.

Danford, E. (2002). Debating the Future of Indochina in 1945: Making Your Case. New Haven, CT: Yale-New Haven Teachers Institute. Available on April 27, 2007 at: http://www.yale.edu/ynhti/curriculum/units/2002/3/02.03.05.x.html.

Donato, R. (1994). Collective scaffolding in second language learning. In J. Lantolf & G. Appel (Eds.), *Vygotskian approaches to second language research* (pp. 33–56). Norwood, NJ: Ablex.

Echevarria, J., & Short, D. (2004). Using multiple perspectives in observations of diverse classrooms: The sheltered instruction observation protocol (SIOP). In H. Waxman & R. Thorp (Eds.), *Observational research in U.S. classrooms: New approaches for understanding cultural and linguistic diversity* (pp. 2–24). New York: Cambridge University Press.

Echevarria, J., Short, D., & Powers, K. (2003). *School reform and standards-based education: How do teachers help English language learners?* Technical report. Santa Cruz, CA: Center for Research on Education, Diversity & Excellence.

Echevarria, J., Vogt, M. E., & Short, D. (2000). *Making content comprehensible for English language learners: The SIOP model.* Needham Heights, MA: Allyn and Bacon.

Gass, S. M., Mackey, A., & Pica, A. (1998). The role of input and interaction in second language acquisition: Introduction to the special issue. *Modern Language Journal, 82*(3), 299–307.

Holliday, L. (1995). *NS syntactic modifications in NS-NNS negotiations as input data for second language acquisition of syntax.* Unpublished doctoral dissertation. University of Pennsylvania, Philadelphia.

Hume, K. (1999). *Sightlines 9,* Prentice Hall Literature Series. New York: Prentice Hall.

Kennedy, X.J., & Gioia, D. (2002). *Literature: An Introduction to Fiction, Poetry, and Drama, Eighth Edition.* New York: Pearson/Longman.

Krashen, S. (1980). *Second language acquisition and second language learning.* Oxford: Pergamon Press.

Krashen, S. (1983). Newmark's ignorance hypothesis and current second language acquisition theory. In S. M. Gass & L. Selinker (Eds.), *Language transfer in language learning* (pp. 135–156). Rowley, MA: Newbury House.

Krashen, S. (1985). *The input hypothesis: Issues and implications.* London: Longman.

LaPierrre, D. (1994) *Language output in a cooperative learning setting: Determining its effects on second language learning.* Unpublished master's thesis. University of Toronto (OISE), Canada.

Lau vs. Nichols, 414 U.S. 563 (1974).

Linnell, J. (1995). *Negotiation as a context for learning syntax in a second language.* Unpublished doctoral dissertation. University of Pennsylvania, Philadelphia.

Long, M. H. (1980). *Input, interaction, and second language acquisition.* Unpublished doctoral dissertation. University of California, Los Angeles.

Long, M. (1983). Linguistic and conversational adjustments to nonnative speakers. *Studies in Second Language Acquisition, 5,* 177–193.

Long, M. (1985a). Input and second language acquisition theory. In S. M. Gass & C. G. Madden (Eds.), *Input in second language acquisition* (pp. 377–393). Rowley, MA: Newbury House.

Long, M. (1985b). A role for instruction in second language acquisition: Task-based language training. In K. Hyltenstam & M. Pienemann (Eds.), *Modeling and assessing second language acquisition* (pp. 77–100). Clevedon, England: Multilingual Matters.

Long, M. (1990). The least a second language acquisition theory needs to explain. *TESOL Quarterly, 24,* 649–666.

Nobuyoshi, J., & Ellis, R. (1993). Focused communication tasks and second language acquisition. *English Language Teaching Journal, 47,* 203–210.

Pica, T. (1994). Research on negotiation: What does it reveal about second-language learning conditions, processes, and outcomes? *Language Learning, 44*(3), 493–527.

Pica, T. (1996). Second language learning through interaction: Multiple perspectives. *Working Papers in Educational Linguistics, 12,* 1–22.

Pica, T., Young, R., & Doughty, C. (1987). The impact of interaction on comprehension. *TESOL Quarterly, 21,* 737–758.

Rutherford, W., & Sharwood Smith, M. (1985). Consciousness-raising and universal grammar. In W. Rutherford & M. Sharwood Smith (Eds.), *Grammar and second language learning* (pp. 107–116). Rowley, MA: Newbury House.

Schmidt, R. (1990). The role of consciousness in second language acquisition. *Applied Linguistics, 11,* 129–158.

Sharwood Smith, M. (1991). Speaking to many minds: On the relevance of different types of language information for the L2 learner. *Second Language Research, 7,* 118–132.

Short, D. (2000). What principals should know about sheltered instruction for English language learners. *NASSP Bulletin, 84*(619), 17–27.

Short, D., & Echevarria, J. (2004–2005). Teacher skills to support English language learners. *Educational Leadership, 62*(4), 8–13.

Swain, M. (1985). Communicative competence: Some roles of comprehensible input and comprehensible output in its development. In S. M. Gass & C. G Madden (Eds.), *Input in second language acquisition* (pp. 236–244). Rowley, MA: Newbury House.

Vecchione, J. (Producer and Writer). (1983). *Roots of a War (1945–1953).* In *Vietnam, A Television History* [film]. Boston, MA: WGBH Public Broadcasting Station.

CHAPTER 8

Developing Academic Language Through an Abundance of Interaction

LORRIE STOOPS VERPLAETSE

English language learners (ELLs) need an abundance of opportunities for interaction. They need to interact with the course content, with other students, and with their teachers. They need to interact orally and in writing. When they are first beginning to learn the language, they need to convey their ideas visually—with graphics and gestures. As they begin to produce language out loud, they need ample opportunities to convey their thoughts in short responses. As they move into an intermediate stage of language development and indicate an ability to produce language in a full sentence, they need plentiful opportunities to express their thoughts extensively and frequently. And at each stage of language development, they need ample opportunities to express their thoughts on paper as well as orally.

This chapter first reviews the literature on the importance of interaction for language acquisition and academic achievement. Then a discussion is provided of six instructional strategies to increase interaction opportunities, followed by a review of the literature that supports these strategies. Finally, the chapter explores the particular importance of interaction through the written form, with teacher recommendations and a review of the current literature on adolescent ELL writing.

Importance of Interaction

As mentioned in the introductory chapter, interaction opportunities are one of the essential ingredients for second-language development (Gass, Mackey, & Pica, 1998; Hall & Verplaetse, 2000; Swain, 1985, 1995). Because linguistic minority adolescent students are developing their second languages at the same time that they need to be developing their academic skills, classroom interaction is particularly important to them for a number of reasons.

Classroom interaction is tripartite in nature (Green & Harker, 1982) in that it leads to the development of content learning, a student's personal and social development, and the development of academic language proficiency (Mehan, 1978). Taking part in classroom interaction affords the student a number of benefits:

- It allows the learner to be part of the co-construction of course knowledge (Rosebery, Warren, & Conant, 1992; Wertsch & Toma, 1990).
- It helps construct the student's classroom identity (Corson, 2001; Norton, 1997; Toohey, 2000) and co-membership in the class (Zuengler, 1993).
- It provides the learner the practice needed to develop academic language communicative skills (Hall, 1993; O'Connor & Michaels, 1993).
- Through such practice, it leads the learner to the mastery of meanings, allowing the student to express ideas in a variety of ways (Lemke, 1990).

The language proficiency required to engage in academic discourse is gained through repeated production practice. Because academic language is often composed of extended text, for such production practice to occur opportunities for extended interaction must be provided to the learner. Given that teachers determine the level of student participation in a classroom, they are responsible for creating the opportunities for students to practice extended interaction.

Unfortunately, far too often teachers—sometimes unwittingly—shelter ELL students from interaction opportunities (Verplaetse, 1995, 1998). They do so for a number of reasons:

- They are trying to protect the students from other students' ridicule.
- They express concern about time issues, thinking that interactions with language learners can be time intensive and feeling pressed with the need to move the curriculum along.
- They sometimes mistakenly misinterpret an ELL student's reticence as a sign that the student does not understand the course content.

Consequently, it is important that teachers recognize the importance of student interaction and consciously employ strategies that will provide rich opportunities for student production of language, both oral and written. The following section identifies six specific ways educators can provide opportunities for student interaction.

Six Strategies to Provide Interaction Opportunities

Modify Teacher Talk in Teacher-Fronted Classrooms

Currently, the class talk of most teacher-fronted classrooms is dominated by the teacher; the teacher can easily monopolize 60 to 90% of the classroom talk, leaving only a small minority of class time for the students to take part in interactions. Teachers have two major ways to alter this disproportionate ratio in teacher-fronted classrooms: (1) modify the questions they ask; and (2) modify the responses they give to students' comments.

Modify Teacher Questions   In teacher-fronted classrooms, teachers lead their students in a variety of activities: They review, summarize, identify main and supporting ideas, signal comprehension of ideas. Activities that lend themselves well to opportunities for student interaction include (1) to wonder, (2) to speculate, (3) to predict, and (4) to explore. In these activities, teachers can ask the larger, higher-order questions such as *why* and *how*.

One very simple, yet effective, technique to increase student interaction is to offer follow-up questions. For example, if the science teacher has asked the class why they think that a particular model of clay boat can float, and a student has offered an opinion, the teacher can follow up by asking that student to justify his or her opinion by asking "Why do you think that?" or "Why do you suppose that's possible?" Far too seldom do teachers follow up on correct student answers. Teachers' follow-up questions most often are reserved for times when a student's comments are in need of correction or redirection. When a teacher follows up on a student's correct answer, the classroom message is clear: The teacher is interested in the content, in the student's ideas, and in engaging in a discussion.

Another very simple yet effective technique to increase student interaction is for teachers to ask questions to which they do not know the answer. Such questions lead to the same type of class activities: to speculate and to wonder. "Why do you think that…" questions rather than "What is…" questions naturally lead to extended student responses. They are asking a student to do more than recall and retell. Higher-order questioning is often correlated to length of student responses.

Modify Teacher Responses My research suggests that the way the teacher responds to students' comments may be more important in producing extended student turns at talk than the type of question the teacher might ask (Verplaetse, 2000). The teacher response most successful in producing student interaction is the response that signals nonevaluative listening on the part of the teacher. This bears repeating. Teachers achieve the most frequent and lengthy student turns at talk when they signal through their own responses that they are listening and not evaluating.

Examples of this kind of nonevaluative response include the following. The teacher can paraphrase what the student has just said or can repeat it. The teacher can offer a simple back channel, like, "Ahhh," or "Uh-huh." Ironically, the teacher can respond with silence. The silent response is a powerful indicator that the teacher need not offer a response to every student comment. This indicator, in turn, signals that the floor is open for other students to react or respond. Another way to accomplish this kind of student response is to openly offer the floor up to other students by saying something like, "Who has a thought about this?"

The most challenging part of this type of nonevaluative listening teacher response is for teachers to refrain from offering their own words of wisdom. So often a student's comments will naturally lead to a teachable moment where a teacher could easily offer further information or more correct information. But if the goal of the class activity is for the students to speculate or to wonder and to produce extended language output, then a teacher's silence is a most effective tool for this purpose. And perhaps that teachable moment need not be lost; perhaps it can be achieved through the use of effective teacher questioning or wondering rather than through telling.

Employ Instructional Conversations One type of teacher-fronted activity, called *instructional conversations* (ICs), employs both of the aforementioned question-and-response strategies. ICs can be conducted in small groups or in a full-class discussion (Goldenberg, 1992–1993; Saunders, Goldenberg, & Hamann, 1992). During an instructional conversation, the teacher takes the role of facilitator, guiding through effective questioning techniques student engagement of interpretations, predictions, and jointly constructed meanings of text. The teacher also makes extensive use of pausing and teacher silence, thus enabling the students to become the primary interlocutors of this conversational event. Small-group ICs are strongly recommended for early elementary classrooms, in particular for English-language-learning students (Damhuis, 2000). They have been equally successful in middle schools.

In one particular study of a seventh-grade math class (Dalton & Sison, 1995), a teacher–graduate student engaged a group of Spanish-speaking nonachievers in four ICs over the course of several weeks. In the course of four ICs, these six nonachieving students who regularly skipped school, and when in attendance sat at the back of the room and did not participate, began to show an interest in measurements by taking part in conversations, using the appropriate math vocabulary, and presenting an identity as an engaged math student. The first IC consisted of social conversation about the sky, planets, and stars prompted by a Star Trek photo. This IC ended with the students and teacher collectively wondering about whether planets can be measured. The second IC consisted of a hands-on measuring event, where students used string to measure the circumferences and diameters of variously sized objects and then graphed their findings while the teacher used the appropriate vocabulary.

The teacher's language and style of talk, not the activities used, are the focus of this example: How this teacher accepted the students' utterances nonjudgmentally and built her own talk from that of the students is the key to this teacher's and students' accomplishments. By the third and fourth IC, the students were regularly using the math lexicon and were issuing spoken turns appropriate to the topic at a rate that far exceeded that of the first IC. "In a sociocultural sense, the language use strongly suggests that the students' points of view have shifted from those of an excluded outsider to those of the included member, the math student" (Dalton & Sison, 1995 p. 12).

The Verplaetse (2000) study shows similar teacher behavior in instructional conversations carried out at the full-classroom level. This research examines an eighth-grade science teacher, whose topics are academically rigorous and whose students are engaged, curious, and highly interactive, including the English language learners in the class.

Increase Student-to-Student Activities—Small-Group Work or Paired Exercises

A second strategy to increase opportunities for student interaction is to move away from teacher-fronted instruction by making frequent use of student-centered, small-group work and paired exercises. Elementary classrooms make frequent use of paired activities, such as shoulder buddies and paired reading assignments. Middle school and secondary school classrooms far too often fall into the traditional lecture and transmission models of instruction, losing the opportunities for student interaction. An important caveat to this recommendation is that in small-group work each member must have a clearly defined role, or the ELL student may be as marginalized in the small group as in the full class.

One small-group activity that is particularly productive for ELL interaction is the jigsaw activity. In a jigsaw activity, students start out in home groups of three to five. Within the home groups, the students determine who will be specialists for a designated portion of reading or a topic to research. The topic specialists from each of the home groups then come together, forming a second small group, the specialist group. This group reviews the material for which they are to become specialists. They discuss how they are going to present this material back in their home groups, and they practice their delivery of this information. After a defined period of preparation time, the specialists return to their home groups. Now each home group consists of a series of prepared specialists on varied topics. Each specialist shares his or her information, and the home group discusses and delivers whatever product the teacher has assigned.

A simple, illustrative summary of the jigsaw is as follows:

Step 1. Students in home groups. Students assign specialist topics.

- Home Group 1: Tran, Susan, Maria
- Home Group 2: Jenn, Brian, Chris
- Home Group 3: Carlos, Yuki, Ashley

Step 2. Students in specialist groups. Students study determined topic and practice presentation to home group.

- Group studying iguana habitat: Tran, Jenn, Carlos
- Group studying koala habitat: Susan, Brian, Yuki
- Group studying white whale habitat: Maria, Chris, Ashley

Step 3. Students return to home groups where specialists share their findings.

What is particularly valuable about the jigsaw activity is that ELL students can become a specialist on a given topic and have the time to practice their delivery before returning to the home group. Teachers can strategically assign group sizes to ensure that weaker students may have a peer from the home group who functions as cospecialist with the weaker student.

Study centers are another way to shift from teacher-fronted instruction to student-centered classroom instruction, which fosters an abundance of student interaction. At each designated center, students are engaged in a particular activity, for example, a particular lab experiment, a writing assignment, and reading assignment, or an exercise to accomplish. Students rotate from center to center knowing that ultimately each student must visit each center by a designated time. This center arrangement can be quite structured, in that a particular defined group moves from center to center on a timed schedule, or it might be loosely arranged, so that students independently move from station to station until all tasks are accomplished. This second arrangement allows for considerable flexibility so that students can spend a longer time, if needed, on particular tasks, whereas other tasks that might be a bit easier for a student can be accomplished in a shorter time. During center assignments, students are encouraged to work together, to discuss questions with other students, to talk with the teacher when questions arise, and, in general, to interact with each other about the learning activities.

Teachers often ask the best way to assign students to work together regarding language abilities. That is, they wonder if they should group students homogenously or heterogeneously. How students are paired or grouped depends on the instructional goals of the activity. At times, pairing an ELL learner with a proficient English speaker will give the ELL a chance to try out his or her abilities with someone more proficient and to hear the excellent usage of the target language by the more expert partner. At other times, teachers purposefully pair ELLs with other students who speak the same first language, allowing the students the chance to engage about the content freely in their first language. This allows the students, at times, to explore the new content in depth, something they are currently unable to accomplish in their new target language—English. Still at other times, language learners might be grouped together intentionally so that the teacher can take some time to work with them on particular language development issues or to help make the course content comprehensible through additional sheltered strategies.

One excellent way to promote student interaction is to make use of ELL students' cultural strengths. Teachers can make it a point to ask ELL students to share information about their own country and background when appropriate. For example, when studying about the Pilgrims, a teacher can first explore why immigrant families have come to America and in that exploration can elicit ideas from the class, including the immigrant students. As a second example, foreign-language classroom teachers could easily invite ELL students to come to their classrooms as guest speakers to share information about their language, home country, and culture.

Vary Questioning Techniques and Assignments Based on Language-Proficiency Level

The third strategy to increase student interaction is to learn how to question students and how to assign tasks differentially based on the student's language proficiency level. As mentioned at the beginning of this chapter, teachers can challenge students intellectually about content, even when students are still in the silent, preproduction, phase of second-language development.

- During a language learner's pre-production (i.e., silent) phase, teachers can ask students to identify information by circling, pointing, or matching. Newcomer students might find themselves in the silent phase of their second-language development for weeks or even months.
- As students begin to produce language at the one- and two-word phase, teachers can ask students either/or questions, yes/no questions, and questions that elicit single word lists.
- Then, as students indicate at an early intermediate phase that they are able to produce full sentences, teachers can ask questions that elicit full-sentence answers (e.g., *what, when, where* questions).
- Finally, as students indicate a mid-level intermediate ability with English—that is, as they begin to speak in one to two sentences, if not in the classroom then in the halls or playgrounds or in the ESL classroom—then teachers can begin to expect more production of them and to create opportunities for their extended production (e.g., *why* questions; questions that ask them to speculate, justify, predict, explain).

Consider an example to illustrate such differentiated expectations, dependent on the student's language-proficiency level. Suppose that students in an eighth-grade health science course are studying the skeletal system and that the lesson on a given day is proper care for the skeleton. The mainstream class members may be expected to write a paragraph about ways to care for one's bones. Once the materials have been made comprehensible to all students in the class through sheltered instructional strategies, ELL students will be able to explore and display their understanding of the material in ways other than writing a paragraph. Preproduction ELL students may have a series of pictures that identify proper and improper ways to care for the skeleton and may be expected to circle the proper ways. Or they may be assigned to look through magazines and select photos that illustrate proper or improper care. Early production ELL students may be expected to respond to short-answer questions about the proper care for skeletons or to select from multiple-choice options. Intermediate-level students may be asked to write the paragraph, but model sentences may be provided for them. (For a detailed discussion on sheltered strategies, see Chapter 7.)

Or, for this same example, if students have been strategically grouped heterogeneously, they might all be responsible for creating a poster to advertise correct ways to care for one's bones, and each student can contribute based on the student's own level of language proficiency: some drawing, some printing out the text, other more proficient students drafting the text. Again, the caveat: Teachers will need to help groups assign appropriate tasks to ensure that each member of the group is engaging and contributing.

In summary, teachers have the right to expect all students to indicate an understanding of materials. But how that understanding is conveyed is language dependent. Consequently, students who are still developing their language may need to show their understanding of material in ways that rely less heavily on language usage. Teachers can provide differentiated ways of asking course questions that enable all students to engage in the content.

In a class I observed recently, the teacher handed out math folders to each student with the understanding that the students were to work on their math assignments in class, using each other for help and using the teacher for help as needed. What I learned later was that the math assignments were not the same for each student; rather, they were differentially determined to meet each student's particular level of math. Similarly, differentiated questions can be asked of students based on their language proficiency: still probing the content at the same level of cognitive complexity yet doing so through various use of questioning and language production.

Model Students' Responses for Beginning and Early-Intermediate ELL Students

Language-learning students often find themselves with ideas they want to express but lacking the language required to express these ideas. At this stage of language development, students need models of how to express academic ideas. The fourth strategy for creating opportunities for student interaction is to provide language models for students. A wonderful example of how to do this comes from Ernenwein, Szyika, & Wellman (2002), from Castleton, New York, schools, who presented at the 2002 TESOL conference. Teachers had created a lesson about insects in which students had identified certain insects and now were writing descriptive paragraphs about the insects. The teacher had provided model expressions for the ELL students, such as

- It has (two, three, four) (legs, eyes, antennas, wings).
- It is (5, 10, 15) centimeters (wide, long).
- It has (a) (big, long, striped) (eyes, body, head).

All students were required to identify and describe their insects in writing, but language learners who needed the descriptive expressions modeled could make use of the expressions provided by the teachers in their written descriptions.

Another example of modeling language expressions comes from an algebra classroom, where the teacher had posted formulas around the classroom (Center for Applied Linguistics, 2002). Below each formula she had written how to say the formula in English. She then asked ELL students to bring in written samples of how to say the same formula in their home languages, which she posted on the wall along with the English expressions and the algebraic formula. The students had all of these mathematical expressions posted on a word wall to consult as needed.

Know When and How to Interactionally Challenge the Intermediate ELL Student

The fifth strategy for increasing student interaction is to recognize when to stop providing crutches and when to start pushing for extended output. Once ELL students have reached an intermediate level of language development, they are able to produce full sentences. However, often such students will be highly interactive in the safety of the ESL classroom or bilingual classroom but will remain painfully silent in the mainstream classrooms.

found that teachers enable this silent behavior by expecting less from ELL
...tionally than they expect from other students. Often this is because the
...are of what the intermediate ELL student is capable of. In fact, I argue that
...re often unaware of their own productive abilities.

Once an ELL student has indicated that he or she can speak at the intermediate level, higher expectations for production are in order. But how does one determine when the student is at that level? A mainstream classroom teacher can ask the ESL teacher. Or the teacher can listen for the student's ability as the student talks in the school hallways. A highly recommended way is to first interact with the student one on one. Once the student has indicated the ability to produce full sentences in one-on-one conversations with the teacher, then the teacher can begin to slowly bring the student into full-classroom discussions. The teacher can bring the student into full-class discussions by telling the student ahead of time, "I'm going to call on you for number 4." Or the teacher can ask the student to answer a question she or he knows the student is prepared to answer. I have seen excellent collaborative efforts between the ESL teacher and content teacher in planning to challenge an ELL student interactively. I have also observed an ELL student go up to the teacher after class to thank the teacher for letting her talk. ELL students want to be a part of the interactive classroom, but often they need the support and encouragement of their teachers to make their interaction a reality.

Let ELL Students Use Their First Languages

The final strategy to increase student interaction is to allow students to speak in their home languages. We all use our language as a tool to help us think. Consider, for example, when you are in the grocery store and have momentarily forgotten what you came to the store for. What do you normally do? You speak quietly to yourself, almost in a whisper, for example, "Let's see, I needed bread, toothpaste, and…That's right!…cat food." That talking aloud helps us to think.

Similarly, language learners can think out thoughts and can problem solve with considerably more facility when they are allowed to do so in their first language. This use of the first language does not interfere with their ability to develop their new language. On the contrary, it allows them to successfully engage in the content topic, thus allowing them to have more extensive thoughts about the topic. In this process, teachers can explicitly provide words in English for concepts students already understand. This, in turn, will allow them to have more to say about the topic, when it is time for them to produce in the new target language. Figure 8.1 summarizes the six teacher strategies, which will provide an abundance of student interaction opportunities.

Research Supporting These Strategies

The field of second language acquisition (SLA) has a long history of interaction literature (for a review, see Pica, 1996). These SLA interaction studies have shown that interaction leads to increased comprehensibility, which in turn has led to

- Improved task accomplishment (Pica, Young, & Doughty, 1987)
- Increased vocabulary (Gass & Varonis, 1994)
- Increased metalinguistic awareness of particular grammatical structures (Swain, 1995; Swain & Lapkin, 1998)
- Improved abilities to carry out certain academic functions (such as giving definitions) (Snow, 1990)

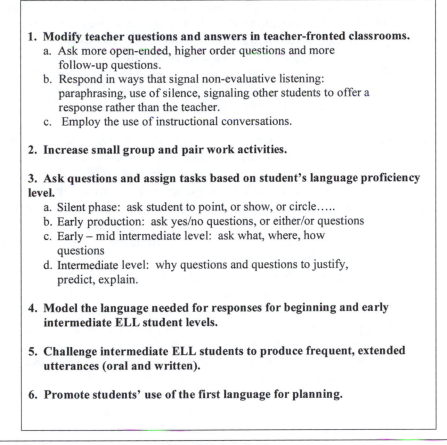

1. **Modify teacher questions and answers in teacher-fronted classrooms.**
   a. Ask more open-ended, higher order questions and more follow-up questions.
   b. Respond in ways that signal non-evaluative listening: paraphrasing, use of silence, signaling other students to offer a response rather than the teacher.
   c. Employ the use of instructional conversations.

2. **Increase small group and pair work activities.**

3. **Ask questions and assign tasks based on student's language proficiency level.**
   a. Silent phase: ask student to point, or show, or circle.....
   b. Early production: ask yes/no questions, or either/or questions
   c. Early – mid intermediate level: ask what, where, how questions
   d. Intermediate level: why questions and questions to justify, predict, explain.

4. **Model the language needed for responses for beginning and early intermediate ELL student levels.**

5. **Challenge intermediate ELL students to produce frequent, extended utterances (oral and written).**

6. **Promote students' use of the first language for planning.**

Figure 8.1 Teacher strategies to promote adolescent ELL student writing

However, the term *interaction* in the SLA literature has been limited most often to a specific type of interaction: the repair work that speakers undertake to provide clarity or to repair confusion in their oral exchange.

In the SLA work of socioculturalist linguists—in particular educational linguists, following the ideas of Vygotsky (Hall, 1993; Lantolf, 2000)—the concept of *interaction* is a broader one, looking at student and teacher talk as it is produced in extended discourse and exploring the notion of communicative competence within classroom settings. Recall from the introductory chapter that the communicative skills required to successfully involve oneself in academic discourse are considered to be more linguistically challenging than interpersonal conversational skills (Cummins, 1981, 1984; Schleppegrell, 2004). Hall (1993, p. 148) states that "language acquisition is bound to the notion of oral practice and proposes that the ability to participate as a competent member in the practices of a group is learned through repeated engagement in and experience with these activities with more competent members of the group."

Unfortunately, middle and high school classrooms are normally not filled with opportunities for extended student talk (Harklau, 1999; Meltzer & Hamann, 2004, 2005; Verplaetse, 1998). Even when teachers believe their classes to be interactive, one study found that "discussions actually averaged less than a minute per day per class" (Williams, 2003, p. 105).

My research has focused on teacher talk in science classrooms and middle and secondary school, examining how mainstream teachers talk to students, both native English and nonnative English speakers (Verplaetse, 1995, 1998, 2000, 2001). In this work I have found that even the most engaging and culturally open teachers modify their talk to ELLs in ways that prohibit the ELL students' opportunities for interaction. Most of the time, these inhibiting modifications occur unwittingly; in fact, quite often teachers are protecting the ELL students from cruel teasing by other students, or they are concerned that to take the time to interact with the ELL students will take away from time on task.

An earlier line of my research focused on native to nonnative speaker interactions (Verplaetse, 1992, 1993). In this work I proposed that native speakers unwittingly modify the manner in which they speak when engaged with a nonnative speaker in ways that minimize the interactive role of the nonnative speaker. For example, the native speaker may change topics more frequently with a nonnative speaker or may not offer as many supportive back-channel moves (e.g., "uh-huh," "yep") as with native speakers. I hypothesize that when native speakers spend so much time on repair work (i.e., the conversational strategies needed to clarify confusion in speech), they then determine the time on topic to be sufficiently spent or even overspent. Consequently, due to this sense of exhaustion on topic, they cut the conversation short before full development of topic.

In more recent work (Verplaetse, 2003, 2005), in an analysis of an extended one-on-one conversation between an adult native English-speaking interviewer and a Vietnamese immigrant high school student studying natural science, I identified a point early in the conversation where the interviewer makes a most unexpected yet influential choice. She and the student have been engaged in what seems to be a very difficult conversation for the ELL student on the topic of mitosis and daughter cells. He continues to pause and hesitate rather than to produce talk freely. She continues to ask him questions about the science topic. The pause times exceed what native English speakers consider a reasonable time to pause in talk. Yet the interviewer persists and insists that the two stay on topic. At one point in the conversation, it appears that the ELL student has given up on his ability to convey his ideas about this science topic. He has produced two lengthy pauses in his turn and now is simply uttering, "mmmmmm," as if he were thinking. At this point in an interaction, research has shown us that it would be natural for the native speaker to switch the topic or to finish the statement for the ELL student (Long, 1981, 1983). But in this case, the interviewer does neither. Rather, the interviewer's response is, "Tell me what you are thinking." Interestingly, this continued insistence on the part of the interviewer unlocks the student's floodgate, and the student begins to talk in English—albeit English that needs a lot of scaffolding assistance—about the science topic. What ensues is an extended conversation of more than 40 turns on the topics of mitosis, daughter cells, and the birth of new cells to replace dead cells, in which the ELL student takes the floor from the native speaker twice and issues extended utterances a number of times. In effect, this ELL student has found his voice as an English-speaking science student. It took the conscious intentions of the adult conversation partner to help this student find this voice.

What I have learned from this collective body of research is that teachers must consciously employ interactive strategies when engaging with ELL students. It is the conscious application of longer wait times after a question, intentional use of follow-up questions, modeling expressions for the beginner ELL, responding to students' comments with a nonevaluative paraphrase, and the gentle persistence and insistence to genuinely engage with the ELL speaker that create the opportunities for ELL students to produce extended utterances.

An Abundance of Writing Opportunities

Although the six strategies previously discussed address oral interaction, ELL students also need an abundance of opportunities to produce written output. Second-language writing research with special attention to adolescent writing recognizes that the secondary schools require far too little writing for their ELL students. In ESL classes, the students are focused on microlevel language issues—primarily issues of grammar. ELL students are then frequently tracked into lower-level, non-college-preparatory courses and therefore are not required to write frequent paragraphs, essays, and papers. Yet many of these ELL students plan to go to college; consequently, they are ill prepared for the writing expectations they face from institutions of higher education (Harklau, Losey, & Siegal, 1999).

In a review of the adolescent ELL writing literature as linked to nationwide standards on writing, Panofsky, Pacheco, Smith, Fogelman, Kenney, & Santos (2005) identify the following recommendations for teachers:

- Explicitly instruct their students in writing in different genres.
- Allow for a prewriting planning process.
- Create opportunities for students to review teacher feedback and incorporate that feedback into subsequent writing.
- Make use of technology, which eases the task of self-editing.
- Spend time on organization and content in student writing, while still in ESL courses, and provide some form of bridge as students move from ESL to mainstream courses to help students produce the extended text required of mainstream content courses.
- Read authentic texts and explicitly analyze the style of authentic texts to learn about English writing style.

Additionally, in a review of two overlapping literatures, one on adolescent literacy development and one on the educational needs of adolescent ELLs, Meltzer & Hamann (2005) identify the following recommendations that are directly related to the issue of writing:

- Model the types of texts students are expected to produce.
- Avoid timed writing tests and instead make use of multiple-draft processes and portfolio assessments.
- Provide frequent opportunities to brainstorm, organize, plan, discuss, and peer edit texts.
- Show ELL students how oral and written texts differ from each other, and provide explicit instruction on how to write academic text that does not sound like informal conversation.
- Provide overt attention to higher-order thinking in literacy activities.
- Guide ELL students on how to answer open-ended questions.
- Engage in learner-centered activities as a means to help students develop positive literacy identities.

To successfully prepare ELL students to achieve proficiency in academic language, middle and high school ESL teachers are encouraged to teach beyond the language lesson. It is recommended that they build into their ESL curricula frequent opportunities for students to write extended text and to write on academic subjects other than personal narratives. ESL students must be exposed to the academic writing styles of a variety of disciplines. Additionally, middle and high school counselors are encouraged to seek out the career goals of the immigrant students and to place ELL students in college preparatory courses accordingly. Finally, secondary content teachers must come to understand that their job is to teach both content and language development to their students. Given the number of language minority students in the public schools, secondary teachers no longer have the luxury to resist teaching language development; it has become part of their responsibility. By learning sheltered instructional strategies, content teachers will find ways to make their material more understandable. Then, the next step is for these same teachers to learn the importance of requiring frequent written activities for their students and of providing the appropriate scaffolding to assist their ELL students in the writing assignments. Figure 8.1 summarizes the teacher strategies that will promote adolescent ELL student writing.

In summary, this chapter has identified six strategies to increase student oral interaction opportunities and has listed a series of teacher recommendations to increase and improve ELL student writing opportunities. Interaction is inextricably intertwined with issues of second-language acquisition, literacy development, and student identity, motivation, and academic achievement. ELL students in particular must have an abundance of opportunities to interact—with the content, with their peers, and with their teachers. If ELL students are to achieve proficiency in academic language skills, they must engage with the content, using higher-order thinking both orally and in written form repeatedly. It is the responsibility of the teacher to provide these opportunities for interaction by consciously and purposefully increasing the amount of times students are required to interact with content, in extended utterances—orally and through writing.

References

Center for Applied Linguistics (2002). *Helping English learners succeed: An overview of the SIOP.* Video. Washington, DC: Author.

Corson, D. (2001). *Language, diversity and education.* Mahwah, NJ: Lawrence Erlbaum Assoc.

Cummins, J. (1981, Winter). Empirical and theoretical underpinnings of bilingual education. *Journal of Education, 163,* 16–29.

Cummins, J. (1984). Wanted: A theoretical framework for relating language proficiency to academic achievement among bilingual students. In C. Rivera (Ed.), *Language proficiency and academic achievement* (pp. 2–19). Avon, England: Multilingual Matters, Ltd.

Dalton, S., & Sison, J. (1995) *Enacting instructional conversation with Spanish-speaking students in middle school mathematics.* Santa Cruz: National Center for Research on Cultural Diversity and Second Language Learning, University of California.

Damhuis, R. (2000). A different teacher role in language arts education: Interaction in a small circle with teacher. In J. K. Hall & L. S. Verplaetse (Eds.), *Second and foreign language learning through classroom interaction* (pp. 243–264). Mahwah, NJ: Lawrence Erlbaum.

Ernenwein, K., Szyika, X., & Wellman, L. (2002). Come back to school for a day. Paper presented at TESOL Annual Conference, Salt Lake City, April 11.

Gass, S. M., Mackey, A., & Pica, T. (1998). The role of input and interaction in second language acquisition: Introduction to the special issue. *Modern Language Journal, 82*(3), 299–305.

Gass, S. M., & Varonis, E. M. (1994). Input, interaction, and second language production. *Studies in Second Language Acquisition, 16,* 283–302.

Goldenberg, C. (1992–1993). Instructional conversations: Promoting comprehension through discussion. *Reading Teacher, 46*(4), 316–326.

Green, J., & Harker, J. (1982). Gaining access to learning: Conversational, social, and cognitive demands of group participation. In L. Wilkinson (Ed.), *Communicating in the classroom* (pp. 183–221). New York: Academic Press.

Hall, J. K. (1993). The role of oral practices in the accomplishment of our everyday lives: The socio-cultural dimension of interaction with implications for the learning of another language. *Applied Linguistics, 14,* 145–166.

Hall, J. K., & Verplaetse, L. S. (2000). *Second and foreign language learning through classroom interaction.* Mahwah, NJ: Lawrence Erlbaum.

Harklau, L. (1999). The ESL learning environment in secondary school. In C. J. Faltis & P. M. Wolfe (Eds), *So much to say: Adolescents, bilingualism, and ESL in the secondary school* (pp. 42–60). New York: Teachers College Press.

Harklau, L., Losey, K. M., & Siegal, M. (Eds.). (1999). *Generation 1.5 meets college composition: Issues in the teaching of writing to U.S. educated learners of ESL.* Mahwah, NJ: Lawrence Erlbaum.

Lantolf, J. (2000). *Sociocultural theory and second language learning.* Oxford: Oxford University Press.

Lemke, J. (1990). *Talking science: Language, learning and values.* Norwood, NJ: Ablex.

Long, M. (1981). Input, interaction, and second language acquisition. In H. Winitz (Ed.), *Native language and foreign language acquisition* (pp. 259–278). New York: Annals of the NY Academy of Sciences.

Long, M. (1983). Linguistic and conversational adjustments to non-native speakers. *Studies in Second Language Acquisition, 5*(2), 177–193.

Mehan, H. (1978). Structuring school structure. *Harvard Educational Review, 48*(1), 32–64.

Meltzer, J., & Hamann, E. (2004). *Meeting the needs of adolescent English language learners for literacy development and content area learning, Part 1: Focus on motivation and engagement.* Providence, RI: Education Alliance at Brown University.

Meltzer, J., & Hamann, E. (2005). *Meeting the literacy development needs of adolescent English language learners through content area learning, Part II: Focus on classroom teaching and learning strategies.* Providence, RI: Education Alliance at Brown University.

Norton, B. (1997, Autumn). Language, identity, and the ownership of English. *TESOL Quarterly, 31*(3), 409–429.

O'Connor, M. C., & Michaels, S. (1993). Aligning academic task and participation status through revoicing: Analysis of a classroom discourse strategy. *Anthropology and Education Quarterly, 24,* 318–335.

Panofsky, C., Pacheco, M., Smith, S., Fogelman, C., Kenney, E., & Santos, J. (2005). *Approaches to writing instruction for adolescent English language learners: A discussion of recent research and practice literature in relation to nationwide standards on writing.* Providence, RI: Education Alliance at Brown University.

Pica, T. (1996). Second language learning through interaction: Multiple perspectives. *Working Papers in Educational Linguistics, 12,* 1–22.

Pica, T., Young, R., & Doughty, C. (1987). The impact of interaction on comprehension. *TESOL Quarterly, 21,* 737–758.

Rosebery, A., Warren, B., & Conant, F. (1992). Appropriating scientific discourse: Findings from language minority classrooms. *Journal of the Learning Sciences, 2*(1), 61–94.

Saunders, W., Goldenberg, C., & Hamann, J. (1992). Instructional conversation begets instructional conversations. *Teaching and Teacher Education, 8*(2), 199–218.

Schleppegrell, M. J. (2004). *The language of schooling.* Mahwah, NJ: Lawrence Erlbaum.

Snow, C. (1990). The development of definitional skill. *Journal of Child Language, 17,* 697–710.

Swain, M. (1985). Communicative competence: Some roles of comprehensible input and comprehensible output in its development. In S. M. Gass & C. G. Madden (Eds.), *Input in second language acquisition* (pp. 235–253). Rowley, MA: Newbury House.

Swain, M. (1995). Three functions of output in second language learning. In G. Cook & B. Seidlhofer (Eds.), *Principle and practice in applied linguistics: Studies in honour of H. G. Widdowson* (pp. 125–144). Oxford: Oxford University Press.

Swain, M., & Lapkin, S. (1998). Interaction and second language learning: Two adolescent French immersion students working together. *Modern Language Journal, 82,* 320–337.

Toohey, K. (2000). *Learning English at school: Identity, social relations and classroom practice.* Clevedon, England: Multilingual Matters.

Verplaetse, L. S. (1992). Modifications of politeness strategies and personal detail in native speaker input to non-native speakers. Master's thesis, Boston University.

Verplaetse, L. S. (1993, April). *Modifications in native speaker input: A hindrance to L2 production*. Refereed paper delivered at the American Association for Applied Linguistics Conference, Atlanta, GA.

Verplaetse, L. S. (1995). Discourse modifications in teacher interactions with limited English proficient students in content classrooms. Unpublished doctoral dissertation, Boston University, ERIC Document ED390254.

Verplaetse, L. S. (1998). How content teachers interact with English language learners. *TESOL Journal, 7*(5), 24–28.

Verplaetse, L. S. (2000). Mr. Wonder-ful: Portrait of a dialogic teacher. In J. K. Hall & L. S. Verplaetse (Eds.), *Second and foreign language learning through classroom interaction*. Mahwah, NJ: Lawrence Erlbaum Associates.

Verplaetse, L. S. (2001). How content teachers allocate turns to limited English proficient students. *Journal of Education, 183*(1), 19–35.

Verplaetse, L. S. (2003, May). Locating the learner's authenic ZPD: Finding the learner's voice. Refereed paper delivered at the First Annual Conference for the International Society for Language Studies, St Thomas, Virgin Islands.

Verplaetse, L. S. (2005, July). Native speaker interactive modifications: Revisited and revised. Refereed paper delivered at the Conference for the International Association of Applied Linguistics, Madison, WI.

Wertsch, J. A., & Toma, C. (1990, April). Discourse and learning in the classroom: A sociocultural approach. Paper presented at University of Georgia, Visiting Lecturer Series on Constructivism in Education, Athens.

Williams, J. D. (2003). *Preparing to teach writing: Research, theory, and practice*. Mahwah, NJ: Lawrence Erlbaum Assoc.

Zuengler, J. (1993). Encouraging learners' conversational participation: The effect of content knowledge. *Language Learning, 43*(3), 403–432.

CHAPTER 9

Through and Beyond High School: Academic Challenges and Opportunities for College-Bound Immigrant Youth

LINDA HARKLAU

When the United States experienced its last major wave of immigration at the turn of the 20th century, college-going was a luxury—the realm of the privileged. First-generation immigrants took unskilled jobs as farm or factory workers, but subsequent generations experienced the American dream of upward mobility (Berrol, 1995; Olneck, 1995). As immigration again peaks today, that agrarian-industrial economy is largely gone. College-going, once considered a luxury of the elite, is now much more necessary. In a postindustrial service economy, three quarters of all jobs require postsecondary education (U.S. Department of Labor, The Secretary's Commission on Achieving Necessary Skills, 1991), and one third demand at least a baccalaureate degree (College Board, 1999). There is also evidence of slowing social mobility (Leonhardt, 2005) with the children of unskilled laborers finding it harder to climb out of the lower rungs of the economy (Portes & Zhou, 1993). At same time, the United States increasingly competes on a global level with countries including China and India where college access and the supply of skilled labor is rapidly expanding. Thus in a real sense our future socioeconomic well-being as a nation depends on educating immigrant youth to their highest potential (Hayes-Bautista, Schink, & Chapa, 1988; Orfield, 2004).

In this chapter I draw on research including my own work in California, New York, and Georgia high schools to make recommendations for educators who are preparing multilingual students to enter and succeed in college. The road to higher education arguably starts in early grades when students' self-concepts as college-going are established, but this chapter limits discussion to what middle and high schools can do to help English language learners (ELLs) along this path. The chapter is organized around the following themes: (1) navigating course placements and the tracking system; (2) providing comprehensible and challenging instruction in English and social studies; (3) preparing students for the culture of college work; and (4) fostering immigrant students' participation in the social and extracurricular aspects of high school. Each section begins with a composite vignette of best practices in high schools in which I have worked, and the chapter concludes with suggestions for further reading.

Navigating Course Placement and Tracking Systems

I'm talking with Dolores, a Mexican American high school sophomore, about her classes for next year. "How many more math courses do you need for college?" I ask. "Two," she responds definitively, pulling something from her bookbag. She unfolds it and reveals a six-page annual newspaper put out by the school counselors with information about courses, tracks, college-entrance requirements, and deadlines. She points to the math section—"See, I need four college-prep math courses. Ms. Brock, my homeroom teacher, asked me what I'm planning to do after high school. I told her I want to go to college and be an engineer so she told me what math courses are college prep and which one to take next. She also told me to 'double up' on math courses and take physics before I graduate. My friend Jorge wants to be an engineer too and he told me about this elective I should take that's, like, architecture and modeling? And then my mom is going to a Hispanic Scholarship Fund meeting next Saturday so she can find out what I should take in my senior year."

Course placement and tracking are key in immigrant academic success or failure in middle and high school (Callahan, 2005). Given the normal course of schooling, immigrant students end up disproportionately placed in low academic tracks. Schools that endeavor to raise expectations for immigrant achievement must take proactive steps to change school-course-placement practices.

Talk Explicitly About Tracking with Students

There is a tendency in American education not to talk with students or their parents about the fact that American schools routinely sort students according to perceived academic ability. Perhaps that is because it goes against an American ethic of equal treatment and makes us worried that we will hurt students' feelings or discourage them. But not talking about tracking or ability grouping does not make tracking go away—it just takes information and choices away from students and families. Tracking is an especially important issue for immigrant families, because they are unfamiliar with American schooling and often do not realize that ability grouping exists (Harklau, 1994b). When we don't talk about tracking, we give unfair advantages to students and families who are most familiar with the American schooling system. Educators need to be frank with English language learners and their families about what tracks are available to their children, what tracks they are currently in, their recommendations for course placement, and why.

Assign an Educator to Be Responsible for Reviewing ELL Course Assignments

Public schools rarely have the resources to provide individual counseling for students about their academic ambitions and plans for the future. As a result, schools tend to rely on a combination of teacher recommendations, standardized test scores, and computer-generated scheduling. However, English language learners can easily founder in this system. For example, standardized test scores may not reflect learners' abilities because of limited English proficiency (Harklau, 1994c). Though most English learners start out in lower mainstream tracks, they may need their track level reevaluated as they become more proficient. In addition, because of their lack of familiarity with the American system, immigrants are more likely than other students not to recognize course placement errors. Though students could seek out counselors to help them, it has been my experience that many middle and high school students rarely if ever speak with a counselor. Some are not even sure who their counselor is or how they would go about initiating a conversation with them. Research has also found consistently that secondary content teachers vary considerably in their willingness and ability to work with English language learners (Harklau, 2000; Reeves, 2004; Verplaetse, 1998). In other words, even content-area classes that are ostensibly exactly the same in terms of curriculum and track level may differ in their suitability for immigrant students depending on the instructor. For all these reasons, designating one well-informed and sympathetic teacher or counselor to be responsible for helping English language learners with course placements and hand scheduling them when necessary is vital in making choices that are best suited to their linguistic and academic needs and ambitions. At many schools this role is taken by an English for speakers of other languages (ESOL) teacher (Harklau, 1994a), but it can also be taken by a homeroom teacher or a designated counselor.

Make Information on Course Choices and College Requirements Accessible

Educators tell me that students receive information repeatedly throughout high school about college and course selections. Nevertheless, I often find that immigrant students at the same schools do not recall being given any of this information. It turns out that many schools present this information through spoken language such as counselor visits to homerooms or morning announcements. For a variety of reasons, including lower levels of listening comprehension and unfamiliarity with the American system, English language learners often do not understand the information they are receiving from schools about course choices and college-preparatory course requirements. It is therefore important to present this information in writing and to distribute it widely.

Schools may already have an abundance of written publications in the form of magazines and leaflets about college-going and requirements provided by outside government and foundation sources (e.g., state university system publications, the College Board). However, these publications have a generic, abstract quality that is not necessarily helpful to students navigating the particulars of course choices in their own school. These materials are also of limited help when they are not distributed widely to students—I have seen many of them end up in a neat pile on a coffee table in the counseling office where they remain untouched for the duration of the school year. The newspaper strategy mentioned in the earlier vignette is one relatively easy and inexpensive way to provide every student with the same information about course choices and college requirements in a readily accessible and reviewable format. Even better, although I have not seen it done, would be to translate this same annual newspaper into immigrant students' home languages.

It is also important for schools to seek out speakers and recruiters from local colleges who speak immigrants' home languages and who can meet with college-bound students and their families to talk with them not only about course requirements but also to address cultural knowledge about developing a college-bound portfolio (Gee, Hull, & Lankshear, 1996) in the United States. Immigrant families and communities vary considerably in their knowledgeability about college-going in the United States. In some communities, there may be well-organized family, church, and community networks that spread information about college-going (Bankston & Zhou, 1997). In others, however, immigrant families may have little understanding of how college works. For example, immigrant families may focus on academic achievement but may not realize that extracurricular activities play a significant role in college admission. In Georgia, organizations such as the Hispanic Scholarship Fund address this gap, regularly scheduling college information sessions for parents at high schools with high numbers of Spanish-speaking, first-generation, college-bound students. At other schools this role may be played by an ESOL teacher or migrant agency (Gibson, Bejinez, Hidalgo, & Rolon, 2004).

Foster Cohorts of College-Bound English Language Learners

By adolescence, peer groups have a significant influence on students' academic self-concept and aspirations (Davidson, 1996; Harklau, 2007; Phelan, Davidson, & Yu, 1998; Suárez-Orozco & Suárez-Orozco, 1995). Peers are often students' main source of information about schooling. Yet immigrant peer cultures vary considerably in their knowledge about college-going and their motivation to achieve in school (Bankston & Zhou, 1997). When college-going is not the norm in English language learners' peer cultures, they can be confronted with difficult choices. They can choose to remain in a peer group where they will not get much information about or incentive for further education, or they can associate with other college-bound students at the risk of being isolated or ostracized. Schools can offer a better option; they can foster the development of a college-bound immigrant peer cohort and culture in which college ambitions are shared, in which students participate in the highest levels of instruction, and where information about college is available through the collective peer group (see, e.g., Gibson, Bejinez, Hidalgo, & Rolon, 2004). Research shows that even peers who are not significantly better off in terms of parental education or socioeconomic measures can serve as effective peer mentors and sources of information about school (Stanton-Salazar, 2004).Many current educational reform efforts aiming to increase the numbers of underrepresented students in higher education emphasize this tactic including the Gates Foundation's Early College High Schools and similar initiatives (Huebner & Corbett, 2004). Creation of cohorts of college-bound linguistic minority students is also a cornerstone of approaches such as Project Advancement Via Individual Determination (AVID), a high school dropout prevention and college-enrollment program that began in California in 1981 (Fashola & Slavin, 2001; Mehan, Hubbard, & Villanueva, 1994). The program features special classes and activities for cohorts of participating students during lunch, elective periods, and after school. Students are also identified with the program through special notebooks and badges.

Providing Comprehensible and Challenging Instruction in Mainstream English and Social Studies Classes

Gary is a Taiwanese immigrant in high school. Gary is in an advanced "sheltered" English class. The class exemplifies a high caliber of reading and writing instruction, including a variety of authentic reading sources and frequent extended writing assignments featuring multiple drafts and feedback. In addition, the class provides focused instruction in several particular trouble areas for ESOL students. As part of their reading, the teacher demonstrates reading strategies to help them approach texts and anticipate content, understand and organize information they get from texts, and synthesize and extrapolate beyond it. Students also learn how to read at different speeds and different ways for different kinds of information. Writing assignments include timed essay questions and extended research papers where students learn how to organize, compare, and write about information coming from multiple sources. Students are given authentic models for their writing; for example, their teacher uses a passage from Asimov's *Guide to Shakespeare* to show them how to write an analysis of *Romeo and Juliet*. Before writing, the class looks at how the text uses things such as verb tense, sentence structure, and paragraphs to organize ideas. The teacher also selects vocabulary from the passage for the week's vocabulary quiz and also reviews academic vocabulary commonly used for hypothesizing and synthesizing such as *doubt, infer, hypothesize, predict, assert,* and *conclude.* She asks students to paraphrase and summarize from selected paragraphs of their reading.

Surveys and interviews confirm that English language learners experience considerable difficulty with the linguistic demands of college-level academic work. English and social studies tend to be the areas of the curriculum that are most language intensive and therefore pose both the greatest difficulty and the greatest learning opportunities for English language learners. Chapters 7 and 8 provide detailed information about developing a challenging and high-caliber reading and writing curriculum for these students. College-bound immigrant students may need additional, focused instruction in several areas including reading strategy and speed instruction, writing timed essays and writing from sources, and having discourse-level instruction on vocabulary and grammar.

Developing Strategic Reading Skills

Research reports that English learners in college experience difficulties reading and studying from textbooks (Smoke, 1988; Spack, 1997). Yet reading researchers report that few content-area teachers in middle or high school actively teach reading skills and strategies (Meltzer & Okashige, 2001). Work in both first- and second-language adolescent literacy instruction (Meltzer & Hamann, 2005; Roe, Stoodt, & Burns, 2004) makes it clear that we can and should teach strategies for approaching academic texts across the curriculum in middle and high school. These might include discipline-specific prereading exercises such as guessing the content from titles and pictures that help students get ready to read a passage and use their existing knowledge about the world and about academic texts to help them interpret. It also includes helping students organize ideas in reading through graphic organizers (i.e., charts or graphs that diagram relationships in a given text) and ideas for helping them show that they understand the meaning of a text and also can speculate or think beyond it (e.g., asking students to create alternate endings for a short story). These are the sorts of skills that students will need to hone for college-level reading. Building reading speed is also especially important for English language learners since students report they have much more—perhaps twice as much—reading in college than in high school and are held much more accountable for the information in texts (Harklau, 2001).

Practice Timed Essays and Writing from Sources

Two sorts of writing tasks pose particular difficulty for English learners in college: timed essays and writing from sources. With increasing standardized testing and accountability, timed essays may be becoming the single most important genre—or form or writing—for English learners to learn to produce. These essays play a prominent role in high school graduation examinations, college-entrance tests, college composition placement and exit tests, and college midterm and final examinations. Studies show that English learners find the composing process less automatic or fluent and more time consuming than native-speaker peers (Silva, 1993). It is therefore vitally important to teach immigrants how to approach timed essays. We know that writing academic essays is a cognitively complex task that entails managing multiple demands on attention (e.g., thinking about what you want to write next, choosing words and sentence structure, reading back what you have already read, thinking about correct spelling and punctuation). The only way students learn how to manage these multiple demands under time constraints is by frequent practice.

Writing research papers from sources (Leki & Carson, 1997; Smoke, 1988; Spack, 1997) appears to be another area of particular difficulty for English learners. In particular, though all students must master the ability to quote and paraphrase appropriately from sources, plagiarism has been identified as a particular issue for English language learners (Pennycook, 1996). In some cases, plagiarism is the result of weak language proficiency and difficulties paraphrasing. However, researchers also point out that different cultures have differing conventions and values about citing sources in writing (Pennycook, 1996). In any case, college-bound language learners require copious experience writing from sources to learn how to appropriately cite, quote, and paraphrase from multiple sources of information.

Provide Discourse-Level Instruction on Vocabulary and Grammar

Vocabulary and grammar instruction are rarely popular subjects for either teachers or students. Yet they are extremely important for English learners. Studies show that bilingual students enrolling in U.S. colleges by way of American secondary schools tend to have significantly smaller English vocabularies than their native-speaker peers (Hinkel, 2003)—although of course their combined vocabularies in English and their native languages may far outpace monolinguals. Nonnative speakers of English also make different types of errors in their written texts than native speakers (e.g., verb-tense choice, subject–verb agreement) and make errors on the average with more frequency (Hinkel, 2002; Silva, 1993). Although linguists tell us that even fluent bilinguals may never sound or write just like monolinguals, our society nevertheless tends—somewhat unfairly—to assess bilinguals' language only by how much they sound or write like monolingual English speakers. It is therefore important to provide English learners with targeted vocabulary and grammar instruction.

In most mainstream English classrooms, vocabulary and grammar are taught in isolation from the rest of the curriculum, for example, weekly word lists or diagramming sentences and labeling parts of speech. These exercises tend to emphasize areas in which native speakers commonly make errors such as run-on sentences. Grammar and vocabulary instruction in ESOL classrooms has likewise traditionally been taught in isolation from content areas; however, in recent years there has been a move toward teaching language structure and vocabulary through content-area instruction (see, e.g., Echevarria, Vogt, & Short, 2000). Schleppegrell (2004) suggests that a good approach is to train mainstream teachers to explicitly present and analyze how good academic texts in their field are put together linguistically. So, for example, teachers can show students the linguistic building blocks—grammar and vocabulary—that make a well-developed explanation, discussion, or argument in history writing or a coherent explanation of cause and effect in a science lab report. Likewise, ESOL teachers can contextualize grammar and vocabulary instruction in a specific content area such as English literature. This approach, Schleppegrell argues, helps all students, but especially English learners, to develop the ability to use grammar and vocabulary as tools to build academic texts in the ways they are actually written in content areas. This approach also takes the emphasis off the unrealistic notion that schools should fix bilinguals and eradicate any trace of nonnativeness. Rather, the emphasis should always be on providing students with the language they need to express and manipulate complex ideas in academic content.

Preparing English Language Learners for the Culture of College Work

Hanh, a Vietnamese American immigrant student, is in an American history class. The teacher has told the class since the first day that when they get to college things will be different from high school. Hanh reports that she assigns homework every night but only checks it once a week. "She says, 'College teachers won't be checking your homework. If you don't do the homework, you'll just fail the tests.'" Hanh also receives explicit scaffolding and instruction on note taking. Her teacher gives the class an outline of the main topics they will discuss with big blanks for them to fill in more information. She tells them, "Write down what you think is important. This will help you take notes in college." Sometimes she tells the class, "Write this down," "Draw a picture of this," or "Write yourself an explanation in your own words in your notes" as she lectures. Her teacher provides the class with explicit strategies for selecting a prompt and writing an essay test in the class, such as "Some of these are easier to compare than others" and "Rank order the goals in your mind, and make a value judgment." One week before the end of the semester, Hanh's teacher has asked students to make a schedule for the week showing when and where they are going to study for final exams and indicating what they will do to review.

Although providing high levels of instruction, high expectations, and language-focused feedback on language production are all necessary to help students get into college, there are also ways schools need to prepare students for a shift in academic culture and expectations in college.

Prepare Students to Work Independently

High school students spend much more of their time than college students in classrooms, and their learning activities are more tightly structured (Harklau, 2001). Frequent assignments and tests are designed to keep them on task. Homework may be fairly rote or mechanical in nature (e.g., math problem sets, textbook comprehension questions). In college, on the other hand, students find that they spend far less time in the classroom and have fewer assignments, tests, and deadlines. Instead, students' entire course grade may depend on three or four tests. However, each of those tests will cover more material than a test in high school and demand that students know the material better than they did in high school. Students may also not realize that they will be expected to spend much more time out of class completing tasks than in high school and will be held responsible for pacing their own learning and seeking assistance when necessary.

All college-bound students need to learn to study independently, to structure their own learning, and to meet deadlines in a timely way. However, English learners may be especially in need of study skills and time-management strategies because they often require more time than native speakers to complete assigned readings (Kiang, 1992; Leki & Carson, 1994, 1997). Studies of successful college students suggest that "there is no single time management plan that works for all students in all learning situations" (Allgood, Risko, Alvarez, & Fairbanks, 2000). In other words, students need practice to learn what plan works for them in various study situations. For example, teachers might ask students to create a study schedule for final exams or to write a contract for when they will complete stages of a major project or report.

English learners, like other college-bound students, also need to become self-aware about what skills they possess, what knowledge they have, and how they prefer to learn (Allgood, et al., 2000). For example, students might be given learning styles inventories to help them identify whether they learn best through visual, oral–aural, or other means. They can also be asked to keep a study journal to explore whether they study best with or without music, what sort of light and other environmental factors make them study most efficiently, and whether they study better with or without peers. Successful college students are also able to adapt their study strategies depending on the demands of specific courses (Allgood, et al., 2000). Immigrant students in high school can begin to develop this ability through, for example, guided practice in making study plans to meet the demands of a particular course or assignment, whether it involves memorization, library research, writing a report or PowerPoint presentation, or coordinating group activities.

Teach Note-Taking Skills

In many high school classrooms, teacher lectures are what Alvermann and Moore (1996) term an *auxiliary* approach to communicating subject matter, only one of a number of ways to achieve content learning. Lectures tend to be redundant, serving to review and reinforce the same material presented in assigned reading. In college, however, teacher lectures become the predominant mode of instruction, employed by some 60 to 90% of faculty instructors (Weingartner, 1992). The nature of lectures also changes. Rather than reviewing textbook material, they are used to add supplemental terms, concepts, and examples to the ones presented in the text. Students are thus responsible for learning new material from both the text and lectures as well as figuring out how it fits together. Moreover, high school teachers often ask students to simply copy verbatim what they write on the board, handouts, or overheads. In college, on the other hand, instructors may provide an outline but the bulk of the lecture material may only be presented orally. These changes pose challenges to many new college students, but research suggests that they are especially difficult for English language learners who are still developing listening comprehension skills (Ferris, 1998; Harklau, 2001; Kiang, 1992; Smoke, 1988). All college students, but especially English learners, need practice developing independent, functional note-taking skills and the ability to study from their notes. High school teachers can model self-questioning and summary strategies that students can use to study from notes. They can also teach students a variety of graphic organizer formats to help them make notes and to see relationships among concepts. English language learners may need additional help developing compensatory strategies for listening comprehension such as forming study groups.

Provide Explicit Instruction on Test-Taking Strategies

In one study I found that multiple-choice and other discrete-point format tests dominated English language learners' school experiences in both high school and introductory college work (Harklau, 2001). Yet none of the students could recall ever receiving any explicit instruction on tactics and strategies for studying for and taking multiple-choice tests. With the recent boom in high-stakes standardized testing at school, it is ever more important to provide English learners with explicit tactics and strategies for taking multiple-choice and other discrete-item format tests.

Fostering the Participation of Immigrants in the Social Life of the School

Javier is a Mexican American immigrant student at a prosperous suburban high school in which the immigrant student population has recently surged. Javier knows that extracurricular activities are important on college applications, but he often feels confused or alienated by the extracurricular activities at his school. He also has to depend on the system's bus transportation to and from school and does not have money to participate in most clubs or activities. The school's teachers are beginning to recognize this as a problem and are taking steps to help include students like Javier in the extracurricular life of the school. The school has capitalized on immigrants' interest in soccer to develop it into a major school sport. Coaches went to the local business community to help sponsor participation fees and costs for immigrant students from lower-income families. The school's foreign language department has created an International Affairs Club where ESOL students predominate and take leadership roles. The school's peer mentoring and leadership program has added bilingualism to its selection criteria. Students in this program will earn elective credit for classes in leadership and serve as aides in the main office and counseling office. The school has funded an activities bus for students who stay late working on extracurricular activities and mandated that school clubs alternate morning, lunchtime, and afternoon meetings so that students with after-school work and family responsibilities can still participate. Immigrant students are also explicitly recruited for the school's elective courses and clubs in technology and media that produce the daily announcements broadcast, PowerPoint school bulletin loop, and the school's Web pages.

Schools do not simply deliver academic content. In fact, public secondary schools were founded in part to socialize youth into civic and social dispositions (e.g., leadership, democracy, teamwork) that are valued in American society. Although most schools give attention to the language needs of English language learners, far fewer take proactive steps to integrate the languages and cultures of these newcomers into the social life of the school. Neglecting students' backgrounds sends a powerful if implicit message to immigrants that they do not truly belong in the school community. Research strongly suggests that students' academic success is dependent on their sense of belonging in the school community (Gibson, Bejinez, Hidalgo, & Rolon, 2004; Valenzuela, 1999). Moreover, a lack of opportunities for immigrant students to participate in and lead extracurricular activities can significantly harm their ability to compete for college admission and scholarships.

Be Aware of Popular Culture and Youth Cultures in the School

In theory, popular culture has little to do with classroom instruction. However, because teenagers are the main consumers of popular culture, most high school activities are peppered with references to movie or television characters, sports figures, popular music, advertising, hobbies, and the like. However, popular culture also tends to be very localized and specific in its audiences; for example, hip-hop appeals to a different audience than country music. English learners, as newcomers to American society, may understand few of the referents to pop culture that come into the classroom. Classroom activities or extracurricular activities that include these sorts of references may inadvertently exclude and alienate immigrant students (Duff, 2001; Zuengler, 2004). Conversely, schools often fail to recognize or incorporate immigrants' interests or their own popular cultures into school-sponsored extracurricular activities. Schools that aim to be inclusive and develop civic participation and leadership in college-bound immigrants need to take a proactive stance and ascertain what clubs, sports, or other activities might be established at the school to give immigrant students an active role and voice.

Be Mindful of Diversity Within Immigrant Groups

We all work with certain preconceptions and notions of who students are. Immigrant students in particular tend to be typecast or seen only in terms of their ethnicity or English learner status (Harklau, 2000). However, teachers need to be aware that just because students are from the same continent or country does not mean that they will share the same socioeconomic, educational, language, or ethnic background. For example, a student from a comfortable middle-class family in Mexico City may have little in common with a student from a poor rural Mexican village. There can also be deep divisions between first- and second-generation students from the same ethnic group (Lee, 1996; Olson, 1997; Valenzuela, 1999). In my work with Taiwanese and Hong Kong immigrants, for example, first-generation students tended to regard their American-born coethnic peers as overly materialist slackers who were woefully ignorant about Chinese heritage and language. For their part, American-born peers tended to ignore or even harass recent immigrants. Teachers can educate themselves about differences in immigrant groups at their school by taking opportunities to talk with students, more knowledgeable educators (e.g., ESOL teachers), and community leaders. They must also exercise caution and sensitivity in class discussions and small-group assignments and be alert to tensions among students.

Remove Barriers to Participation in Extracurricular Activities

First-generation immigrant families may struggle financially, creating barriers to the participation of children in extracurricular activities. For example, students may lack the money for all of the necessary extras that tend to come with extracurricular involvement such as special clothing or sports or music equipment. They may also be under considerable pressure to work before or after school. In suburban and rural areas, transportation is also a major issue, and many students do not have any option other than the school bus. In my experience, immigrant students will rarely raise this issue at school or ask for help. They will simply opt not to participate based on the cost. It is therefore important for schools to take a proactive stance, anticipating potential obstacles and incorporating solutions into the standard operations of extracurricular activities at the school. This may include club fundraising, limits on how much any club or activity requires students to spend, going to local businesses to sponsor team activities, or organizing carpools.

Make a Place for Home Languages and Cultures in the School

Americans historically have had a conflicted relationship with the notion of bilingualism. We laud monolingual English-speaking students who achieve high levels of foreign-language proficiency. We love it when spies in movies or on TV jet around the world switching effortlessly among languages. But at the same time we neglect immigrant students' home languages and insist that they do everything in English. Research shows, however, that the students who value home-language skills and work on bilingualism as part of schooling are the ones who tend to do best academically in the long run (Cummins, 1981; Davidson, 1996; Thomas & Collier, 2002; Valenzuela, 1999).

Dual-language schooling is an ideal option, but even if that is not feasible there are other ways to show that students' home languages and cultures are valued at the school and considered an academic asset. Some of these include advanced heritage language classes specifically for students who already speak the language at home, bilingual aide and peer mentoring programs, multilingual school signs, materials, and other school-based communication. Schools can capitalize on existing service learning electives or can develop new ones where students can work in a variety of communities including immigrant communities and can develop credentials in civic leadership. Perhaps most important is to give students strong role models: bilingual teachers, community members, or graduates of the school from the same immigrant group who have gone to college themselves.

Additional Resources on Getting Multilingual Students Ready for College

General references on college readiness for immigrants and other underrepresented groups include Slavin & Calderón (2001), Gándara, Bial, and the National Postsecondary Education Cooperative's Working Group on Access to Postsecondary Education (2001), Lucas (1997), Tierney, Corwin, & Colyar (2005), and Kazis, Vargas, & Hoffman (2004).

An excellent source on how tracking affects classroom instruction is Jeannie Oakes's (1985) classic text, *Keeping Track*. Other useful sources include Oakes, Gamoran, and Page (1992), Oakes and Lipton (1992), and Wheelock (1992). See Harklau (1994b) for examples of immigrant student experiences with tracking and Callahan (2005) for a broad view of how tracking practices affect immigrant achievement. See Mehan et al. (1994) for information on how the AVID program works to counteract tracking.

Sources of information on providing English language learners with high-caliber, challenging academic and linguistic preparation can be found throughout this volume, specifically in Sections I and II. Also useful is the report of California's "ESL Intersegmental Project" (California Pathways Project, 2000), a task force that looked across high school and college curricula for English language learners.

Middle and high school educators interested in preparing English language learners for the academic culture and literacy demands of college work can consult the *Handbook of College Reading and Study Strategy Research* (Flippo & Caverly, 2000). Especially relevant is a chapter (Pugh, Pawan, & Antommarchi, 2000) explaining typical reading demands on new college students. Carson (2000) also provides an overview of reading and writing demands of college tasks for English language learners.

A great deal of research has appeared in recent years on the interconnection of immigrants' social worlds and academic achievement in North American high schools. Some of these include Duff (2002), Gibson, Gándara, and Koyama (2004), Harklau (2000), Lee (1996, 1997, 2001), Olson (1997), Suárez-Orozco and Suárez-Orozco (1995), Suárez-Orozco and Todorova (2003), and Zuengler (2004).

References

Allgood, W. P., Risko, V. J., Alvarez, M. C., & Fairbanks, M. M. (2000). Factors that influence study. In R. F. Flippo & D. C. Caverly (Eds.), *Handbook of college reading and study strategy research* (pp. 201–219). Mahwah, NJ: Lawrence Erlbaum.

Alvermann, D. E., & Moore, D. W. (1996). Secondary school reading. In R. Barr, M. L. Kamil, P. Mosenthal, & P. D. Pearson (Eds.), *Handbook of reading research* (Vol. 2) (pp. 951–983). Mahwah, NJ: Lawrence Erlbaum Associates.

Bankston, C. L., & Zhou, M. (1997). The social adjustment of Vietnamese American adolescents: Evidence of a segmented-assimilation approach. *Social Science Quarterly, 78*(2), 508–523.

Berrol, S. C. (1995). *Growing up American: Immigrant children in America, then and now.* New York: Twayne Publishers.

California Pathways Project. (2000). California Pathways: The second language student in public high schools, colleges, and universities. Updated with revised writing proficiency descriptors, writing samples, and user's guide. Sacramento, CA: California Community Colleges Chancellor's Office. Retrieved May 2, 2007 from http://http://www.catesol.org/pathways.pdf

Callahan, R. (2005). Tracking and high school English learners: Limiting opportunity to learn. *American Educational Research Journal, 42*(2), 305–328.

Carson, J. G. (2000). A task analysis of reading and writing in academic contexts. In D. Belcher & A. Hirvela (Eds.), *Linking literacies: Perspectives on L2 reading–writing connections* (pp. 48–83). Ann Arbor: University of Michigan Press.

College Board National Task Force on Minority High Achievement. (1999). Reaching the top: A report of the National Task Force on Minority High Achievement (No. 201635). New York: College Entrance Examination Board.

Cummins, J. (1981). The role of primary language development in promoting educational success for language minority students. In Office of Bilingual Bicultural Education, California State Department of Education (Ed.), *Schooling and language minority students: A theoretical framework* (pp. 3–49). Los Angeles: Evaluation, Dissemination, and Assessment Center; California State University.

Davidson, A. L. (1996). *Making and molding identity in schools: Student narratives on race, gender, and academic engagement.* Albany: State University of New York Press.

Duff, P. A. (2001). Language, literacy, content, and (pop) culture: Challenges for ESL students in mainstream courses. *Canadian Modern Language Review, 59*(1), 103–131.

Duff, P. A. (2002). The discursive co-construction of knowledge, identity, and difference: An ethnography of communication in the high school mainstream. *Applied Linguistics, 23*(3), 323–347.

Echevarria, J., Vogt, M., & Short, D. (2000). *Making content comprehensible for English language learners: The SIOP model.* Boston: Allyn and Bacon.

ESL Intersegmental Project. (1997). *California pathways: The second language student in public high schools, colleges, and universities.* Glendale: California Teachers of English to Speakers of Other Languages (CATESOL).

Fashola, O. S., & Slavin, R. E. (2001). Effective dropout prevention and college attendance programs for Latino students. In R. E. Slavin & M. Calderón (Eds.), *Effective programs for Latino students* (pp. 67–100). Mahwah, NJ: Lawrence Erlbaum.

Ferris, D. (1998). Students' views of academic aural/oral skills: A comparative needs analysis. *TESOL Quarterly, 32*(2), 289–318.

Flippo, R. F., & Caverly, D. C. (Eds.). (2000). *Handbook of college reading and study strategy research.* Mahwah, NJ: Lawrence Erlbaum Associates.

Gándara, P. C., Bial, D., & National Postsecondary Education Cooperative. Working Group on Access to Postsecondary Education. National Center for Education Statistics. (2001). *Paving the way to postsecondary education: K–12 intervention programs for underrepresented youth.* Washington, DC: National Center for Education Statistics, Office of Educational Research and Improvement U.S. Dept. of Education.

Gee, J. P., Hull, G. A., & Lankshear, C. (1996). *The new work order: Behind the language of the new capitalism.* Boulder, CO: Westview Press.

Gibson, M. A., Bejinez, L. F., Hidalgo, N., & Rolon, C. (2004). Belonging and school participation: Lessons from a migrant student club. In M. A. Gibson, P. Gándara, & J. P. Koyama (Eds.), *School connections: U.S. Mexican youth, peers, and school achievement* (pp. 129–149). New York: Teachers College Press.

Gibson, M. A., Gándara, P. C., & Koyama, J. P. (2004). *School connections: U.S. Mexican youth, peers, and school achievement.* New York: Teachers College Press.

Harklau, L. (1994a). ESL and mainstream classes: Contrasting second language learning contexts. *TESOL Quarterly, 28*(2), 241–272.

Harklau, L. (1994b). Jumping tracks: How language-minority students negotiate evaluations of ability. *Anthropology and Education Quarterly, 25*(3), 347–363.

Harklau, L. (1994c). Tracking and linguistic minority students: Consequences of ability grouping for second language learners. *Linguistics and Education, 6*, 221–248.

Harklau, L. (2000). From the "good kids" to the "worst": Representations of English language learners across educational settings. *TESOL Quarterly, 34*(1), 35–67.

Harklau, L. (2001). From high school to college: Student perspectives on literacy practices. *Journal of Literacy Research, 33*(1), 33–70.

Harklau, L. (2007). The adolescent English language learner: Identities lost and found. In J. Cummins & C. Davison (Eds.), *International handbook of English language teaching.* Norwell, MA: Springer.

Hayes-Bautista, D. E., Schink, W. O., & Chapa, J. (1988). *The burden of support: Young Latinos in an aging society.* Stanford, CA: Stanford University Press.

Hinkel, E. (2002). *Second language writers' text: Linguistic and rhetorical features.* Mahwah, NJ: Lawrence Erlbaum Associates.

Hinkel, E. (2003). Simplicity without elegance: Features of sentences in L1 and L2 academic texts. *TESOL Quarterly, 37*(2), 275–301.

Huebner, T., & Corbett, G. C. (2004). *Rethinking high schools: Five profiles of innovative models for student success.* San Francisco: WestEd for the Bill & Melinda Gates Foundation.

Kazis, R., Vargas, J., & Hoffman, N. (2004). *Double the numbers: Increasing postsecondary credentials for underrepresented youth.* Cambridge, MA: Harvard Education Press.

Kiang, P. N.-C. (1992). Issues of curriculum and community for first-generation Asian Americans in college. In L. S. Zwerling & H. B. London (Eds.), *First-generation students: Confronting the cultural issues* (pp. 97–112). San Francisco: Jossey-Bass.

Lee, S. J. (1996). *Unraveling the "model minority" stereotype: Listening to Asian American youth.* New York: Teachers College Press.

Lee, S. J. (1997). The road to college: Hmong American women's pursuit of higher education. *Harvard Educational Review, 67*(4), 803–827.

Lee, S. J. (2001). More than "model minorities" or "delinquents": A look at Hmong American high school students. *Harvard Educational Review, 71*(3), 505–528.

Leki, I., & Carson, J. (1997). "Completely different worlds": EAP and the writing experiences of ESL students in university courses. *TESOL Quarterly, 31*(1), 39–69.

Leki, I., & Carson, J. G. (1994). Students' perceptions of EAP writing instruction and writing needs across the disciplines. *TESOL Quarterly, 28*(1), 81–101.

Leonhardt, D. (2005, May 14). A closer look at income mobility. *New York Times.*

Lucas, T. (1997). *Into, through, and beyond secondary school: Critical transitions for immigrant youths.* Washington, DC: Center for Applied Linguistics and Delta Systems.

Mehan, H., Hubbard, L., & Villanueva, I. (1994). Forming academic identities: Accommodation without assimilation among involuntary minorities. *Anthropology and Education Quarterly, 25*(2), 91–117.

Meltzer, J., & Hamann, E. T. (2005). *Meeting the literacy development needs of adolescent English language learners through content area learning. Part Two: Focus on classroom teaching and learning strategies.* Providence, RI: Education Alliance at Brown University, Northeast and Islands Regional Educational Laboratory.

Meltzer, J., & Okashige, S. (2001). *Supporting adolescent literacy across the content areas: Perspectives on policy and practice* (ERIC Document Reproduction Service. Providence, RI: Northeast and Islands Regional Educational Laboratory at Brown University. ED459442).

Oakes, J. (1985). *Keeping track: How schools structure inequality.* New Haven, CT: Yale University Press.

Oakes, J., Gamoran, A., & Page, R. N. (1992). Curriculum differentiation: Opportunities, outcomes, and meanings. In P. W. Jackson (Ed.), *Handbook of research on curriculum* (pp. 571–608). New York: Macmillan.

Oakes, J., & Lipton, M. (1992). Detracking schools: Early lessons from the field. *Phi Delta Kappan, 73*(6), 448–454.

Olneck, M. R. (1995). Immigrants and education. In J. A. Banks & C. A. M. Banks (Eds.), *Handbook of research on multicultural education* (pp. 310–327). New York: Macmillan.

Olson, L. (1997). *Made in America: Immigrant students in our public schools.* New York: New Press.

Orfield, G. (2004). *Dropouts in America: Confronting the graduation rate crisis.* Cambridge, MA: Harvard Education Press.

Pennycook, A. (1996). Borrowing others' words: Text, ownership, memory, and plagiarism. *TESOL Quarterly, 30*(2), 201–230.

Phelan, P., Davidson, A. L., & Yu, H. C. (1998). *Adolescents' worlds: Negotiating family, peers, and school.* New York: Teachers College Press.

Portes, A., & Zhou, M. (1993). The new second generation: Segmented assimilation and its variants. *Annals of the American Academy of Political and Social Science, 530,* 74–96.

Pugh, S. L., Pawan, F., & Antommarchi, C. (2000). Academic literacy and the new college learner. In R. F. Flippo & D. C. Caverly (Eds.), *Handbook of College Reading and Study Strategy Research* (pp. 25–42). Mahwah, NJ: Lawrence Erlbaum.

Reeves, J. (2004). "Like everybody else": Equalizing educational opportunity for English language learners. *TESOL Quarterly, 38*(1), 43–66.

Roe, B. D., Stoodt, B. D., & Burns, P. C. (2004). *Secondary school literacy instruction: The content areas* (8th ed.). Boston: Houghton Mifflin Co.

Schleppegrell, M. J. (2004). *The language of schooling: A functional linguistics perspective.* Mahwah, NJ: Lawrence Erlbaum.

Silva, T. (1993). Towards an understanding of the distinct nature of L2 writing: The ESL research and its implications. *TESOL Quarterly, 27,* 657–678.

Slavin, R. E., & Calderón, M. (Eds.). (2001). *Effective programs for Latino students.* Mahwah, NJ: Lawrence Erlbaum Associates.

Smoke, T. (1988). Using feedback from ESL students to enhance their success in college. In S. Benesch (Ed.), *Ending remediation: Linking ESL and content in higher education* (pp. 7–19). Washington, DC: Teachers of English to Speakers of Other Languages.

Spack, R. (1997). The acquisition of academic literacy in a second language: A longitudinal case study. *Written Communication, 14*(1), 3–62.

Stanton-Salazar, R. D. (2004). Social capital among working-class minority students. In M. A. Gibson, P. Gándara, & J. P. Koyama (Eds.), *U.S. Mexican youth, peers, and school achievement* (pp. 18–38). New York: Teachers College Press.

Suárez-Orozco, C., & Suárez-Orozco, M. (1995). *Transformations: Immigration, family life, and achievement motivation among Latino adolescents.* Stanford, CA: Stanford University Press.

Suárez-Orozco, C., & Todorova, I. L. B. (Eds.). (2003). *Understanding the social worlds of immigrant youth. New directions for youth development, no. 100.* San Francisco: Jossey-Bass.

Thomas, W. P., & Collier, V. P. (2002). *A national study of school effectiveness for language minority students' long-term academic achievement: Executive summary.* Santa Cruz, CA: Center for Research on Excellence and Diversity in Education.

Tierney, W. G., Corwin, Z. B., & Colyar, J. E. (Eds.). (2005). *Preparing for college: Nine elements of effective outreach.* Albany: State University New York Press.

U.S. Department of Labor, The Secretary's Commission on Achieving Necessary Skills. (1991). *What work requires of schools: A SCANS report for America 2000.* Washington, DC: Government Printing Office.

Valenzuela, A. (1999). *Subtractive schooling: U.S.–Mexican youth and the politics of caring.* Albany: State University of New York Press.

Verplaetse, L. S. (1998). How content teachers interact with English language learners. *TESOL Journal, 7*(5), 24–28.

Weingartner, R. H. (1992). *Undergraduate education: Goals and means.* New York: American Council on Education and Macmillan.

Wheelock, A. (1992). *Crossing the tracks: How "untracking" can save America's schools.* New York: New Press.

Zuengler, J. (2004). Jackie Chan drinks Mountain Dew: Constructing cultural models of citizenship. *Linguistics and Education, 14*(3–4), 277–304.

III: School and Community Collaboration

Editor's Introduction

This section examines the linkages between schools and their communities and how the linkages can effectively engage students, especially English language learners (ELLs). Each chapter focuses on a different kind of community involvement, and each takes a different perspective on what it means to be part of a school community. Though the traditional view might be that the community is the neighborhood of families and businesses immediately surrounding the school, the chapters in this section invite the reader to broaden the definition of *community*. Through the perspective of the traditional view, school personnel usually expect that the parents of students will be involved in particular ways: attending parent–teacher conferences, participating in school events, and helping students with homework, to name a few. Furthermore, the traditional view often defines the community as the source of potential funding, limited as the resources of the family and local businesses might be. Unfortunately, many teachers and administrators view the parents of ELLs through the same cultural lens as mainstream American students. They have the same expectations for both groups without taking into account that the ELL community may differ vastly in terms of cultural background, expectations of schools, and ability to provide resources, whether financial or in terms of time availability. This section provides three chapters that defy the traditional view of school–community involvement.

Challenging the notion of the community as local neighborhood only, the interview with Colón bids the reader to consider how a large national organization—the National Council of La Raza (NCLR)—works to empower Latino students and families in myriad ways. NCLR works with community-based organizations (CBOs) in local regions but has the strength of a national organization. Whether large or small, the CBOs provide high-quality services including voter registration, funding, policy analysis, and educational programs of all types. The advantage of such an organization lies in the fact that the agenda and commitment to the education of Latinos is clear. For example, Colón points out that bilingual education as a viable option is not debated among Latinos. Taking educational philosophy and cultural background into account are strengths of this organization as it works to foster community–school linkages.

In Chapter 11, Migliacci challenges the idea that the public school is the seeker of community partnerships and that funding comes only from businesses. This chapter illustrates that the community can provide unique professional development opportunities for public school teachers through creative partnering. The reader learns that the community partner in this chapter is a large university that initiates the collaboration and provides training for high school teachers, funding for the partnership, and education for parents on what their children need for success in a university medical program. The ongoing success of this partnership has prompted a large insurance company to collaborate with the public schools and to extend the program to include middle schoolers, giving students an even better chance at academic success. The insurance company not only provides funding but also training in the medical insurance field, showing students the wide range of medical careers available within the city and state.

Finally, in Chapter 12 Wei shows how Asian Americans United in Philadelphia's Chinatown had to figure out ways to leverage its way into the school, not the other way around. In addition, this parent-led activist organization sought out ways they could participate in the school community. Ultimately, the members of the organization decided to ensure that as parents and as members of a particular cultural group they would create a charter school. In this way, the community would feel that a school they created would value, respect, and honor the cultural ways and beliefs of the community, thus challenging the traditional notion that parents have to accept the status quo or that it is the school that dictates its expectations for parent involvement.

CHAPTER 10

Community-Based Organizations: Partnerships for Student Success

ANTHONY J. COLÓN

Editors' note: Having heard Mr. Anthony Colón speak at the 2003 Brown University/ Annenberg Research Symposium on Educating English Language Learners, we were anxious to have the opportunity to discuss his ideas concerning school/community linkages further. Mr. Colón has a warm, pragmatic manner about him; he has years of experience, and there is much work to be done. But with these years of experience comes a wisdom and a temperance that seasons his pragmatism. We met Mr. Colón at the National Council of La Raza headquarters in Washington, D.C., in August 2004 to interview him in his office. When he arrived he was with his daughter, a young grade-school child, who was no stranger to the office. They were on their way to a summer vacation, but Mr. Colón had made the time for us to speak. Mr. Colón found an office for his daughter to work in while we conducted our interview.

Editors: Can you tell us what the National Council of La Raza is all about?

The National Council of La Raza (NCLR) is the largest Latino civil rights and advocacy organization in the United States. As a national organization, we work to improve life opportunities for Latinos throughout the country in many different ways. At the heart of NCLR are our affiliates—more than 300 Latino-focused, community-based organizations (CBOs) to which we provide assistance, such as capacity building, policy analysis, and funding. These organizations range in size from very small, $200,000 budget, single-service, mom-and-pop organizations providing voter registration information in lower California to multimillion-dollar, multiservice organizations providing mental health services, a charter school, an adult education program, and a welfare-to-work program all in one. No matter the size or service offered, they all have one thing in common: They provide high-quality services to Latinos in the United States and Puerto Rico. By far the majority of these organizations are led by Latinos, so the agenda and commitment are clear.

Let me give you an example of what I mean by that last statement. If someone is talking about building a school, developing a school with a CBO that's an affiliate of ours, we don't have to convince them that bilingual education is the correct thing for children. It's understood; it's a done deal, so we go beyond that. In other instances, when an organization or community is trying to start a school and may not be Latino—may not have that cultural competence—we spend a lot of time trying to convince them why bilingual education is a good thing for English language learners.

NCLR is one of the largest small-school developers in the country and the largest that is Latino led. We have about 90 schools in our network, the majority of which have been developed in collaboration, cooperation, and consultation with a CBO affiliate. At some point an affiliate comes to us and says, "We are interested in running a school." We don't say, "Let's go to Missouri because they need a charter school there," or "Let's go to Texas because we know the statistics and Texas has a lot of Latinos, so we should go to El Paso and open a school." That's not how it works at NCLR. We promote a grassroots approach that is not imposing; our CBOs and affiliates come to us; these are the programs that will be successful and sustainable over time.

Before going any further, I would like to talk a little more about something I just mentioned—about the majority of our schools working in collaboration with a CBO. I want to establish the fact that there's a difference between community-run schools and CBO schools. In the first instance, community-run schools, there is a group of people in a particular community who come together—these could be teachers or parents or other community members—who are really wonderful and want to do something for the community. They want to build a school, and although they may even live in the community, they are not linked to any local community-based organizations. Meanwhile, there are already community-based organizations in the area, which are linked directly to the community; they are providing culturally and linguistically relevant services and have already developed relationships—understanding and trust—with community members. While a community-run school is of course something we support, we are convinced that if you work with CBOs that are linked directly to the community, the school will be much more successful because the foundation has already been laid.

I'll give you an example that shows what I mean by this. In Oakland, California, we have a school called Lighthouse Community Charter. When we say it's our school, that means we (NCLR) provide funding for it, but they have affiliations with a lot of other people, not just us; we don't manage the school. But it's our school in the sense that we provide funding for them, and we work closely with them. When they came to us originally we were hesitant because they were not tied to a community-based organization. They were two incredibly bright, young entrepreneurs who wanted to start a school in their community. We were reluctant; we said, "What are your ties to the community? What do you know about the Latino community? How are you going to tie the services to the community?" And do you know what they did? They went out and started making those linkages with the community—with CBOs and different groups of people. And because they established ties in the community from the beginnning, those two incredibly wonderful and committed people are now responsible for starting one of the best schools in our charter school network; it is a real success.

So what I'm trying to build here is a sense that for us at the National Council of La Raza, the community-based organization work is critical whether we are focusing on health or education programs or advocacy work around immigration or housing rights. This piece is critical for us because of the cultural competence that's built into the work of the CBOs— this cultural and linguistic relevance and understanding. All of those things are built in. We also believe that the more supports, the more wrap-around services you can provide to the children and to the family, the better off they're going to be, because so many issues are interconnected and are directly connected to the family.

Editors: Could you describe how, exactly, CBOs and schools can be effectively woven together? How is that manifested?

Let me try. Nueva Esperanza in Philadelphia, for example, is one of the largest, if not the largest, Latino CBO in Philadelphia, providing all kinds of services, including education services with linkages to higher education. About four years ago they came to us and said, "We're ready to start a charter school. We think it will be a great idea. We think we have all the competencies we need to do that." So we started working with them four years ago, and it has been an ongoing process, because you are really never finished.

The very first thing that they provide that lots of other groups don't provide is community buy-in. You don't need to do new grassroots work because that has already been done by the CBO. So when they develop a new program, in this case a school, they didn't need to go out and get new buy-in from the community. There was already community support and community buy-in, because this CBO had been working with this community for years. That is a central element, I think, of building a school that really works for a community: buy-in from the community and from the parents.

Now the school is running. The CBO provides the school facility, and the school is a separate 501(c)(3). Sometimes the school is housed in the CBO, or vice versa; sometimes the CBO is housed in the school. Or the school and CBO could be in separate locations all together. In many cases CBOs have several different venues, with specialized services offered at each.

We require that our schools become a 501(c)(3), although there's nothing in the law to my knowledge that obligates anyone to do that. We've seen situations where the CBO gets into financial problems, and everything goes down, so we want to ensure solid financial viability and governance. We think it's important because we don't want our funds to be commingled with other things going on in the community. Our funds are earmarked because of funder restrictions and our own restrictions, to develop the school. So the school is a separate 501(c)(3), but the parent, the umbrella agency, is the CBO. In the case of Nueva Esperanza, they literally provide the school with mental health services for the entire family—guidance for not only the children but the entire family. They provide leadership development for the school as well as all of their other programs, which parents are a part of. They do focus groups with parents around educational issues so that all of the services that are provided by that CBO to the community are provided to the school. That is the right link.

Editors: Can you talk a little more about what makes the services offered by these CBOs so special? Can you help us understand what cultural competence really looks like?

Sure. Let's look at the SeaMar Community Health Centers. They have a $60 million budget and they provide health services to the Latino community in 15 different locations around the state of Washington. I visited one of their centers, a nursing home in Seattle, which specializes in providing care for elderly Latino patients with Alzheimer's and AIDS. I'll tell you, I was so blown away, because you walk into this place and it really celebrates the Latino culture. It celebrates the language; it's not a problem to speak Spanish in this place. They hire staff that can speak the language so they can communicate with the patients however they are most comfortable; their prescriptions are written in Spanish. It's just an incredible and wonderful thing because they're providing dignity—the intangible things that you can't touch, that you can't measure. What's so important about it? People who are elderly go to this place and, maybe for the first time in their lives, are treated like real human beings and completely valued and respected for who they are, culture and language and all. It's an incredible place.

For another example, a totally different type of group is the Parent Institute for Quality Education (PIQE) in San Diego, California. They've been around for more than 13 years, and they focus all of their work on providing information, training, and parent awareness for parents of children in the traditional public school system. They help parents understand that no matter what their situation in life—no matter what their economic status, no matter what language they speak—they are the primary caregivers and providers, the first teachers of their children, and that nobody in this world is going to advocate for that child more than the parent. So they have a very unique type of training. I've seen it work; I can't talk enough about it. I've been in this business for 30 years, and this is probably one of the best, if not the best, parent education programs in the country. There's no mystery about what makes it so successful: It honors parents. One of the requirements, for example, for those who are going to be instructors in the program, is that they must have experience with poverty. Why? Because by far the majority of parents they serve are living in poverty. So when the instructor is sitting across from a parent, an immigrant parent who doesn't speak English, hasn't had a formal education, and is experiencing the difficulties of poverty, the instructor can not only communicate but can also relate and understand where that person is coming from. It's just an incredible program because it's very parent centered.

I always smile when I say that because in education someone came up with the term *child-centered education* a hundred years ago, and what I always say to people is, "If you really want to know whether you're child centered or not, dissect your entire program. Look at your hiring practices, look at your curriculum, look at how you deal with conflict in school, look at how you deal with the school schedule. Look at all those things. List them, and see who you are centering those things around." Let's look at the school schedule for example. Traditionally schools go on vacation in July and August. This is a practice that began in the agricultural days many years ago, but is this really best for today's children and communities? What do the children do whose parents don't get vacation in the summer, who work year round? Do children really learn best this way, or would they retain more knowledge and skills if they attended school year round? A school that is adult centered is very different than a school that is child centered. When you walk into a school that is child centered and you walk into kindergarten you notice that things will be at the eye level of the children, not adults.

So when we work with our schools and CBOs, these are the kinds of things that are so critically important—that they really become child centered when they claim to be child centered and parent centered when they need to be parent centered and not the reverse. Let me tell you a little bit about a school I worked at that I believe truly exemplified the term *child centered.*

After 20 years of working in education in New York City, the last 10 of which I worked as an administrator for the district, I realized, "I can't do this anymore. I want to have more direct impact and work directly with the kids. I want to be able to implement the things that I really believe I should be working on in education." So I went to work in a school in Oakland, California. It was the first time in my life that I worked in a school that wasn't focused on minority or inner-city kids, and I was extremely hesitant at first. I thought, "I just don't know how to do this; I've always worked with Latino and African American kids; that's all I'm good at." Well, needless to say, that's not true. I went to work in this school—a small, independent, nonprofit school with approximately 500 kids, pre-K through 12th grade—and I spent the next three years of my life in a lab learning about real education. The two women who founded the school—one from California and one from New York—had experiences similar to my own. They got fed up and said, "We want to start our own thing because we believe education should be done differently." They founded the school and were able to operationalize the concept of child-centered education.

It is a year-round school that follows block scheduling, and although it includes pre-K–12th grade, the school does not group the children by age or grades as we have done traditionally. Some people think this would be complete chaos, but it isn't. There are rules and guidelines so that we don't put a 14-year-old with a 5-year-old; it's not craziness. We did a lot of authentic testing, in addition to all of the regular standardized testing required by the state. Then at the end of the year we did profiles for every single child and said, "You know what? We got 'x' done, we didn't get 'y' done, and we got 'z' done." We identified the most important concepts that we wanted to cover with the kids, looked at their abilities and needs, and then grouped them depending on how we would get that particular group from point A to point B and identified the teacher whose skills best matched the group of students' needs. That's the way teachers were assigned. It was much different from having a third-grade vacancy and hiring someone who had absolutely no connection to the children he or she was going to be teaching. There was a curriculum and a syllabus, but they weren't written in stone; they were flexible. If we didn't get through New York history with our sixth graders, it didn't mean that the world was going to end. The fine arts became part of the core curriculum, because we don't learn just through reading and math, you know? The strategies we used were effective and totally different than those used in the traditional system. It was just incredible.

Now let's look at governance and conflict mediation. This particular school, the independent school in Oakland, dealt with conflicts through a massive training program in conflict resolution for the entire school. When I say the entire school, I mean children, parents, teachers, and school administrators. This was different from what I was used to and admittedly difficult to adjust to at first. I had come from a world where I was in charge. I was the director; I had a $50 million budget; I had thousands of people who worked for me. If there was a conflict, I was the one who took care of it, and I told people what they needed to do. I then found myself in this school in Oakland, where, if there was a conflict between a teacher and the principal, they had to sit down and talk about it. If there was a conflict between a teacher and a child, they had to sit down and talk about it. There was nothing demeaning; there was no loss of respect whatsoever. The kids called me and all the teachers by our first names. This may sound like a bad idea, like it wouldn't promote respect, but I have to tell you, it created an intimate, family-like environment, and there was absolutely no loss of respect. So I was working in this incredibly supportive and innovative environment, and I kept saying, "I'm getting paid to do this. This is so wonderful." I bring that experience with me wherever I go; it reinforced the whole concept of education, which I believe in so much—that we need to be able to meet the needs of each child. So that is what we try to do with our schools and community-based organizations at NCLR. There's a holistic approach.

Holistic approach, those are loaded words, you know? I try not to use them because it turns certain people off. I always love to say I use that phrase differently; I don't mean the fluffy stuff, which is what people think of immediately. Our organizations and schools are embedded in the community, and the community response is a holistic response. So, if a part of the childrens' educational issues is a need for better nutrition, then we have to meet that need. And there is something in the community that ties back to that need, and that may be a breakfast program that addresses the nutritional needs of children. So we embed those breakfast, lunch, and snack programs into the school. If the issues are around a high prevalence of domestic abuse, violence in the home, abuse of all kinds, then it's very difficult to educate children if those needs aren't being met too. If the school or its CBO doesn't have the wraparound services to meet the children's or parents' needs, they partner with other CBOs to bring the needed services to the school. And it needs to be more than a referral system, because it is usually not enough to simply tell people where other services are offered. There are so many factors that can hold them back from taking advantage of these services—finances, transportation, childcare—just to name a few. I'm talking about actually providing them access to these services. We have to either bring the services to the community and its people or bring the people to the services. That's how it has to be. That's the link—that physical movement back and forth. And that means, for example, that the school develops a program with a CBO, and every Friday a bus load of parents goes to this center to do a training. It is that specific.

When I left the independent school in Oakland I was just describing, I became the principal of a charter school in Oakland. I went from a pretty affluent community school to an extremely poor community in a poor area of Oakland. The school was housed in portables, bungalows, in an industrial park. Almost all of the parents—99%—were undocumented Mexican immigrants, which brings a whole collection of problems to the table, which many of us, including myself at the time, are unaware of. So I went to work there, and that experience was very different because the academic programs also needed to include feeding and clothing children. I mean clothes and a whole myriad of other issues, which if you are middle class and you have some money, you don't have to deal with. We knew that we couldn't do this alone, so we linked with a local CBO, the Spanish Speaking Unity Council in Oakland, California, which is a huge community-based organization that could then provide us with some of those services and that had expertise working with people who are undocumented.

Editors: Can we ask you a specific question? Imagine a new principal assigned to that school or a school like that, wanting to make that link, having read your chapter and understanding the importance of linking the school with some local CBOs. Where do they get started? What do they need to do?

I didn't know this at the time either; I didn't have a manual, but I knew, for example, that national organizations like NCLR exist, as well as similar, smaller local organizations. If you're interested in starting a school in a Latino community, NCLR is a great resource. It's as easy as going to their Web site and searching their affiliate database for CBOs in your area or picking up the phone and calling them. Once you get the information about groups in the community, you go out and you walk the streets and you make those ties. You ask to meet with the executive director or the education director, and you sit and you talk to them; I have found that they are usually more than willing to share their experiences and offer guidance.

Having a school linked with a CBO really helps connect the school with the community, which is so important for its success and sustainability. Ideally the community will be not only supportive but also involved in the development of the school, from the beginning. That was one of the things that I found most fascinating about the charter school in Oakland: When I tell you that this is a poor school and poor community, it was poor only in material things but the richest school I have ever been in, in my life, in terms of energy, in terms of willingness to go every step of the way. One of the biggest problems we have in education in this country is getting parents involved in the Parent Teacher Association (PTA) or other similar parent engagement groups. However, we had more than 80% attendance at every single parent meeting we held. If something happened, say a water pipe broke, and we needed to get a message to the parents that we were calling an emergency meeting for the next evening, I could actually put that message in the kids' backpacks; they would take it home, and 80% of the parents would be there the next night or would pick up the phone and ask, "What's the issue? How can I help?"

Editors: Why? And How?

Because it was their school. Six years prior to my getting there, they got fed up with the local public school. Now, I want to make sure it is clear that I am not suggesting that it is not worthwhile to work with the traditional public schools in our attempts to improve education in this country. I really believe that they can and must be a part of that effort. We can't just find fault with the system; we need to work with them, do good things with them. On a local scale, if a community is not finding success with its traditional public school, as in this case, it may decide that the most effective and fastest way to bring about the desired changes in the community is to create a charter school. The parents in this Oakland community were fed up with a lot of issues at their local public school—particularly security and safety. So a group of organizers—community people, parents, teachers, and staff—got together and said, "We need to respond to this. We can't let our children get hurt and beat up." So they created the idea of the school and then got it up and running, which of course was a struggle. So this became their school, which they worked hard for, and their response was, "This is our school. This is for my child." There was huge investment.

Let me share another story about that school, which exemplifies the parents' and community's investment and ownership. When I was there we applied for the 21st Century School Program Grant from the Department of Education. We got it. The grant funders required a separate, dedicated venue for the program, but we didn't have any extra rooms. What we needed to do was rent another portable, which we managed to do. We rented another portable, and it came in—except we had one problem. Where the last portable was positioned, the electricity ended. This is stuff that you don't learn in books, and what do I know about this stuff, you know? I was the principal; I had no clue. So we brought in an electrician to give us an estimate, and it turned out to be a lot more money than we had in the budget; it would be impossible for us to afford. We called a meeting to explain the problem to the parents and the parents said, "No problem, we'll come in. We'll dig the ditches. We're plumbers; we're electricians; we'll lay everything down; we just won't hook it up, because that's illegal. Then you get someone to hook it up for $20."

So the next weekend 100 parents and community members came out to the school, to the portables in the industrial park: 50 men and their wives. The women set up barbecues and cooked for us, and the men started to dig. I offered to rent a John Deere tractor or backhoe, but they refused. "We are not going to rent that; we'll do it with our own hands," and they did; we did. They did it all with picks and shovels. When I asked why, there was one common answer: "Because this is for our children."

Meanwhile, in many other areas of the country, in other schools, we can't even get 10 parents to a PTA meeting—and we wonder why. That's because there is no ownership, and we're not showing them that there can and should be ownership. We're trying to bring in 50 parents who have never had bagels and cream cheese in their lives, and we serve them bagels and cream cheese to feel welcome and comfortable? We don't give them dulces, pan dulce. We talk to them in English and they can barely understand what we're saying, so it's no wonder they don't feel ownership; it's not theirs; it's ours. Latino parents are very grateful; they want the best for their children. But that doesn't necessarily translate into, "It's mine," "It's for my child," or "It's something that I can do." So even though this community in Oakland was one of the poorest in terms of materials, I have to tell you, it was one of the richest places in terms of what people had to offer and were willing to do to help. It was just incredible.

Editors: I'm almost frightened by what you are saying. The piece that frightens me is that the answer seems to be in charter schools as opposed to the district public schools. Why that frightens me is because my job is to train educators in traditional public schools, and I want desperately to find some answers for public schools. I felt a little bit of hope when you said just a minute ago something along the lines of, "We can't just find fault with traditional public schools; we have to do good things with them." Could we play with that for a few minutes? Could you talk about that?

Oh, absolutely. I tell my colleagues who are involved in the school choice movement—which includes charter schools and scholarships or vouchers to independent schools—"If we continue to talk about this movement in negative terms, as a direct response to the traditional public school system, it's going to fail. I'm talking about an approach to education; I'm talking about the competencies in education; I'm talking about how we do it. This has to translate into how we do it in all of our schools, including the traditional public school system." There's no question about that, and I'm a firm believer that it's possible. I think it's going to take time; I think the system needs to be shocked to make the radical changes that it needs to make, and I think that charter schools can provide some of that shock. From my perspective charter schools are not in lieu of traditional public schools or to replace them or even to say, "You guys are doing a miserable job, so we are going to do this over here because we just can't stand it." I prefer to say, "Look, we haven't done a good job of educating all our children in this country; we all share in that responsibility." We have an opportunity here to develop these charter schools—another kind of public school (all charter schools are public), with more flexibility to move away from the things that I think currently constrain and restrict us in the traditional system.

For example, charter schools can be and tend to be smaller. We cannot possibly have a successful school building with 3,000 kids; I don't care where it is. Even the idea of having small, separate learning communities within large buildings that house a total of 3,000 students—I think that's a problem too. I think the latter would be more successful, but for the most part we still have the same building with the same resources—same library, auditorium, and cafeteria. When we have kids eating lunch at 10 o'clock in the morning because we have to stagger the lunches to accommodate so many kids, it doesn't work. That is not meeting the needs of kids. When we have a city of people there is a loss of identity; there's more anonymity, and it becomes more impersonal. Those are the things that we need to chip away at from the old system and build on. When the school is smaller and the school's community is smaller, it is easier to create the linkages we need with the community and allow people to become empowered. I think there are lots of people and lots of different groups who are working on that.

Are you familiar with Aspire Public Schools in California? They are a charter management organization (CMO), so they actually run the schools, which is different than what we do at NCLR. We are not a CMO; we have very strong relationships with our affiliates, our grantees, but we don't run them; we don't manage them. Don Shalvey, cofounder and chief executive officer of Aspire Public Schools, was previously superintendent of the San Carlos, California, traditional public school district for many years. He knows that his charter schools will flourish if the traditional public schools flourish. No school system, no school, is an island. If you're flourishing but nothing else is flourishing around you, it's a matter of time before it collapses.

It's not easy to create linkages between the traditional public school systems and the charter and community-based school movement, because they have unfortunately become adversaries. That's because we do such foolish things as to have the traditional public school system act as the only charter school authorizer in the state, as many do. This is a conflict of interests and creates competition. If people within a community are not satisfied with its traditional public school, they have to go to the district schools and tell them that, and then ask them to authorize a school that will compete with theirs for resources. That doesn't make sense. Who would authorize this? And if a charter school is authorized, it is basically up to its leaders to know their rights and seek the money that they deserve, as it is passed through the traditional public school system. When I was the principal of the charter school in Oakland, California I was telling you about, we experienced a lot of difficulties because of the big adversarial relationship that was created between the community members requesting the charter and the public school district. So I think how we authorize and govern schools is important.

The charter school movement is special work. It gives us the ability to develop new models, to experiment, to do lots of great things, but at some point in time this has to be translated to the public school system. I believe with all my heart that we can do that. I think that traditional public education in this country as it's known today needs to change. There is no question about it and all of the systems with it. And change is difficult, but it has to happen. I believe the underlying pillars of what American education has always strived to provide will always be there: a free, appropriate education that is child centered, that addresses the needs of children, wherever they come from. Those are the things that made American education wonderful from the beginning. You didn't have to pay; it was free. It was a right and not an entitlement. So I think those things will remain; I'm very hopeful about that. When charter and traditional public schools work together they can learn from each other. Traditional public schools can learn new effective strategies from charters, which have more liberty to try new strategies and are more likely to be directly linked to the community; and charter and community schools can benefit from the wealth of knowledge and information, and links to other services that the traditional public schools have. So I think it would be to everyone's advantage to develop partnerships across school sectors and realize that we are all in this together.

Editors: Let's continue by asking you the nonbeliever question: Do these community linkages really help the kids? Isn't our job to help the immigrant children become English speaking—to give them the power that they need to succeed in the American system? What good would it be for them to perpetuate a non-English-speaking experience?

I agree with everything you said except that when we are talking about education some of these questions become more philosophical rather than educational. Our job is to educate children and to use whatever sound educational approaches we have at our disposal. That's what education is about—about teaching children how to learn. Education is not about the language of instruction. It's not about English; it's not about Spanish; it's not about any language. Language is the method of instruction—the means by which we reach the end. And the end is to have children become learners and to learn. I think this point is even more important than whether or not they have learned the content. The most important part of learning is learning how to access the content because in one school year we probably impart one millionth of the content that the child will learn by the end of his or her life. The real purpose of education is to teach children how to become learners—how to access information, how to apply concepts and make inferences, how to think critically—so that when they don't know all of the content facts they can say, "I'm not exactly sure, but I think this is the answer—for these reasons. Let me explore that." That's what education is about.

That's the American experience, and the children who are immigrants, who come rich with another language, use that as one of the ways to get to the end product, to become learners. Do you know this term—*rich with another language*? It's not a deficit. They come rich with another language, another culture, other customs, and energy. It doesn't matter in what language you learn the concept of honesty; once you've learned it, you know it in any language. That's America. Samuel Betances, a sociologist from Northwestern University in Chicago, spoke at a conference once on bilingual education; at the end he said, "I can defend this country in two languages; that's good for me and good for America." There is no question that being English speakers is not only critical; it's absolutely necessary in our country to be able to function, to be able to communicate, to be successful American citizens. No question. That is important, but not at the expense of everything else, don't you agree?

That's why bilingual education makes the most sense. Several reputable studies have shown this to be the most effective method to educate English language learners, but it has unfortunately turned into a political issue By promoting bilingual education we are not saying, "Bilingual education is going to save us; it will help us save our culture, our language, and everything else so that we can remove ourselves from America; we don't want to assimilate, and we don't want to learn English." Bilingual education is none of those things. Bilingual education is an educational tool that research has shown to be extremely effective when truly implemented—I have seen this with my own eyes; it is incredible; it works. Bilingual education is the means to the end: It meets English language learners and Latino children where they are and successfully helps them learn to think critically—in two languages. It brings them to where we want them to be in this country: able to access the American dream, able to graduate from high school prepared for college or career, able to get that job, able to buy that house.

Here's the irony: From many mainstream, middle-class people in our country, the first thing you hear is, "We don't believe in bilingual education"; they'll give you the whole spiel; "It doesn't work; they won't learn English." However, that is not at all the case; in a true bilingual program, students become proficient in two languages. The problem is not bilingual education. It's not the theory of bilingual education, but rather the implementation of the program and all the pieces that go into it, that can be a problem. People will tell you everything that can go wrong with it. I'm going to ask you a question now: Should we abolish it? Let's look at the alternative. The Latino population is the largest growing minority population in the United States—a population that will clearly impact the future of this country. There are currently more than 5.5 million children in our schools whose first language is not English. If we are truly meeting the educational needs of children, why not use their native language as the context for learning? Doesn't it make sense that children must be literate in their first language to have a basis for learning a second language? Let's look at this from another perspective.

You know how all of us in this country had to take at least one foreign language to graduate from high school? So should we do away with that foreign language requirement also? Of course not. Everybody should learn another language, so what's the difference? The difference is the audience. With the high school concept of learning a foreign language, the target audience is middle-class mainstream America, who should all learn a language because that's a good thing. But the target audience in bilingual programs is usually people of color—minorities, low-income populations—and it's not okay for them to know two languages because some people believe they are not going to use it the same way. Why?

So I think I'm trying to respond to the nonbelievers. I think we all—the believers and the nonbelievers—want the same thing: the ability to access this wonderful country and everything that it provides us and to realize equality and everything that goes along with it. But it's the way we're getting there that we are not articulating to each other because there's so much mistrust. I think the issue is that we do not really understand each other. We need to build bridges, and then we need to go beyond that. We need to walk across them—meet each other halfway. I'm convinced we can do that. We need people who are softer and gentler about conveying the messages rather than the extremes on both sides.

Editors: You've answered this in other ways, but could you really crystallize it for us? In our training of district superintendents, school principals, and other educators, we meet caring, concerned professionals who are open to the fact that schools are not currently doing what they need to be doing for our immigrant children and they are asking, "What do I need to do?" One of the things that we're hearing you say is, "If they look to these wonderful CBO-based charter schools there may be some real, interesting ideas traditional public schools could learn from or take from them." As someone who knows those CBO schools intimately, could you come up with some specific, immediate recommendations that you could give a principal, from Anytown, USA?

Certainly, but before looking directly to the CBO-based charter schools once again, I want to mention several other resources that I think could be helpful to schools—traditional public, charter, or independent—working with Latino and English language learner populations.

We (NCLR) have just completed a Parent as Partners curriculum in Spanish and English for parents of elementary and middle school Latino students. The essence of it comes from the PIQE program, which I spoke about earlier. It's been written and worked on by experts in the field of Latino education and guides parents in working with their children's schools as early as possible to ensure that they are prepared for college or a career after high school.

Another resource NCLR can offer schools who are working with Latino English language learners is a series of guides titled "Educating English Language Learners." This series of three guides, expected to be published in 2007, is being developed by NCLR, the Education Alliance at Brown University, and education consultants, with support from the Annie E. Casey Foundation. These guides will assist teachers and schools leaders, as well as charter school founders, in building their capacity to design high-quality programs, implement effective instructional practices, and use relevant and meaningful assessments—all specifically for English language learners.

NCLR has also just begun working on a program called *Lee y serás*—"Read and You Shall Be"—with Scholastic and Verizon. It's a Latino early childhood literacy initiative that engages parents and communities in the literacy development of their children. Research shows that children who are exposed to early literacy activities have a better chance of becoming successful learners in school and throughout their lives; however, Latino children are less likely than their counterparts to be enrolled in early childhood education programs and, due to high poverty rates, are often not exposed to many literacy resources before they enter school. And unfortunately this achievement gap, which begins before Latino children even enter kindergarten, increases exponentially as these children progress through school. *Lee y serás*, which is expected to launch in 2005, will help close the achievement gap that young Latino children face today. Among the resources offered in this program will be three published curricula and trainings in Spanish and English for preschool teachers, parents, and community leaders, which will guide these groups to implement successful literacy strategies with preschool-aged children.

In addition to these programs and resources offered by NCLR, there are several others that I have found to be quite exceptional as well. For example, Sesame Street has a wonderful early literacy tool kit, available for purchase, in Spanish and in English. It is family oriented and is great for administrators and school principals to use for professional development and to base fellowship programs around. Another organization, the National Center for Family Literacy, also does incredible work around literacy in both children's and adult education. They have an institute called the Hispanic Family Learning Institute, which distributes lots of helpful resources and materials in these fields.

As I mentioned earlier, I think one of the best ways for teachers and principals working with Latino students or English language learners—in traditional public, charter, or independent schools—as well as potential charter school founders to learn effective child-centered strategies for this population is to visit a local CBO or a school where this is being done: to talk with organization or school leaders, teachers and staff, students and parents; to observe classroom instruction or a typical day at the CBO; and experience the culture of the school or organization first-hand. These are things I have found very helpful and incredibly inspirational in my career; I always encourage friends and colleagues to do the same, and NCLR's programs and affiliated school cohorts also incorporate school and CBO site visits, because there is just so much to take away from the experience. We can read words and strategies on paper, but to actually see what success looks like in action, to experience it being realized, is incredible. Not only will this experience resonate with you, but often you can walk away with specific ideas or strategies that inspire a new way of thinking, that you can implement in your classroom or school.

NCLR has some incredibly wonderful charter schools, and we are happy to help connect you to one that would be most meaningful and relevant for you to visit. One of our exemplary schools is IDEA Academy, located in the Rio Grande Valley of Texas, one of the poorest communities in the state. I spent the day there last year and had a wonderful learning experience. I was totally mesmerized by the work they were doing. The five-year-olds were reading, and I know what that means, because I have two little ones. The five-year-olds were reading—in English and in Spanish. The idea that our children—Latino children and other poor children—can't do this, which is actually believed by some, is ludicrous.

During a discussion with one of the teachers she mentioned that the school picks up the kids in the *colonias*, and I said, "The *colonias*? What are the *colonias*?" I wasn't familiar with this term, and I have to tell you, I'm a Latino; cultural competence starts here. The *colonias* are these developments that have very little infrastructure—little or no electricity, no running water, latrines, shacks—extreme poverty. And there are tons of them in the Rio Grande Valley. Ninety-five percent of the kids this school served came from the *colonias*.

One's first instinct might be to think that because these kids came from poverty their school wouldn't be high quality, but that was clearly not at all the case. What an amazing experience to listen to these kids. I walked into a ninth-grade science classroom, and they were studying the Periodic Table of Elements, but they weren't just repeating them and memorizing them. They were talking about the parts of oxygen and how those parts, when combined with another substance, would react. These were ninth-grade students in a poor, rural area of Texas, and it felt like I just walked into a classroom in Beverly Hills or something. I was just so totally taken by the whole thing. I said, "What is the secret?" "There is no secret," the teacher said. "You honor who they are. You work with them. You involve the parents. You continue to involve the entire community. You have to provide the students with some of the things they don't have, like transportation for example. These students don't have any way of getting here, which means we can't have school unless we find a way to transport them." So transportation is an issue, and resources become an issue; facilities are an issue for a lot of these schools. Another thing that impressed me about this school was that it demonstrated that lots of non-Latino teachers have become totally culturally and linguistically competent in teaching Latino kids. So this doesn't only happen when there are Latinos doing the teaching or Latinos doing the leading. This can very much happen when we have people that are willing to look at things a little bit differently.

I also want to tell you a story about a traditional public elementary school, because there are great things happening in some of these schools as well. Some colleagues and I were visiting the University of Texas at Pan America in the Rio Grande Valley; we were working with them to help build the capacity of schools in need of university training. I told the dean that I was so anxious to visit a really great bilingual program. She said, "Go over to Donna, Texas, a few minutes away." She said it was a "suburban school." First of all, to give you a sense of the place, we couldn't find it because it was down a dirt road, and we thought we must have been in the wrong place. We tried to ask someone, and they told us to stay on the road—go to the end and we'd find it. So we went to the end, and sure enough, we eventually got to the school; it was in the middle of nowhere, I mean in the middle of nowhere. We went into the school, and it was Spanish Day. There were signs on everything that told us so, and on the reverse they said, "Today is English Day." On Spanish Day they do everything—think, talk, eat—in Spanish, and on English day they do the reverse. It's the most incredible program—totally bilingual.

We had not made an appointment but rather just walked into the school, and they happened to be having a leadership in-service day, so the teachers and students were there, but the principal and administrators were gone. The person who took us around the school and told us about the programs—the academic programs—was the custodian. I said, "Listen, I've got to tell you this. You're the custodian and you know all about the programs—you can tell us all about the academics. I'm honestly a little surprised, and really impressed." And he said, "That's because their job," and he pointed to the teachers, "is to teach in the classroom, and my job is to keep the school clean and safe. Other people are responsible for other things, but no matter who, no matter what, it's all about the children; they are the most important thing so we all have to know about everything that goes on in this school. I couldn't go in and teach in a classroom, but I've got to tell you, I know about everything they do in those classrooms."

So we look at our country's public schools—our CBO charter schools, our community-run charter schools, and our traditional public schools, our schools in the poorest areas of the Rio Grande Valley, Texas, and in Oakland, California—and these schools show us what education is all about. They show real-life connections; dedicated parents, teachers, principals, and custodians of all backgrounds; critical thinking that teaches us how to learn; bilingual classrooms; child-centered classrooms; communities that truly own and run their schools; empowerment and sustainability. It can happen.

We had come to the end of our interview. Mr. Colón had just this left to say:

This is my job. I keep saying, "I can't believe I get paid to do this."

High School and University Partnerships: The Strengths and Challenges for ELLs

NAOMI MIGLIACCI

This chapter focuses on the factors that contributed to the successful link between a university and a high school and provides ideas for how other schools can collaborate with institutes of higher education. These partnerships are not without their challenges, however, and they are also raised in this chapter. In addition, the chapter looks at practices related to including English language learners (ELLs) in themed academies and factors that contribute to their success as they relate to the link between the high school and the university.

The trend toward creating smaller, more personalized environments in large comprehensive high schools can be achieved many ways. One popular method of reform is to create themed academies whereby course work centers on student interests. The academy, or small school, is a hook to motivate students to do well in and graduate from high school, to think about and apply their learning to their future careers, and to help make their dreams a reality by providing realistic support and guidance during the high school experience.

In one of Connecticut's urban high schools, the Health Professions Academy has a long-standing reputation as a place where students can prepare for further education toward fulfilling their dreams in the medical field, or they can prepare to enter the health-care industry more immediately by studying first aid and other certificate programs and courses. In addition to courses directly related to health care, the Health Professions Academy requires students to take all subjects for graduation such as English, history, math, and physical education. However, these students take more science courses than students enrolled in one of the other academies, such as the Business and Finance Academy or the Technology Academy.

A unique feature of academies and smaller learning communities (SLCs), especially those with a theme, is their connection with the local community. Academies often link with organizations that can provide resources not often available in the large, traditional school. Community-based organizations (CBOs) and other institutions can provide student internships, a professional who can teach or provide workshops, and funding. In fact, without these resources, some academies may not be able to sustain themselves.

The Health Professions Academy located at Bulkeley High School is just such a smaller learning community within the larger school with an established relationship with the University of Connecticut (UConn), a university of national reputation. The partnership allows students to connect with the university's medical and dental schools and their respective resources. Although the ultimate benefit is to the students, faculty in both schools benefit from the relationship as well. In addition, UConn provides significant funding for the academy. On the university's side, the relationship with the high school is borne out of the university's desire to attract more prepared students from an ethnically diverse urban environment who will add to the future population of the university as well as, hopefully, service the state's medical needs in that local area.

The academies at Bulkeley High School are open to all students as required by grants that fund small learning communities. English language learners (ELLs) enrolled in academies receive services appropriate to their test scores, length of stay in the United States, and state mandates. In fact, there is controversy over just how ELLs can and should be included in general in SLCs, especially those with a theme, since they could spend several hours a day studying English or receiving bilingual services and possibly not taking all the required courses of the academy. Usually, an academy's curriculum is based on the traditional four-year model, but some offer different time frames. Several ELLs have successfully completed the program at the Health Professions Academy. They have participated in the university-based part of the program and have been able to continue their education with an eye toward a medical degree. Several factors have contributed toward their success.

- The leadership within the academy, which ensures that students can take advantage of English as a second language (ESL) services and the unique programs of the academy
- The connection with the university, which provides funding as well as the added benefit of catering to a hands-on learning style associated with the internships and other programs offered to students of the academy but at the university
- The flexibility of the program in terms of scheduling and its ability to provide a personalized curriculum for a diverse population

The next section provides information on the Health Professions Partnerships Initiative (HPPI, pronounced *hippy*), how it got started, the kinds of resources each party brings to the partnership, the program design, and the integration of ELLs. Following that, an outline is provided of school and university linkages more generally, with illustrations from other projects with which I have been associated. Next, ideas are provided for overcoming some of the challenges that face these types of partnerships, and, finally, the chapter concludes with ideas for partnering for school reform.

HPPI Case Study[1]

Bulkeley High School is one of three large, comprehensive public high schools in downtown Hartford, Connecticut. Like so many schools in Hartford, it is home to a diverse population of students, yet it is a neighborhood school. Of the three large, comprehensive high schools, Bulkeley is probably the most diverse in terms of the numbers of ELLs enrolled there. Since the year 2000, more than 5,000 Bosnian and Albanian peoples, mostly refugees, have moved to Hartford in neighborhoods near the school. Bulkeley boasts more than 100 ethnicities with 45 different languages spoken at school. More than 70 Liberian and Somali students are enrolled there since the city received 30 families from each country. Due to the large

numbers of recent immigrants at the high school age, Bulkeley has recently created a New Arrival Center.

Although Hartford's diversity sounds like an exciting place to be, attending school there can be a challenge for many students, especially those with interrupted schooling, for those whose school cultures and learning backgrounds differ so vastly from the U.S. system, and for so many who come to the city with little or no English skills and often limited literacy skills. In fact, many of the schools in the district are not faring well as indicated by the numbers of schools not making adequate yearly progress under the federal No Child Left Behind Act. Add this to the fact that the large, diverse population found in the city is home to children who live in low-income neighborhoods in a wealthy state that is rich in economic and other resources. Many of Hartford's teachers do not live in the city but live in wealthier neighborhoods, and their understanding of the needs of the ELL population is limited. Recent newspaper articles and local television programming has criticized Connecticut as having one of the largest achievement gaps of all states between its white and minority public-school-age population, especially in the large cities of Hartford and New Haven. However, Hartford Public Schools see their students as rising stars. The mission of the district follows:

> Hartford Public Schools: Our Students! Our Community! Our Future! The Hartford Public School System must be a community of active learners that nurtures self-confidence, respect and excellence in all its members. Within such a community all students:
>
> Master communication, computation, analytical and problem solving skills
>
> Develop their physical and artistic potential
>
> Acquire strong ethical values
>
> Learn to act creatively, responsibly, and effectively in meeting the challenges of a diverse and changing world.

One might look at the school-age population in Hartford and have two different thoughts. The first might be that the students are not motivated and not doing well academically, with low test scores, and even if they stay in school and graduate from high school, they do not amount to very much in terms of finding careers that would provide them with economic successes. One might think that these young people will not have many choices in life in terms of fulfilling dreams for a future with a satisfying career or of being able to attend college, travel, or make things happen for themselves. In this scenario, youngsters work in dead-end jobs, repeating the lifestyles of their parents and guardians. Most of them certainly will not go to college or earn advanced degrees, and even if they get admitted, they will drop out. These are students who allow things to be done to them. They do not create their own destinies. They do not know any other way.

On the other hand, one might look at the students in Hartford and have a completely different response. The youngsters could be seen as a future pool of college applicants and potential nurses, doctors, and dentists. One might say that the students, the faculty, the structure of the program, and the facilities just need some resources and some support, and this could happen. One might say that these students just need to be engaged and motivated. They need to see possibilities for their futures, and they need to know how to realize them. And if a university with a medical and dental school wanted to increase its pool of applicants and start training them at a young age, as well as to pour resources into an economically depressed environment, Hartford could be just the place. The university's desire might also be to increase the numbers of doctors and dentists in the state, especially bilingual medical professionals who would work in their home communities.

This way of thinking is the basis for HPPI. With Bulkeley High School as its partner, UConn helps to support high school students in academic content areas so they might be successful at the university level. It is UConn's hope that more underrepresented minorities will continue on to UConn's medical or dental school. The following is from UConn's information on Innovative Programs Section 46a-68-49 (n.d.):

> The Dept of Health Career Opportunity Programs' mission is to develop innovative and supportive programs that encourage underrepresented minority and disadvantaged students to pursue careers in the medical, dental, nursing, pharmacy, and allied health fields by providing the opportunity to participate in a broad spectrum of educational and mentoring programs. In response to the Association of American Medical Colleges' *Project 3000 by 2000*, an initiative to increase the number of students from underrepresented groups in the health professions, the University of Connecticut Health Center, the Hartford and New Britain School District, Central Connecticut State University, University of Connecticut and Wesleyan University have developed the Health Professions Partnership Initiative (HPPI).

This is a formal consortium offering a comprehensive program of educational enrichment and support activities for minority students. Its goal is to increase the number of Connecticut underrepresented minority students applying to medical and dental schools; graduate programs in biomedical sciences; and nursing, pharmacy, and allied health programs. Program elements form a continuous pipeline for upper elementary, middle and junior high school, high school, and college-level students. The goals are to increase awareness and proficiency in science and to provide a continuous mentoring and support system for students interested in pursing health professional careers.

Incidentally, partnerships are not new to the Hartford schools, and they do bring in much-needed resources and funding. In fall 2004 under Superintendent Robert Henry, the Office of Strategic Alliances counted $8.6 million in funds from business. Partnerships with institutes of higher education are up from 8 in 2003 to 14 in 2004. UConn has four school partnerships with the Hartford Public Schools: law, social work, education, and the medical and dental school. Due to UConn's success in partnering with the Hartford high schools, Aetna has joined the collaborative efforts of businesses involved in school reform efforts. This new infusion of funds from Aetna has provided the impetus to back up the help students receive by offering programming in the sixth to eighth grades. These programs are also offered in the summer so that very young students can go to UConn and get a head start in thinking about their futures and in getting excited about learning.

All three of Hartford's comprehensive, public high schools have received grants to establish SLCs, and it is the desire of the district to place students in SLCs wall to wall in all four grades. This means that the entire high school will be made up of small learning communities or academies, with no large, comprehensive high school model. The Health Professions Academy had been established before the city-wide SLC initiative and, due to its success, served as a model for other themed SLCs throughout the city. The academy is housed in its own building just down the street from the main campus, but students enrolled in the academy take physical education and a few other subjects at the main campus. SLCs are meant to support the school's mission. Bulkeley's mission statement follows:

> Bulkeley High School provides a safe and nurturing environment that encourages active learning and delivers educational experiences for an academically and culturally diverse community. We serve the needs of all students through a variety of programs for a lifetime of intellectual, physical, and emotional well being, and nurture students' aesthetic, social, ethical, and moral values.

The Health Professions Academy

The Health Professions Academy provides high school students with college preparation with an emphasis on the health professions. Ultimately, the partnership hopes to accomplish several goals including the following, which come from planning information on the UConn side of the partnership.

- Provide students with educational enrichment activities that will stimulate their interest in the health-care professions.
- Provide students with training that would lead to Red Cross certification.
- Provide career guidance through designated meetings and e-mail communication.
- Reinforce an understanding of the role and function that the department plays in the health-care profession.
- Enable students to experience varied laboratory settings where the student can participate in scientific projects.
- Provide the students with clinical rotations that would serve as an opportunity to expose the student to the various areas of the health professions.
- Provide an informative series of presentations on the health-care professions that would assist students in making more informed decisions concerning their career choices.
- Get students involved in community service programs that are affiliated with the health center, which would enable them to become active in the community and to form an alliance with area agencies.
- Provide informative medical and dental topic presentations that students are interested in and that will stimulate independent outside research.
- Involve students in an internship program sponsored by the health center that would provide a hands-on experience.

The following information is taken from the academy's Web site (http://www.hartnet.org/health/) and provides information on the features of the academy, who they are, and what their goals are.

- The Bulkeley–UConn partnership program is a collaboration between the Bulkeley High School Center of Excellence for Health Professions and the University of Connecticut Health Center through the office of Health Career Opportunities and is operated as a school within a school.
- The partnership is the marriage of high school students that have expressed an interest in the medical field and a large health center that encompasses a hospital, medical school, dental school, and a research facility.
- All of the planned activities are educational and have been designed for students to learn and be challenged in a real-world environment.

- Students take part in field trips and numerous other programs designed to assure their success, to challenge their intellects, and to sustain their interest in health professions.
- On returning from their field trips, students complete assignments based on their health-center activities.
- Academy administrators, teachers, students, and parents function as a team to foster student learning and achievement with the ultimate objective being for students to go on to higher postsecondary education.
- Parents are invited to become involved in the partnership by attending sessions with their children.
- Summer programs, like "Medical Camp," (a program offered as a result of collaboration among the Central Area Health Education Center, Bulkeley High School's Health Professions Academy, and St. Francis Hospital and Medical Center) allow students to shadow doctors. Students are introduced to various other areas within the medical field. They also participate in an educational component administered by the Institute for Community Research.
- The Health Professions Academy teachers receive fellowships at UConn Health Center, where they complete courses (e.g., a course in epidemiology).
- UConn faculty present courses to academy students. One is on health risks (a primer in epidemiology). This instruction develops skills in writing and critical and analytical reading. This course is developed by the academy faculty as a part of its core curriculum and is integrated across all disciplines.
- Future projects include teleconferencing capabilities to augment the direct relationship between Bulkeley High School and UConn. Students and their mentors will be able to meet face to face on an ongoing basis. Programs such as the UConn Mini Medical Series will be presented, and distance-learning programs will be offered to enhance offerings for students.
- Students participate in service-learning activities. The academy feels that students should learn responsibility to their community and should give back by becoming active, productive citizens. To this end, each student becomes a volunteer. Students participate in many volunteer activities with such groups as the Red Cross, Hartford Hospital, and Riverfront Recapture.
- The academy is presently in the planning stages to work with the State of Connecticut Department of Social Services to train pupils to become student ambassadors for the Healthcare for Uninsured Kids and Youth (HUSKY) initiative. This opportunity will allow students living in the insurance capital of the world to learn firsthand about this facet of health care, its opportunities, and career paths while performing a worthwhile service to their community.

One fundamental tenet of themed SLCs is that they be inclusive and allow all students to choose which theme is of interest to them. The point is that student interest is a motivating factor for choosing an SLC or academy, for desiring to study the subject, and for staying in school. Faculty in the academy use student interest as a hook whereby all subjects are taught in an integrated manner and relate to a student's postsecondary future. Students explore career options, and several are presented to them with shorter and longer terms of future study. For example, in the Health Professions Academy, a student with strong academic skills and the wherewithal to continue another four to eight years in school might choose a set of college-track courses that will take them down a path to become a nurse, a pharmacist, a doctor, or a dentist. Another student might choose a course of study that leads to a career as an x-ray technician, whereas another might choose to work as an emergency medical technician immediately on graduation by taking classes from certified instructors while still a high school student. The academy makes these kinds of opportunities and connections with real-world experiences possible.

Bulkeley is committed to including all students in its SLCs and offering all students their choice. The question is how does a school establish equity for all its students, and in this case the diverse population of ELLs? There are several challenges to this commitment, and Bulkeley is still trying to work out the details. Several structural barriers exist that promote a challenge to being able to offer students a choice of academy. Many would just as soon place ELLs in an international academy, but that would mean many closed doors for this population. International academies tend to focus on language and, to some degree, culture. This would be fine for students who want to be linguists or multilingual. The other problem with international academies is that they do not typically attract native English speakers. These academies, although diverse because of the immigrant population, often become the holding tanks, or dumping grounds, for ELLs. That is not to say that the teachers are not caring or good instructors. What it means is that the rest of the school becomes closed to nonnative speakers of English.

Other structural barriers include schedules, transportation, class-size ratios, the physical location of the SLC on the campus, and mandated tests. According to Mary Giuliano, former English teacher and director of the Health Professions Academy and now liaison to all three of Hartford's high schools for SLCs, "the students know where they want to go but the structures aren't there to support them" (personal communication, 2005). In other words, the students know they need to learn English—and many know their academic skills are lacking and they might need remediation. At the same time, the students want to attend an academy in their area of interest, like the Health Professions Academy. Students have goals for their futures and they want the opportunity to attend the UConn programs and learn what it means to work in the medical health field.

The staff at Bulkeley would like ELLs to enroll in the Health Professions Academy, but for many newly arrived immigrants, the language of the academic work is challenging. The ELLs need what Bulkeley calls *skills class* every day, or ESL instruction. Although Bulkeley High School promotes transitional bilingual education and sheltered instruction, there are no sheltered classes offered in the academy, and often the numbers of students enrolled do not support these types of classes, especially if ELLs are spread throughout the school and the desire is to keep them within their academy or SLC. Sheltered courses offered in the larger high school environment, whereby students receive content instruction with attention to their linguistic needs, may not be appropriate for this group as well, since the courses, like science, are so specialized for the students enrolled in health professions. However, sheltered instructional strategies in the health-professions-content classrooms could alleviate this problem. For more on sheltered strategies see Chapter 7 in this volume.

Another problem with enrolling in courses outside of the academy and taking classes on the main campus with other students is that the academy, or SLC, does not remain pure. When students have to move between academies scheduling can become a nightmare, even where academy schedules do not differ from one another. In some instances, students are scheduled out of lunch. Pure academies are desirable for several reasons. There is evidence to suggest that schools with students who stay within their own domains report decreased instances of violence and other disruptions like pulled fire alarms. Also, in a pure academy everyone knows everyone, so there is no slipping through the cracks or students reporting ey did not have homework in a particular class. All the teachers in an academy orate on curriculum and on knowing the strengths and weaknesses of each student.

The personalized learning environments of SLCs and academies are not the norm in many large, traditional, comprehensive high schools, although they are becoming more popular. Though teachers may have had a workshop on differentiated instruction, a one-day professional development opportunity is not enough to realize classrooms with teachers fully differentiating their lessons. In addition, without the specific knowledge of the linguistic needs of ELLs, much of the lessons, even if differentiated, are still beyond the reach of the newly arrived student with limited English skills or with limited literacy skills due to interrupted schooling. Workshops in differentiating lessons do not necessarily speak to making content comprehensible to ELLs or how to engage ELLs so that they can showcase their learning even when their English skills are limited. These types of instructional strategies, however, are essential if ELLs are to participate fully in a themed academy.

Though Bulkeley High School and other SLCs around the nation continue to address the challenges, there are advantages to ELLs. In addition, the Health Professions Academy has experienced a series of successes, yet it continues to consider the best options for including ELLs who have lower literacy levels, interrupted schooling, beginning levels of English-language proficiency, and other challenges.

For one thing, the structure of an academy or SLC can be advantageous to the ELL for many reasons. The small size of the academy allows for students to be known by the adults in associated with the community. The fact that the academy provides an integrated curriculum on a theme allows students to connect to the content in meaningful ways that will impact their futures. For ELLs without knowledge of the opportunities and how to attain their goals, the academy provides visits to the university, interactions with faculty, courses that count toward graduation and university admissions requirements, and guidance on how to negotiate the postsecondary world depending on what the student's goals are.

The Health Professions Academy has graduated several nonnative-English-speaking students over the years with great success. In 2005, an Albanian student who came to the United States in 1998 not knowing any English was named valedictorian of the high school. She won UConn's Nutmeg Scholarship and wants to be an endocrinologist, conducting research after she earns a Ph.D. and M.D. In addition to this student, other students, especially from Bosnia, have been successful. They take ESL classes as well as content classes and are able to experience academic success.

The next section considers school and university partnerships more generally and how they can be advantageous for ELLs. It includes examples from a variety of collaborative efforts. Some include a small schools or small learning community model, but not all. They share programmatic features that put the needs of ELLs in the forefront. Unlike many programs that focus only on the needs of the majority population, or on native English speaking students, these programs include non-native speakers in the planning stages and are committed to inclusive pedagogy.

School–University Linkages

According to the National Network of Partnership Schools, there are two types of community collaborations between schools and CBOs: Schools can receive services from the community, and they can also provide services to the community. These can be student centered, family centered, school centered, or community centered. Community partnerships with schools are many and varied and include some of the following types:

- Businesses and corporations
- University and educational institutions
- Health-care industries and organizations
- Government and military
- National service and volunteer
- Faith-based organizations
- Senior citizens
- Cultural and recreational organizations
- Other community organizations
- Various individuals in the community

Though these partnerships can exist for all students, schools that use these alliances for the welfare of its ELLs uniquely design the collaborations. For students, community partnerships provide several outcomes:

- The partnerships provide enrichment in curricular and extracurricular activities. In Philadelphia, heritage-language programs provide students with the opportunities to maintain their linguistic and cultural heritage.
- Students are able to gain knowledge and explore careers as well as options for future educational work. UConn provides high school students with trips to the medical school to explore careers in health.
- Students gain a sense of self-confidence and a feeling of value and of belonging in the community. Students from Cristo Rey High School in Chicago readily entered the job market after successful internships.
- Students form positive relationships with adults. College and university students provide positive role models for high school students.

Teachers also benefit from the relationships formed with the university partner. In the HPPI case, all of these were realized:

- Teachers gain knowledge of resources that enrich the curriculum.
- Teachers gain skills in working with university faculty and others to assist students as well as improve their teaching practices.
- Teachers gain knowledge of admissions requirements and new careers in the field.

High schools that link with universities provide students with experience in various careers through internships at the university during the academic year and through summer programs. Students can also participate in courses or course work with college-bearing credit that mimic college courses or in high school courses held on college campuses or can attend colleges that provide tutors or mentors.

For example, Cristo Rey High School in Chicago, in an effort to increase the connections between young people and adults and in effect to reduce class size, exemplifies the partnerships formed between business and corporations and the language minority students. All students participate in several internships as part of their course of study.

In another example, the connection between UConn and Bulkeley's Health Sciences Academy in Hartford, Connecticut not only includes funding from the university but also partnerships in curriculum design and teaching. New arrivals to the United States are able to join the academy and participate in the hands-on curriculum even while learning English.

A community partner does not just include those with children in the schools but all interested in and affected by the quality of education. Parents of many ELLs work at least one job and some more than two. Their time and resources are limited. Hundreds of college students from the surrounding area of Cambridge Rindge and Latin School in Massachusetts provide homework help to ELLs. Most of the ELLs attend the International Academy. It is a two-way street in this alliance since many of the college students wish to travel to, or eventually to work with, students who come from the many countries represented at the school.

During the late 1980s I worked for the Lynn Public School and North Shore Community College in Massachusetts. I taught a class of high school students at the college. The local high school and the community college formed a partnership whereby ELLs, who enrolled in the high school after the start of the school year and were classified as at risk juniors and seniors, attended half of their school day at the community college. Students were classified "at risk" because they had limited English language skills, were overage for the grade, had missed at least one month of school, and often hadn't been to school for a year or more. Since the students would be graduating from high school in a year or two, this particular program was designed to assist students in familiarizing them with a college environment in the hopes that they would want to attend after they finished high school. This group traditionally did not attend college. By attending classes while in high school with instructors they would have in college, the students would have established relationships that would enable them to comfortably transition to college—a now familiar environment.

Forming a Partnership and Overcoming the Challenges

Several challenges exist when forming community partnerships, and many problems need to be solved for students to reap the benefits of the collaborations. According to the National Network of Partnership Schools (2005), there are four types of challenges to overcome.

- Partners need to solve turf problems. Each partner needs to know its role, responsibility, the funding sources, and the locations where the collaborations will take place, as well as what activities will take place.
- The school and its community partners need to inform families about the programs and services. Families need to know the roles, responsibilities, funding sources, locations, and activities mentioned in the first bullet.
- The school and its community partners need to assure equal opportunities for students and families to obtain the services offered by the partners and how they can participate.
- The partners need to know that their services and resources have to match their efforts with the school's or program's goals.

Another step in forming community partnerships is for schools to rethink, or redefine, what it means for schools to collaborate with the various community constituents. A community partner does not just exist in the immediate neighborhood where the school is located. The school community includes all locations that influence students' learning and development. These might include virtual communities found online, for example. Bulkeley High School is not located in the immediate neighborhood of UConn. In fact, the university is located in a more rural part of the state but is certainly convenient to travel to and from in a day. Other schools may need to avail themselves of online communities or televised programming for the collaborations to work.

The Bulkely High School Health Professions Academy illustrates how it attempts to provide support for all its students through its partnership with UConn. English language learners from high-poverty neighborhoods are often at risk of dropping out of high school or, even if they do graduate, of not receiving an adequate education that prepares them for college should they desire to attend. In addition to limited proficiency in English, students are unfamiliar with the university system, its processes, personnel, and curriculum. Furthermore, high schools cannot do it all. Even if they have guidance and career counselors, these resources are spread thin with the large case loads of the counselors; ELLs do not always know how to use the counselors; there is often a language barrier between the students and counselors; and most counselors are not trained to work with and to understand the position of the English learner population.

The desire to integrate ELLs into the school community for the benefits they reap when involved with a small learning community is a goal of many restructuring efforts in high schools around the country. The redesign efforts of South Boston High School in Massachusetts is one to emulate; however, they are still faced with the challenge of integrating bilingual students into their three SLCs (National Association of Secondary School Principals, 2004). The school community needs to think differently about what ELLs can accomplish and what they want to accomplish. As other chapters in this volume have shown, teachers need a bank of instructional strategies through ongoing professional development opportunities to serve this population in regular classrooms. With students who are motivated to attend school because the subject matter and the connection with their futures is so real, this is an enjoyable task for teachers. Although it is not part of the case for this chapter, UConn does offer programs for science teachers as part of its outreach program to reach minority students in which HPPI takes part.

A community partner is not just rated by social or economic qualities but also by its strengths and talents to support families and schools. Since UConn is a nationally recognized university in the field of medicine, it is able to provide status, economic assistance, and unique medical opportunities to the Health Professions Academy at Bulkeley. This relationship exemplifies a partnership whereby the university provides specific resources in hopes that it will have a hand in educating potential scholars who might one day attend UConn. Since UConn knows what it needs and wants, it is in a good position to work with the high school students who could be future applicants. This, in turn, benefits the high school faculty so that their standards are maintained and they are able to communicate to students what colleges need and want.

In fact, many ELLs have a desire to go to college or pursue careers that require advanced degrees. For most, they will be the first in their families to graduate from high school and to apply to college. Without the support of the high school and the university, these students will not know what is expected and required of them. Their parents and guardians have not negotiated this road and are unable to provide more than encouraging words. Financial support from the family is out of the question for most ELLs, who live in high-poverty neighborhoods in urban and rural areas throughout the United States. High schools that link with university programs give an advantage to these students by familiarizing them with the university, which had previously been unknown to ELLs and their families. The high school's partnership provides ELLs with visits to the university to make the place and structures more familiar and comfortable, with access to faculty so there is a familiar person on campus, with high academic expectations and a path to achieving those standards, and with a curriculum similar to what they can expect in university. For the uninitiated ELLs, knowing what to expect and how to be successful in a university environment will help them achieve their goals.

Large, comprehensive high schools are hard pressed to support the academic achievement of all students without community sponsors. High schools, such as Bulkeley with its small learning communities and academies within the larger school, that create these learning environments to support specific curricular and instructional goals for targeted student interests are better able to provide their students with meaningful, relevant curriculum. However, these schools may only be able to provide this kind of educational experience through a partnership, especially a high school with a medical interest. The partnership with a university medical school and its faculty helps motivate students and ensure their success through the resources, staffing, and programs offered that exist at the university that would otherwise not be available to high school students. In addition, if the student has an interest in higher education and little if any background on what universities and colleges require for admissions, what kinds of academic behaviors are expected, and how what they are learning in high school connects with a future career, a partnership with an institute of higher education can provide these kinds of supports. Ultimately school partnerships "help to broaden the base of support for language minority students" (Adger, 2000, p. 2). Whether the support is provided through mentoring and tutoring, experiences with an institute of higher education, or funds for future study, the educational piece for ELLs is not secondary to their high school experience but is often essential to their success in school.

School Partnerships and School Reform

In the book titled *Inside High School Reform: Making the Changes That Matter,* Jordan Horowitz (2005) outlines the "Top Ten Tips for Improving High Schools." The tips come as a result of a research project that included the evaluation of several types of school partnerships through a variety of means, but all of the partnerships were in place to increase college attendance among schools underrepresented in colleges in California. The goal was to see what kinds of students benefited from what kinds of programs. One of the main concerns is that high school students are not being prepared for their futures and that those with only a high school diploma will not earn as much as those with a college degree. One of the outcomes of the project is to motivate schools to prepare students for college whether they choose to attend or not. Several of these tips can be more easily attained when high schools work with university partners. In fact, one of the problems is that high schools are expected to provide so much but without all the necessary resources. Horowitz argues that "there are a lot of resources and a great deal of knowledge held by individuals and organizations outside the high school systems, and that's where we should look." One goal for high schools is to "hold students to high expectations." When universities are involved, especially in the HPPI case, the expectations are to enter a profession with skills for work immediately on leaving high school or to obtain an advanced degree. Horowitz recommends creating an "optimistic, college-going culture and help students understand how high school work affects their future college and career choices" (p. xx). With the university as the partner, frequent visits and interactions with university faculty create an environment where students are motivated to attend college. Horowitz says, "Whether their goal is going to college or not, they should be planning to succeed in a college-preparatory course of study…Also, they should

Table 11.1 Checklist schools can use to link with community partners

- Resources
  - What kinds of resources does the partner provide?
  - Do they provide funding?
  - Do they provide staff/faculty?
  - Do they provide materials?
  - Do they provide technology?
  - Do they provide extra-curricular programming (i.e., summer programs, Saturday academies, lectures, guest speakers, etc.)?
  - Does the partner provide structures needed to support the program(s)?
- Flexibility
  - How flexible are the programs?
  - Do partners require funds to be applied in a particular way?
  - Does staff/faculty have to be qualified or certified by a particular organization?
- Program Design
  - Are the programs appropriate?
  - Do the programs respond to our needs?
  - Is the program responsive to our particular population?
  - Do the programs support the linguistic and cultural identity of our population?
  - Are the programs accessible?
  - Are the programs familiar?
- Evaluation
  - How do the partners help us to monitor our progress?
  - How do the partners help us to improve our services?
  - How do we help the partners serve our needs?
  - How do we assist in our partners' needs?
  - What kind of record keeping do we have/need to measure our success?

visit some colleges and see that there are students there who are just like they are" (p. xx). And, they see the direct link between their work in high school and how it will help them in future course work. They see what college classrooms look like, what kinds of behaviors are expected, and who their potential professors might be. The HPPI case exemplifies Horowitz's suggestion to "find partners such as local colleges, businesses, other schools, and parent groups to provide help" (p. xx).

School–community partnerships are characterized by the resources, program flexibility, client responsiveness, and evaluation (Adger, 2000). Table 11.1 shows a checklist schools can use when looking to link with community partners.

In summary, this chapter examined a case whereby a highly ranked university medical and dental school provides resources to a large urban high school with a diverse population of generally low-income families to raise the academic skills necessary to attend this prestigious university. The university provides funding, materials, organizational support, curriculum assistance, teaching, hands-on experiences, school-to-college assistance and information, and motivation. The success of the structure of this very successful academy has spawned other theme-based academies and partnerships throughout the rest of the school and in other high schools in the city. In general, partnerships with institutes of higher education help ELLs and their families by making direct connections between course work in high school and their futures by familiarizing them with the curriculum of a university, the location, the faculty and the admissions requirements and process and by motivating them to set goals with clear paths to reach them.

Notes

1. The information on the HPPI case study comes from work I did for Secondary School Redesign at Brown University's Education Alliance with the Small Learning Communities (SLC) initiative in Hartford, Connecticut, high schools. Information also comes from personal communication with those associated with HPPI at the Board of Education in Hartford, at UConn, and at Bulkeley High School's Health Professions Academy, as well as from Web sites and other communiqués.

References

Adger, C. T. (January 2000). School/community partnerships to support language minority student success. Center for Research on Education, Diversity & Excellence. Available at: http://www.cal.org/crede/pubs/ResBrief5.htm.

Bulkeley High School Health Professions Center of Excellence. Available at: http://www.hartnet.org/health/.

Horowitz, J. (August 2005). Inside high school reform: Making the changes that matter. WestEd. Available at: http://www.wested.org/cs/we/view/rs_press/38.

National Association of Secondary School Principals. (2004). Breaking ranks II: Strategies for leading high school reform. Reston, VA.

National Network of Partnership Schools. (2005). Center for social organization of schools. Baltimore, MD: Johns Hopkins University. Available at: http://www.csos.jhu.edu.

University of Connecticut (n.d.). Innovative programs: Section 46a-68-49. Available at: http://www.csos.jhu.edu.

CHAPTER **12**

Activist Organization and Parental Engagement in Philadelphia's Chinatown

DEBORAH WEI

Editors' note: Deborah Wei was one of the speakers at the 2003 Brown University/ Annenberg Research Symposium on Educating English Language Learners in Providence, RI. When we heard her talk about how public schools need to respond to and reflect the culture of the community, we were determined to contact her as one of the authors for this volume. When she graciously agreed to an interview we were delighted to meet with her in Philadelphia the following year to discuss with her how she views school–community partnerships. Ms. Wei is gregarious, witty, and forthright in demeanor. She works hard for the Chinatown community as well as for all children. We met Ms. Wei at the Board of Education in Philadelphia in August 2004. The interview was audio- and videotaped.

Naomi: Thank you so much for taking time to talk with us about community connections and partnerships in the Philadelphia area and how they benefit English language learners (ELLs) and their families. Lorrie and I have several items we'd like to discuss with you. Let's start with the first one. Can you please describe the services and supports your program provides to ensure community–school linkages? You can tell us mainly about your program.

Deborah: Unfortunately, in the past, my experience has been that it is not the school that's reaching out to the community. It's the community group trying to figure out how to leverage their way in, and that's what's always been an extremely difficult process. Even though I worked for the school district, it's still difficult. In fact, our community organization, Asian Americans United (AAU) just started this charter school. This effort has to do with the community's perspective of not feeling as though we are able to get things done in the ways that we think are really important to have done in order to honor our families. I think I could talk about what we've done in the past organizationally and what we envision for the charter school that we've started.

Lorrie: I think that sounds great! Can you tell us about how you build in parental involvement?

Deborah: AAU is an activist organization, and you really can't be successful as an education activist organization unless you build parent engagement into the program right up front. AAU is committed to developing indigenous leadership and empowering folks within the community to be active participants.

In Chinatown we tried to, as much as possible, not only ensure that there's translation available, but that it's simultaneous translation for the parents in the community. To that end, we borrowed the equipment necessary to provide translation services. We didn't have the funds to actually buy the equipment, but many public schools would. In fact, it was one of the first things we purchased with our planning grant money so that we could communicate with our parents even in the planning and recruitment process. Simultaneous translation allows people to take a more active role in what is happening in the schools. It allows the meeting to happen in real time. We try to ensure that every dialect is covered, because Chinatown has three different dialects: Fujianese, Mandarin, and Cantonese. Even though we give it our best effort, a lot of times we find that it's very hard to get all the translation we need. Sometimes it's only in one dialect, but we usually manage to get at least two. And now, in our school, in addition to Chinese, we have Indonesian, Spanish, Vietnamese, and one or two Cambodian-speaking families as well. We made sure our staff is linguistically diverse, and we have all those languages covered right now except Cambodian.

By and large, in the community organization, we try to conduct our meetings in Chinese. In other words, the people who are disadvantaged at the meetings are the English speakers. And that really changes the dynamic of power in the context of the meeting. However, it's not always possible to conduct the meetings the way we would like, for example, when we're meeting with city officials. And lots of us who were born here—our Chinese isn't good enough to talk about some things. We know *in the house* Chinese but not technical or academic language. But to the extent possible, we conduct the meeting in Chinese, and the English speakers just have to wait for the translation. Again, this sets up a different dynamic about who has the power to speak and who needs assistance to be heard.

I think psychologically we need to be conscious of language and how even accommodations to language still reflect power dynamics. Even in an English-speaking environment that provides translation, there is still a powerful dynamic of who speaks and who feels empowered to speak. It's not just that, though. Many of our parents come from a culture where people don't address things directly. It's very indirect. The meetings take longer. So we plan on our meetings to last at least twice as long as an English-only meeting would be, not simply because of the translation issue but because of the cultural issue of getting to the point. Asians don't get to the point. It's rude. That's not the way things are done. And a lot of what Asians look for is your patience and your willingness to establish a relationship before you start moving into more difficult topics or needier areas. You've got to talk about what might be seemingly innocuous things, but they are not innocuous because they're ways that you're creating a sense of who the participants are at the meeting. In other words, how do the participants interact with each other? How do they mark the ways they respect or don't respect people?

And we try to have food at our meetings—healthy food, a balanced meal. We try to have the kind of food we would want our children to eat because children are always welcome. We always have child care. The parents who attend our meetings are working 10 to 12 hours a day. It's a privilege for us to welcome their participation in the educational process. It's a privilege for us that they can come to a meeting because, Lord knows, if I was working 10 to 12 hours a day, it better be pretty damn important for me to get my energy up to come to a meeting. So we enter into any meetings that we have with our parent participants from a great sense of humility and recognition of the sacrifice that they're making to be there. We do whatever we can to make it easier for them. We have established relationships with restaurants in the community, and they know the work that we do. And sometimes they donate a meal or give us food at a very low price, but we try to make sure that there's a meal.

Many of our Chinatown meetings are on Monday nights because that's when a lot of the restaurants are closed, and so folks that are restaurant workers can attend. Also, we usually don't start till 7:00 or 8:00 p.m. because parents are working, like I said, 10, 12, or even more hours, so by the time they get off of work at 6:00 or 7:00, get home, take a shower, do a few little things, they are not ready to go until 7:00 or 7:30 at the earliest. The city officials may say, "You are having your meeting when?" It wreaks havoc on your life but certainly not more havoc than it does on folks that really can't afford the time or energy.

What I'm trying to say is that in promoting community–school linkages we need to consider the people we are asking to engage with us. I also think we really need to understand what the community is. A lot of times when I talk to folks, they say, "We want community involvement." What they really mean is they want the involvement of the business community. They say, "We need to get the museums involved and the banks, and the corporations and the 'this' and the 'that.'" And I say, "That's not community to me." I mean, it's not their children in the public schools. When I hear *community*, I think of the neighborhood in which we sit—the people who we are supposed to be serving. So sometimes, in discussion of *community involvement* I feel like asking, "Are we in the right book, never mind on the right page?" We should make sure there is a common understanding of the community we want to address in the discussion.

My primary goal is making sure that the children feel like school is part of who they are—part of their community. I've attended discussions, conferences or whatever at universities, where they talk about how can we bring the community more into the school, and if I could visually encapsulate what the conversation looks like, I would draw on a piece of paper a school right in the middle of the paper and all these orbits around it. The discussions focus on how to draw the family into the picture. How should we draw the church in? How should we draw this and that other thing? But the important thing I hear in these conversations is that the center is the school. I think that's really an inaccurate way to talk about who we are and what our work should be about. I think that what should be in the middle is the child, and then around the child are things like his family, his community, his church, his school. But school is embedded in this much broader picture. In fact, maybe I wouldn't even put the child in the center. Maybe I would put the community in the center, because it's not just about the child. It's about the families. It's about that whole thing. School is just a piece of that.

If you're going to be part of a community you have to have a whole different kind of mindset. You need a different way of thinking about what it means to be part of a community. In other words, what does it mean to be a responsible citizen? A responsible community member? I want to be in a school where as a staff person if I walk outside I know everybody there. We'll all say "Hi!" Everyone will know that I'm at the school. It would be like going to a neighborhood store where you know everyone, or saying hello to the neighbor sitting outside on the stoop. That's the idea. That's what school should be.

Naomi: It sounds like the television program, "Cheers," where "everybody knows your name."

Deborah: Yeah, kind of like "Cheers" without the alcohol. Let's talk about small towns and the way the one-room school used to function. That's what we should be about even in urban schools. We should be both in the community and of the community. We should be devoting our resources to these schools as if they exist as parts of small towns. Schools are really one of the few intact places left in our communities. Our communities have been totally decimated by crazy economic policies in the past 20 years. Our sense of community has been destroyed. It's our role to rebuild our communities even as we talk about educating the children. This is a big piece of it.

Some people might ask, "How is it our responsibility to rebuild community? What is our role?" I'm not talking about just inside the building but inside the entire kind of community neighborhood. Here's what I mean. Everyone knows the difference between a house and a home. Your house is just a place. Your home has all the heart to it. To me that's like the difference between a neighborhood and a community. A neighborhood is a geographic set of streets. A community is history, relationships, stories that you tell 10, 20 years down the pike, and everybody knows what you're talking about and they're contesting your version of the events, saying, "No, that's not how it happened. It happened this way!" That's a community. So if we're talking about linking schools to communities, it's more than just a feeling of hanging out here at school. Schools should be places where the community just couldn't imagine existing without the school. It should be such a sacred space for relationships and for history and for memory. We should ask ourselves, "What would this community be without this school here?" That's the idea.

In our charter school now, this question becomes more of a challenge because we aren't only a neighborhood school. We draw from the neighborhood and then from all over the city as well. We have a challenge to both create a relationship within the community we are located, which is Chinatown, and also to reach out to other communities our children are from as well as creating a sense of community among our children and parents as well. We are simultaneously trying to be part of this community of Chinatown and build community beyond Chinatown with the children and families in our school.

Naomi: What challenges does your school face? What are some barriers to getting community members involved in the school?

Deborah: Let me start by giving some context. Starting the charter school wasn't an easy decision to make. We're going on 20 years trying to do educational advocacy in the system. What we see is stuff that you work so hard for dismantled in about six months' time. It's just that you work, you work, you work, and nothing happens. Now we have No Child Left Behind. You feel like everything you worked for is gone. And then you ask yourself, "What was the past 20 years about?" So I think our decision to move to a charter school was a function of age. Twenty years ago I was a lot more patient probably. Well, no. When you're young you're actually less patient. Maybe I was more idealistic or had the idea that I could change things. You know, I used to think, "It's got to be a big change. And it's got to be overnight, and it's got to be so huge and … ." I think I was stuck.

A friend of mine, Grace Lee Boggs, who is the most amazing woman and now in her 90s and still thinking about these issues, told me that we base a lot of our thoughts about how social change happens on scientific understandings about change. We used to operate on the belief that there are causes and effects—in other words, big change, big effect; small change, small effect. So, in all the big social movements of the past centuries, there are big markers to look for. Take for example, civil rights: big, huge marker. The Vietnam War is another big, huge marker of social change. Then Grace told me that we based our social thinking on Newtonian physics: big cause, big effect. But these days where there's globalization and things are so big, you feel powerless to change things. Grace said, "But we know that scientific understanding has changed and quantum physics now tells us that things are related even if you don't see they're related. And like a small movement in a web, it vibrates throughout the entire web. Things will change and you don't even realize that they are changing." It's like that whole thing where people are looking at biodiversity now. They say, "What's the loss of a species?" And now we're suddenly realizing, "Oh, if you lose this little mosquito it's going to affect things all the way up the food chain." I think what Grace was saying was that we need to start thinking about our politics in a different way, and we really need to start to think about how we reclaim just one space—one small space. It doesn't have to be the entire educational system. It doesn't even have to be the whole city. It has to be one small space where you care enough and love the children there enough to make sure that they're going to get what they deserve. Just concentrate on that. To me, that feels so much more doable and so much more hopeful. What happened was that I was talking with Grace and others, and at some point we all said, "Ahhhh," and took a deep breath and decided to work on a small piece of the web.

That's when we all decided to do a charter school. Our idea is to build a space where we can do what we think is best instead of fighting against things that we have little power to change. We are setting out to create something the way we would like it to be. And it's not going to be perfect. We're going to make mistakes and we'll mess up, but there are things we also passionately believe about in education that we know will make a difference. So we worked to get this charter school in Chinatown here in Philadelphia. The theme of the charter school is around folk arts for many reasons.

For one thing, we want to be able to honor local knowledge, and we want to be able to say to a parent, "Look, you know who this person is in our culture, our history." This point links to some of the challenges we face. Some of the greatest teachers that are in our communities don't speak English. They don't have a college degree. They never went to formal educational institutions, but they can teach us values, skills, things about life that we don't want to lose. And we don't want to privilege one type of knowledge over another. When this traditional knowledge is lost, it's an incredible tragedy because these are the lessons which for generations have supplied our children with the resilience they need to survive. So we are building a school where alternative ways of knowing and doing can be honored and respected. So one of the reasons why we are focusing on folk arts is precisely to build this community–school linkage, but I think it's even much deeper than that. We're trying to look at how values get taught and preserved, and it really is in folk arts.

I'm a multiculturalist. I went through the whole tip-of-the-iceberg thing. Some say, "The tip of the iceberg is just the foods and festivals, and we never get to the deep stuff." And then I realized, "This is so wrong." The tip of the iceberg is so fundamental to who we are. It is in the foods that we eat—the foods that we have passed on from our grandparents. Who we are is in the ways of knowing and doing our past. These are the vessels, the vehicles that pass the stuff on. So here we're pooh-poohing these things. I also came to the realization that, as antiracist educators, we said that foodways, folktales, and all that stuff are just fluffy, backward stuff and what we really need to do is talk about racism in the classroom. That's the dangerous stuff. That's where I suddenly realized, "Wait a minute—I talk about race every night around the table with my kids. That's not dangerous. It's life." It's dangerous in school because people are so uptight about it, but in the community you talk about it all the time. It's not dangerous at all in the community. It's just a matter of fact. What's dangerous is sustaining these traditions, because people think they can't make money. You don't get recognition. You get teased. You get criticized. Kids are taught at a young age that this stuff isn't hip—it's not marketed to them.

Let me tell you about this Cambodian dancer that the Philadelphia Folklore Project did this book about. He gets called a *fag*. He gets vilified, not just by non-Cambodian people but by Cambodian people as well. Even the young people would laugh at him for dancing. So what kind of courage does that take? The fact is that he danced in secret. Under the Pol Pot regime in Cambodia, the dancers were targeted for genocide, but he believed he needed to practice because if he survived it would be up to him to pass the dance on. So he would practice in secret knowing he could be killed. I thought, "So when did this become fluffy? Who made that decision, because it certainly wasn't Cambodian folks that made that decision." So it started me really rethinking what I was calling safe and superficial. All the folks that we're working with have been struggling around these issues of folk arts and cultural traditions and sustainability, and we recognize that folk arts are so subversive in so many ways and so counterinstitutional.

Folk art exists because it's not just old stuff. It is art that is useful because it's collective. So it could be graffiti arts; it could be hip-hop. It is the stuff that a group has decided, for whatever reason, that is important to hold on to and pass on. It's almost always passed on informally. It falls outside of the domains of educational institutions. It uses time-honored pedagogies outside of what we teach about in our universities. My colleagues and I have been thinking, "Wow, folk art teaches a number of things. This is not an art form that you're going to get a million dollars from, or get on MTV, or get rich and famous. And you don't do folk art for those reasons. You don't do it because one is an artist, or an individual. You do folk art because the community needs it. It needs it in order for messages to be passed on—for lessons to be taught. You do it out of love for your community." That's a good set of values. That's what we want our children to learn. Of course, we want them to learn math and English and all that stuff, but we want them to learn how to be good people, especially now under the present political conditions, where kids are so bombarded by materialism, by individualism, by entitlement, by things that I never had to deal with as a child. Looking at kids growing up now, materialism has so corrupted and invaded every facet of their lives. What does it mean to be around elders who give up stuff to save something, who value things that money can't buy, who value these things that are about memory and tradition and being a good person? My point is that when we tell people we're doing a school around folk arts, they think, "This is going to be fluffy." It's not.

Lorrie: In fact, your explanation is so rich, both theoretically and conceptually.

Deborah: I hope so. What we really want is to create a school where elders have space and time, because like folk-art traditions, the other thing that we value is time. In fact, what I value in folk art is not fast and easy. This is not about two-week residences, where you test something out. It is about understanding time. It is taking an 80-year-old artist, who is sitting in front of you, and hearing him say that he still hasn't finished learning. It's like my son, who's studying Chinese opera. He's been studying this one jump that the actor does on stage. It takes maybe five seconds on stage. He's been studying this jump for four years. His teachers tell him that he is still not good enough to perform it. It takes persistence just to do things right—to get it right. I want young people to honor the art enough that they're just going to stick to it until it's right.

Once, I was observing this kindergarten teacher, and these children were scribbling and running up to her and she would just say, "That's so lovely. That's so wonderful." And it wasn't lovely. It wasn't wonderful. They were wasting paper, and they were being thoughtless, and they just won this empty praise that at a certain point becomes meaningless. It's the evolution of entitlement. I could see it happening right in front of me. It's where kids can do something silly, like blow a bubble, and get a trophy. Society has become so sick with this message, and young people have grown to expect it. We're saying, "Not in our school. Not in our school. No, no, no, no, no." Students are going to learn that things take hard work. It takes passion and commitment and compassion and caring. You need all these things to be able to say that you are doing any of these things even a little bit. Forget about doing it well—just do it even a little bit. In fact, the first thing a lot of the artists and elders say is, "If you're not a good person, you can never learn this. It's not about the skill. It's about the heart that you bring to it. And if you are not a good person, I can teach you how to do these things and you'll do them, but you won't really get it." So, we say, "Oh, that's the lesson we want for our kids."

Lorrie: Imagine being able to talk about being a good person in the context of schooling.

Deborah: Well, imagine if that was the basis for our schooling. Actually, it has to be that way in a democratic society. That's the other piece of it. We're looking at a democratic society where half the people don't vote—where it didn't matter if you voted last time because who cares if you win or lose. You're looking at a society where people feel so disempowered and where high stakes testing and standardized answers to questions are considered what it means to be a well-educated person. We say, "No, no." Democracy will die if we don't have people that understand that it's about responsibility. It's about being thoughtful. It's about patience. It's about plodding along and working hard and uncovering stuff. Those are the values we want to promote.

There are other things that we're talking about, too. They range from the deep philosophical to almost the mundane. We want to have ritual in our school. I think people need ritual. They need to have ways to mark things. We have this whole list of things we're thinking about creating but haven't yet. For example, how do we start our day? How do we end our day? How do we acknowledge when new people come into the school, such as staff or students? How do we acknowledge when someone has left? How do we mark any kind of significant thing? These are the traditions that we have to create. It's a new school, but we are really conscious about the need for ritual, because it's what creates community. It's like when you start singing, "We shall overcome," and everyone knows the words. There are reasons why that song has some kind of meaning and significance, and it carries something with it because it's been used in ritual practice across various movements around the world for at least 50 years now.

Well, if I go back to your original question about challenges, there are many. I'm just kind of rambling about all these things we think about on a day-to-day basis. And then there is the very real challenge of funding. It's something often discussed—the funding gap between wealthy districts and poorer districts. It's a very real problem. Our children have so many needs, and we feel committed to trying to address those needs. If we really want to pay attention to academic achievement, we need to be able to pay attention to the things a child needs in order to be able to focus on school. If the child is hungry or cold or enduring physical or emotional trauma—these are very real issues facing our kids. To run our basic programs—to pay folk artists equitably in order to be a presence in our school, to find resources for healthy food services for our children and so on—it does often boil down to funding. That's always an issue.

Lorrie: How are students selected for the school?
Deborah: They are chosen through a lottery. The school is located in Chinatown, but we're recruiting from everywhere. We are a multiracial school.

So, we have students from Chinatown and South Philadelphia and northeast Philadelphia where there are a lot of Chinese immigrants because they can't afford Chinatown. We also have a lot of Indonesian, Vietnamese, Lao and Cambodian students, African American, Latino, and European American kids. We're about 90% free and reduced lunch, so it's a low-income community for the most part.

Lorrie: Is it your sense that once you have this charter school, that there may be a butterfly effect? For example, you wave the wings of the butterfly and over here in my arms later a movement occurs. Do you have, say, a hope or a wish that maybe the Philadelphia public schools will in some way be aware and respond?
Deborah: I have come to believe—and I probably shouldn't say this on the record but I'll say it anyway—that this society as it is constructed is not designed to have public schools that work for children that are poor. That won't happen unless there's a significant shift in the social structure, and that means the economic structure. I can't say that it is never going to happen. But I think that it isn't going to happen because of the inequity in our society. I don't think anyone would say that we want inequity. Everybody in this country would say, "Yes, we want equity in our society." What they don't acknowledge is that when you have things that are unequal—that in order for one side to come up and balance out—the other side has to come down a little bit. Unless people are willing to give something up, or are forced to give something up, there's just no way that we will have an equitable situation. It's something intellectually new for me, and I didn't internalize until maybe the past two years. So, in terms of the butterfly or the web effect it's hard to say.

Let me give another example. I went to this wonderful National Coalition of Education Activists (NCEA) conference where civil rights veteran Vince Harding was speaking. At the conference, he was saying that in 1967 or '68, Thich Nhat Hanh, who is this amazing Zen Buddhist monk from Vietnam, came to Spelman College in Atlanta because he wanted to meet Dr. King because Dr. King had nominated him for the Nobel Peace Prize for his work to try to oppose to the war in Vietnam. As Thich Nhat Hanh was making his way across the United States, he stopped off in San Francisco and saw all these antiwar rallies. When he arrives at Spelman, he finds himself in a room full of civil rights activists, and he declares that he was so moved when he stopped in San Francisco and saw the immensity of the opposition to the Vietnam War—just the intensity of it and the amount of students, taking risks, being vocal, saying, "Out of Vietnam now!" As he was speaking he began looking around the room at all these veteran civil rights activists in the midst of this incredible struggle, and he said, "I don't know what I can offer you, but I can offer you this. I want you to know that Vietnam has been fighting colonialism—1,000 years under the Chinese and 500 years under the French. And the thing with Americans is they always want something now, but the thing Vietnamese have learned is that you have to struggle with patience."

I put these two pieces together: what my friend, Grace, said about quantum physics and what Thich Nhat Hanh said about struggling with patience. I know that I'm not sure what the effect is going to be. It certainly will be in the lives of the children of the school or else at that very most basic level we failed, but if we've got 200 to 400 kids who come through the school, learning another way of thinking and in opposition to some of the stuff that's out there now, that's 200 to 400 more than what were there before. If what we do strikes some kind of chord, even in this interview with you, if there's some kind of resonance that you feel—or if there's something that happens where people start to feel, "Wait a minute. There's another way of being. There's another way. It doesn't have to be like it is now"—that's good. It doesn't have to be this kind of thing where we're totally defeated if it's not big enough to move some of these societal forces. It's better, you know, to know whose feet are on our necks now. There are large multinational corporations with a whole lot of power who really are thinking only in terms of profit—no matter what the human or environmental cost. Vince Harding said something like, "You can't dance if your foot is on somebody else's neck." And what I'm trying to say is that at a certain point we have to show what it is like to still be able to dance. Maybe they will see that they can't dance because their foot is on our neck. But we're dancing. We're alive. We're oppressed but we're alive. And what have you lost now that you can't dance trying to hold us down?

I'm trying to think what it would mean to take back our humanity—whatever pieces of it we can. What would it look like if we can take back the fact that our elderly will not be neglected? What would it look like to know that their knowledge won't be disrespected? What would it be like to know that their presence in our schools will be honored and that they would be treated with the respect that elders deserve? If we just take back that much, I'd feel like I've won a small battle.

Lorrie: In fact, when I listen to you talk I'm thinking about what education leaders will think when they read your words. My fear is that when you took the courage to share your sense of public schools and what they are willing or will be able to do for the oppressed, that it might even give education leaders license to say, "Oh well. See here's an activist who even agrees public schools can't address that solely. We don't have to address it." But then, when I hear you speak the way you just did, saying, "Even if we could just learn about the respect of the elders and understand," I can't help but think to myself, "Couldn't leaders hear that? Couldn't educational leaders hear that and understand there may be some way within the schools where they can show respect for the elders? Is that not still possible?" I mean, it was you who fired me up into understanding that that has to be possible.

Deborah: Maybe that's the web that's shaken a little bit. I think the thing is that we can't afford to say anymore, "There are our children, and there are their children." They're my children and your children. They are all our children. I think that we're seeing two opposing forces. One is getting a whole lot more air time than the other. In places like gated communities, I see vouchers that are clearly designed to suck the public schools dry. There's been such a defunding and a turning the back on what we used to call the *commonwealth*.

Someone told me once that the best way to cook frogs is to put them in a pan of cold water and slowly turn the heat on because they won't even realize they are being cooked. And I feel like we're the frogs in the water. That if we go back to 30, 40 years ago, the social sucking out of the common good has taken place, and it has taken place slowly but relentlessly and we haven't even realized it. That's why I can go into public school buildings in this district and not think about it. So many of our schools are so old and outdated—children in buildings that are well over 100 years old. This is the richest country in the world, and that's the best we can do for our children? That's the best? Everybody knows damn well it's not, but where is the outrage? Then I talk to people from the suburbs who say, "Oh well, money doesn't matter. You can't fix anything by throwing money at it." To some degree I agree with them, but then I say to them, "I guess if money doesn't matter you should give me your money, because if we just equalize the spending between schools, you wouldn't miss it because money doesn't really matter." And then they get indignant and say, "Oh, no, no. They will just abuse it."

What we hear is a tacit understanding that it's okay to write off whole segments of this society and largely because these are children of color we're talking about. Not solely, but largely. I like to think that there is a group out there who is saying, "No. This is not what we want. This is about what it means to be human." We're social beings. Human beings have survived throughout time because we recognize that we're fundamentally social beings and we can't break society down to this hyperindividualist thing because we'd destroy ourselves. We can't consume at the rate that we're consuming. We can't. We're going to destroy the planet. It's something that I think the human species has always known but it's been kind of marketed to us to forget. So, if there's any kind of vibration that we can do across the web, it's at this end.

Our vision for this charter school, and for schools in general for the public, is that when we're talking about public education, it has to have a bigger vision than test scores. It really has to reflect a vision of the kind of society we want, what kind of people we want our children to become. It's not just what kind of kids we want to feed into a society that's consuming itself into extinction but what kind of children we want for our survival and for the survival of the world.

Lorrie: When you thought about participating in this book, you brought up the idea for a chapter that talks about putting community back in the community–school linkages. Were you thinking about your model school?

Deborah: I think so, because it's been on our minds for a while. We had been talking about doing a charter school for probably at least five years, and for many years we resisted it. A lot of the initial thinking was charter schools are used for divesting support from the public schools. It wasn't as if we didn't think about it, but then I think we just came to the realization that we're never going to really change the system because of what I said earlier. We just don't have the power to do that.

Lorrie: Let me tell you about what I believe about the population that will be reading this book and the population that I've been working with in our training at the university. I actually have found a group of administrators on this side of this large group who, through training, are becoming aware of the needs. That may be hard to believe but they understand and say, "We're not serving certain groups well enough yet," and the next question they ask is, "How do we do it?" I believe there is a small portion of people who are asking, "How do we link better to the ethnic communities that populate our schools? I don't know how to do it." And I'm hoping you will help us think about that.

Deborah: If I take myself out of this face where I kind of mentally put myself—which is, "This is what I want" and go back to "this is what is"—I think that the educational leaders can't honestly do it without looking at diversity. You are not really going to address cultural inequity unless you start looking at power dynamics in the school. In other words, for example, how are you committed to affirmative action in your school? Do adults in the building reflect who the children are? That's a hard conversation for folks because a lot of them are just starting to ask, "What can the white teachers do to be more sensitive?" I say, "Well, maybe they can step aside." That's a hard conversation to have. But would you send your daughter to a school that was only taught by men? I wouldn't. Would you send your daughter to a school where every single person that they saw in the district was a man? Maybe there are a couple of women cleaning the building? I wouldn't do it. I don't care how caring and genuine they are. I don't care if every man in that building says he's a feminist. What's my daughter going to learn from this situation? And I think we have to be able to say, "Wait a minute then. This is what we're doing with race and language and culture and a whole bunch of other stuff, and we're saying we have good intentions." I understand you have good intentions, but this is what it feels like.

Lorrie: And is your intention good enough to step aside?

Deborah: And that's the hard conversation. That's why I'm saying we can talk about equity, but we've got to talk about the structures. I guess I jumped right into the hardest part of it, because there's all the stuff that you can do and tinker around the edges, but it's still tinkering around the edges and that's the hard part of it. I remember putting my son in a daycare center in Chinatown when he was two. Probably 70% of the kids in that daycare center were Chinese, and the remaining 30% were a mixture of other races. It was a good daycare center with caring teachers. My son came home one day and said, "I'm not going to speak Chinese anymore. I'm only going to speak English." And I asked, "Why?" He said, "English is better than Chinese." And I said, "Why are you saying that?" He told me, "Because if you speak English the teachers understand you." So I sent him to this center that was largely Asian so he could have a better sense of his own identity and he comes home with this? It's a complex thing. And even harder, you can't just have one person of color on the staff or even two because they'll just die. They'll die without more support.

I attended a workshop with California Tomorrow, and they had this really nice opening exercise where you were paired up with a partner to answer some questions asked by the facilitator. One of the questions was, "Tell us a time when you felt like a fish out of water." And I went first, and I said, "I feel like that almost every day—at work, in the school district. I'm Asian American. I'm Chinese. I work fundamentally in a building that's pretty black and white, with maybe a little attention to Latinos on the side. But that's about it, and everyday I feel like I'm not home. It's not something that I'm conscious of, but it's like carrying around grains of sand. It's as if with every incident of feeling a little bit marginalized there's a grain of sand. After a while you're carrying around a couple thousand pounds, but you don't notice it. It's not something I notice until I'm not in it anymore. You say to yourself, "Ahhh." My partner at the workshop, an attorney, couldn't quite understand, and then she said, "Well, I'm kind of politically liberal, progressive. When I'm in my office and I'm talking to people, we are all the same. It's really good, but sometimes I have to go to these meetings with corporate lawyers and stuff and I feel like I just can't be myself. I have to watch what I say. I have to watch what I do, and it feels so crappy." And I said, "That's it. That's how I feel every day." And she said "Oh my God, you feel that every day? That must suck." I said, "Yeah, it does."

I would start with addressing the cultural issues of the kids. How are they made to feel like they're coming home? Where are these spaces where you feel like "Ahhhh, I can relax." I'm a proponent of personal spaces. For example, if I have a group of young women in a school who feel that they need to talk about what it feels like to be an adolescent young woman facing some of life's issues, there should be a space for them. And boys are not going to be allowed in that space because the girls need some space and time to talk about these confusing issues. And I often use the gender analogy because then people get it right. They say, "Oh yeah, that makes sense." Let's translate that to race and culture and language because people need those spaces sometimes. They need a safe space. If schools don't intentionally create spaces for folks to feel that comfort zone, it happens anyway. You know that book by Beverly Tatum, *Why Are All the Black Kids Sitting Together in the Cafeteria?* That's the phenomenon I mean. And it's funny, because in a lot of schools where that happens, teachers or administrators will say it's bad or wrong and want everyone to mix together. But I think it's actually normal because people need spaces to call home sometimes, and they will create those spaces if the spaces aren't there for them.

Naomi: What would you say to somebody asking you for advice? What would you tell them? Imagine just one school asks you for advice; one principal comes to you and he says, "What can I do?" Earlier in our conversation you said that it's the community organizations that are doing the reaching out; the schools aren't really reaching out to the communities at all. How could they change that in your opinion?

Deborah: I think you need to be involved with the community, and I think what that means is if I were the principal assigned to a new school, the very first thing I would do is come down to the community in the evenings and on the weekends and walk around and introduce myself. I would sit down on the stoop with folks. I would go into the local corner stores. I would talk to folks. I would offer my services. I would let them know that I'm around. I would ask how the school could be of help in the neighborhood. I would find out if there is a clean-up going on and where I should show up. I would've loved if the principal of the local public school that serves Chinatown would have come down and said, "What can I do to help you guys stop the stadium from being built? Do you need to use the school for meetings? Maybe I can talk to the art teacher about volunteering some time to silk screen some T-shirts. We can come out on the street, and work with the kids; we can do it in class." It's like when I was saying that you've got to be of the community. Not in the community but of the community. It's got to be your community—whatever it is that's going on in this place. It matters to me because it's my family. This is where I live. This is my school. If you lived in this place, if that was your house, not your school, how would you do civic engagement? How would you be involved? What's a good model of what a democratic citizenry looks like? And if nothing's happening, why not? Because there isn't a single community in the country that can say that everything is hunky-dory and we don't need to have some meetings and talk about how we improve stuff in the community. I'm not talking about the school but the community overall. I guess that would be one of the approaches I would have. And I would try to encourage that in my faculty. I would try to recruit faculty that felt that way. I would try to recruit faculty who either grew up in that neighborhood or still live there.

There are all these other little things that I heard from other people like Ellen Wolpert, who conducted an early childhood workshop once for a conference several years back. She told us that a lot of school districts still have shop classes where sixth, seventh, eighth graders go to the wood shop or something. She said that in the schools that she works with, on the first day of school or the first week of school, she gets a camera—before she was using film but I guess it'd be much more easier with a digital camera these days—and she takes a picture of the front and the back of every child in the school and then of all the adult staff and then she walks around the neighborhood and gets the front and back of the neighborhood grocer, the police officer, the firefighters, and anyone around the neighborhood. She gets parents, too, if they would like to volunteer. She develops those pictures, and then she gets the kids who are in the wood shop to cut out wood-block figures, and then they laminate the front and the back. Those become the play blocks that are used in the kindergarten. How cool is that?

I remember one of my student teachers who had done a unit that I thought was just wonderful. She had been doing research on community heroes. She was up near the Church of the Advocate, which was really an activist church all through the civil rights movement. She asked the children to imagine Malcolm X and Martin Luther King. She asked them to talk about the qualities that these leaders had, for example, courage, commitment, passion, and caring for the community. Then she had them figure out which contemporary people in their community were community heroes. The students did a whole newsletter about community heroes in the neighborhood, and then she had them create want ads. This was the one that I thought was really cool. Who do we need in our community now? The children wrote want ads for community heroes and included qualifications and job requirements. It was the cutest thing. I thought, "Oh, that's wonderful. That's just wonderful." It's using the community in terms of both assets and possibilities as the basis for the curriculum in the classroom.

Naomi: Can you tell us about children that you've worked with or children where you've seen some positive behaviors or received some positive feedback that might be directly tied to community linkages? What I'm asking for may actually be success stories that relate more indirectly to community involvement. I know that right now you're thinking and dreaming about the possibilities of linking to the community for the success of children. But do you know of any successes right now that can be linked to increased academic achievement?

Deborah: Yeah. I'll just tell you about one more teacher story, and then I'll tell you the kids' stories. My favorite activity was done when I was actually running a program. The Children's Defense Fund has Freedom Schools, which operate in the summer. They've been primarily African American schools, and in recent years there's been some Latino ones, but AAU operated the first and only Asian American Freedom School—two actually, one in Chinatown and one in south Philadelphia. One year they asked me to be the educational director on site for the Chinatown Freedom School, and it happened to be the year that we were fighting for that building and against the baseball stadium in Chinatown. The fight to keep the school became a very important part of the work that we did on our school.

We needed school uniforms because the kids were going on trips. So first we asked the kids to write essays. Remember, this was in the context where the children were constantly hearing about the threat of the stadium. There were demonstrations constantly. We asked the children to respond to the question, "What does Chinatown mean to you? These were little kids between 4 and 10 years old. The youngest was a little four-and-a-half-year-old girl named Pinkie. Because she still couldn't write, she dictated her entire essay. It read, "If they build the stadium in Chinatown Pinkie will be mad." That was her entire essay, and I still remember it because the teachers went through the essays and pulled out sentences or phrases that really jumped out at them.

We got white T-shirts at a dollar each. And because we had no money, these T-shirts were going to be the school uniform. We got a laser printer and asked an artist to design a logo with "No Stadium in Chinatown." Each kid's statement was typed on the computer and laser printed onto an iron-on transfer. The school uniform became these statements that children were saying about how much this community meant to them. And they ran the gamut from Pinkie's to another one that said, "I can buy candy for five cents a piece. I love Chinatown." Another said, "My family of seven lives in two bedrooms. We need housing. We don't need a stadium." Each one had its own thing. Every kid got a T-shirt, and we gave them crayons to draw pictures that could be ironed onto the T-shirt. Anytime we went on a school trip—and we took many that summer—the children became a walking billboard of protest, and they became spokespersons for their community. For example, we'd go to the science museum with these kids, and we were walking with them and it was comical because you'd see people and first they'd say, "Oh, look, cute little Chinese kids." Then they'd look at a kid's T-shirt, and then you'd see them stare, and then they looked at the next one. Then you could see the realization that every single T-shirt was different, and then you'd see them looking up and down at each one. The kids would be on the subway, and people would just spend the subway ride reading the T-shirts. Everywhere we went with these kids we were

taking the power to humanize this community and say, "You know what? There are reasons why we don't want the stadium. And it's in these 50 children right here, and if you can still support building it after reading these 50 children's T-shirts then you don't have a heart at all." It's with projects like that I just look back at it, and I think, "Oh my God, that was wonderful." And the kids were so proud of their shirts. It was nice. And they didn't build the stadium. No, they did not.

Lorrie: Then that school really linked with the community.
Deborah: Oh, yes. But it was a summer school. It was independent of regular school. It was our Freedom School. It wasn't a school-district school. I wonder if schools feel they can't support communities in these ways because of the politics involved. But if we think of schools as integral parts of a community and an entire community is concerned about an issue, schools need to have the ability to get involved. But in this case, it was a school for 50 children, and that was one of the projects. In fact, it was a small project because it was really just creating the school uniforms.
Naomi: But that's your web example—something seemingly small that has a huge effect. It affected an entire city, a major building project.
Deborah: It wasn't just the kids though. It was all of us.
Naomi: It was a piece of the whole puzzle. The kids are part of the puzzle, part of the community.
Lorrie: I recall the striking comments you made at the symposium where you said that schools always think they have to start with curriculum and you said, "Where I would start would be the lunchroom." You were talking about why schools couldn't arrange to have a time so that the mothers or the grandmothers could come in to be with their children. There's a message to me about making time and space for the elders of the community.
Deborah: Well, there also needs to be time and space for community, right? My question is how do we rebuild the sense of collectivism and community and greater responsibility? What I was thinking about the lunchroom is this: We have these lines and the kids get their trays and everybody gets a designated lunch item and then they go and they sit. I was thinking why don't we eat family style? You know, our kids never eat like families anymore. Their parents are working too hard, and food is too hard to come by because there are no grocery stores in poor neighborhoods and we've been McDonalded to death. For 100 different reasons, family meal time no longer exists for a lot of kids. Why don't we have family-style dinning in our schools? Why don't we sit around the table? In my culture, that's what you do. You have food in the center, and people take according to their needs. Sitting around a table you take the time to talk. In my ideal school, the eighth graders would be with the kindergarteners and the fifth graders. There would be family units, and the older children would learn that they need to be responsible for the little ones and the senior citizens. We have a food service in Chinatown for low-income seniors. Why does it have to be separate from the children's feeding? Why couldn't they be together? Why couldn't it be culturally appropriate food, for goodness sake? Why couldn't it be a whole bunch of things?

I'm concerned about the nutrition and quality of food given to our kids. I am concerned about the quality of a lot of the school lunch food. Eating is an important marker of community time. It always has been, until recently with fast food and processed foods, but if you go back in time, it took a long time to prepare food, and it wasn't economical or a good use of time to prepare just a single serving. You did it big, and meal time was an important time when you sat around and talked and shared. Schools can play a big role in reclaiming that time and space for children who've lost it and for families who've lost it. I see an increasing interest and concern in school lunches—both in how they are presented and what the contents are. I think it's a really positive development.

Lorrie: Is there any research that drives your own thinking or that has affected your own thinking?

Deborah: A lot of my thinking is driven by noneducation stuff. Believe it or not, there was a funky reading on Buddhist economics. You see, I can't separate my thinking about schools from the larger picture of society. We have to think about the bigger things in society. What kinds of schools do we want then? What really struck me in this reading on Buddhist economics is a point made about Sanskrit, the Buddhist language. There are two words for *production* and two words for *consumption,* and they are totally different words. There's good production and bad production and good consumption and bad consumption. In our society there's only one word, and so when we do any of our economic analysis it's based on a formula that's mathematically driven. It's different in Buddhist economics. For example, if I have five dollars, I can buy a pack of cigarettes or I can buy a book to read. In Sanskrit people would use very different words for those two acts, because one is destructive to your body, to the environment, to a number of other places, and one is constructive. It's the same thing with the words for production. There isn't just production because you have to weigh the environmental costs. How would it contribute to building families and communities? What does it contribute to making the world a better place? If you're producing toy guns, you couldn't use the word for *production* that is a good word. You just couldn't. There's no way to justify it. After reading this Buddhist economics book I thought, "That's what I want my children to know. I want them to have two words for production and I want them to have two words for consumption. I want them to know that there are consequences to actions and that we can't always look at things one way and think that it's the only way."

There's so much that we can learn from other cultures, and it's not just about the multicultural idea that some have, which is "Let me make you feel good about yourself." It is about how I become a better human being. I do it by understanding the way the rest of the world thinks. It's how I become a better world citizen. Other folks have some really good answers. I'm also a Rethinking School junkie.

Lorrie: I want to ask you a really basic question, and it actually comes from my father, but it's the question that I also get from educational leaders who don't think as you do. Why do schools have to link more with communities? What evidence is there from the children that in fact it's necessary? I mean, isn't our goal to Americanize children? What grounds do we have that tell us that schools do in fact need to link more effectively with their ethnic communities?

Deborah: The first thing I would ask them is, "What does it mean to Americanize?" I really don't know what that means. I think that multicultural education is not just for schools that have students of color. It's part of living in a global society. Part of it is being a competent human being. We can't walk through the world anymore thinking, "I only have to learn only one way of doing things and one way of being, and that's good enough." We could, but I think we would ultimately destroy ourselves and the planet. I would start right there.

It depends on what you measure as success. It depends on what you measure as important. I think it's okay to disagree, but you've got to be clear about what your goals and purposes are in education. If it's just for test scores and just for academics, you might get away with it. I think we have to go back to the questions, "What are our schools for? What kind of children do we want our kids to be? And what kind of people do we want our faculty and ourselves to be?"

My litmus test uses the gender analogy. It's always a good litmus test because people can see it and they feel it better—women better than men, but most at this stage of the game can get it. Let's take a girl that goes to a school that has all male teachers. Let's say that you need a jock strap to get in the door. Imagine that every cultural thing in the school screams male dominance and the tokenizing of women. Or, perhaps the school is more benign than that and simply has an environment where women are invisible. Do we honestly believe that the girls going to that school would grow up without some kind of damage to their sense of self? I don't think so. I would just offer that analogy.

Whenever you are in a situation and you are not sure how it deals with race, switch it. Switch the oppression. Make it somebody else's experience, and do it several times. Pretend it's a gay person, which is even harder sometimes for people to see. Pretend it's someone with a disability. Just switch it around a little bit, and if in any of those scenarios it feels like that wouldn't be right, then it ain't right. It's hard to see from somebody else's lens. Sometimes you've got to practice with a bunch of different lenses until you hit it. I think it's much easier for me to do this with folks by just flipping into the gender thing because then they feel it more.

Lorrie: Thank you. I'm very satisfied with how you answered that. That would help me when I'm posed with that question.

Deborah: Well, I think most people would get that. It'd be pretty hard not to get that. Maybe it wouldn't fly. Maybe it flies for us because we are all women.

Naomi: Is there anything else that you feel a burning need that you should say or share?

Lorrie: Educational leaders and future educational leaders will be reading your thoughts—principals or principals in training or superintendents.

Deborah: Well, first it occurs to me that I didn't answer your earlier question about successes. Well, again, I can point mostly to the work with AAU and the youth we worked with in our different programs. But what about this: In our school right now, there are 18 teachers. Of those 18, three are former youth in our programs. We had an interview process with a committee made up of various folks, and these individuals were chosen because of how they articulate their vision for education. When I look at that, I'm pretty amazed. In terms of sowing seeds for carrying on building and developing our communities, being able to know some of our youth went on to become teachers who choose to come back to the community is just really a wonderful thing.

And another final thought: I guess another piece of all this cultural stuff has to do with hierarchy power structures. I think the way that a principal's role is constructed creates a very vertical power arrangement that closes itself off. Have you ever seen the doctor, and you're kind of intimidated? You go to see the doctor and you're feeling like crap, and the doctor explains the problem and then you kind of feel like you don't understand. But you don't want to waste his valuable time. I don't know what it is about doctors. I'm a well-educated person. I'm not the type of person that isn't going to talk. But when I get with the doctor, no matter what he says, I nod my head and pretend that I understand him.

I think a lot of times in education, because we in public education feel disrespected as professionals, we don't realize the doctor effect we have on parents and the community. We don't realize that we need to practice our bedside manner a little bit and understand the fact that because we're teachers or principals that is enough to shut people down. We don't have to open our mouths. I know public educators in this country feel disrespected and powerless. As educators we feel like that but in the communities that we work in we carry so much power. It's the power to intimidate. So I guess one of the things that we really need to think about is how to connect with the people—like I said earlier, sitting on the stoop, walking on the sidewalks with grandmas. What we say now is, "My door is open. You can come in to see me." The barrier has to be broken down by educators, not by parents. I don't think we realize the power of our positions.

Lorrie: I don't think you realize the power that you have had on me and how you influenced me when you spoke a year ago at the symposium. I hadn't thought about this butterfly or web effect, but it opened my eyes. I train ESL teachers, and now I train principals and superintendents for the federal grant about how to work with ELLs, and after you spoke I realized there's an entire whole area that I'm unaware of, that I need to explore further and I didn't know where to begin. I knew even before the book that I had to have a conversation with you to know where to begin. I just needed for you to know. I want just to thank you. Thank you for helping me shape my ideas and understand.

IV: School and District Reform

Editor's Introduction

This section examines reforms at the school and district levels that impact the academic success of English language learners (ELLs). Throughout the country several movements are under way to reform and redesign schools to meet the needs of all students. The authors in this section discuss ways school and district personnel can rethink how best to serve the needs of ELLs. The chapters in this section provide information on quality programming for ELLs, bilingual education, special education, and professional development for teachers who work with ELLs.

The researchers at the Education Alliance and Lab at Brown University promote successful learning environments for ELLs by outlining several principles that must be taken into consideration when planning programs for non-English-speaking students. The authors consider the goals of schooling for ELLs as well as the roles of language and culture in teaching, learning, and the assessment of learning. They consider factors that impact the education of ELLs, including research-based, age-appropriate literacy instruction that ELLs need to develop good literacy skills. Finally, they consider the importance of parental and community involvement in the education of ELLs.

Bilingual education is usually thought of as a program for non-English-speaking students only. In Chapter 14, Miranda reminds us that school administrators need to be cognizant of their responsibility to prepare all students to contribute meaningfully to a world that is increasingly interconnected. He challenges the idea that bilingualism is only for ELLs. The chapter illustrates how teachers and administrators can capitalize on the assets ELLs bring with them—their languages and cultures—and how these resources can be used for the success and benefit of English monolingual students as well. The chapter looks at bilingual education as a benefit for all students.

In Chapter 15, deGeorge helps the reader distinguish between academic difficulties due to language issues and those due to learning disabilities. The author, a practitioner in the field, often receives requests on how to determine if an English language learner should be referred to special education professionals for services. He provides a checklist of questions to consider for school personnel to best plan services for ELLs.

In Chapter 16, Hamann considers the fact that the education of ELLs is the purview of all teachers, yet many are not trained in how to work with them. The chapter outlines the author's research in two school districts on responsiveness to ELLs as measured by their academic performance. Unfortunately, most teachers and administrators in the districts did not see the education of ELLs as part of their own professional task. Hamann seeks to explain why the educators responded the way they did and, in addition, outlines the missed opportunities that would most likely have increased the number of teachers willing and capable of contributing to the success of ELLs.

The concluding chapter by Migliacci and Verplaetse not only offers a summary of the chapters in this book but also examines how what we learn from each one can be applied in a mandate-driven climate to ensure the academic achievement for ELLs. The chapter provides the reader with a new set of myths to consider to better answer the question of how educators can achieve inclusive pedagogy when faced with standardized testing.

CHAPTER 13

Successful Schooling for ELLs: Principles for Building Responsive Learning Environments

MARIA COADY, EDMUND T. HAMANN, MARGARET HARRINGTON, MARIA PACHECO, SAMBOEN PHO, AND JANE YEDLIN

Guiding Questions

- What are the goals of schooling in general and for ELLs in particular?
- What roles do language and culture play in teaching, in learning, and in the assessment of learning?
- How do we measure the successfulness of schooling for ELLs?
- What factors besides the quality of classroom instruction impact the education of ELLs? How?
- In addition to research-based, age-appropriate literacy instruction, what more do ELLs need in order to develop good literacy skills?
- What is the importance of parental and community involvement in the education of ELLs?

While measurable academic gains in reading and mathematics are certainly central to the notion of successful schooling, we must not conceptualize success too narrowly. The famous educator John Dewey (1916) considered education a tool that would enable the citizen to "integrate culture and vocation effectively and usefully." Dewey cautioned that assessing the success of such an education is not simple or one-dimensional.

Reprinted with permission from the Education Alliance at Brown University. This chapter originally appears in a publication by the Education Alliance at Brown University entitled Claiming Opportunities: A handbook for improving education for English Language Learners, 2003, Brown University, Providence, Rhode Island. This publication was based on the work supported by the Institute of Education Sciences (IES), U.S. Department of Education, under Contract Number ED-01-C0-0010. Any opinions, findings, and conclusions or recommendations expressed in this material are those of the authors and do not necessarily reflect the views of the IES, the U.S. Department of Education or any other agency of the U.S. Government.

...in dealing with the young...it is easy to ignore...the effect of our acts upon their disposition, or to subordinate that educative effect to some external and tangible result. (p. 7)

Supreme Court Justice Earl Warren's 1954 decision in Brown v. Board of Education emphasized that test scores are only benchmarks, not ends in themselves. He asserted that our educational system should prepare students for "public responsibilities, awakening the child to cultural values...and...helping him to adjust normally to his environment." More recently, Williams (1999) described the scope of the challenge that we face in successfully educating English language learners for the world of tomorrow:

[It is] an awesome challenge for society and educational institutions...to adequately prepare the diverse population of students we are not successfully educating with recognition and respect for their individual human rights...and to enable all students to participate in and contribute to the growth of the nation and the world community in a future that demands cross-cultural interdependence and new social interactions—global human opportunities (pp. 89–90).

Mindful of these broader definitions of success, this section outlines several major principles of successful ELL education. Successful education for ELLs means that the academic and social development of each student is supported in culturally and linguistically responsive ways. A standardized test score may not fully or accurately represent school success. Other quantitative data, such as reduced dropout rates, improved attendance, continuation on to higher education, and rubric-scored portfolios and performance assessments, also offer direct and indirect evidence of success (Pellegrino, Chudowsky, & Glaser, 2001).

More fundamentally, however, the success of ELLs must be thought of in broader terms than their success at mastering the language, customs, and knowledge of the dominant culture (Miramontes et al., 1997; Halcón, 2001; Hamann, 2001). As Gibson (1997) wrote, "We must measure school success in terms of the ability of students to move successfully between their multiple cultural worlds" (p. 446). In a similar vein, Portes and Rumbaut (2001) argued that it is in the best interest of society and the individual ELL to allow students to acquire new knowledge without ignoring, displacing, deprecating, or diminishing existing linguistic and cultural knowledge. Portes and Rumbaut wrote:

In this new world order where multiple economic, political, and cultural ties bind nations more closely to one another, it is not clear that the rapid extinction of foreign languages is in the interest of individual citizens or of the society as a whole. In an increasingly interdependent global system, the presence of pools of citizens able to communicate fluently in English plus another language and bridge the cultural gaps among nations represents an important collective resource (p. 273).

As Miramontes et al. (1997) pointed out, a student who becomes bilingual and biliterate is more accomplished than one who masters only one language.

Moreover, García (1998) wrote: "There is some evidence that assimilation may actually inhibit academic success. Studies of Mexican immigrants suggest that those who maintain a strong identification with their native language and culture are more likely to succeed in schools than those who readily adapt to U.S. ways" (p. viii). Trueba (1999) echoed that sentiment, saying, "If children manage to retain a strong cultural self-identity and maintain a sense of belonging to their socio-cultural community, they seem to achieve well in school" (p. 260). Both of these scholars are aware of troubling data that suggest second-generation students (i.e., children of immigrants) often do not fare as well in school as the immigrant generation did, despite their greater familiarity with "American" ways (Suárez-Orozco & Suárez-Orozco, 1995; Portes & Rumbaut, 2001). Maintaining a sense of pride in self aids the acquisition of new competencies and new cultural ways; thus, a definition of ELL success could incorporate maintenance of first language and culture for practical as well as pluralist reasons.

In her book *White Teacher* (1979), Vivian Gussin Paley discussed her realization that shared language and cultural knowledge make it easier to recognize intelligence in young children of one's own cultural group and language community. Moreover, intelligence, learning, and good behavior are all conceptualized somewhat differently across cultures. Cultural assumptions determine whether a "good" student is expected to be talkative, inquisitive, and independent or, on the other hand, observant, cooperative, and a good listener. The Northeast and Islands Regional Educational Laboratory (2002) has identified the following cross-cultural differences as significant for schooling:

1. How children are expected to interact with each other and adults
2. How language is used by adults and children
3. How knowledge is acquired and displayed
4. What counts as knowledge (pp. 51–52)

School practices that disregard these cross-cultural differences or discount ELLs' first language, literacy, cultural identity, or self-esteem are not likely to create effective learning environments. First-language vocabulary, oral language, and literacy skills all support successful English literacy development (Dickinson & Tabors, 2001; Moll, 1996). At the same time, Delpit (1988) and Bartolomé (1998) caution educators that not teaching minority students mainstream ways or academic forms of discourse is doing them a disservice. ELLs' prior knowledge and first-language proficiency provide the foundations for achievement in U.S. schools. Success for ELLs means being able to function well in mainstream academic settings and in their home communities.

Given multiple criteria for ELL success, multiple measures may be needed to evaluate it. It is widely agreed that ELLs' scores on standardized tests of subject knowledge are often not valid (August & Hakuta, 1997; García, 2001; Hurley & Tinajero, 2001; LaCelle-Peterson & Rivera, 1994; Stefanakis, 1998). The Standards for Educational and Psychological Testing (American Educational Research Association, American Psychological Association, National Council on Measurement in Education, 1985) state:

> Every assessment is an assessment of language…This is even more so given the advent of performance assessments requiring extensive comprehension and production of language. For example, "mathematical communication," one of seven subtests, … requires the student to use appropriate mathematical terms, vocabulary, and language based on prior conceptual work (p. 120).

This seldom-recognized linguistic dimension of (even math) tests often limits the ability of ELLs to fully demonstrate their content knowledge and understandings (García, 2001). Moreover, tests designed for native English speakers may lack the sensitivity to represent initial gains or incremental growth in English language acquisition.

August and Hakuta (1997) found that although ELLs can and should reach the same high standards as other students, they may need more time:

According to the law, the same high performance standards that are established for all students are the ultimate goal for English language learners as well. On average, however,

English language learners (especially those with limited prior schooling) may take more time to meet these standards. Therefore additional benchmarks might be developed for assessing the progress of these students toward meeting the standards. Moreover, because English language learners are acquiring English language skills and knowledge already possessed by students who arrive at school already speaking English, additional content and performance standards in English language arts may be appropriate (p. 127).

It is important to understand that the label "ELL" encompasses diverse individuals and groups in a variety of school settings. A Chinese-speaking kindergartener born in a U.S. city has different needs, abilities, and attributes than a 17-year-old from a Central American preparatory school attending high school in a rural U.S. community. Clearly, recommended practices and educational challenges vary according to student characteristics and school/community settings. Despite this diversity, educators and researchers have identified some practices common to most contexts where ELLs experience effective schooling. From these research-based practices we have derived a set of principles for building responsive learning environments that support ELLs. The principles serve as guides for the development of teaching strategies, reform models, programs, and research questions in settings where ELLs are part of the school population.

PRINCIPLES FOR BUILDING AN ELL-RESPONSIVE LEARNING ENVIRONMENT

Principle 1.   ELLs are most successful when...

School leaders, administrators, and educators recognize that educating ELLs is the responsibility of the entire school staff.

- School leadership's support of the education of ELLs can be seen in the explicit inclusion of ELLs in a school's vision, goals, and reform strategies as well as in its promised accountability regarding retention and dropout rates, test exemption rates, and enrollment in special programs.
- ELLs are neither programmatically nor physically isolated; rather they are an integral part of the school and they receive appropriate targeted services such as ESL and/or literacy instruction.
- ESL and bilingual teachers have equitable access to all staff development resources and materials.
- All staff have access to appropriate professional development in educating ELLs.
- Linguistic and cultural needs of ELLs are included in decisions regarding comprehensive school reform. School reform teams include members who are knowledgeable about ELLs.

Research supporting Principle 1: Brisk, 1998; Dentler & Hafner, 1997; Grey, 1991; Hamann, Zuliani, & Hudak, 2001; IDRA, 2002; Lucas, 1997; Miramontes et al., 1997; Olsen et al., 1994; Stringfield et al., 1998.

Principle 2.   ELLs are most successful when...

Educators recognize the heterogeneity of the student population that is collectively labeled as "ELL" and are able to vary their responses to the needs of different learners. ELLs differ greatly in terms of:

- Language background
- Place of origin

- Rural or urban background
- Previous school experience
- Home language literacy skills
- Proficiency in conversational English
- Proficiency in academic and written English
- Age
- Age on arrival
- Family circumstances and responsibilities
- Living situation
- History of mobility
- Employment and work schedule
- Immigration or refugee experience
- Trauma and resiliency
- Family legal status
- Family educational history
- Family social organization
- Birth order in the family
- Size and resources of the local ethnic enclave
- Identification with local ethnic enclave
- Religious beliefs and practices
- Continued contact with place of origin and language
- Gender roles and assumptions
- Aspirations and expectations
- Interests, talents, skills
- Funds of knowledge and community support

Research supporting Principle 2: Lucas, 1997; Tabors, 1997; Portes & Rumbaut, 1990; Suárez-Orozco & Suárez-Orozco, 1995, 2002; Miramontes et al., 1997; Olsen, 1997; Yedlin, 2003.

Principle 3.   ELLs are most successful when...

The school climate and general practice reinforce the principle that students' languages and cultures are resources for further learning.

- Hallway conversations, displays of student work, and school activities are multi-cultural and multilingual.
- Adults from students' heritage communities play important roles in the life of the school.
- Teachers integrate students' first language and literacy and other "funds of knowledge," including their individual areas of interest and curiosity, into the learning process, helping them make connections between their prior and new knowledge.

Research supporting Principle 3: Au, 1980; Brisk & Harrington, 2000; Cloud, Genesee, & Hamayan, 2000; Escamilla & Coady, in preparation; González, et al., 1995; Hammond, 1997; Miramontes, et al., 1997; Moll et al., 1992; Ruíz, 1984; Roseberry, Warren, & Conant, 1992; Um, 2003.

Principle 4.   ELLs are most successful when...

There are strong and seamless links connecting home, school, and community.

- Educators foster family participation in ways that truly value parents' knowledge and priorities.
- Educators communicate regularly with families, exchanging information and points of view through newsletters, calls, interpreters, and presentations at ethnic, community-based organizations and houses of worship. Meetings are conducted multilingually.
- The school staff includes adults from students' heritage communities and speakers of their languages.
- Educators recognize the importance of family participation in education and, through family and community activities, reinforce connections among students' home, school, and the broader community in which the school operates.
- Educators understand that across different cultures and settings the roles of parents in their children's education vary. In some cultures parents' responsibilities center around the provision of necessities, protection, discipline, and moral guidance in the home and community. They may view schooling as the responsibility solely of professional educators.
- Educators have some familiarity with and show interest in learning about the cultures, languages, places of origin, demographic patterns, reasons for immigration or migration, naming patterns, and interactional styles of the communities they serve.
- Educators make explicit to ELLs' parents the new opportunities and expectations that exist for parental involvement.
- Educators are aware of potential linguistic, cultural, economic, and logistical obstacles to the participation of ELL families in school-based programs and events.
- Educators try to address obstacles energetically, creatively, and in culturally sensitive ways. They provide ethnic community liaisons, interpreters, child care, and transportation.
- Educators understand that in some families the provision of necessities, protection, and moral guidance consumes all of the parents' time and resources.
- Educators do not disparage parents whose support of their children may not be evident because of its lack of alignment with local expectations.

Research that supports Principle 4: Ada & Zubizarreta, 2001; Delgado-Gaitán, 1990; Epstein, 2001; Epstein, et al., 2002; Heath, 1983; Henderson, 1987; Miramontes et al., 1997; Moore, 1992; Siu, 1995; Valdés, 1996; Valenzuela, 1999; Villenas, 2001.

Principle 5.   ELLs are most successful when...

ELLs have equitable access to all school resources and programs.

- ELLs have access to all programs and levels of instruction, including special education, gifted and talented education, or high-level courses such as calculus.
- Curricula, teaching strategies, grouping strategies, and other reforms are implemented in ways that increase their accessibility, comprehensibility, and meaning to ELLs.
- ELLs have access to prerequisites for acceptance into higher education.
- ELLs have access to all enrichment and extracurricular activities.

- ELLs have equal treatment from guidance counselors and equitable access to the full range of services they provide, such as planning for postsecondary education.

Research that supports Principle 5: Northeast and Islands Regional Educational Laboratory at Brown University, 2000; Olsen & Jaramillo, 1999.

Principle 6.   ELLs are most successful when...

Teachers have high expectations for ELLs.

- Particularly for ELLs with previous school experience, this principle means educators need a clear sense of what students have already mastered in a different language or in a different country.
- The need to adapt curriculum to match achieved language proficiency cannot be an excuse for denying ELLs access to challenging academic content.

Research supporting Principle 6: García, 1997; Verplaetse, 1998; Valdés, 2001.

Principle 7.   ELLs are most successful when...

Teachers are properly prepared and willing to teach ELLs.

- Teachers should have high-quality professional development experiences in topics pertinent to working with ELLs, including:
    - First- and second-language acquisition
    - Reading and writing in a second language
    - Methods for teaching content subjects to ELLs
    - Alternative assessment
    - Sociocultural issues in education
- Staff development is long term and job embedded.
- Teachers can differentiate among developmental issues in language acquisition, gaps in prior schooling, and learning disabilities.
- Teachers are culturally responsive, building on students' linguistic and cultural knowledge both for purposes of scaffolding new knowledge onto students' existing knowledge and earning learners' assent.
- Teachers foster meaningful relationships with students.
- Teachers understand and incorporate standards for ELLs.

Research supporting Principle 7: Cummins, 2001; Erickson, 1987; García, 2001; Gay, 2001; González et al., 1995; Ladson-Billings, 1995; Miramontes et al., 1997; Moll et al., 1992; Nieto, 1999; TESOL, n.d.; Wong Fillmore & Snow, 1999; Yedlin, 2003.

Principle 8.   ELLs are most successful when...

Language and literacy are infused throughout the educational process, including curriculum and instruction.

- Teachers explicitly teach and model the academic skills and the thinking, learning, reading, writing, and studying strategies that ELLs need to know in order to function effectively in academic environments.
- Teachers act as "educational linguists" and pay attention to uses and functions of language in their own classrooms and disciplines.

- Students are taught which styles of speaking, writing, reading, and participating apply in a given setting, genre, or subject area, including text books and story books, friendly letters and essays, personal narratives, and persuasive essays.
- Children are enabled to make overt comparisons of linguistic meanings and uses in one environment versus another, such as the playground and the reading group, or in English and their home languages.
- ELL students have opportunities to hear comprehensible language and to read comprehensible texts. Texts are reader friendly and make links to students' prior knowledge and experiences.
- Teachers employ a variety of strategies to help students understand challenging language, texts, and concepts. These may include linguistic simplification, demonstrations, hands-on activities, mime and gestures, native language support, use of graphic organizers, and learning logs.
- Students have opportunities to interact with teachers, classmates (both ELL and English proficient), and with age-appropriate subject matter through instructional conversation, cooperative group work, jigsaw reading, writing conferences, peer and cross-age tutoring, and college "buddies."

Research supporting Principle 8: Brumfit, 1997; Cummins, 2000; Kohl, 2002; Wong Fillmore & Snow, 2000; Yedlin, 2003.

Principle 9.   ELLs are most successful when...

Assessment is authentic, credible to learners and instructors, and takes into account first- and second-language literacy development.

- Multiple forms of assessment measure not only students' academic achievement but also their progress, effort, engagement, perseverance, motivation, and attitudes in the school and classroom setting.
- Because first-language development positively impacts English language literacy (Snow, Burns, & Griffin, 1998), tests assess literacy in the first language along with students' English language proficiency and content area knowledge.
- Assessment is used frequently and formatively, with results allowing the instructor—perhaps in direct consultation with the learner—to refine subsequent teaching strategies.
- Teachers include first-language competence in assessment of an ELL's overall academic accomplishment.

Research supporting Principle 9: Ascher, 1990; Escamilla & Coady, 2001; García, 2001; Hurley & Tinajero, 2001; National Research Council, 2000; O'Malley & Pierce, 1996; Snow, Burns & Griffin, 1998; Stefanakis, 1998; Yedlin, 2003.

References

Ada, A. F. & Zubizareta, R. (2001). Parent narratives: The cultural bridge between Latino parents and their children. In M. L. Reyes & J. J. Halcón (Eds.), *The best for our children: Critical perspectives on literacy for Latino students* (pp. 229–244). New York: Teachers College Press.

Ascher, C. (1990). Assessing bilingual students for placement and instruction. ERIC Digest No. 65. Retrieved February 19, 2002 from the ERIC Clearinghouse on Urban Education. Access: http://eric-web.tc.columbia.edu/digest/dig65.asp.

Au, K. (1980). Participation structures in a reading lesson with Hawaiian children: Analysis of a culturally appropriate instructional event. *Anthropology and Education Quarterly, 11*(2), 91–115.

Brisk, M. (1998). *Bilingual education: From compensatory to quality schooling.* Mahwah, NJ: Lawrence Erlbaum Associates.

Brisk, M. E. & Harrington, M. M. (2000). *Literacy and bilingualism: A handbook for all teachers.* Mahwah, NJ: Lawrence Erlbaum Associates.

Brumfit, C. (1997). The teacher as educational linguist. In L. van Lier & D. Corson (Eds.), *Encyclopedia of language and education,* Volume 6. Dordrecht, the Netherlands: Kluwer Academic Press.

Cloud, N., Genesee, F., and Hamayan, E. (2000). *Dual language instruction: A handbook for enriched education.* Boston: Heinle & Heinle.

Cummins, J. (2000). *Language, power, and pedagogy: Bilingual children in the crossfire.* Clevedon, UK: Multilingual Matters.

Cummins, J. (2001). *Negotiating identities: Education for empowerment in a diverse society* (2nd edition). Los Angeles: California Association for Bilingual Education.

Delgado-Gaitán, C. (1990). *Literacy for empowerment: The role of parents in children's education.* New York: The Falmer Press.

Dentler, R. A. & Hafner A. L. (1997). *Hosting newcomers: Structuring educational opportunities for immigrant children.* New York: Teachers College Press.

Epstein, J. L. (2001). *School, family, and community partnerships: Preparing educators and improving schools.* Boulder CO: Westview Press.

Epstein, J, L., Sanders, M. G., Simon, B. S., Salinas, K. C., Jansorn, N. R., & Van Voorhis, F. L. (2002). *School, family, and community partnerships: Your handbook for action* (2nd edition). Thousand Oaks, CA: Corwin Press.

Erickson, F. (1987). Transformation and school success: The politics and culture of educational achievement. *Anthropology and Educational Quarterly, 18*(4), 335–356.

Escamilla, K. & Coady, M. (2001). Assessing the writing of Spanish-speaking students: Issues and suggestions. In S. Hurley & J. Tinajero (Eds.), *Literacy assessment of second language learners.* Boston: Allyn & Bacon.

Escamilla, K. & Coady, M. (in preparation). Beyond skills and strategies: Assisting Spanish-speaking students in their transition to English literacy.

García, E. (1997). Effective instruction for language minority students: An exploratory study of six high schools. In A. Darder, R. D. Torres, & H. Gutierréz (Eds.), *Latinos and education* (pp. 362–372). New York: Routledge.

García, E. (2001, July). *Student cultural diversity: Understanding and meeting the challenge* (3rd ed.). Boston: Houghton Mifflin.

Gay, G. (2001). *Culturally responsive teaching: Theory, research & practice.* New York: Teachers College Press.

González, N., Moll, L., Tenery, M. F., Rivera, A., Rendon, P., González, R., & Amanti, C. (1995). Funds of knowledge for teaching in Latino households. *Urban Education, 29*(4), 443–470.

Grey, M. (1991). The context for marginal secondary ESL programs: Contributing factors and the need for further research. *The Journal of Educational Issues of Language Minority Students, 9,* 75–89.

Hamann, E.T., Zuliani, I., & Hudak, M. (2001). *English language learners, the comprehensive school reform demonstration project, and the role of state departments of education.* Providence, RI: Northeast and Islands Regional Educational Laboratory at Brown University.

Hammond, L. (1997). Teaching and learning through Mein culture. In G. Spindler (Ed.), *Education and cultural process: Anthropological approaches.* Prospect Heights, IL: Waveland.

Heath, S. B. (1983). *Ways with words: Language, life, and work in communities and classrooms.* New York: Cambridge Press.

Henderson, A. (1997). *The evidence continues to grow: Parent involvement improves student achievement.* Columbia, MD: National Committee for Citizens in Education.

Hurley, S. R. and Tinajero, J. V. (2001). *Literacy assessment of second language learners.* Needham Heights, MA: Allyn and Bacon.

Intercultural Development Research Association. (2002). *Good schools and classrooms for children learning English: A guide.* San Antonio, TX: Author.

Kohl, H. (2002). Topsy-turvies: Teacher talk and student talk. In L. Delpit and J. Kilgour-Dowdy (Eds.), *The skin that we speak: Thoughts on language and culture in the classroom*. New York: The New Press.

Ladson-Billings, G. (1995). Toward a theory of culturally relevant pedagogy. *American Educational Research Journal, 32*(3), 465–491.

Lucas, T. (1997). *Into, through, and beyond secondary school: Critical transitions for immigrant youths*. McHenry, IL: Center for Applied Linguistics and Delta Systems.

Miramontes, O.B., Nadeau, A., & Commins N. L. (1997). *Restructuring schools for linguistic diversity: Linking decision making to effective programs*. New York: Teachers College Press.

Moll, L. C., Amanti, C., Neff, C., & González, N. (1992). Funds of knowledge for teaching: Using a qualitative approach to connect homes and classrooms. *Theory into Practice, 31*(2), 132–141.

Moore, D. (1992). The case for parent and community involvement. In G. A. Hess (Ed.), *Empowering teachers and parents: School restructuring through the eyes of anthropologists*. Westport, CT: Bergin & Garvey.

National Research Council, Commission on Behavioral and Social Sciences and Education. (2000). How people learn: Brain, mind, experience, and school. Washington, DC: National Research Council.

Nieto, S. (1999). *In the light of their eyes: Creating multicultural learning communities*. New York: Teachers College Press.

Northeast and Islands Regional Educational Laboratory at Brown University (LAB). (2000). Student Voices: English language learners (Video and guiding materials). Providence, RI: Author.

Olsen, L. (1997). *Made in America: Immigrant students in our public schools*. New York: The New Press.

Olsen, L. et al. (1994). *The unfinished journey: Restructuring schools in a diverse society*. San Francisco: California Tomorrow.

Olsen, L. & Jaramillo, A. (1999). *Turning the tides of exclusion: A guide for educators and advocates for immigrant students*. Oakland, CA: California Tomorrow.

O'Malley, J. M., & Pierce, L. V. (1996). *Authentic assessment for English language learners: Practical approaches for teachers*. Reading, MA: Addison-Wesley.

Portes, A. & Rumbaut, R. (1990). *Immigrant America: A portrait*. Berkeley and Los Angeles: University of California Press.

Roseberry, A. S., Warren, B., & Conant, F. (1992). Appropriating scientific discourse: Findings form language minority classrooms. *Journal of the Learning Sciences, 2*(10), 61–94.

Ruíz, R. (1984). Orientations in language planning. *NABE Journal, 8*, 15–34.

Siu, S. F. (1995). Final report, Center on families, communities, schools, and children's learning, Volume 2. Patterns of Chinese American family involvement in young children's education. Boston: Wheelock College.

Snow, C. E., Burns, M. S., & Griffin, P. (Eds.). (1998). *Preventing reading difficulties in young children*. Washington, DC: National Academy Press.

Stefanakis, E. H. (1998). *Whose judgment counts? Assessing bilingual children, K-3*. Portsmouth, NH: Heinemann.

Stringfield, S., Datnow, A., Ross, S., & Snively, F. (1998). Scaling up school restructuring in multicultural, multilingual contexts: Early observations from Sunland County. *Education and Urban Society, 30*, 326–357.

Suárez-Orozco, C. and Suárez-Orozco, M. (1995). *Transformations: Migration, family life, and achievement motivation among Latino adolescents*. Stanford, CA: Stanford University Press.

Suárez-Orozco, C. and Suárez-Orozco, M. M. (2002, April). *Children of immigration: The developing child*. Cambridge, MA: Harvard University Press.

Tabors, P. O. (1997). *One child, two languages*. Baltimore: Paul H. Brookes.

TESOL. (n.d.). The ESL standards for pre-k-12 students. Retrieved April 29, 2002 from http://www.tesol.org/assoc/k12standards/it/05.html.

Um, K. (2003). *A dream denied. Educational experiences of Southeast Asian American youth: Issues and recommendations*. Berkeley, CA: Southeast Asia Resource Action Center (SEARAC).

Valdés, G. (1996). *Con respeto: Bridging the distance between culturally diverse families and schools. An ethnographic portrait*. New York: Teachers College Press.

Valdés, G. (2001). *Learning and not learning English: Latino students in American schools*. New York: Teachers College Press.

Valenzuela, A. (1999). *Subtractive schooling: U.S. Mexican youth and the politics of caring.* Albany, NY: State University of New York Press.

Verplaetse, L. (1998). How content teachers interact with English language learners. *TESOL Journal, 7*(5), 24–29.

Villenas, S. (2001). Reinventing educación in new Latino communities. In S. Wortham, E. Murillo, & E. T. Hamann (Eds.), *Education in the new Latino diaspora: Policy and the politics of identity* (pp. 17–35). Westport, CT: Ablex.

Wong Fillmore, L. & Snow, C. (1999). What teachers need to know about language (ERIC special report). Retrieved March 19, 2003 from the ERIC Clearinghouse on Languages and Linguistics. Access: www.cal.org/ericcll/teachers.pdf.

Wong Fillmore, L. & Snow, C. E. (2000). *What teachers need to know about language.* Washington, DC: Center for Applied Linguistics.

Yedlin, J. (2003). Teacher talk and writing development in an urban, English-as-a-second-language, first-grade classroom. Unpublished doctoral dissertation Harvard Graduate School of Education.

CHAPTER **14**

Bilingual Education for All Students: Still Standing After All These Years

TOMÁS Z. MIRANDA

Introduction

As school administrators in the new millennium, we are cognizant of our responsibility to prepare all students to contribute meaningfully to a world that is increasingly interconnected. Our newer students bring with them valuable resources: their languages and their cultures. We can capitalize on these resources for the success and benefit of our English monolingual students as well. This chapter seeks to provide a discussion of bilingual education and its benefits for all students at a time when bilingual education is under attack because many public policy makers and school administrators do not understand it and at a time when local school districts and state legislatures across the United States pass policies, regulations, and laws outlawing the use of other languages for purposes of instruction.

I have been involved in bilingual education for the past 40 years. Starting out as an English as a second language (ESL) resource teacher with bilingual skills in the Midwest, I became the key point person in my school to address the educational needs of the students attempting to acquire English. These students, from a variety of countries, were placed in regular classrooms, and I had a chance to see them for part of the day to tend to their English language and academic needs. Fortunately, I was also involved in the evenings working with their parents as they met the challenges of acquiring English. At that time, my daytime ESL students were failing; they were being identified as students with special needs, and, in addition to me, all of the remedial teachers in the building were seeing them. In 1968, when the first Title VII of the Elementary and Secondary Education Act legislation in bilingual education was approved, our district received one of the very first grants. I was selected to become the head teacher for this program that was to work with preschool and primary school English- and Spanish-dominant children in learning together. This program, like many of the projects of that day, intended to provide a bilingual education in English and

Spanish for all of its children. The goal was to make all of the children proficient in two languages by the time they completed fifth grade. To implement the program, we had to request a change in the Indiana state law forbidding the use of a language other than English for the purposes of instruction.

A lot has occurred since those early days of full bilingual education for all students. Midstream through the project, the policy makers decided that bilingual education should only be for those students who were limited in English proficiency, and thus all of the English dominant students had to be removed from the program. This ended the integration of English-dominant (i.e., Anglo) and Spanish-dominant students learning together while acquiring each other's languages. Bilingual education was to become a compensatory program only for students who needed to learn English. The goal at that point in time was changed. From bilingualism for all students in the project we now had to focus on making the Spanish-dominant students English proficient.

Through the years, I have seen bilingual education from a variety of perspectives. As a teacher, I saw the potential for all students to become fully bilingual and bicultural. It was confusing for me to suddenly be a part of a plan to assimilate students into an all-English existence. It was very frustrating. I saw it as a contradiction that policy makers and politicians wanted to have students acquire a foreign language while at the same time obliterating the very native language that our students brought with them. It got to the point that once our Spanish-dominant students acquired sufficient English to engage in mainstream instruction, they were not allowed to participate in any kind of Spanish instruction at all. When these same students could study a foreign language in middle school, they were counseled to take French or another foreign language—not Spanish. I never understood why, in this country, we have to wait until middle school to initiate instruction in a foreign language. As a program administrator, I advocated for the equal education of all English language learners (ELLs), and I never lost my vision of having bilingual education programs that would benefit both English- and Spanish-dominant students. So when I became a school principal, I looked for ways of providing bilingual education opportunities for all of my students. I implemented late-exit models of bilingual education and supplemented this program with after-school Spanish as a second-language instruction for my Anglo students and multicultural activities for my Spanish-dominant students. Little by little, I began to move in the direction of dual-language instruction, again involving both English- and Spanish-dominant students.

Late-exit transitional bilingual education programs and dual-language programs in existence across the United States and across various languages continue to demonstrate academic success for student participants (Collier, 1992; Thomas & Collier, 1998; Medina & Escamilla, 1992; Willig, 1985). Nevertheless, the U.S. Congress, influenced by the English-only and the English-first movements, has entertained the notion of a constitutional amendment making English the official language of the United States. In addition to this, educators, politicians, and policy makers fail to value the benefits that bilingual education has for all students. At one end, we have the upper class advocating for their students to develop a foreign language and to work toward proficiency in that foreign language to the point of valuing semesters abroad so they may develop their bilingual skills. And at the other end, we have politicians, educators, and policy makers advocating for our lower-class ELL students to limit their home language use, as if it were a detriment to the development of their second language, English. What appear to be contradictions present a challenge to all school administrators who continue to receive a multitude of ethnolinguistic students with varying levels of formal prior schooling and from diverse cultures.

How we can lead a school using bilingual education as a positive force to benefit all students is discussed here in detail. This chapter first offers six principles for effective practice. These principles seek to translate bilingual education and second-language-acquisition research into effective practice for the benefit of school administrators with the challenge of educating all students. Each of the principles is followed by an explanatory discussion. The six principles for effective practice are as follows:

1. Each second-language-learning student has his or her own individual language and content-learning profile. Therefore, schools must attain a full profile of each student's language and academic background to make the best instructional decisions for their English language learning students.
2. Second-language acquisition occurs in stages similar to the acquisition of the first or primary language. Therefore, effective programs for English language learners and their English-speaking peers take into consideration each stage of language acquisition when planning for instruction.
3. To ensure that young second-language learners (SLLs) acquire language naturally, their instructional environment should be acquisition rich, that is, an environment that is comprehensible and meaningful.
4. For young bilingual students, second-language literacy develops best when the child has had the opportunity to develop literacy in his or her first language; however, if the child is developing literacy in both languages simultaneously, she or he must first have oral proficiency in the new language.
5. Older students, who are more cognitively mature and who have developed some level of first-language proficiency, need classroom experiences that offer a balance of language development and formal content learning.
6. A thorough assessment (i.e., speaking listening, reading, writing) of a student's language proficiency in the student's first and second language is essential for appropriate placement.

Following the discussion of the six principles for effective practice, the chapter presents four practical program models that reflect these principles. It is important to note that the four practical program models are inclusive of all students within the school. The four models to be discussed are (1) dual-language programs; (2) gradual-exit transitional bilingual education programs in combination with foreign-language programs; (3) in-school second-language resource centers; and (4) after-school second-language enrichment programs.

Six Principles for Effective Practice

Principle 1: Each language learner has his or her own language and content profile

Acquisition of a second language is relative to each student. Therefore, administrators and teachers need to be aware of student background and language dominance, as well as language proficiency in the primary language and the second language, prior schooling, socioeconomic levels, and prior experiences to make the best instructional decisions for their students.

What students bring with them to the learning and language-acquisition situation is just as important as what they have to learn or acquire. Knowing students' language dominance—what language they are stronger in and use most of the time—is critical for purposes of instruction. Practitioners in bilingual education generally begin the student identification process with the determination of language dominance. This is done through a combination of steps, getting information from parents about the students as to the language used in the home, what language was spoken first, and what language is used in communicating with parents, siblings, and peers. To obtain this information, schools usually use what is called a *home language survey*. This survey is part of the student registration procedure. Of course, for those families and students coming brand new from another country, one might assume that the responses to the home language survey will indicate 100% use of the non-English language. However, this is not always the case. It may be that a student may have been exposed to numerous languages prior to coming into our school. Nevertheless, knowing the language-use situation at home is important because it provides a perspective on whether the student is coming from a bilingual or a monolingual home language situation. It also provides a perspective on the student's language preferences, the comfort level in using a particular language, and how the student may use one or two languages to communicate.

Knowing the student's socioeconomic level provides another perspective on what resources and home support systems may be in place at home. Generally speaking, students who come from low socioeconomic levels do not have access to books or computers at home. They may not have the full-time attention of their parents, as both parents may be out of the home working and an older sibling acting as the caretaker is supervising young children. This affects students' ability to complete homework, to engage in computer activities, or to interact with parents regarding the experiences in school, all of which affect language and learning. Students with the least resources and support systems at home require more time and support for language acquisition and general learning.

General experiences and prior schooling are determinants of students' potential success in language acquisition and general learning. How much students bring with them academically determines how much they are able to transfer into the language acquisition or academic learning situation. Have the students had preschool experiences? What formal prior schooling have they had, and in what language? Do they know key basic concepts? Do they know how to read? These important questions must be asked of the parents at the time of registration in school. Knowing this information provides the opportunity to offer instruction that will be challenging to the student and will move students along in terms of language acquisition and general learning at a faster pace.

What does this mean for administrators? It means that we must ensure that all of the intake process for students and their families is sufficiently thorough and asks the right questions to gain all of the information needed. In addition, this information has to be accessible to all staff that is expected to have an impact on the success of the student.

Principle 2: Education Programs Reflect the Consideration of Language-Acquisition Stages

Stephen Krashen (1981), expert researcher in language acquisition, bilingual education, and reading, has done extensive studies on language acquisition and has maintained that acquiring a second language is very similar to acquiring the first language. The acquisition of the first language is a process that begins at birth, and through a series of developmental stages a child acquires the sounds of the language, isolates and learns language fragments that contain meaning, and eventually produces them in trying to convey a meaningful message. According to Krashen, this process is based on reinforced meaningful interactions between children and their primary caretakers and key people with whom the children interact in the surroundings. Key to Krashen's work is the concept of comprehensible input: language delivered by the caretaker in an understandable and meaningful way. In the process of language acquisition, Krashen identifies four sequential stages: (1) preproduction; (2) beginning speech; (3) early fluency; and (4) fluency. Anyone going through the process of acquiring a second language goes through these stages. Krashen's work is significant for us as administrators promoting bilingual education or dual-language in our schools, because these stages apply to our students acquiring a second language. Therefore, we must assure that the conditions conducive for second-language acquisition are created in our classrooms. These conditions include an environment that reduces the students' anxiety levels and that offers many opportunities for listening to understandable language, engaging in hands-on activities with peers, and producing language as needed.

Once identified as second-language learners, students can be categorized according to their second-language-acquisition stage.[1] Once categorized, appropriate instructional strategies can be implemented, and reasonable student performances can be anticipated. By understanding that varying language levels require varying performance expectations, teachers can begin to appreciate how they can engage ELL students in a particular content, at a high cognitive level but can expect those students to be able to show an understanding of that content in various ways depending on if the students are using their first or second language. Table 14.1 describes each second-language-acquisition stage (Krashen, 1981) and lists the realistic performance expectations for our acquirers of a second language.

What does this mean for school administrators? We must ascertain that all the ELL students in our schools are receiving differentiated instruction that realistically allows them to engage in lessons at their appropriate level of language acquisition. Furthermore, each administrator should see to it that the teachers have the professional development they need to learn about these language-acquisition levels and to learn how to differentiate instruction targeted toward these stages of language acquisition.

Principle 3: Young Language Learners Require an Acquisition-Rich Environment

Young second-language learners acquire language naturally; therefore, their environment and instruction for learning and acquiring a second language should be acquisition rich. An acquisition-rich environment is one that is both meaningful and comprehensible. It includes visually demonstrable subject-matter activities such as science experiments, role playing, story telling, collaborative problem solving, interactive games, arts and crafts, music, and physical movement conducted in the target language.

Educators of bilingual children support and promote conditions that reduce the anxiety level on the part of students and that offer many opportunities for viewing relevant information, for listening to understandable language, for engaging in hands-on activities with peers, and for producing language as needed. Current practice in bilingual education and dual-language programs is to teach content through the second language. Therefore, in our schools we provide opportunities to English-dominant and other-language-dominant students to come together in an integrated way to study particular content together taught in the second language. This may be in content-area subjects such as mathematics, science, social studies, and literature. As we walk into our bilingual education classrooms, we expect to see these conditions in place. Practitioners and researchers Echevarria, Vogt, and Short (2004) in *Making Content Comprehensible for English Learners* outline what to look for in a good second-language lesson using their sheltered instruction observation protocol (SIOP).

Table 14.1 Second language stages and performance expectations

Second Language Acquisition Stage	Performance Expectations
1. Pre-Production and **2. Beginning Speech** **0-10 months; newly entered student; initial stages of exposure to second language acquisition**	• Produces no speech. • Indicates comprehension physically/non-verbally • Comprehends single words only. • Depends heavily on context. • Responds by pantomiming, pointing, gesturing, or drawing. • Says only yes, no, or single words. • Produces one or two words in isolation. • Verbalizes key words "heard." • Depends heavily on context. • Responds with one/two word answers or in phrases. • Makes "errors of omission." • Mispronounces words.
3. Early Fluency **11-30 months; student has been exposed to second language acquisition for at least a year.**	• Produces whole sentences. • Often makes some pronunciation and basic grammatical errors. • Discriminates smaller elements of speech. • Shows good comprehension (given rich context). • Uses language to function on a social level. • Uses limited vocabulary.
4. Fluency **30 months and beyond; student has been exposed to second language acquisition for three years.**	• Produces whole narration. • Makes complex grammatical errors. • Hears some subtle elements of speech. • Shows good comprehension (given some context). • Functions somewhat on an academic level. • Uses expanded vocabulary.

Although this teacher observation protocol was prepared for teachers involved in the teaching of content through English as a second language, it has application for all teachers and certainly may be applied to all second-language teachers. A more detailed discussion of sheltered instruction is given in Chapter 7 of this volume.

Following the recommended practices of sheltered instruction, a good bilingual educator will have done the lesson preparation necessary so that the lesson being delivered includes

- Specific content objectives
- Specific language objectives
- Age- and grade-level-appropriate curriculum concepts
- Visuals such as pictures, graphs, and models
- Differentiated instruction according to the language-acquisition levels of the students
- Integration of hands-on activities with opportunities for language practice

Following this process, effective bilingual teachers increase second-language acquisition and the development of content-area proficiency. This is conducive to the ongoing development of bilingualism and biliteracy, which are the primary goals of bilingual education or dual-language instruction for all students.

What does this means for us as administrators? It means that we, along with all of our teachers, need to learn about sheltered instruction; we need to learn the procedures, and we need to include these strategies when we do our teacher observations and evaluations. Certainly, as administrators we must support continuous professional development in this area for all of us.

Principle 4: Young Students and Literacy Development

Second-language learners need to acquire English within the confines of a demanding academic environment. Not only must they quickly become adept at social interaction for simple survival, but they are also expected to be able to understand, read, write, and explain concepts at an academic level appropriate to their age and cognitive development at an increasingly rapid rate. Cummins (1981, 1989) contrasts the differences between these registers of language use as (1) basic interpersonal communication skills (BICS), or social or conversational language used in face-to-face everyday communication; and (2) cognitive academic language proficiency (CALP), or academic language used in educational settings. Once the difference between these uses for language is understood, it is easier to value the research used in developing effective programs to promote the acquisition of a second language. Acquiring a second language for academic purposes (i.e., CALP) is a complex process, which all of the research has shown to take a significant length of time. The development of social language (i.e., BICS) may take anywhere from one to three years, whereas the development of academic language (i.e., CALP) may take up to seven or nine years (Cummins, 1991).

Another construct important to understanding second-language literacy is Cummins's Threshold Hypothesis. Cummins (1981) suggested that two thresholds exist between first- and second-language development. The lower threshold is the minimum amount of first-language academic proficiency necessary to make a positive impact on second-language academic proficiency. The higher threshold is the amount of first-language competence necessary to reap the cognitive benefits of bilingualism.

The task of the bilingual teacher is to ensure attainment of the lower threshold and, as much as possible, to help students attain the higher threshold. When implemented properly, an effective bilingual education or dual-language program accomplishes both of these goals. As children reach the threshold for a particular subject matter using their first language, they then proceed to follow instruction in the second language in that subject matter, beginning with the kind of instruction described in the acquisition-rich environment section of this chapter. Once bilingualism is achieved, continued development in both languages through the use of the two languages—in content instruction as well as direct language development instruction in each language—effective bilingual teachers may attain the higher threshold and may produce bilingualism at its highest levels.

For young students in a bilingual education program, literacy is developed in the first and second language. Once students are able to read and write in their primary language they begin to transfer their skills into the second language. With some children, due to exposure and experiences, this biliteracy may occur simultaneously.

A review of the research that has been done in literacy development among bilingual children, and particularly students who are acquiring English as a second language in schools, reveals that much may be applied to literacy development for all second-language learners. The National Clearinghouse for English Language Acquisition & Language Instruction Education Programs published a detailed article in the Spring 2002 edition of *Directions in Language Education* titled "Implementing Reading First with English Language Learners" (Antunez, 2002a). In this article, Beth Antunez cites study after study that have demonstrated that this is a strong and positive correlation between literacy in the first or native language and learning English and that the degree of children's native language proficiency is a strong predictor of English language development. Citing the studies of other researchers, Antunez claims that literacy in a child's native language establishes a knowledge, concept, and skills base that transfers from native-language reading to reading in a second language.

Antunez's article continues examining reading research for young children. She includes a study by Hiebert, Pearson, Taylor, Richardson, and Paris (1998) that synthesized this research for the Center for the Improvement of Early Reading Achievement (CIERA). These researchers recommend that ELLs first learn to read in their native tongue. On the other hand, Antunez's article balances this finding with those from the Committee on the Prevention of Reading Difficulties in Young Children, National Research Council, which found that "learning to speak English should be a priority before being taught to read English." Other research findings cited in Antunez's article support the fact that "oral language development provides the foundation in phonological awareness and allows for subsequent learning about the alphabetic structure of English." We apply this research to the teaching of any second language within a bilingual education situation.

Furthermore, the report, entitled *Preventing Reading Difficulties in Young Children* (Snow, Burns, & Griffin, 1998) and quoted in Antunez (2002a), explains that "hurrying young non-English speaking children into reading in English without ensuring adequate preparation is counterproductive. The report outlines a two-pronged recommendation, strongly emphasizing the importance of native-language oral proficiency, and when feasible, written proficiency." (Antunez, 2002a, p.3) The recommendations from the report as cited in Antunez are given below to provide teachers guidelines for the placement and teaching of ELLs.

"If language-minority children arrive at school with no proficiency in English but speaking a language for which there are instructional guides, learning materials, and locally available proficient teachers, these children should be taught how to read in their native language while acquiring oral proficiency in English and subsequently taught to extend their skills to reading in English.

If language-minority children arrive at school with no proficiency in English but speak a language for which the above conditions cannot be met and for which there are insufficient numbers of children to justify the development of the local capacity to meet such conditions, the initial instructional priority should be developing the children's oral proficiency in English. Although print materials may be used to support the development of English phonology, vocabulary, and syntax, the postponement of formal reading instruction is appropriate until an adequate level of oral proficiency in English as been achieved" (p. 324).

Current effective practice in literacy development in the first and second language has identified five essential components of reading instruction: phonemic awareness, phonics, vocabulary development, reading fluency (including oral reading skills), and reading comprehension strategies. In the "Directions in Language Education" article, also available as an article prepared for *Reading Rockets* (Antunez, 2002b), Antunez discusses each of the five essential components and what teachers should consider when instructing English language learners. A few examples taken from this article follow:

1. Phonemic awareness: "Some phonemes may not be present in the student's native language and, therefore, may be difficult for a student to pronounce and distinguish auditorily, or to place into a meaningful context. ..." (p. 5).
2. Phonics: "Students may have learned to read and write in a native language in which the letters correspond to different sounds than they do in English, or they may have learned to read and write in a language with characters that correspond to words or portions of words..." (p. 6).
3. Vocabulary development: "... When a student comes to a word and sounds it out, he or she is also determining if the word makes sense based on his or her understanding of the word. If a student does not know the meaning of the word, there is no way to check if the word fits, or to make meaning from the sentence" (p. 7).
4. Reading fluency, including oral reading skills: "When developing fluency...second language learners should learn to read initially in their first language..." (p. 8).
5. Reading comprehension strategies: "... Second language learners may be working diligently to translate concepts literally, figurative language such as 'crocodile tears' or 'sweet tooth' or any idiomatic language can be perplexing ..." (p. 9).

An article with specific suggestions as these should be required reading for all elementary teachers and administrators. Education leaders should make this article available and should schedule brown-bag luncheon discussions or in-service training around this information.

Principle 5: Older Students Require a Balance of Language Development and Formal Content Learning.

When I speak of older students, I am referring to students who enter our schools beyond the third or fourth grade. These students may have entered our bilingual education or dual-language programs at the very beginning—preschool or kindergarten—and may be part of the language-acquisition and content-learning continuum already in place in our school. Others may be newly arrived students coming from another country or from another school where the education they received may have been different from the program in our school. It is possible that some of these students will not have had the opportunity to attend school at all.

For school administrators, the challenge is to have in our school buildings a bilingual curriculum program that meets the linguistic needs of the older student and at the same time moves the student along in the learning of content across all areas as required by the school district. In meeting this challenge, we count on older students to be more mature cognitively, to possess a more fully developed first language (dependent on previous formal schooling), and to acquire cognitively demanding aspects of the second language faster than younger students do. The one skill in which older learners do not have an early advantage over young learners is pronunciation. Therefore, we can anticipate that older students will retain an accent; teachers and students should be assured that this accent is not a sign that the student is not learning; rather, it is the natural result of being introduced to a second language at an older age.

Because older students are more cognitively mature, teachers of older students must provide an appropriate balance of language-acquisition opportunities as well as formal language and content learning. This means that in addition to promoting an environment that is conducive to language acquisition, there needs to be the formal study of vocabulary, grammar, and literacy skills in English as well as the target language. This instruction can be programmed during the school day in mixed classes of students who may be dominant in English, dominant in the target language, or bilingual. This immersion environment allows for learning to take place through teacher-to-students interaction as well as student-to-student interactions where they negotiate meaning and support each other in the common learning. Similarly, content classes (schoolwork in the content areas, such as math, science, and social studies) need to be made available to these students—content that is both meaningful and comprehensible. Classroom activities that focus on tasks rather than on language itself (e.g., role playing, collaborative learning and problem solving, literacy development) and that deploy sheltered instructional strategies (as mentioned under Principle 3 in this chapter and Chapters 7 and 8 in this volume) will yield better results.

Principle 6: A Thorough Assessment of a Student's Language Proficiency Is Essential for Appropriate Placement.

Principle 1 already covered the importance of attaining a full profile on a student's language and education history. In addition to knowing the home language and the language dominance of the student, language proficiency is used as part of the criteria for entry into a bilingual education or a dual-language program. Language proficiency refers to how well the student demonstrates listening comprehension, speaking, reading, and writing skills in the primary language and in the second language. Language proficiency is determined through tests that measure listening, speaking, reading, and writing in English and in the second or target language of our bilingual program. Though we may not have available a test that will measure all of these four areas, we can get a language-proficiency profile through the use of the following:

1. An interview conducted in English and in the second language. Through this interview, we may confirm personal identification data, a measure of the student's listening comprehension and sound discrimination between the two languages of our program, and (if the student is beyond the second grade) a student's ability to read in either language with short reading selections in both languages.
2. If the student is beyond the second grade, we may use a writing sample produced by the student in both languages: English and the second language.
3. Norm-referenced tests in English and in the second language if available.

Once we know where the student is performing in both languages, we can make better decisions for placement for instruction within our program. This information becomes an invaluable tool for our teachers, who must consider all of the student's linguistic characteristics and all of the other information available about each student for planning an effective program of studies and for making instructional delivery modifications. As mentioned in Principle 1, the responsibility on ensuring adequate and appropriate testing for the purpose of placement lies with the administrator. Unfortunately, too much is misunderstood relative to language acquisition, and it has been my experience that incorrect instructional decisions have been made based exclusively on a student's conversational skills as opposed to the academic language skills acquired by the student. Far too often, students are placed or exited from a program based on their oral conversational ability. Similarly, content teachers make assumptions about students' language abilities based on their oral conversational skills.

However, oral conversation skills develop two to three times faster than a student's reading and writing skills, or the student's oral and written proficiency in academic language (CALP language abilities), as mentioned in Principle 4. So, unfortunately, it is far too easy for second-language learners—particularly English language learners—to be inappropriately placed based on oral conversational skills and then to find themselves unable to keep up with the rest of the class because they are still developing their academic-language proficiency skills. Consequently, thorough assessment and appropriate placement are crucial to assure a student's success.

Practical Program Models

All of the aforementioned principles may be incorporated into an effective bilingual education program of studies within the school. School administrators have the advantage of setting the tone for the type of school culture we want to see. It is possible to have a school environment conducive to bilingual education for all students. Certainly, with the support of the parents, the community at large, and the district administration, we can be in a position to provide second language acquisition opportunities for all. As school instructional leaders, we determine what happens in our schools in terms of curriculum, staffing, instruction, assessment, the use of time, and the use of the first and second language.

I recommend that we consider any of the following four practical program models in providing second-language acquisition opportunities to our students: (1) dual-language programs; (2) gradual-exit transitional bilingual education programs in combination with foreign-language programs; (3) in-school second-language resource centers; and (4) after-school second-language enrichment programs. Note that these programs promote the development of bilingualism not just for the English language learners but for all students.

Model 1: Dual-Language Programs

A dual-language program, also known as two-way bilingual education or dual-language immersion, is an educational program that delivers instruction across the curriculum through the use of two languages. It is possible for administrators to integrate our English-dominant students with those students who are dominant in another language in our school (e.g., Spanish) so that both groups of children may learn and acquire each other's language together. For example, if my school has a sizable population of students who are Spanish dominant and who are in the process of acquiring English, I can organize my school building in such a way that allows for all of the students to study the curriculum in English and in Spanish. This allows me to serve both groups of students within a single dual-language program. Here, the students learn side by side, assist each other, and have the opportunity to become fluent bilinguals in English and Spanish while making good progress in all subjects.[2]

In dual-language programs, ideally a classroom consists of 50% English dominant and 50% Spanish dominant. Table 14.2 illustrates the distribution of language across the grades and subject areas in a typical English–Spanish dual-language model in an elementary school.

Other models offer course content in both languages from the first year so that, for example, a class might study math in Spanish for one week and proceed in math the next week in English. Note that they do not redo the math in the second language but rather move ahead in the curriculum, alternating languages. Thus, the curriculum is delivered through the use of two languages, not necessarily at the same time.

Table 14.2 One possible way to distribute language in a dual language model

Key: E = English; S = Spanish; E/S = English and Spanish

Grade	Students	Lang/ Lit. Devel.	Math	Soc. Stud.	Science	Music	Phys. Ed	Second Lang. Devel.
Pre-K + K.	English Dominant	E	E	E	S	E/S	E/S	S
	Spanish Dominant	S	E	E	S	E/S	E/S	E
1	English Dominant	E	S	S	E	E/S	E/S	S
	Spanish Dominant	S	S	S	E	E/S	E/S	E
2	English Dominant	E	S	E	S	E/S	E/S	S
	Spanish Dominant	S	S	E	S	E/S	E/S	E
3	English Dominant	E	E	S	E	E/S	E/S	S
	Spanish Dominant	S	E	S	E	E/S	E/S	E
4	English Dominant	S	S	E	S	E/S	E/S	S
	Spanish Dominant	S	S	E	S	E/S	E/S	E
5	English Dominant	E	E	S	E	E/S	E/S	S
	Spanish Dominant	E	E	S	E	E/S	E/S	E

Some comments about this model follow.

- Once approval of the concept of a dual-language program for your school has been given, the implementation of this model, as with any effective instructional program, requires careful planning with and among the entire school staff and the community at large. The long-term planning should carefully consider the following: the overall curriculum, instruction, assessment, staffing, the allocation of time, and the distribution of the two languages to be used for instructional delivery.

- Also very important is the preparation of a training program for all staff, volunteers, and the community at large to address dual-language-related themes as first- and second-language acquisition, bilingual education, comprehensible instruction, language immersion, and student assessment.

- To implement this dual-language model, the administrator of the school will need to identify English–Spanish bilingual staff. This can be done by filling existing vacancies within the school as they become available. If the school has access to paraprofessionals (e.g., teacher assistants, tutors), it would be good to hire staff members who already possess prior training such as a certificate in child development, an associate's degree, or other college-level preparation in English and Spanish.

- When beginning to implement this program, I suggest that the school administrator begin with one grade level at a time, preferably at the prekindergarten and kindergarten levels.
- Throughout the pre-K through third-grade levels, students receive their language and literacy development in their dominant language. Though bilingual students (i.e., students already proficient in both languages) are not reflected as a separate group within the model, I suggest that these students be integrated within the English-dominant and Spanish-dominant groupings on an equal basis. In terms of language and literacy development, these students will continue their development in both languages.
- In the model charted, in the fourth and fifth grade and beyond, language and literacy development as a subject is alternated between English and Spanish from year to year. We count on students continuing their language and literacy development throughout the content-area subjects as well as through the second-language development course.
- Note that throughout the model, the language used for instruction is alternated in the subject areas of math, social studies, and science. This means that English-dominant, Spanish-dominant, and bilingual students are integrated in these classes where instruction is delivered in a context of immersion. When a particular class is taught in English using the sheltered, comprehensible instructional strategies already discussed, the Spanish-dominant students will be able to participate with English-dominant students in learning, which enhances their own acquisition and application of English. In addition to being English-language models, the English-dominant students become providers of the information as well for their Spanish-dominant peers. The same thing is true for Spanish-dominant students when the course is being taught in Spanish. On the other hand, bilingual students included become a valuable resource as interpreters and models of bilingualism and biliteracy. When these students are placed in collaborative groups to do some problem solving or to complete a task, the teacher should divide the class into triads (i.e., groups of three) and assure that each triad contains one English-dominant student, one Spanish-dominant student, and one bilingual student. This sets the stage for students helping each other in negotiating meaning and achieving the common learning.

Model 2: Gradual-Exit Transitional Bilingual Education Programs in Combination with World Language Programs

Administrators of urban schools with large enrollments of language minority students who enter not able to comprehend, speak, read, or write the English language usually have to provide a bilingual education or English as a second-language program of support for those students. Unfortunately, these programs tend to separate out the English language learners from the rest of the school population for most, if not all, of the school day. They usually exist with time limitations placed on how long a student may participate in the program. The usual scenario has the ELLs enrolled in the program for three school years, or 30 months. By the end of this time, these students are expected to have achieved academic English language proficiency and are to be placed in the regular mainstream classroom integrated with mainstream students with whom they have had little or no contact. These quick-exit programs do very little to prepare students for the rigorous demands of an academically focused classroom where academic English is required. Consequently, these ELLs become frustrated because they are not able to keep up with the academic load; they feel isolated because the have not had the opportunity to socialize and develop positive relationships with their English-monolingual peers; they lose their self-esteem because now that they are in the mainstream, they may be in the lowest-performing group.

An alternative to these quick-exit transitional bilingual education programs is a gradual-exit transitional bilingual education program where students are exited into the mainstream classroom gradually, subject by subject, as they are ready to understand the instruction delivered in a comprehensible, contextualized way. In these gradual-exit programs, the students never need to exit the bilingual education program. They have the option of continuing first-language development. In addition, ELLs are exposed to mainstream students from the very beginning.

Here is a concrete example of what I am talking about using a school setting in which there is a sizable enrollment of Spanish-dominant ELLs.

- New arrivals and beginning-level ELL students will study ESL; take their content subjects (i.e., language arts, math, science, and social studies) in Spanish; and take their art, music, and physical education classes integrated into the mainstream.
- Intermediate-level ELLs will study ESL; take social studies in Spanish; study language arts, math, and science through content-based ESL instruction; and take their art, music, and physical education classes integrated into the mainstream.
- Advanced intermediate ELLs will study ESL; continue with language arts in Spanish; study social studies and additional language arts through content-based ESL; and take art, music, physical education, math, and science classes integrated into the mainstream.

Good planning of this program can take into consideration the involvement of the English-dominant mainstream students in learning Spanish during the school periods when English dominant and ELLs are integrated for instruction in art, music, and physical education at first and then eventually in the core subjects (i.e., literacy and language arts, mathematics, social studies, and science). This can only happen if the school has bilingual staff so that Spanish can be taught through these subjects using a very comprehensible instructional approach. English- and Spanish-dominant students can be taught together in this immersion situation. In fact, English and Spanish may be alternated as the language of instruction from day to day or from week to week.

Additionally, the world languages department can offer Spanish language arts (i.e., Spanish for Hispanics). In this course, Spanish-dominant students may continue their literacy development in Spanish. The curriculum for this course focuses on high-level Spanish language arts and literature. At the high school level, efforts need to be made to include Spanish-dominant students in advanced Spanish course work.

Careful programming and planning can result in a program that is conducive for the Spanish-dominant ELLs to develop in Spanish and in English and for the English-dominant students to acquire Spanish. Given both groups and the expectations of the program, it is advisable to seriously monitor second-language acquisition for all students. The rate of second-language acquisition is relative to the formal prior education and needs of the individual student. There will be students who may not conform to the English or Spanish language-acquisition continuum or rate described. Such students must be provided with an intervention program appropriate for second-language learners.

Model 3: In-School Language Resource Centers

Any school having access to a full-time ESL teacher and SSL teacher can set up an in-school language resource center where English- and Spanish-dominant language learners can come together for a period to learn Spanish as a second language or English as a second language. Using team teaching, thematic units, and a comprehensible second-language teaching approach, English- and Spanish-dominant students may be scheduled into the language resource center on a daily basis for continuous language-acquisition opportunities. The center would receive students from the different mainstream home-rooms. Because the focus of the instruction being delivered is language, grade levels are not important. English-dominant, Spanish-dominant, and bilingual students are identified to participate in the program in the center. While in the center, the students are integrated in a nongraded setting. Table 14.3 demonstrates an in-school language resource center model within a K–8 school.

Model 4: After-School Second-Language Enrichment Programs

A school can organize a second-language enrichment program on an after-school basis. After-school programs have been found to be very effective in supporting regular school-day educational programs. Most after-school programs focus on areas for which there is little time during the school day. They also provide opportunities for students to apply the skills they have learned in their core courses in areas to which they may not ordinarily be exposed. These areas may be the arts (e.g., music, dance, drama, painting, illustration), creative writing, cooking, physical education, or computer science. After-school programs help the school become a more community-based organization, and in providing these programs they attract parents and community youth services thus linking the school to the family and to the community at large.

Having an after-school program that includes English language learners does not exempt the school from having a fully staffed program to address the English-language acquisition and bilingual education needs of these ELLs. It is imperative that these students receive a program of instruction addressing their English language needs during the school day. For ELLs, their participation in an after-school program provides them with the opportunity to teach others about their own language and culture, and this goes a long way toward enhancing students' self-esteem, exposure to a multitude of other English-language models, and better integration with the mainstream population of the school.

An effective after-school language-enrichment program may be organized around the themes of art, music, physical education, and drama. Organizing after-school activities delivered in English and the other dominant language of the ELLs in the school (e.g., Spanish) may allow English-dominant students to acquire the second language and to apply the language skills they may be already acquiring in their world language classes held during the school day. Similarly, Spanish-dominant students who may be receiving one or two periods of direct English as a second-language instruction daily and who may already be immersed in all-English classes during the day will benefit from after-school sessions that are conducted in their own language and where they have the opportunity to assume a leadership role in helping others learn material through Spanish.

Table 14.4 illustrates a suggested model for an after-school language enrichment program delivered through the arts. Three days per week through the school year, English-dominant, Spanish-dominant, and bilingual students come together with the staff who teach English, Spanish, and the arts.

Table 14.3 One in-school language resource center model

Time	English as a second language teacher	Spanish as a second language teacher
8:45 to 9:15 AM	K-1 Spanish Dominant Students receive English as a second language (ESL) instruction.	K-1 English Dominant Students receive Spanish as a second language (SSL) instruction.
9:15 to 9:45 AM	K-1 Students are integrated to receive a content lesson based on a thematic unit. Using a comprehensible language approach, the language used for delivery of the lesson is alternated from day to day or from week to week. If the 30 min. lesson is taught in Spanish, the lesson would serve as a review for the Spanish dominant students and it would be an opportunity for the English dominant students to receive the information in their second language. Using cooperative learning and comprehensible language instruction, students engage in language and help each other in the common learning.	
10:00 to 10:30 AM	Grade 2-3 Spanish Dominant Students receive ESL instruction.	Grades 2-3 English Dominant Students receive SSL instruction.
10:30 to 11:00 AM	Grade 2-3 : Same as K-1 above	
11:15 to 11:45 AM	Grade 4-5 Spanish Dominant Students receive ESL instruction	Grade 4-5 English Dominant Students receive SSL instruction.
11:45 to 12:15 PM	Gr. 4-5 : Same as K-1 above	
12:15 to 12:45 PM	Lunch	
1:00 to 1:30 PM	Grade 6-7 Spanish Dominant Students receive ESL instruction	Grade 6-7 English Dominant Students receive SSL instruction.
1:30 to 2:00 PM	Gr. 6-7: Same as K-1 above	
2:15 to 2:45 PM	Grade 7-8 Spanish Dominant Students receive ESL instruction	Grade 7-8 English Dominant Students receive SSL instruction.
2:45 to 3:15 PM	Grade 7-8: Same as K-1 above.	

Table 14.4 One after-school language enrichment program model

Time	English Dominant Students	Spanish Dominant Students
3:00 to 3:40 PM	These students receive a forty-minute lesson in Spanish as a second language focusing on the activities they will be involved with later in the after school session.	These students receive a forty-minute lesson in English as a second language focusing on the activities they will be involved with later in the after-school session.
3:40 to 5:00 PM	English dominant and Spanish dominant students engage in activities in any of the following areas: theater arts, cultural dancing, playing soccer, singing, cooking, etc. These activities are conducted in Spanish in a very understandable way.	

This same model may be expanded for use during the summer as a language camp, which may be carried out for four to six weeks. Meeting daily from 9:00 a.m. to 12:00 noon, integrated groups of students may continue their participation in direct second-language instruction and language-based activities in the arts, physical education, and so forth.

Conclusion

This chapter has presented school administrators with six principles for the provision of opportunities for all students within the school to acquire a second language using *bilingual education for all* models. Guided by these principles, school administrators may be able to implement programs that provide all students with access to acquiring the second language of the school. Any of the four programs described in the previous section may be implemented by the school administrator to achieve bilingual education for all. In other words, having any of these programs in a school produces a school environment that is a positive contributor to excellence for all students, the school staff, their parents, and the community at large.

A school that has looked at its entire population and the community it serves and values the cultural and linguistic resources that each student and the student's family brings creates an environment that engages all participants in providing opportunity and respecting diversity. This environment has the following characteristics:

- There is equity in the use of the two languages of the school.
- Cross-cultural awareness is infused within the curriculum.
- Opportunities for the integration of all students occur several times throughout the school day.

This kind of school environment is critical to the academic success of all: native speakers of English as well as English language learners. Thus, the teaching and learning process for English language learners can be envisioned as a bridge. It is a bridge that links the students' home countries and cultures with their new country. It is a bridge that connects the languages and cultures the ELLs bring with English and the American experience. In turn, it is a bridge that connects English monolinguals with the rest of the world.

Notes

1. See Principle 6 for a discussion on appropriate assessment procedures to ensure accurate identification of language levels.
2. For this discussion, I continue to use Spanish as the second language, only for the sake of convenience of expression. It should be noted, however, that school systems have dual-language programs in a number of other languages, including Arabic, Chinese, French, Italian, Japanese and Portuguese.

References

Antunez, B. (2002a). Implementing reading first with English language learners. In *Directions in language and education* Spring (15), 1–12.

Antunez, B. (2002b). English language learners and the five essential components of reading instruction. *Reading Rockets*, WETA-TV, Washington, DC. Available at: http://www.readingrockets.org.

Cloud, N., Genessee, F., & Hamayan, E. (2000). *Dual language instruction: A handbook for enriched education.* Boston: Heinle and Heinle Publishers.

Collier, V. (1992). A synthesis of studies examining long-term-language-minority student data on academic achievement. *Bilingual Research Journal, 16*(1–2), 187–212.

Crawford, J. (1997) *Best evidence: Research foundations of the Bilingual Education Act.* Washington, DC: National Clearinghouse for Bilingual Education

Crawford, J. (1999). *Bilingual education: History, politics, theory, and practice.* Los Angeles: Bilingual Education Services, Inc.

Cummins, J. (1981). The role of primary language development in promoting educational success for language minority students. *Schooling and language minority students: A theoretical framework.* Sacramento: California State Department of Education

Cummins, J. (1989). *Empowering minority students.* Sacramento: California Association for Bilingual Education.

Cummins, J. (1991) Conversational and academic language proficiency in bilingual contexts. *AILA Review 8*, 75–89.

Echevarria, J., Vogt, M., & Short, D. (2004). *Making content comprehensible for English learners.* Boston: Pearson.

Hiebert, E. H., Pearson, D., Taylor, B., Richardson, V., & Paris, S. (1998). *Every child a reader: Applying reading research in the classroom.* Washington, DC: US Department of Education. ERIC Digest # ED 429269.

Krashen, S. D. (1996). *Under attack: The case against bilingual education.* Culver City, CA: Language Education Association.

Krashen, S. D. (1981). *Second language acquisition and second language learning.* Oxford: Pergamon Press.

Medina, M., & Escamilla, K. (1992). Evaluation of transitional and maintenance bilingual programs. *Urban Education, 27*, 263–290.

Rodriguez, A. (1988). Research in reading and writing in bilingual education and English as a second language. In Am Ambert (Ed.), *Bilingual education and English as a second language: A research handbook* (Garland Reference Library of Social Science, Vol. 634). New York: Garland Publishing, Inc.

Snow, C, Burns, S., & Griffin, P. (Eds.) (1998). *Preventing reading difficulties in young children.* Washington, DC: National Academy Press.

Thomas, W., & Collier, V. (1996). *Language minority student achievement and program effectiveness.* Fairfax, VA: Center for Bilingual/Multicultural ESL Education, George Mason University.

Thomas, W., & Collier, V. (1997). *School effectiveness for language minority students.* Washington, DC: National Clearinghouse for Bilingual Education.

Thomas, W., & Collier, V. (1998). *School effectiveness for language minority students.* Alexandria, VA: National Clearinghouse for Bilingual Education.

Willig, A. (1985). A meta-analysis of selected studies on the effectiveness of bilingual education. *Review of Educational Research, 55,* 269–317.

CHAPTER 15

Is It Language, or Is It Special Needs? Appropriately Diagnosing English Language Learners Having Achievement Difficulties[1]

GEORGE P. DE GEORGE

Whether English language learners (ELLs) having achievement difficulties in English should be referred for special education is a question that I frequently receive from school districts, especially from those that have minimal experience in educating such students or that do not have English as a second language (ESL) or bilingual education programs. The question is not trivial and, if not properly addressed, can have unfortunate consequences for the ELL, despite the well-meaning intentions of staff. This chapter, which addresses the referral process for ELLs, is composed of two sections: (1) a guide of recommended questions about ELLs having achievement difficulties from a practitioner's perspective; (2) a review of the supporting research literature.

Guidelines for Deciding on Referral or Nonreferral

The purpose of this first section is to provide educators with guidance in addressing this question of referral or nonreferral of ELLs. Although much that is worthwhile has already been written on this subject I will not attempt to summarize or to duplicate it here (Artiles & Ortiz, 2002; Cloud, 1994; Garcia & Ortiz, 1988; Roseberry-McKibbin, 1995; Scribner, 2002). Rather, I address the issue by explaining and demonstrating how I help educators, and sometimes parents, who call me for assistance in determining whether an ELL may or may not need to be referred for a special education evaluation and what should be done to help the child. The calls are most frequently about ELLs who have been in the district for one or more years. This group of ELLs is the focus of this chapter.

The question of whether an ELL may need a special education evaluation and how to avoid misdiagnosis in that process can be daunting, and the search for an answer can be complex (Artiles & Ortiz, 2002; Cloud, 1994; Garcia & Ortiz, 1988; Roseberry-McKibbin, 1995). However, the knowledge and awareness of several factors can help educators and parents arrive at a more informed response. Among these factors are first- and second-language acquisition as aspects of cognitive development and an acquaintance with the student's life and educational history. This chapter addresses these and other relevant factors, lists the kinds of questions I ask to get information, and explains why I need this information to assist the caller.

The challenge and the necessity in approaching a case are to uncover what lies behind the questions that staff and parents ask and to keep the focus on the ultimate goal, which is the student's linguistic and cognitive growth and academic achievement. Persons who call from school districts are usually caring teachers, administrators, and special educators. The parents who contact me are concerned about their children and are often in disagreement with school authorities that wish to refer the child for special education. My task is to help these individuals see what is not immediately apparent with respect to what may be preventing the desired student achievement, to provide feedback on the analysis they may have already made, and to identify relevant questions they may not have thought to ask.

Common Scenarios

Though each child and case is unique, I have encountered situations that repeat themselves over the years. The following scenarios are typical of the calls that I receive.

Teacher: Mr. De George, we have a Korean- (or Spanish- or Portuguese- or Albanian-) speaking child who has been with us for two years. The child is having difficulty in reading textbooks and literature and in understanding math problems. We think there is something more than just learning English and want to have the child tested. We need your help and advice.

Administrator: We have a student, Rafael, whose parents are from Colombia. He is in third grade and does not seem to understand what to do with reading and writing assignments. We do not understand why because his older sister came to us three years ago and has done wonderfully. We think he has a processing problem and ought to be tested. Should we bring in a tester who speaks his native language as well as someone who can test in English?

Parent: Mr. De George, my daughter is in fifth grade, and they want to put her into special education. We know there is nothing wrong with her. When she was in school in Puerto Rico she was fine. Here, she is failing. What can we do?

To help callers such as these, I must enable them to see the achievement difficulties in the context of the child's life and educational history. The child may or may not have difficulties attributable to a disability that can be classified under, and addressed through, special education. Moreover, the presence of such a disability is only one possible explanation of why the ELL is having achievement difficulties in English. There is a more than equal chance that non-special education factors may explain the child's difficulty or that the problem is not within the child and that the achievement difficulties may be attributable to gaps in the child's educational experience or to the instructional response of the school (Artiles & Ortiz, 2002; Garcia & Ortiz, 1988; Short, 2000). Therefore, all possibilities and avenues must be explored to obtain an informed answer to the question and to assist staff in providing more effective instruction.

To get to what is really happening in the types of scenarios just outlined, I need to ask questions that will reveal who the child is, what life and educational experience the child brings to the situation, how the school and its staff have addressed the child's educational needs, and what has worked and not worked. It is also essential that I help school staff and parents build a balanced view of the child's school performance. Therefore, in addition to delineating achievement difficulties, it is equally important to have acknowledged the child's progress, assets, and capabilities—that is, what the child knows and can do (Artiles & Ortiz, 2002; Cloud, 1994). This information will help determine the next steps in the student's instructional program.

Opportunity to Learn Versus Disabling Condition

At issue, then, especially in contexts where English is the sole language of instruction for an ELL, is whether the child has had opportunities to acquire expected language and academic skills or whether a genuine disabling condition has impeded such acquisition. My approach to this question is pragmatic because callers need guidance and must take steps to rectify a child's situation immediately. Because of their time constraints and mine, I have only a short while over the telephone to address their concerns and to follow up with written information and perhaps further telephone calls. In essence, I am providing a crash course in avoiding misdiagnosis.

However, to identify the range of questions that need to be asked to determine why an ELL is having achievement difficulties, we must first have a more detailed understanding of what is meant by, and the difference between, the terms *opportunities to learn* and *disabling conditions*.

The question of which opportunities a given ELL has had to develop the language and academic skills needed for achieving in his or her current school situation is, on the surface, deceptively straightforward (Cloud, 1994)—that is, until we probe more deeply. *Opportunities to learn* may be defined as occasions, circumstances, and experiences that stimulate, enable, encourage, motivate, and, on occasion, compel us as human beings of all ages to acquire facts and information (i.e., knowledge that) and to develop skills, abilities, and proficiencies for performing any number of tasks, functions, and operations (i.e., knowledge how to).[2] These operations can be physical, linguistic, intellectual, and artistic. They occur in the students' daily lives, in and out of school. Further, such opportunities can be greatly influenced by students' life situations: the families they are born into (e.g., parents, siblings), families' education and socioeconomic levels, the community, society, culture, and geographical area. For instance, physical, verbal, and nonverbal interactions with parents and others provide the opportunities for children to become proficient in their home language; to learn how to feed and dress themselves, walk, play, and perform manual tasks; and to behave and socialize, among other things. Clearly, schooling and schools open up whole worlds of learning opportunities, such as learning how to read and write; developing mathematical knowledge and skills; learning about the physical world and science, human history, industry and business, the fine and performing arts, and literature and world languages; and preparing for entering various trades and professions.

On the other hand, educators are well aware that not all children come to school having had all or most of these types of learning opportunities. Some students come from well-educated and literate families; some do not. Because of family displacement or other reasons, some students have experienced interruptions and gaps in their schooling. Others have had previous schooling that is inadequate or of questionable quality.

Disabling conditions, on the other hand, include mental retardation, hearing and vision impairments, physical and health impairments, emotional disturbance, deafness and blindness, and specific learning disabilities (Cloud, 1994). Such conditions often prevent or limit students who have them from profiting from the learning opportunities with which they are presented. Educators are aware that the causes or reasons for such conditions are varied, that they often result in achievement difficulties, and that students with disabilities require special instructional strategies and methods to assist them in learning despite the disabling conditions. What is more, by definition, such background differences as lack of English proficiency and literacy, low socioeconomic levels, and cultural differences are not disabling conditions (Garcia & Ortiz, 1988) but rather are situations or matters of fact that may provide challenges in classroom instruction for students and their teachers.

This discussion suggests that a student's life and education history can be useful guides for identifying the questions that will help educators obtain the information needed to answer the central question of this chapter (Artiles & Ortiz, 2002; Cloud, 1994). However, with ELLs there are additional considerations. For instance, ELLs come from homes where a language other than English is commonly spoken. Their proficiency and literacy in English, if they have had an opportunity to acquire them, usually vary widely. Some come from abroad with or without adequate education or literacy in their native language. Others may come from extreme situations such as war or internment in refugee camps. Others are born in this country but may have attended schools that did not address their needs effectively or at all. Clearly, ELLs are quite diverse with respect to language, culture, life experience, socioeconomic status, educational background, and preparedness for schooling in this country. With respect to an ELL's life and educational history, consequently, educators need to become aware of questions that, in the case of English-speaking students, they may never have thought to ask.

The remainder of this first section presents nine major areas that I cover with educators, and sometimes with parents, and the thinking process that I undergo as we work to determine the source of a student's achievement difficulties—that is, a disabling condition or the lack of opportunity to acquire expected knowledge and skills, or both.[3]

Initiating the Information-Gathering Process with a Caller:
Child's Age and Current Placement

My initial response, after I have listened to a caller and depending on what information has been conveyed to me, is something like the following:

> That really is quite a situation. But, to help you out, I will need some more information and will ask you a few questions to try to separate out some of the things you have told me. Is that okay with you?

The caller usually agrees, and we move on.

> I think we need to put aside for a moment the question of testing and whether or not the child may have a genuine disabling condition and may need special education. This may or may not be the case, but my first recommendation is that testing should be the last resort. Even if testing is eventually done, the results will be difficult to interpret unless they are seen in the light of the student's background.

There may be some discussion on this point, but usually the caller agrees to move on, and I continue.

> How old is the child, and in what grade or class is the child at the present time?

I need this information to move backward in time and to ask more pertinent questions about the student's life and educational history. The responses I receive may vary considerably, depending on the child's age, which may be 6 or 7 years old to 14 or 15. I then explore the factors discussed in the following sections, but not necessarily in the order presented.

Cultural Background of the Child and Family

To obtain information on this factor, I ask the following:

- Of what ethnic or cultural background is the child?
- Where do the child and the family come from?

Responses to these questions put the child in a cultural context that will help me activate any knowledge I may have about the cultural background. It may help me understand any of the child's or parents' behavior that the caller may describe. Whether or not my caller and I know anything about the culture, it is important for me to remain open and nonjudgmental. I may ask questions about parent behavior, such as which parent may have stepped forward as the authority in the matter—the mother, the father, or both—and whether the father requires that all proposed actions be submitted for his approval and not just the mother's.

I also listen for evidence regarding whether the parents seem to defend the child or are willing to describe the child's behavior at home and in previous educational settings. Depending on the cultural background or other circumstances, the idea of a child having deficits, disabilities, problems, or needing special assistance may carry a stigma for the parents and the family (Artiles & Ortiz, 2002). In such cases, much discretion is needed to obtain parental trust, cooperation, and support.

The child's gender is another factor that may be significant because different cultures have divergent views on the roles of males and females as children and as adults (Artiles & Ortiz, 2002). Often, the caller will perceive such dimensions as culturally based. At this point, I may also ask the caller about how the child behaves with teachers and other students. A behavior such as shyness, for example, may be culturally based, and I will need to point this out to the caller who may or may not be aware of this.

Nevertheless, in observing cultural characteristics and behaviors, it is important to acknowledge that in dealing with children and adults from diverse backgrounds, we are dealing with individuals. Cultural characteristics are group tendencies, and what may be true for the group may not be true for every individual that is part of the group. For instance, Americans are often characterized as being individualistic and competitive. But, there are many Americans who are very group oriented and deferential to the wishes of the group as well as cooperative by nature rather than competitive (Harris & Moran, 1991; Hofstede, 1984).

Therefore, in observing the characteristics of individual children or adults, care must be taken to avoid overgeneralizing and assuming that all individuals of a given cultural group behave similarly. Again, one must suspend judgment and remain open, get to know the persons involved, and appreciate them as individuals as well as members of a particular cultural group. One must also bear in mind two additional caveats in relating with culturally diverse individuals: (1) the only difference among cultures is that they are different from one another; and (2) we tend to view the actions and behaviors of diverse individuals from our own cultural perspectives and expectations (Harris & Moran, 1991; Hofstede, 1984).

An example will illustrate. In American cultural contexts, we expect children and adults with whom we are speaking to look at us and to make eye contact as a sign of attention and respect. In some other cultures, looking too intently at those who are talking to us—especially if they are older individuals, authority figures, or members of a higher social class—is seen as a sign of defiance and disrespect. Children from other cultures who look down or away from us when we talk to them may, in their minds, believe that they are showing respect. On the other hand, those of us who are culturally American may interpret such behavior as evasive and impolite (Nine Curt, 1976).

Therefore, in matters of culture and cultural behavior, we must suspend judgment, keep an open mind, and seek more information from those who understand the culture to discern the meaning of the behavior we observe or that is described. We may also need input on which behaviors of our own may unintentionally offend others. An instance of this is touching the heads of children. I have been advised by those familiar with Asian cultures, whose members are often followers of Buddhism, that the heads of children, especially older children, should not be touched because the head is considered sacred (Language and Orientation Resource Center, 1981; Thuy, 1976). I frequently refer callers to other sources and knowledgeable individuals for information on a specific cultural group, such as school districts with teachers from a given cultural group or universities that have relevant area studies departments or programs.

Parents' Educational Background and Careers

Another area of questioning that may produce helpful information is the parents' educational background and careers or employment. One reason for pursuing such information is to determine the values or attitudes toward education that the parents and children may exhibit. Most parents, regardless of the extent of their own education, place great value on education and on that of their children. However, depending on such background, we may have to approach parents differently in suggesting ways in which they can support the education of their children. To elicit such information, I will ask such questions as,

- What grade or level of education did each parent complete?
- What type of work did each parent do abroad, and what type of work do they do in the United States?

Again, in asking these questions of parents, one must do so with discretion and respect.

It is important to bear in mind that children from poor or modest families with lower levels of education are just as capable of excelling linguistically and academically as children from well-off families. Such factors do not predetermine their capabilities or achievement patterns. In any case, an important school goal is to solicit parental support for their children's education. Respect for parents and children as individuals, for the assets that the children bring to the classroom and for their diverse cultural ways, as well as showing genuine concern for the child's welfare and education are the best ways for obtaining parental trust and cooperation. It may be necessary for the caller from a district to seek further information on how to communicate effectively with individuals from a specific cultural background. Cross-cultural communication can be a challenging area for everyone (Harris & Moran, 1991; Nine Curt, 1976).

Child's Life, Language Development, and Educational History

With the aforementioned types of information, I am now more prepared to proceed to the next step, which is to delve more deeply into the life, language development, and educational history of the child. Questions and analyses concerning these three areas are intertwined, since information from one area leads to questions and implications for the other. The process begins by asking questions about the child's life history. To get at this, I begin with the following questions:

- When was the child born?
- Was the child born abroad or in the United States?
- At what age did the child come to the United States (if the child was born abroad)?

Often, there is a range of responses to these questions that can be quite revealing. For example, some children are born abroad and come here at a young age, anywhere from infancy to around seven to eight years of age. Others arrive during the upper elementary grades or during adolescence. Some children are born in the United States, but their home language is not English, whether or not their parents are recent immigrants. This chapter concentrates on children who come to the United States at a young age, with or without education, or who are born in the United States into a non-English speaking home.

Viewing Achievement Difficulties of ELLs in English from a Language-Acquisition Perspective
Contrary to what might be expected, the children who come to the United States at a very young age with little or no education abroad, or who are born in the United States, are among those who experience the most difficulty when they attend a school in which English is the only language of instruction (Cummins, 1984; Freeman & Freeman, 2002; Hakuta, 1987). Many teachers and special educators express surprise when I tell them this, and they react by saying something like, "But I thought that by watching television and growing up here, the children would just pick up English." Sometimes they do, but very often they do not or may not do so sufficiently for school learning purposes.

Some ELLs become quite verbal in English but often experience difficulties with reading, writing, and academics in English. Several factors explain this phenomenon, not the least of which is integration with English-speaking children, whereas minimal or no instructional time is dedicated for them to learn English as a second language or additional language (Short, 2000).

For young children raised in a home where another language is spoken, they acquire that language from parents, older siblings, other adults, and children. The children's neighborhoods may contain a high percentage of linguistically similar households. Until such children first enter school at the age of five or six, they have been surrounded with, and have acquired, the other language, not English.

When these children do enter an all-English-speaking school, they are immersed in an English-speaking ambiance. Most likely, such children understand little of what is being said. However, they are about to begin the process of acquiring English alongside speakers who have already acquired five to six years of English at home. When these ELLs return home at the end of the day, they reenters the world of the home language. In addition, the home language is spoken on weekends, holidays, and vacations at home and in the homes of friends and relatives. But in all this, such children are surrounded by an English-speaking world. If any literacy development occurred in the home, most likely it was in the other language. When the young ELLs enter school, they are ready to learn school language and literacy in the home language, not in English. Even if adequate ESL instruction is provided, it will take some time before these children reach a level of English proficiency equal to that of their home language and to that of English-speaking classmates. In the meantime, the English-speaking children will have moved on.

By way of contrast and comparison, let us take a closer look at the situation of the English-speaking child. On entry to school, such a child has had five to six years of English language development surrounded by English-speaking adults and children. English is heard and seen on television and radio, while viewing videos and playing video games, over the Internet, on the street, in shopping centers and stores, in the park, on the playground, and in the homes of friends and relatives. All of these early life experiences work together to support the child's acquisition of English. In school, the process continues: Teachers and administrators speak English, as do other students and their parents. All instruction is conducted in English, and English literacy is developed. The child begins to internalize English school and academic language, advances in English reading and writing, and penetrates more deeply the world of English literature.

Linguistic World of ELLs in the United States   From a life history as well as a linguistic vantage point, the language-minority children we are looking at are about to become ELLs, and their linguistic world is not that of the English-speaking child—it is divided. Had these children remained in the country from which their family came, their Spanish, Portuguese, Albanian, or Vietnamese—whatever the language—would have developed in a world in which that language was encountered at every turn. They would have gone to schools in which that language was the language of instruction, and they would have developed their literacy in that language. But that did not happen or was interrupted. They live in two linguistic worlds. The world outside of their home does not support the language they first acquired in the home, and the schools they enter necessitate the acquisition of another language—English—whether or not they are offered a bilingual education, an ESL program, or some other assistance to facilitate that acquisition and to increase their chances of success.

That these children are capable of acquiring English and achieving academically is not in question. But for this to happen, they need an instructional program that supports what they need over time (Artiles & Ortiz, 2002).

The Advantage for ELLs Educated Abroad   Most children that have received an adequate education in their country of origin, it has been observed, do quite well in American schools if given an instructional program that meets their needs (Short, 2000; Thomas & Collier, 1995, 1997). From a language and cognitive development point of view, this makes sense. Such children's native language is well developed; they are literate in that language and have achieved academically through that language in such areas as mathematics, literature, social studies, and science. Academic concepts and the language in which they are expressed have been acquired. They have solved mathematics problems, read academic texts, and written academic assignments in their language.

When such children come into American schools, they acquire oral English and literacy and usually proceed to transfer over to English what they acquired and learned in their native language. This includes the knowledge of language, literacy, and communication that they acquired through their first language (Short, 2000). In the beginning, then, they do not have to struggle with learning new content through a language they are in the process of learning; they have already learned a lot of content. Rather, they need to take what they achieved in one language and to learn how to express it in the new language they are acquiring. Provided that they achieved adequately, they also have a cognitive structure in which to incorporate new knowledge. However, in time they will have to learn new content through the new language they are acquiring.

This is not to say that all is smooth sailing for such children. Learning a new language, transferring what one knows to that language, and continuing one's education in that new language are in themselves challenging tasks. In addition, some children are better students than others, and some are better at, or more interested in, learning an additional language than others (Short, 2000). In general, however, most students who come from abroad with an adequate education in their native language come with assets that will serve them well, given an appropriate instructional program, personal motivation, and parental support (Thomas & Collier, 1995, 1997). Nevertheless, even some students with adequate education from abroad need an appropriate program over a longer or extended period of time.

Understanding the Achievement Difficulties of Young ELLs with Little or No Education Abroad   We can now appreciate, from this life history and language acquisition point of view, what may not have happened (i.e., lack of opportunity) and what needs to happen (i.e., provision of opportunity) with respect to the education of young ELLs who had no education abroad.

We can also understand that the expectation on the part of school staff that such children should be able to acquire English quickly and to meet the same academic standards as native English speakers within a short period of time (e.g., one to two years) may be neither feasible nor realistic. Undoubtedly, some ELLs in this category do meet this expectation, but, for most of them an appropriate program over a longer period of time is usually needed (Collier, 1989; Cummins, 1981a; Thomas and Collier, 1997).

Detecting Impairments and Disabilities From Early Childhood

The ELLs we are focusing on should be checked for hearing, vision, physical, and health impairments (Artiles & Ortiz, 2002). Of course, these factors need to be considered for all children, but they should not be overlooked in the case of ELLs. The sources for such information about a child are usually the parents, guardians, relatives, and any other individuals familiar with the child and the family, such as church groups that sponsor the immigration of individuals from abroad. Questions such as the following can be asked to obtain information.

- Did anything unusual happen during the time the mother was pregnant with the child?
- Was the pregnancy difficult in any way?
- Were there any accidents, injuries, problematic illnesses, or traumatic experiences while the mother was pregnant? Did the pregnant mother have any serious falls?
- Did the young child have any accidents, injuries, or serious illnesses that caused impairments, or were any difficulties detected with respect to sight and hearing?

If the responses suggest that impairments were congenital or resulted from early childhood experiences, then further investigation and medical examinations may be warranted. Some impairments require relatively simple adjustments, such as eyeglasses; others may entail more in-depth interventions. My experience has been that sight and hearing impairments can go unnoticed. In another state, I was once called in by a school district that had been cited by state authorities for overrepresentation of Hispanic children in special education. I read many cumulative folders and was astonished by the evidence on early hearing and visual impairments that had been overlooked and attended to only many years after their early entry into the child's record. As a result, unfortunately, a number of children experienced several years of unnecessary academic failure. When at last the impairment was investigated, corrective measures such as eyeglasses and hearing aids were prescribed, and the academic achievement of the students improved.

In addition, evidence of emotional disturbance also needs to be checked. Some children have lived through traumatic situations, such as war (Artiles & Ortiz, 2002; Cloud, 1994). The question or the possibility should be raised, especially if children come from countries or areas where the occurrence of armed conflict has been reported in recent years. Instances of acting out, extremely aggressive or other unusual behavior should be noted, and, if children from such countries or areas experience academic failure, then emotional disturbance should be investigated as a possible cause. Such investigation is a very sensitive area for parents and children, so expert psychological and cultural assistance may be necessary in approaching parents, investigating the matter, and deciding what course of action needs to be taken. It goes without saying that much discretion will have to be exercised. Although not all children from such countries or areas will have emotional disturbances that result in achievement difficulties, the possibility should not be overlooked.

Adequacy of Education Obtained Abroad by ELLs

If discussions suggest that a student was educated abroad, then it is important to gather as complete a picture as possible of the schooling that did take place (Freeman & Freeman, 2002). Such information will provide an idea of what opportunities the student had for learning in school before coming to the United States and may provide clues regarding any achievement difficulties the student is having in an American school, including disabling conditions or achievement difficulties that may have been detected or experienced abroad. Among the principal items of interest in this area are the extent to which literacy in the native language was developed and how other types of cognitive development occurred, especially in mathematics, science, and social studies.

Very often, school records from abroad are difficult to obtain or take a long time to arrive and are challenging to interpret when they are available. For these reasons, the student, the parents, and informed relatives, including an older brother or sister, frequently are the sources of such information. Where possible, teachers and others familiar with the educational system of the child's country of origin should be consulted.

Sometimes parents display a reluctance to provide information by withholding or by responding yes to all questions. Such behavior is not unusual for several reasons. Some parents may be distrustful of revealing information about their children to unknown individuals whom they perceive as authority figures because of uncertainty or fear of what may be done with the information if they do provide it. Others wish to present the most positive picture of their child that they can and so communicate that everything is all right even if a given child had previously had achievement difficulties. Respect, patience, demonstrating a genuine concern for the child's education, and explaining in simple terms how such information will help the school educate the child more effectively are among the strategies that will win over parental trust and cooperation.

In any case, among the important questions to ask concerning the child's education abroad are:

- Did the child attend school in her or his native country?
- How old was the child when he or she began school? (Sometimes children abroad do not start school until seven years of age.)

- For how many years did the child attend, and which grades did the child complete?
- Were any grades interrupted, or were there any years when the child did not attend school for the whole year?

It is important to ask these questions specifically and directly because very often parents are reluctant to volunteer information without a direct question. If the parents do indicate that certain years or grades were not completed, this may be, but is not necessarily, a clue that the child experienced difficulties. It may be so for other reasons, such as war or displacement, which may become apparent in the discussion. In addition, the following questions should be asked:

- Did the child learn to read and write? For how many years or grades?
- What other subjects did the child study? For how many years or grades?
- Did the child study English, and was the child introduced to English literacy? For how many years or grades?
- Did the child attend school in an urban or rural area, and how would you describe the school that the child attended?

This last question often reveals the quality of the education the student has received. In some countries, schools in urban centers are better equipped in terms of materials, facilities, and qualified staff, whereas rural schools are not well equipped and the quality of education suffers (Short, 2000). Individuals familiar with the school system of a particular country, such as bilingual education teachers in American schools who happen to be from the country in question, are usually good sources of information regarding such schools.

The list of questions just provided were framed with the child's parents and guardians in mind. Notice that no question asks directly whether the child had a problem or difficulty, because very often the response will be no or an answer will be avoided. In looking for clues (e.g., a certain grade was not completed and asks why), the interviewer is more likely to obtain information about possible achievement difficulties, if there were any. Also, it is often difficult for parents whose child had achievement difficulties to acknowledge this. For some, the matter is shameful or carries a stigma, whereas others are concerned about how the child will be viewed (Artiles & Ortiz, 2002). It is necessary to be sensitive to this and to assure parents that every effort will be made to help the child. Being sensitive may mean that one should not probe too deeply at first regarding clues that the child had difficulties and that a general indication is at least sufficient for the moment.

After obtaining a picture of the child's education abroad through responses to this list of questions, the information needs to be scanned in the light of the following questions:

- Is there evidence that the child had an adequate education abroad and is literate in her or his native language?
- Is it the case that education abroad was very brief, less than one year?
- Is there evidence that the child had achievement difficulties abroad and to what may these be attributed (e.g., disabling condition, poor quality education, frequent absences, low achievement despite adequate education)?

Again, the important point here is to determine whether any achievement difficulties reported from abroad may be due to genuine disabling conditions or to lack of opportunity to learn. A child that experienced serious educational gaps, poor quality education, or a brief period of education abroad has more than likely had less opportunity to learn. The way to deal with this now is to provide the opportunities to learn with appropriate instructional programming in the mainstream program. If poor attendance was the problem, but the child seems normal in all other respects, then the issue to work on is attendance and attending to learning in school (Artiles & Ortiz, 2002). Put another way, lack of opportunity to learn is not a disabling condition as previously defined and should not be dealt with through special education but in the mainstream program with support such as ESL, literacy instruction, bilingual education, and sheltered content-area instruction.[4]

Adequacy of Education Obtained Elsewhere in the United States

Some students, with or without education abroad, come to a particular district after having been enrolled in one or more other school districts in the United States. School records for most of these children should be available and should provide information on achievement and possible disabling conditions. In cases such as these, I ask the caller the following questions:

- In which districts did they attend school, for how long, and which grade levels were completed?
- In which type(s) of program were they placed: ESL, bilingual, mainstream, or special education?
- What kind(s) of opportunities did they have to acquire English proficiency, literacy, and academics?
- What do school records and other sources of information indicate regarding achievement, achievement difficulties, or the presence of disabling conditions?

Appropriateness and Adequacy of Opportunities Offered by the Caller's School District

As already indicated, the ELL about whom I am contacted most often has been in the caller's school district for one or more years and is experiencing achievement difficulties. There is a point in our discussion—after we have discussed the child's life, language development, and educational history prior to coming to the caller's district—when I must ask what learning opportunities the caller's district has provided. I must also help the caller determine whether those opportunities have been appropriate and adequate (Artiles & Ortiz, 2002). Obviously, this is an area in which I must ask frank questions but must also exercise a certain amount of discretion.

Depending on our conversation about the child, I may ask the following questions:

- What information on the child's life and educational history were sought when the child first came to the district?
- Were the child's knowledge, skills, and language proficiencies verified and screened, possibly by a certified bilingual education teacher, when the child entered the school district?
- What kinds of instructional decisions were made on the basis of such information in the beginning? Describe the program that has been provided for the child.
- What adjustments in the instructional programming have been made in response to the child's lack of progress and to address the child's achievement difficulties?

Very often these questions will be answered in the course of our conversation. As expected, the extent to which districts address these areas varies greatly for many reasons, including awareness, the experience of the district and staff in serving such students, and the number of ELLs they have.

In some cases, students' needs have been very well addressed, and considerable resources have been allocated; in others, some but not all of the elements of an adequate program have been implemented. Sometimes the caller realizes that more information is needed and seeks my help in how to obtain it and in how to rethink what should be done on behalf of the child. In still other instances, as a result of our discussion, the caller is better able to formulate a plan of what to do. Often, the caller has more insight and information to bring to a planning and placement team (PPT) meeting that has been scheduled for the child. Last, in some instances a school district does call at the time that an ELL first arrives and asks what it is obliged to do on behalf of such a child or what it should do.

At this point, the reader may very appropriately ask how one determines whether learning opportunities for ELLs in a school district are appropriate and adequate. That can be done by asking the following types of questions:

- Have ELLs received double periods of ESL instruction in their first year and at least one period daily in succeeding years? (This is a good practice recommendation in the ESL teaching field.)
- Does the ESL teacher hold ESL certification?
- Has the student received specific instruction in English literacy from a certified teacher or reading specialist?
- Have classroom teachers made instructional modifications to facilitate student understanding of academic areas, to assist the student in acquiring English academic language (Artiles & Ortiz, 2002), and to help the student with the reading and writing aspects of content learning? (This is the sheltered content teaching approach previously mentioned [Short, 2000].)
- Has the student been given an opportunity to continue her or his native language development or been provided with content-area instruction in that language?
- Have classroom and other teachers received any professional development in serving ELLs (e.g., in sheltered content instruction techniques in helping students acquire English)?
- What kinds of support are provided to teachers responsible for instructing ELLs?
- Which relevant in-district and out-of-district resources and services are employed to assist the student and his or her teachers?
- Have the parents been actively involved by the school in supporting the student's education?

Acknowledging an ELL's Progress and Assets

At the beginning of this chapter I stressed the importance of acknowledging whether the student has shown any academic progress or a pattern of progress while in the district, despite his or her achievement difficulties (Artiles & Ortiz, 2002). If the caller does not raise the matter in the course of our discussion, then I take it upon myself to do so by asking such questions as:

- Has the student made progress while in the district? If so, in which areas—especially in English proficiency and literacy—and to what extent?
- Has the student demonstrated any particular assets or aptitudes or talents, whether they are related to academic learning or not?

In addition to providing a more balanced picture of the ELL as a student and as an individual, such information may:

- be an indicator that, given an opportunity, the student does achieve academically, at least in some areas.
- constitute evidence at least in some areas that the instruction provided has been effective, should be continued, and may provide clues for improving instruction in other areas.
- be used to motivate students since it points out areas in which they have experienced success.
- in the case of assets not related to academic achievement in school, such as artistic ability and excellence in sports, be used to promote student self-confidence despite achievement difficulties and as bridges to academic learning.

Drawing Conclusions

After a fairly detailed discussion on each of the previous points (See Table 15.1 for a summary list of questions), the caller can then review the student's achievement difficulties in the light of all the available background information and, at the time of the call or at a later time, make one or more determinations. These can be summarized as follows:

- The evidence points to lack of opportunity, whether before or after the student came to the district. What specific factors account for this, and what further steps can the district take to improve its program or student achievement?
- The evidence points to a possible disabling condition and a referral for special education evaluation is appropriate.
- The evidence points to both a lack of opportunity and a disabling condition. A referral for special education is appropriate, and, at the same time, opportunities for acquiring relevant knowledge and skills must be devised.
- After reconsideration and all factors considered, the student is making adequate progress, the district's expectations may have been too high, or instruction that has been effective should be continued and ways to enhance further student achievement should be sought and implemented.

Although in a real situation matters may not be so clear-cut, these basic conclusions will serve as reference points.

Summary

The interview process presented in this section was developed in response to requests for help from school district personnel and parents concerned about the achievement difficulties of ELLs. It is the product of much research, study, and experience in working with practitioners in bilingual education and ESL programs at the local level. Clearly, it is very much rooted in the insights of language-acquisition researchers such as Cummins (1981b), Krashen (1981) and of bilingual special educators such as Garcia and Ortiz (1988), whose model for preventing inappropriate referrals of ELLs I have drawn on substantially.

The interview process is, of course, an informal assessment device intended to be part of a comprehensive assessment that employs tests, observations, student records, and work samples to gather information about students. To provide a picture of the whole child in a meaningful context and to pinpoint the sources of learning difficulties, the process solicits information about an ELL's life and educational history, language development, and family and cultural background. In doing so, it also creates a framework whereby all data collected as part of a comprehensive assessment can be interpreted and analyzed from a broad

Table 15.1 Interview question checklist

I.   **Initiating the Information-Gathering Process with a Caller**

- How old is the child and in what grade or class is the child at the present time?

II.   **Cultural Background of the Child and Family**

- Of what ethnic or cultural background is the child?

- Where do the child and the family come from?

- How does the child behave with teachers and other students?

-

III.   **Parents' Educational Background and Careers**

- What grade or level of education did each parent complete?

- What type of work did each parent do abroad and what type of work do they do in the United States?

IV.   **Child's Life, Language Development and Educational History**

- When was the child born?

- Was the child born abroad or in the United States?

- At what age did the child come to the United States (if the child was born abroad)?

V.   **Detecting Impairments and Handicaps from Early Childhood**

- Did anything unusual happen during the time the mother was pregnant with the child?

- Was the pregnancy difficult in any way?

(continued next page)

perspective on the student. This is especially important in the case of standardized test data that may indicate the absence or presence of knowledge and skills but may not be able to indicate which factors account for such findings (Artiles & Ortiz, 2002; Cloud, 1994).

As with most interview processes, the responses given by interviewees, whether school personnel or parents, may suggest further questions or avenues of inquiry. Though interviewers need to be attuned to these possibilities and to pursue them, it also suggests that there is a certain art to questioning that is acquired with time and experience. Last, it is clear that educators conducting such interviews need to have considerable background and understanding regarding the education of ELLs, language acquisition and development, cognitive development, special education, diverse cultural backgrounds, the process of

Table 15.1 (continued) Interview question checklist

> - Were there any accidents, injuries, problematic illnesses or traumatic experiences while the mother was pregnant? Did the pregnant mother have any serious falls?
>
> - Did the young child have any accidents, injuries or serious illnesses that caused impairments or were any difficulties detected with respect to sight and hearing?
>
> **VI.   Adequacy of Education Obtained Abroad by ELLs**
>
> - Did the child attend school in her or his native country?
>
> - How old was the child when he or she began school? (Sometimes children abroad do not start school until seven years of age.)
>
> - For how many years did the child attend and which grades did the child complete?
>
> - Were any grades interrupted or were there any years when the child did not attend school for the whole year?
>
> - Did the child learn to read and write? For how many years or grades?
>
> - What other subjects did the child study? For how many years or grades?
>
> - Did the child study English and was the child introduced to English literacy? For how many years or grades?
>
> - Did the child attend school in an urban or rural area, and how would you describe the school that the child attended?
>
> (continued next page)

acculturation, cross-cultural communication, and familiarity with educational systems outside the United States. This suggests that a team of individuals with complementary skills and areas of expertise may be needed (Artiles & Ortiz, 2002; Cloud, 1994).

In any case, many school districts do have regular and special educators with these sorts of qualifications and who use them to benefit ELLs. It is hoped that what has been presented here will provide experienced practitioners with material for further reflection and newcomers with some of the insight and knowledge they need in serving ELLs in their schools and classrooms.

Research and Professional Literature Review

The preceding was written from a practitioner's perspective. The remainder of this chapter reviews some of the current research that informs the process presented and its various

Table 15.1 (continued) Interview question checklist

VII. Adequacy of Education Obtained Elsewhere in the United States

- In which districts did they attend school, for how long and which grade levels were completed?

- In which type(s) of program were they placed: ESL, bilingual, mainstream, or special education?

- What kind(s) of opportunities did they have to acquire English proficiency, literacy, and academics?

- What do school records and other sources of information indicate regarding achievement, achievement difficulties or the presence of handicapping conditions?

VIII. Appropriateness and Adequacy of Opportunities Offered by the Caller's School District

- What information on the child's life and educational history were sought when the child first came to the district?

- Were the child's knowledge, skills, and language proficiencies verified and screened, possibly by a certified bilingual education teacher, when the child entered the school district?

- What kinds of instructional decisions were made on the basis of such information in the beginning? Describe the program that has been provided for the child.

- What adjustments in the instructional programming have been made in response to the child's lack of progress and to address the child's achievement difficulties?

- Does the ESL teacher hold ESL certification?

(continued next page)

---

components. The research findings have been grouped under five relevant topics derived from the first section of this chapter.

Overrepresentation of ELLs in Special Education Due to Misdiagnosis

For Warger and Burnette (2000, p. 1) overrepresentation in special education is "one of the most troublesome issues associated with the growth of children from culturally and linguistically diverse backgrounds." Thus, the assessment of such students "has become one of special education's major issues" (Burnette, 2000, p. 1).

Table 15.1 (continued) Interview question checklist

- Have ELLs received double periods of ESL instruction in their first year and at least one period daily in succeeding years? (This is a good practice recommendation in the ESL teaching field.)

- Has the student received specific instruction in English literacy from a certified teacher or reading specialist?

- Have classroom teachers made instructional modifications to facilitate student understanding of academic areas, to assist the student in acquiring English academic language, and to help the student with the reading and writing aspects of content learning (the sheltered content teaching approach)?

- Has the student been given an opportunity to continue her or his native language development or been provided with content-area instruction in that language?

- Have classroom and other teachers received any professional development in serving ELLs, e.g., in sheltered content instruction techniques in helping students acquire English, etc.

- What kinds of support are provided to teachers responsible for instructing ELLs?

- Which relevant in-district and out-of-district resources and services are employed to assist the student and his or her teachers?

- Have the parents been actively involved by the school in supporting the student's education?

IX. **Acknowledging an ELL's Progress and Assets**

- Has the student made progress while in the district? If so, in which areas (especially in English proficiency and literacy) and to what extent?

- Has the student demonstrated any particular assets or aptitudes or talents, whether they are related to academic learning or not?

Many attribute this situation to inappropriate referral, poor placement, inappropriate use of test results, and misdiagnosis (Allen, 2002; Garcia & Ortiz, 1988; Scribner, 2002). More specifically, Garcia and Ortiz (1988, p. 1) maintain that their examination of the characteristics of ELLs in programs for the learning disabled and the speech and language impaired "suggests that neither the data…gathered as part of the referral and evaluation process nor the decisions made using these data reflect that professionals adequately understand limited English proficiency, second language acquisition, cultural and other differences which mediate student learning." They see growing support in the literature for the idea "that many students served in special education experience difficulties which are 'pedagogically induced.'"

According to Utley and Ubiakor (2001, p. 21), "Pinpointing academic strengths, multiple intelligences, and weaknesses of multicultural learners may be difficult" because of cultural and linguistic differences. They feel that "the majority of standardized tests do not include standardized and normative information on multicultural groups," and, consequently, such students are often "misidentified" and "disproportionately placed and misinstructed in general and special education classes (Utley & Ubiakor, 2001, p. 2)."

The report of the National Symposium on Learning Disabilities in English Language Learners (USDE, 2004, p. 1), however, finds a "puzzling paradox in the data." The report finds "widespread, informal evidence" (p. 1) that ELLs who do have disabilities are bypassed because teachers assume that the child's achievement difficulties are due to language difference. Conversely, evidence is seen that ELLs may be overrepresented because of "placements based upon inaccurate measures and ill-conceived procedures (USDE, 2004, p. 1)."

In addition, the report points out that "a smaller proportion of ELLs, compared to students in general, were identified for special education services" (USDE, 2004, p. 3). This statement is based on data from a report published by the Office of English Language Acquisition (OELA) in 2003 (USDE, 2003) and another by the Office for Civil Rights (OCR) in 2000 (USDE, 2000). Both publications report that approximately 13.5 percent of all students are referred to special education and that about 9.2 percent of ELLs have learning disabilities. Although these percentages "vary widely across the states," the National Symposium report indicates a need to investigate three possible explanations for these data: (1) "ELLs may be under-identified nationally as needing special education services"; (2) "ELLs in special education programs may not be identified as both ELLs and ELL/Ds [ELLs with learning disabilities]"; and (3) "there actually may be a lower disability rate among those identified as ELLs" (USDE, 2004, p. 3).

Achievement Difficulties of ELLs

"Many ELLS are failing school in the United States, even though most of them are not learning disabled," reports the National Symposium on Learning Disabilities in English Language Learners (USDE, 2004, p. iv). The national dropout rate for all students in the United States is 11%; that of Hispanics, who form three quarters of ELLs, is 28% (Allen, 2002, based on reports from the National Center for Educational Statistics [NCES]).

The dropout rate for students who did not speak English well in 1991 was 35% for Spanish-speaking students ages 16 through 24. For students who did not speak English at all, the rate in 1992 was 83%. Only 1 in 10 of recent immigrant youth in 1989 was enrolled in college. Of these, Spanish speakers were half as likely to enroll in college as other immigrants (Chamot, 2000, based on NCES reports of 1993, 1994).

The question is what underlies this and other indicators of low achievement among ELLs? Allen (2002), surveying districts in the South and Midwest, found that ELLs were often not literate in their native language or English. In addition, because of the perception of their inability to handle English, they are often placed in lower-track classrooms. These "rely heavily on individual work and question-and-answer formats" causing students to miss out on the "collaborative opportunities they need to improve their English" (p. 6).

Children lacking native language literacy experience great obstacles in learning a second language and in managing and processing academic information. Moreover, "their academic and learning difficulties often resemble that [sic] of the learning disabled child, yet the root of their problem in learning is very different (Gopaul-McNichol & Thomas-Presswood, 1998, p. 67)." In addition, achievement difficulties appear when teachers assume that ELLs who communicate in English well should have no difficulty when academic concepts are presented in English. Thus, students who are exited from ESL and bilingual programs after two or three years with just conversational skills and the ability to follow simple directions do not function well in a monolingual academic setting and fall progressively below grade level in academic subjects (Gopaul-McNichol & Thomas-Presswood, 1998).

Freeman and Freeman (2002) examine in depth two groups of secondary-level students that experience achievement difficulties: (1) newly arrived students with interrupted or limited formal schooling (LFS); and (2) long-term English learners (LTELs) who have been in American schools for seven years or more. Although the achievement difficulties of these two groups of students overlap, the authors find some significant differences.

LFS students may not read or write well in their native language or may not be literate at all. They lack basic concepts in various subject areas, may be two years below grade level in mathematics, do not have an academic background to draw on, struggle with coursework, perform poorly on standardized tests, and often lack an understanding of how schools are organized and how they are supposed to act. They must develop conversational English, become literate in English, and, like LTELs, need to acquire academic language.

LTELs, Freeman and Freeman (2002) state, experience the highest failure rates and often leave school as early as the eighth or ninth grade. They do poorly on tests and written assignments, have not developed high levels of literacy in their native language or in English, and are often below grade level in reading, writing, and usually in mathematics, despite seven or more years of attendance in U.S. schools. Though they score low on high school exit examinations and standardized tests, they do receive passing grades if they do their class work, which can give them a false sense of their academic achievement. In general, they lack the English proficiency they need to compete academically. They converse fluently in English but often lose fluency in their native language. They have difficulty in talking about and reading and writing in academic subjects and, therefore, need to develop academic language.

Need to Distinguish Achievement Difficulties Attributable to Lack of Opportunity Versus a Disability

However it is phrased, there is widespread awareness of the need to distinguish between ELLs having achievement difficulties attributable to a lack of opportunity or a language difference as opposed to those attributable to a disability or genuine disabling condition (Allen, 2002; Burnette, 2000; Chamot, 2000; Garcia & Ortiz, 1988; Laing & Kamhi, 2003; Roseberry-McKibbin, 1995; Scribner, 2002; USDE, 2004; Utley & Obiakor, 2001; Wilson-Portuondo & Hardy, 2001). Burnette (2000, p. 1) states that "if a student is having difficulties, information should be gathered to determine whether these difficulties stem from language or cultural differences, from a lack of opportunity to learn, or from a disability."

Roseberry-McKibbin (1995, p. 123) holds that "distinguishing a language difference from a language disorder is often a challenge," whereas Wilson-Portuondo and Hardy (2001, p. 1) see the need to "recognize normal difficulties resulting from the process of acculturation or to learning a second language from a disability." Finally, the report of the National Symposium on Learning Disabilities in English Language Learners (USDE, 2004, p. v) states that in striving to educate all students "there is the responsibility of determining whether a student's academic difficulties stem from learning a second language or from the presence of a learning disability or both."

Opportunity to Learn

Opportunity to learn as defined in the first section of this chapter encompasses all forms of education and formal and informal learning. In advising educators to determine whether a student has had an opportunity to learn prior to referral, Burnette (2000, p. 2) stipulates that this should be done by

> examining both the quantity of schooling (whether the student has been in school continuously and has received instruction) and the quality of schooling (including teacher variables and instructional variables). Among teacher variables are experience, expectations, teaching style, and track record with diverse students. Instructional variables include approaches that support the active involvement of the student. Examples are reciprocal teaching and instructional conversation that provides for 'comprehensible input'—instruction or conversation that is conceptually and linguistically comprehensible to the learner.

Burnette's (2000) advice is well taken but contextually seems to be centered on looking at a student currently enrolled in a district. Nevertheless, the questions that the author raises for examination may be applied to education a student has received abroad or in other school districts.

Scribner (2002, p. 1485) points out that about one third of ELLs in the United States receive "no tailored training" at all, many do not receive instruction in their native language, and others receive only ESL or immersion, both of which are conducted solely in English. She states that ELLs are often placed in lower-level courses and in ESL courses that "emphasize segmented skills, work sheets, and little opportunity for oral language development" (p. 1489). Similarly, Allen (2002, p. 6) indicates that when placed in lower-track classes, ELLs are denied "the collaborative opportunities they need to improve English skills" because such courses rely on individual work and question-and-answer formats. Scribner (2002) considers quick exit of ELLs from ESL classes after two years without further support as insufficient opportunity to develop native-like fluency. She feels that shortages of teachers for ELLs and "related services," such as school psychology, exacerbate "the academic vulnerability of LEP students" (p. 1485). For Scribner, all these indicate a lack of opportunity to learn.

Roseberry-McKibbin (1995) focuses on lack of opportunities in the homes of some students, such as limited exposure to books, limited opportunities for language enrichment, and families that may be nonliterate and that may have had few or no opportunities for education in their native countries. Other ELLs come from groups with no written form of language. She believes that staff must consider the impact of such experiences on children and provide them with opportunities to learn through instruction in "relevant and comprehensible contexts" (p. 165). Although what Roseberry-McKibbin (1995) states here is not true of all ELLs, she is correct in saying that when students come from such backgrounds, it must be recognized and dealt with appropriately in mainstream contexts. Finally, Freeman and Freeman (2002) highlight the inadequate education that many older students experienced from abroad with the consequent lack of opportunity they had to develop high levels of native-language and English literacy and to achieve academically.

Investigating Opportunity to Learn by Examining the Life, Language Development, and Educational History of ELLs

The screening process for incoming ELLs varies considerably from school to school. Its discussion in the literature has been grouped under the following six themes.

Overall Processes   One theme is the concept of a comprehensive process for screening and assessing ELLs. Burnette (2000, p. 1) proposes "conducting a tailored, appropriate assessment of the child and the environment" in which "non-biased, appropriate instruments should be combined with other sources of information (observations, interviews) from a variety of environments (school, home, community) to produce a multidimensional assessment." This assessment should comprise both formal (i.e., standardized) testing and informal (e.g., interviews, observations) testing, administered in a number of environments (e.g., home, community).

Roseberry-McKibbin (1995) recommends a case-history approach involving input from parents and a large team of professionals. Members of the team would examine the student's linguistic proficiencies in the native language and in English, including literacy skills and the child's background. Background information is especially important if a referral for special education testing becomes necessary. In addition, "nonstandardized assessment procedures" should be conducted to "provide information about the child's ability to function effectively in the instructional environment and in various social situations" (p. xx).

Scribner (2002) lays out a process that includes prereferral and referral documentation (e.g., background and educational history, assessment of literacy skills, quality of instruction, clinical observation), oral language and literacy proficiency in native language and English, and the level of acculturation of students and their families.

Freeman and Freeman (2002) emphasize examining the types and quality of education that new arrivals have had abroad and whether it is adequate or inadequate. For LTELs, they look mainly at the student's current level of functioning and educational history in the United States. For both groups, they find it important to gather life history information and information on attitudes toward education and themselves as learners.

Life History   In terms of life history or general background, several categories of information are mentioned: information from a variety of environments such as the home, school, and community (Burnette, 2000; USDE, 2004); how long the student has been in the United States and general background, and educational history (Roseberry-McKibbin, 1995; Scribner, 2002); where the child was born and educated, age, and education history in the United States and abroad (Freeman & Freeman, 2002; Chamot, 2000); home environment and parent information (Freeman & Freeman, 2002; Roseberry-McKibbin, 1995; USDE, 2004); school records (Allen, 2002; Freeman & Freeman, 2002); medical history (Allen, 2002); language and cultural background (Burnette, 2000; Roseberry-McKibbin, 1995; Scribner, 2002; Wilson-Portuondo & Hardy, 2001); and attitudes toward school and the United States (Chamot, 2000; Freeman & Freeman, 2002).

Language Development   All agreed that information was needed on the use of, and proficiency in, the native language and English and on language interaction patterns between parents and children. All agreed on the necessity of measuring language proficiency, in the native language and English, with respect to oral language skills, reading, writing, and the use of academic language (Allen, 2002; Burnette, 2000; Freeman & Freeman, 2002;

Gopaul-McNichol & Thomas-Presswood, 1998; Roseberry-McKibbin, 1995; Scribner, 2002; USDE, 2004). The need for making the distinction between conversational language and academic language is well documented in the writings of Cummins (1979, 1981b).

Most concurred that proficiency information in both languages is needed for placement and instructional planning but also to detect whether a student's language difficulties appear in both languages rather than just in English. This is considered a key factor in determining whether or not a language disability can be ruled out.

Education and Academic Background Most of the authors felt that information was necessary regarding content-area study and students' understanding of academic concepts. The latter went hand in hand with proficiency in the use of academic language. Scribner (2002, p. 1487) feels that it is important that students be able to draw inferences, make evaluations, and analyze information "with native like fluency." Freeman and Freeman (2002) feel that it is important to determine whether long-term English learners understand pre-academic and academic concepts. A related category was the quantity and quality of instruction received by students (Burnette, 2000), whether abroad or in the United States.

Parental Background and Roles Information on the educational background of parents, on their role in the education of their children, and on their relationships with their children was considered important by all the researchers and writers surveyed. Of particular interest was the involvement of parents in the assessment of children experiencing achievement difficulties (Allen, 2002; Burnette, 2000; Freeman & Freeman, 2002; Roseberry-McKibbin, 1995).

Others saw great value in parents as sources of information about children at home and with respect to language usage and behavior (Burnette, 2000; Freeman & Freeman, 2002; Roseberry-McKibbin, 1995). For Burnette (2000, p. 2), "parents can provide information that forms a framework for understanding the information about the student, and the parents' perspective can be invaluable for accurately interpreting data as well as for subsequent planning and instruction."

Burnette (2000) and Roseberry-McKibbin (1995) seek to explain ways to involve linguistically and culturally diverse parents. Burnette (2000) says that such parents may not be aware of the school's expectations of them and their part in the process and perhaps might experience frustration due to linguistic and cultural differences or might not have the time to participate.

Roseberry-McKibbin (1995) says that parents must understand the purpose of interviews with school personnel and of the questions being asked and that some might feel that the questions are too personal and therefore inappropriate. Developing rapport with parents, making them feel comfortable, and avoiding their being overwhelmed by meeting with a large team of school professional were also matters of concern. The National Symposium on Learning Disabilities in English Language Learners (USDE, 2004) is concerned with parents' access to information about their child's academic progress whereas Gopaul-McNichol & Thomas-Presswood (1998) see a need to know about the literacy level of the parents.

Culture and Acculturation The need for information on acculturation, "the change that can occur as a result of continuous contact between two distinct cultures" (Scribner, 2002, p. 1487), was indicated by several authors. In practical terms, acculturation refers to the degree to which immigrants identify with the new society they have entered. Some assimilate (i.e., identify highly) whereas others integrate by involving themselves in the new culture while retaining their traditional culture. Others separate themselves from the dominant culture. Acculturation, therefore, depends on "the importance new arrivals place on maintaining cultural characteristics of their ethnic groups" and on "the importance they attribute to maintaining positive relationships with the larger society and other ethnic groups (Scribner, 2002, p. 1487)." One reason for gathering information on culture and acculturation is to determine whether any students may be experiencing achievement difficulties or failure because of acculturative stress such as adjustment problems and feelings of isolation and loss (Scribner, 2002).

Freeman & Freeman (2002) are concerned about this phenomenon and how it affects student achievement, especially in the case of long-term English learners who continue to experience achievement difficulties. Drawing on the work of John Ogbu, they consider the difference between immigrant minorities who are recent arrivals, retain their traditional values, discount poor treatment and believe that education will lead to success and involuntary minorities. The latter have lived in the United States for many years, view themselves as placed in a low social status, place a low value on education, do not see education as leading to improvement of life conditions, and see few examples of success because those that do succeed move away. One result of these attitudes is school failure.

Cummins's (1979b) analysis of sociocultural determinants of school achievement is also instructive. He proposes that socioeconomic status (SES) and acculturation could not entirely account for school failure or success. Rather, he contends that "an examination of the sociocultural characteristics of minority groups that tend to perform poorly in L2-only school situations suggests that the attitudes of these groups toward their own identity may be an important factor in interaction with educational treatment" (p. 35).

Freeman & Freeman (2002) propose that teachers need to help students, such as long-term English learners, who fail because of sociocultural factors by helping them learn to value school and begin to see themselves as learners.

Summary

The current research reviewed in this second section clearly indicates attention and concern about several issues regarding ELLs, namely, the overrepresentation of ELLs in special education due to misdiagnosis, the achievement difficulties of many ELLs, the need to distinguish between a lack of opportunity to learn and a disability, the need for an assessment process that includes a student's life and educational history, language development, educational and academic background, parental background and roles, cultural background, and acculturation. However, the same research also pinpoints other important dimensions not mentioned or emphasized in the first section that practitioners need to be aware of.

One of these is that some students in special education classes have difficulties that are pedagogically induced. Arguably, this can occur when an ELL with achievement difficulties attributable to lack of opportunity is misdiagnosed as having a disability and is placed in special education classes. This, of course, underscores the importance of assessing ELLs appropriately by staff well acquainted with the special factors discussed in the first section.

Other observations of researchers and writers include placement of ELLs in lower-track classrooms and the disadvantages of this practice; the harmful effects caused by assuming that ELLs fluent in oral English are also proficient in reading and in academic language when they are not; early exit from bilingual education and ESL programs before English literacy and academic-language proficiency are solidly developed; the need for ELLs to function effectively in educational and social environments; acculturation stress; the attitudes of ELLs toward their own identities and toward themselves as learners; and the beneficial role that parents can play in interpreting assessment data about their children and in planning for their instruction. Although this is not the place to enter into an in-depth discussion of these issues, the research surveyed in the second section of this chapter does suggest that staff responsible for providing instruction and for assessing ELLs and their administrators are well advised to prepare themselves through training, research, and study to serve this growing population in American schools effectively if they have not already done so.

In the last analysis, the test of effectiveness for the education of any student is whether that student is progressing, learning, and experiencing success at an acceptable rate. If not, then all elements involved in the educational process need to be considered: the student and her or his background, the current educational and assessment programs, and the staff serving the student. The purpose of this chapter has been to provide some guidance for those faced with the challenging task of helping ELLs with learning difficulties.

Notes

1. An earlier version of this article originally appeared in *ConnTESOL Newsletter,* Summer, 2001.
2. The distinction between *knowledge that* and *knowledge how to* is found in Cazden (1971).
3. See Table 15.1 for summary of all questions used in interviewing callers from school districts.
4. Sheltered instruction, or sheltered content-area instruction, refers to "an approach for teaching content to ELLs in strategic ways that make the subject matter concepts comprehensible while promoting the students' English language development" (Short, 2000, p. 17). For more information on *comprehensible input* and its implications for teaching and learning language and subject-matter instruction, see Krashen (1981). These terms are used frequently in this chapter. It is highly recommended that professional development in sheltered instruction be provided for English-speaking classroom teachers with ELLs.

References

Allen, R. (2002, Fall). Schools seek ways to strengthen language learning. *ASCD Curriculum Update,*1–2, 6–8.

Artiles, A. J., & Ortiz, A. A. (2002). *English language learners with special education needs: Identification, assessment, and instruction.* Washington, DC: Center for Applied Linguistics and Delta Systems Co.

Burnette, J. (2000). *Assessment of culturally and linguistically diverse students for special education eligibility.* Arlington, VA: Council for Exceptional Children. ERIC/OSEP Digest #E604.

Cazden, C. B. (1971). Evaluation of learning in preschool education: Early language development. In B. S. Bloom, J. T. Hastings, & G. F. Madaus (Eds.), *Handbook on formative and summative evaluation of student learning* (pp. 345–398). New York: McGraw-Hill.

Chamot, A. U. (2000). Literacy characteristics of Hispanic adolescent immigrants with limited prior education. In *Proceedings of a research symposium on high standards in reading for students from diverse language groups: Research, practice & policy* (pp. 188–199). Washington, DC: U.S. Department of Education.

Cloud, N. (1994). Special education needs of second language children. In F. Genesee (Ed.), *Educating second language children: The whole child, the whole curriculum, the whole community* (pp. 243–277). New York: Cambridge University Press.

Collier, V. P. (1989). How long? A synthesis of research on academic achievement in a second language. *TESOL Quarterly, 23,* 509–531.

Cummins, J. (1979). Cognitive/academic language proficiency, linguistic interdependence, the optimum age questions and other matters. *Working Papers on Bilingualism, 19,* 121–129.

Cummins, J. (1981a). Age on arrival and immigrant second language learning in Canada: A reassessment. *Applied Linguistics, 2,* 131–149.

Cummins, J. (1981b). The role of primary language development in promoting educational success for language minority students. In California State Department of Education (Ed.), *Schooling and language minority students: A theoretical framework* (pp. 3–49). Los Angeles: Evaluation Dissemination and Assessment Center.

Cummins, J. (1984). *Bilingualism and special education.* San Diego: College Hill Press.

de George, G. (2001, Summer). Connecticut Teachers of English to Speakers of Other Languages. Is it language or is it special needs? *ConnTESOL Newsletter,* p. 1, 14–22.

Freeman, Y. S., & Freeman, D. E. (2002). *Closing the achievement gap: How to reach limited-formal-schooling and long-term English learners.* Portsmouth, NH: Heinemann.

Garcia, S. B., & Ortiz, A. A. (1988, June). Preventing inappropriate referrals of language minority students to special education. In *New Focus, The National Clearinghouse for Bilingual Education, (5).* Silver Spring, MD: National Clearinghouse for Bilingual Education.

Gopaul-McNichol, S., & Thomas-Presswood, T. (1998). *Working with linguistically and culturally different children: Innovative clinical and educational approaches.* Boston: Allyn & Bacon.

Hakuta, K. (1987). Degree of bilingualism in cognitive ability in mainland Puerto Rican children. *Child Development, 58*(5), 1372–1388.

Harris, P. R., & Moran, R. T. (1991). *Managing cultural differences* (3rd ed.). Houston: Gulf.

Hofstede, G. (1984). *Cultures consequences: International differences in work-related values.* Beverly Hills, CA: Sage.

Krashen, S. (1981). Bilingual education and second language acquisition theory. In California State Department of Education (Ed.), *Schooling and language minority students: A theoretical framework* (pp. 51–79). Los Angeles: Evaluation Dissemination and Assessment Center.

Language and Orientation Resource Center. (1981). *The peoples and cultures of Cambodia, Laos and Vietnam.* Washington, DC: Center for Applied Linguistics.

Laing, S. P., & Kamhi, A. (2003). Alternative assessment of language and literacy in culturally and linguistically diverse populations. *Language, Speech, and Hearing Services in Schools, 34,* 44–55.

Nine Curt, C. J. (1976). *Non-verbal communication in Puerto Rico.* Cambridge, MA: National Assessment and Dissemination Center (Lesley College).

Ogbu, J. Immigrant and involuntary minorities in comparative perspective. In M. Gibson & J. Ogbu (Eds.). *Minority status and schooling: A comparative study of immigrant and involuntary minorities.* New York: Garland Publishing.

Roseberry-McKibbin, C. (1995). *Multicultural students with special needs: Practical strategies for assessment and intervention.* Oceanside, CA: Academic Communication Associates.

Scribner, A. P. (2002). Best assessment and intervention practices with second language learners. In A. Thomas & J. Grimes (Eds.), *Best practices in school psychology* (vol. 4) (pp. 1485–1494). Washington, DC: National Association of School Psychologists.

Short, D. J. (2000). What principals should know about sheltered instruction for English language learners. *National Association of Secondary School Principals Bulletin, 84*(619), 17–27.

Thomas, W. P., & Collier, V. P. (1995). Language minority student achievement and program effectiveness: Research summary of ongoing study, results as of September 1995. Handout presented at National Association for Bilingual Education Conference.

Thomas, W. P., & Collier, V. P. (1997). *School effectiveness for language minority students.* Washington, D.C.: National Clearinghouse for Bilingual Education.

Thuy, V. G. (1976). Getting to know the Vietnamese and their culture. New York: Frederick Ungar.

U.S. Department of Education, Office for Civil Rights. (2000). *Elementary and secondary school civil rights compliance report.* Washington, DC: Author.

U.S. Department of Education (USDE), Office of English Language Acquisition, Language Enhancement and Academic Achievement of Limited English Proficient Students. (2003). *Descriptive study of services to LEP students and LEP students with disabilities.* Washington, DC: Author.

U.S. Department of Education (USDE), Office of Special Education and Rehabilitative Services, Office of the Assistant Secretary. (2004). National Symposium on Learning Disabilities in English Language Learners, October 14–15, 2005: Symposium Summary. Washington, DC: Author.

Utley, C. A., & Obiakor, F. E. (2001). Multicultural education and special education: Infusion for better schooling. In C. A. Utley & F. E. Obiakor (Eds.), *Special education, multicultural education, and school reform: Components of quality education for learners with mild disabilities.* Springfield, IL: Charles C. Thomas.

Warger, C., & Burnette, J. (2000). *Five strategies to reduce overrepresentation of culturally and linguistically diverse students in special education.* Arlington, VA: Council for Exceptional Children. ERIC/OSEP Digest # E596.

Wilson-Portuondo, M. L., & Hardy, P. R. (2001, January). When is a language difficulty a disability? The assessment and evaluation process of English language learners. Paper presented at the conference of the Massachusetts Association for Teachers of Speakers of Other Languages (MATSOL), Chestnut Hill, MA, (January 12, 2001).

CHAPTER 16

Meeting the Needs of ELLs: Acknowledging the Schism Between ESL/Bilingual and Mainstream Teachers and Illustrating That Problem's Remedy[1]

EDMUND T. HAMANN

Introduction

Nationwide, education researchers, policy makers, and school reformers agree that the education of English language learners (ELLs) is an increasingly important issue as (1) more students in more districts fit in that category (Ruiz-de-Velasco, 2005; Suárez-Orozco & Suárez-Orozco, 1999; Wortham, Murillo & Hamann, 2002); as (2) they, in aggregate, continue to fare less well than most other student populations (August & Hakuta, 1997; Callahan & Gándara, 2004; NCES, 1997); and as (3) policy compliance with the No Child Left Behind Act holds their schools accountable for their cumulative average yearly progress (Abedi, 2005; Crawford, 2004). There is also an emerging understanding that the education of ELLs should be a concern of all educators (Miramontes, Nadeau, Commins & Garcia, 1997), not just a specialized and often marginalized segment of the staff (Grey, 1991). That issue—whether ELL education is viewed as a shared task among all educators, including school and district administration—is the focus of the two short case studies presented here.

This chapter considers my experiences in two school districts in two different regions of the United States. Although both districts were making substantial responses to ELLs when I last studied them, neither was an exemplar of responsiveness as measured by the academic performance of ELLs, nor did most teachers or administrators in either district see the education of ELLs as part of their own professional task. In my sketches of both cases, I seek to explain why the response was not more efficacious and to outline missed opportunities and next steps that would have increased the number of teachers willing to and capable of contributing to the success of ELLs.

I situate my analysis within the domains of policy implementation studies (McLaughlin, 1987) and ethnography (Erickson, 1984). Education researchers and school reformers acknowledge that it is human nature to make sense of new ideas and to learn new practices by reconciling them with what one already thinks and knows (Spillane, Reiser, & Reimer, 2002; Stritikus & Garcia, 2003). Thus, if we posit that ELLs are not regarded by all educators as part of their responsibility and if we ask how the learning and school success of ELLs can become the concern of all educators, we can see that we are outlining a learning task for many educators: to have them learn a new orientation towards the task of educating ELLs as well as to learn the specific skills and tactics to do so well. In turn, this sets up some important follow-up questions: How will those not currently much concerned with educating ELLs react to this charge? How will those who currently work primarily with ELLs react to this support or potential intrusion? Strategically, what needs to happen to get educators who currently have different responsibilities for and experiences with ELLs to align their efforts so that ELLs are most effectively supported? This chapter speaks to these issues.

Some Demographic Reminders

In October 2002, the National Clearinghouse for English Language Acquisition (NCELA) estimated that there were 3,908,095 limited-English-proficient students attending U.S. public schools (excluding Puerto Rico and other outlying jurisdictions) of whom 1,146,154 were attending grades 7–12 in U.S. public schools.[2] This tally represented 10.5% of all elementary enrollment and 5.6% of all public secondary enrollment (Kindler, 2002). Despite their large numbers, ELLs at the secondary level are not served as well by their school experience as are other student populations (NWREL, 2004)—as measured by secondary school completion rates (August & Hakuta, 1997; NCES, 1997), participation in advanced classes (Cadeiro-Kaplan, 2004; Harklau, 1994a, 1994b), or postsecondary educational pursuits (Callahan & Gándara, 2004; Harklau, Losey, & Seigal, 1999). Nor are ELLs necessarily served well at the primary level, as measured by achievement and by the long-term persistence of many learners in special programs for identified ELLs, even though these programs are ostensibly designed to exit ELLs into the mainstream (Gándara, Rumberger, Maxwell-Jolly, & Callahan, 2003).

Important explanations for this problem can be found in national survey data that discovered that 11.7% of identified ELLs receive no special support services—despite laws requiring service—and that 36.4% receive only some services. However, 86.2% of surveyed ELL services coordinators indicated that the general curriculum materials provided to teachers were aligned with state standards, but only 56.7% felt that materials specifically designed for use with ELLs were aligned with standards (Zehler, Fleischman, Hopstock, Stephenson, Pendzick, & Sapru 2003, pp. ix–x). This same survey found that the number of teachers who have identified ELLs in their classes is rapidly increasing, with almost 43% of all teachers having at least one in their class, three and half times as many as in 1991–92. Of these 1.27 million teachers, 23.2% had bilingual, English as a second language (ESL), or other ELL-related certification, and 5.6% had a master's or doctorate in a relevant field, but 9.8% were working with just provisional certifications. Also, 39.9% reported having had no in-service development related to ELLs in the last five years, and an additional 20.8% of teachers reported less than 10 total hours of in-service related to ELLs in that period. Schools with more than 30 identified ELLs had higher percentages of new teachers than did schools with less than 30. Middle school and high school teachers of identified ELLs were substantially less likely to have had significant training for working with ELLs than their elementary colleagues (Zehler, et al., 2003, pp. 69–73).

In other words, in many parts of the United States, ELLs attend schools where there is an insufficient supply of trained and qualified educators for them. And even if there are a number of qualified teachers, this does not mean that the curriculum is most appropriate or that the trained teachers have latitude to pursue all of the practices that, per their training, they are supposed to draw on when they work with ELLs (Hamann, 2003; Stritikus & Garcia, 2003). Nor is it the case that extensive-service or standards-aligned programs for ELLs automatically work well. Still, there is a substantial body of research showing that ELLs can do well at school (e.g., Ernst, Statzner, & Trueba, 1994; Lucas, 1997; Lucas, Henze, & Donato, 1990; Mehan, Villanueva, Hubbard, & Lintz, 1996; Pugach, 1998; Romo & Falbo, 1996; Walqui, 2000), and some emerging research highlights the overlap between some change strategies currently being targeted at mainstream teachers—for example, a focus on adolescent literacy development across the content areas—and those practices that work particularly well with ELLs (Meltzer & Hamann, 2004, 2005). The current relative lack of success of ELLs illustrates that key educators have lacked needed information and skills to serve ELLs well, that they have lacked the will to serve ELLs as well as other students, or that the current arrangement of most school systems inhibits the prospects of many ELLs.

The Cases

The two cases presented here both illustrate responses to ELLs, but responses that were incomplete; responses where many teachers and administrators were neither trained nor oriented toward assuring that ELLs perform well. In both cases, the response to ELLs was precipitated by the requirements that emerged from the 1974 *Lau v. Nichols* U.S. Supreme Court decision. That decision, however, was not relevant to the first district described until 1989 when changes in local employment patterns first brought identified ELLs into the schools. *Lau v. Nichols* defined identified ELLs as a special population requiring specific modification of the regular educational program. As with special education students, identified ELLs were a don't fit population (Deschenes, Cuban, & Tyack, 2001)—that is, a population for whom the regular program was deemed inadequate—and special staff were recruited and hired to take the lead on their education.

The first case comes from a large town with a manufacturing dominated economy in the U.S. South, a part of the United States that historically has not been a major destination for newcomers. But that tradition changed dramatically in the last two decades, as changes in hiring practices at local factories precipitated the arrival of more than a thousand Mexican immigrant families—and a handful of families from other non-U.S. locations. The second case comes from a medium-sized city in the Rustbelt that has newcomers from all over the world, although four fifths are native Spanish speakers, a change from that city's previous patterns of immigration.

A Dramatic Response with Incomplete Leadership—A Large-Town District

Since its creation in the late 1800s as a town school district carved from a then-rural county district that surrounded it, the large-town district was better funded and more successful—in terms of student achievement outcomes—than any other district in its region. This Southern district served the children of local professionals and business executives as well as the Anglo working class that labored in the mills. Corporate paternalism, in terms of scholarships and donations, complemented the generous tax base and set a tone for the district to focus on the substantial college-bound portion of its enrollment. Working-class students who were not in college-preparatory tracks were not as well attended to. Indeed, in the 1980s, in an effort to stem the high dropout rate of working-class students, the district and several large local employers signed an agreement to stop employing during school hours youth (i.e., dropouts) who had not finished high school. At that time, the district's pay to teachers exceeded the average of nearby districts, and multiple top-notch applicants usually competed for every opening.

Just as the dropout accord went into effect, a large immigrant influx began. In 1990 the district hosted less than 200 Latino students (in this case, *Latino*, *ELL*, and *immigrant* were substantially overlapping categories); by the year 2000, Latino enrollment had surpassed 2,500, forming the majority of enrollment, a status that had been accelerated by a net decline in white enrollment. Teachers who had been hired to work with one kind of student (i.e., a largely Anglo middle class) and who had done so effectively found themselves during the 1990s increasingly expected to serve a different enrollment (i.e., Mexican newcomers). They had not been prepared for this latter task, and many were resistant to it (Keyes, 1999).

A local civic leader, however, was not resistant, although he was as underprepared as any of the teachers. Inspired by the complaint of his daughter, who said that teachers and students could not communicate at the suddenly majority ELL elementary school where she was a paraprofessional, in 1996 this leader led a grassroots response to his community's demographic transition. He successfully goaded local business leaders and a new superintendent to help form a partnership with a university in Mexico. The tie to Mexico built on a partnership between a local company and an industrial conglomerate in Mexico. The leader of that Mexican conglomerate, in turn, had ties to the Mexican university.

The new partnership had multiple components. These included plans to (1) train U.S. teachers in summer courses hosted at the Mexican university; (2) write a bilingual version of the state-approved curriculum; (3) have bilingual teachers from Mexico serve year-long terms in the large town's schools; and (4) have Mexican partnership leaders engage in community research initiatives. In short, the district was poised to be exceptionally responsive to its ELLs.

One of the district's elementary school principals provided crucial support for what from the very beginning was an unorthodox collaboration. She had just written a dissertation about the professional development needs of schools experiencing growth in their ELL enrollment, so she endorsed the proposed curricular changes, the recruiting of qualified staff from Mexico, and the idea of local educators taking summer courses there. The first year of the summer training in Mexico, she and her assistant principal led a delegation of 10 educators from her building. Most of these teachers were not in the district's formal ESL program. The district's remaining seven schools—some as impacted as the principal's— sent seven teachers combined, an average of one per school. When visiting instructors came from Mexico, the principal had her building host four of them. Per the proportion of enrolled ELLs and the interest of other principals, the remaining nine visiting instructors were divided at the other seven schools. In short, one of the eight principals demonstrated the kind of mobilization that was possible to respond to the new presence of ELLs, and her school was later recognized as an exemplary Title I school. But the district-wide response was more measured.

When the first group of 17 American teachers returned from their training in Mexico that first summer of the project, they were greeted by TV and newspaper reporters, and the story of their experiences dominated local news. Although all 17 were eligible for the district to reimburse their incidental expenses from their four weeks away, only three applied. Sharing the sentiments of several, one of those not seeking reimbursement explained that she had been so favorably overwhelmed by the district's willingness to invest in the most amazing professional development experience of her life—an investment of nearly $5,000—that it seemed petty to seek compensation of her investment of $200 or so.

On return, most of the summer institute veterans indicated that they expected to continue convening as a group and that they expected to share their experiences and learnings with colleagues. But no such formal follow-up experience was ever organized. Enrollment of educators for the second summer of training in Mexico declined by half, even though three veterans of the first experience repeated. When the superintendent told me he wished he could learn what his teachers were learning—he was monolingual, had never received training for working with ELLs, and had never taught in or presided over a district with a significant ELL population—I asked him why he did not participate in the summer training himself. He demurred, saying he did not think his board would want him to take that much time away from the district. In accordance with the local business community's support for the binational project, he had gone along with some unusual and intriguing programs, but he was not sufficiently convinced by them that he needed to be a learner to participate directly. As such, he missed a chance to know better how to lead his part of the binational project.

Other components of the project slowly withered or never got off the ground. A two-year effort by the Mexican university at bilingual curriculum development was ultimately rejected without even pilot implementation. Efforts to coordinate with the district's ESL teachers never amounted to much; at a large business-sponsored event that was supposed to celebrate the project's early successes, the district's ESL coordinator made a 20-minute presentation that scarcely mentioned the novel binational collaboration, setting the collaboration up as a rival rather than aligned effort. The number of visiting instructors from Mexico was capped, and then, after four years, the program was ended when under a new superintendent the district determined it was not willing to provide transportation or housing or other supports that distinguished the trained teachers from Mexico's compensation from that of local paraprofessionals.[3] There were a few more years of shortened summer trainings in Mexico—shortened from a month abroad to two weeks—but district participation declined, even as neighboring districts started to participate.

When last I checked, the district's scores on state tests and the SATs had declined, and the Latino dropout rate remained high. On the state's 11th-grade-administered exit exam, in 2003–04 the town district underperformed state averages in all four content areas—English language arts, mathematics, social science, and science—for all students, Hispanic students, and identified ELLs. The Hispanic failure in each subject ranged from 18 to 62%, whereas the ELL failure rate spanned from 33 to 88%—although, per Abedi (2005), even my limited use of comparing district ELL scores to state ELL scores on an exam offered in English is probably scientifically inadequate in that the validity of such an assessment is absent for showing what an ELL knows.

Some ELLs in the district were succeeding, but not in the proportion as other populations the district served. As it ended its participation in the binational collaboration, the district created a multiage newcomer school that enrolled ELL newcomer students for up to a year before turning them over to the ESL programs at the regular schools. Though commenting on the efficacy of newcomer schools can introduce a debate that would be tangential to purposes of this piece, it does not seem controversial to claim that the creation of newcomer programs is consistent with a logic that ELLs should be the concern of a specially trained small proportion of educators rather than of all educational personnel. Many teachers and administrators still did not see meeting the needs of ELLs as their major charge, even as the language background of enrollees had changed, with the majority of students now coming from Spanish-speaking households. In short, the majority of teachers were not conceptualizing that the majority of the district's enrollment was a main responsibility of theirs. And district leadership, including board leadership, was not challenging this presumption.

Separate Systems—An Urban District

This profile is based on my reflections from a formative evaluation I helped conduct of an urban school district's response to ELLs. At the time I was involved in the evaluation, approximately two thirds of the district's enrollment came from households where English was not the first language. Roughly, that ELL population divided into 5,000 identified ELLs and 10,000 who had exited programs for ELLs or who were deemed sufficiently English proficient to never have been placed in the district's ESL or transitional bilingual education (TBE) program.

Measured on separate rubrics, both ELL groups were not achieving well. The population of 10,000 unsupported ELLs (i.e., ELLs in the mainstream) was faring dismally. On tests aligned with the state standards, adding together *exceeds standard, meets standard,* and *almost meets standard,* in none of the categories were more than 15% successful. Phrased another way, at least 85% of 10,000 students were not even almost meeting standards in any category. In the various tested categories, native-English-speaking students from the district were two to three times likelier to almost meet, meet, or exceed standards—not a high success rate, but one well ahead of their nonnative-English-speaking peers.

Looking at identified ELLs who were in supported programs and measuring success by progress toward the exit criteria of those programs, half were deemed to be making adequate yearly progress toward their exit from the special language support program. That figure, however, obscured a wide discrepancy in performance: In some classrooms all students were deemed to be making progress, and in others none were. Moreover, it is useful to juxtapose the in-program success rate (50% adequately progressing) and the success rate of those out of the program on standards-aligned tests (15% almost meeting, meeting, or exceeding standards). This juxtaposition suggests that the criteria for success within the ESL and TBE programs were not aligned with state standards; if they had been, the success of ELLs in the mainstream should have matched that of the whole student population.

According to the district's written policy, all students who were not native speakers of English were to be subjects of a special ELL support framework, which, because the district had more nonnative than native speakers of English, sets up the irony of there being a special support program that targeted the majority of enrollment. But in practice the framework was only used in the ESL and TBE classrooms for identified ELLs. In a survey of all teachers in the district, teachers overwhelmingly indicated that they felt the framework and the responsibility of supporting ELLs were the responsibilities of the ESL and bilingual teachers. On the same survey, many non-ESL and nonbilingual teachers indicated a frustration that students exited from the ESL and TBE program were not ready for mainstream work.

More generally, there was a fracture in this district between ESL and bilingual teachers and mainstream ones that was a source of problems at the time of the evaluation and that had pertinent historic antecedents. Within the larger structure of the district, there was a subunit—the language and culture division (LCD)—that was semiautonomous from the larger district. All of the ESL and bilingual teachers were within LCD, and LCD had the charge of implementing the ESL and bilingual framework. LCD took lead responsibility for the 5,000+ identified ELL students who were receiving support services and kept data on these students' progress in regards to the framework. It did not claim responsibility for non-native-English speakers in the mainstream, although the previously referenced framework included such students in its stated purview. LCD also kept different data sets than those of the district writ large. LCD's data sets included all students who received language support during the academic year, whereas the larger district's ELL tally, like its other statistics, were a point-in-time count (on October 1), so even the official counts of supported ELLs in the district varied depending on data source.

As I wrote in the evaluation,

> From the beginning and throughout this evaluation, we have repeatedly been struck by the division between the programs/structures we were charged to evaluate (ESL/Bilingual and [LCD]) and the larger programs and structures that these endeavors and structures were to fit within (i.e., mainstream education and the whole Central Office). Before data collection began, we were told by the now former director of [LCD] that once a student exited the ESL/Bilingual Education program they were not her responsibility anymore; their proficiency in English had been empirically demonstrated and they were ready for whatever 'mainstream' teachers had to offer. When we tried to collect information about how exited students fared, we realized that data on ESL/Bilingual Education students were kept separately from data on all students in the district so that cross-referencing district-held performance indicators with in-program or exited status was nearly impossible.

Clearly the split between LCD and the rest of the district was partially a product of personality clashes, but it also was a result of the history of LCD's creation and of the pro-ELL stance of the educators within it, which varied from many regular program teachers. LCD was created shortly after the 1974 *Lau v. Nichols* decision. At that time the number and proportion of ELLs qualifying for services and the number of students from non-English backgrounds who were in the regular program were both much smaller, and many teachers still saw themselves as primarily teaching to a native (i.e., white) working and middle class, a population that steadily diminished thereafter. ELLs were a marginal population and not the concern of most teachers, so, as Grey (1991) found in a Kansas study, those who specialized in working with ELLs were also regarded as marginal and peripheral by many in the regular program.

At that time, many schools did not enroll enough ELLs to merit a full-time ESL or TBE teacher. So the ESL or TBE teacher at these schools was itinerant, responsible for multiple schools, and not positioned to feel much connected to the stable staff. Even as ELL enrollments grew allowing a full-time ESL or TBE teacher and then multiple full-time ESL/TBE teachers to work in a given building, such teachers still did not connect much with the rest of the staff, or vice versa. ESL and TBE classes tended to be sorted by English proficiency as a first criterion, so, unlike most regular program teachers, ESL and TBE teachers often had multigrade classrooms. Because the ESL and TBE teachers' tasks and challenges differed from regular program teachers, because ESL and TBE teachers went to the same in-services with each other, and because they shared a commitment to a group of students that were not a main focus of their non-ESL and TBE colleagues, the ESL/TBE teachers found camaraderie with each other, which established them as a group within a group.

LCD, in many ways, functioned as a parallel structure to the rest of the district, almost as a minidistrict within a larger one, organizing its own data collection, professional development, and professional support networks. Perhaps as a legacy of nonresponsiveness by teachers in the regular program, ESL and bilingual education teachers were accustomed to bypassing traditional routes of support (e.g., the literacy coach, the principal) and dealing directly instead with ESL and TBE administrators in the district's central office. During school visits that were part of our evaluation, ESL and TBE teachers and regular program teachers we talked to both said that many regular program teachers did not understand the curriculum framework for ELLs and did not know the identified ELLs in their schools. Similarly, many regular program teachers reported not knowing which of their students had exited out of previous ESL and TBE placements.

Unfortunately, all of these dynamics preserved the noncollaboration between ESL and TBE teachers and those in regular education, and they left uninterrupted the hazards of incomplete alignment between the ESL and TBE curriculum and that of the regular program. As I wrote in the evaluation, "This separation needs to be remedied, but that remedying cannot mean the unwitting suppression of the skills and capacities that LCD has steadily assembled. The remedying of the separation needs to instead emphasize the pertinence of the skills of some ESL and Bilingual educators to challenges faced by nearly all of their peers." That is the part needed to be reconnected to the whole but not as an act of unilineal assimilation; there were good reasons for the skepticism of LCD-affiliated teachers toward the district's regular program, and there was expertise for working with ELLs that needed to be preserved and expanded on rather than ignored in a re-merger.

Considering the Two Cases

The nature of an analysis of two unsuccessful cases, or of cases that highlight what did not quite happen and what was not quite realized, is that a researcher can say this factor existed, and it appeared to be associated with what went wrong. It is more speculative to ask, what are all of the necessary ingredients to have changed the cases, to have made those districts sources of successful rather than cautionary accounts? We return then to the questions outlined at the beginning of this chapter: How will those not currently much concerned with educating ELLs react to the charge of becoming educators of ELLs too? How will those who currently work primarily with ELLs react to this support/potential intrusion by other teachers? And, strategically what needs to happen to get educators who currently have different responsibilities for and experiences with ELLs to align their efforts so that ELLs are most effectively supported? The cases illustrate more about missteps and missed opportunities than about all that should have been pursued.

Ironically, in both districts there was evidence that the majority of teachers (i.e., those teachers who were not part of the ESL or bilingual programs) did not see themselves as educators of the majority of students. That is, they did not see themselves as educators of ELLs—though ELLs formed the majority of enrollment—and did not see a need to be trained in the areas of second-language acquisition, content-area instruction in a second language, and the like. Nor did their leaders, with the exception of a rare principal, see a need to compel, enable, endorse, or prioritize that their teachers acquire such skill sets and orientations. In the meantime, at least based on outcomes on standards-aligned tests, identified and mainstream ELLs were faring shockingly poorly.

Yet perhaps reflecting a frustration or skepticism because of their historic marginalization by their peers, credentialed teachers who worked with identified ELLs hardly seemed enthusiastic about collaborating with their mainstream colleagues or supporting those colleagues' efforts. An unfortunate habit of distrust was in play that meant, in the first case, staying aloof from a dramatic but ultimately ephemeral binational collaboration and, in the second, keeping separate data sets and not advocating for the broader implementation of the ELL support framework outside of ESL and TBE.

Thus, this chapter's case evidence in relation to the first two questions was that there was little likelihood that mainstream teachers would see ELLs as appropriately within their charge. There was also little evidence that special program teachers wanted much to do with the mainstream teachers. Yet neither of these postures is inevitable; thus, both are interruptable, though perhaps only with difficulty. Leadership, if provided, can compel different and better outcomes for ELLs. In a crucial comparative study of 11 districts that saw substantial growth in their ELL populations between 1980 and 1990, Dentler and Hafner (1997) noted that the three districts that saw their standardized test scores rise during that period all were led by administrators with expertise on ELL-support issues.

Dentler and Hafner's (1997) study did not find that intensive professional development, per se, helped districts succeed in the face of changing enrollments. The three improved districts had intensive professional development, but so too did the five they studied that lost ground; 3 of their 11 districts neither improved nor declined. As one key, in the successful districts the intensive professional development was purposeful and coherent rather than scattershot. Because the mainstream leadership of the districts was advocating for responsiveness, there were also some core climatic differences between Dentler and Hafner's successful districts and the two that I have just described. We can imagine how the two cases just shared might have differed if:

- Large portions of the faculty could not claim that ELL education was not their task too.
- Those with special training and credentials for working with ELLs saw their work institutionally valued and embraced, so they were not guided by a learned skepticism and skittishness in their relations with administrators and nonspecialist colleagues.
- There was less of a gap to breach between ESL programs and regular programs, which meant better coordination and alignment and less of a transition to negotiate for ELLs exiting Lau-required programs.
- Teacher hiring was both more purposeful in terms of the sought-after skill sets and more competent—in that those doing the hiring knew what the appropriate skill sets to be ELL responsive would look like.

There are good teachers who work well with ELLs in almost any district, and there were in the two districts featured here. But the districts that are more successful with ELLs are systemically competent—professional development is consistent, purposeful, and ELL focused. Cooperative communication between those in ELL-focused programs and the mainstream is prioritized and cultivated. District managers know why, vis-à-vis the education of ELLs, they are doing what they are doing (Schecter & Cummins, 2003).

In both districts profiled here the number of ELLs was rapidly growing. However, in both districts there had been few identified ELLs until relatively recently, so there had been little impetus to recruit staff trained in ELL-responsive pedagogies or to retrain many existing staff to work effectively with ELLs. As the districts began their response to the presence of ELLs, or, as accurately, as the districts began their compliance with federal requirements that they make special accommodation to students who did not speak and read English well enough to succeed academically in an unsupported classroom, ELLs were viewed as a minor population. Mainstream educators could be professionally successful without attending much to ELLs. These habits and orientations persisted even as they were no longer as apt.

In both districts the first direct attempts—beyond hiring paraprofessional interpreters—to meet the needs of ELLs were to hire and train ESL or bilingual teachers. Initially these specialists worked with ELLs in multigrade settings, in multiple classrooms, often in multiple schools. The special population they worked with and their mobility made these teachers different from most of their colleagues. Mainstream and ESL and bilingual staff interacted little with each other and the much smaller group (i.e., the ESL and bilingual teachers) quickly became accustomed to providing collegial support to each other rather than trying to derive it from their less trained mainstream colleagues. Held together both by the common experiences of working with ELLs and being misunderstood and ignored by mainstream peers, the program staff formed an alternative culture, a system within the larger district.

In short, these two districts, like hundreds of others, have gone through three phases: (1) nonresponse, none needed; (2) nonresponse, but response needed; and (3) creation of a special program for an identified special population (i.e., ELLs). But these phases have never led all or most educators in both districts to see the education of ELLs as partially their task too; to see that the regular curriculum aligns with the curriculum that exited ELLs previously encountered in ESL/TBE; or to assure that professional development is consistent and coherent in regards to helping teachers understand how to meet the needs of ELLs. These districts needed to be led to a fourth phase, one in which the expectable challenges that logically emerged from the earlier phases were identified and addressed. Only in this leadership-involving, schism-mending fourth phase is the large-scale, long-term, and deserved success of most ELLs likely.

Notes

1. I want to thank Lorrie Verplaetse and Janelle Reeves for their thoughtful editing of earlier drafts of this chapter.
2. The word choice *limited English proficient* is intentional here. Although that term has been aptly identified as embedding a deficit label (i.e., defining students by what they do not know), it is the formal term used in the education law and policy that stem from the *Lau v. Nichols* (1974) Supreme Court decision. That formal embedding of a deficit orientation in federal jurisprudence should be noted. Here, *identified ELLs* refers to those receiving support per Lau-originating regulations, whereas the term *ELL* is slightly more inclusive than the *limited English proficient* or *identified ELLs* labels. As the General Accounting Office (2001) notes, there are ELLs who have been exited from ESL and bilingual education support systems that are still not as proficient in English for academic purposes as are native-English-speaking peers. *ELL* here refers to all students who are not native speakers of English and whose academic performance is impeded by not being fully proficient in English.
3. The Mexican teachers qualified for H1-B visas, a category reserved for skilled professionals in work categories with limited domestic supply. However, ironically, state education laws did not recognize Mexican credentials so the visiting teachers officially served as paraprofessionals. The payment of housing and transportation costs was an informal way to try to work around the limits created by the state law.

References

Abedi, J. (2005). Issues and consequences for English language learners. In J. L. Herman & E. H. Haertel (Eds.), *Uses and misuses of data for educational accountability and improvement: The 104th Yearbook of the National Society for the Study of Education*, Part 2 (pp. 175–198). Malden, MA: Blackwell.

August, D., & Hakuta, K. (Eds.). (1997). *Improving schooling for language minority school children: A research agenda*. Washington, DC: National Academy Press.

Cadeiro-Kaplan, K. (2004). *The literacy curriculum and bilingual education*. New York: Peter Lang.

Callahan, R. & Gándara, P. (2004). On nobody's agenda: Improving English-language learners' access to higher education. In M. Sadowski (Ed.), *Teaching immigrant and second language students: Strategies for success* (pp. 107–127). Cambridge, MA: Harvard Education Press.

Coady, M., Hamann, E. T., Harrington, M., Pacheco, M., Pho, S., & Yedlin, J. (2003). *Claiming opportunities: A handbook for improving education for English language learners through comprehensive school reform*. Providence, RI: Education Alliance at Brown University.

Crawford, J. (2004). No Child Left Behind: Misguided approach to school accountability for English language learners. Paper presented at the Center on Educational Policy's Forum on Ideas to Improve the NCLB Accountability Provisions for Students with Disabilities and English Language Learners, September 14, Washington, D.C. Available at: http://www.cep-dc.org/pubs/Forum14September2004/CrawfordPaper.pdf.

Dentler, R. A., & Hafner, A. L. (1997). *Hosting newcomers: Structuring educational opportunities for immigrant children*. New York: Teachers College Press.

Deschenes, S., Cuban, L., & Tyack, D. (2001). Mismatch: Historical perspectives on schools and students who don't fit them. *Teachers College Record, 103,* 525–547.

Erickson, F. (1984). What makes school ethnography "ethnographic"? *Anthropology & Education Quarterly, 15,* 51–66.

Ernst, G., Statzner, E., & Trueba, H. T. (Eds.). (1994). Theme issue: Alternative visions of schooling: Success stories in minority settings. *Anthropology and Educational Quarterly, 25*(3), 200–207.

Gándara, P., Rumberger, R., Maxwell-Jolly, J., & Callahan, R. (2003, October 7). English learners in California schools: Unequal resources, unequal outcomes. *Education Policy Analysis Archives, 11*(36). Available at: http://epaa.asu.edu/epaa/v11n36/.

Grey, M. A. (1991). The context for marginal secondary ESL programs: Contributing factors and the need for further research. Journal of Educational Issues of Language Minority Students, 9, 75–89.

Hamann, E. T. (2003). *The educational welcome of Latinos in the New South*. Westport, CT: Praeger.

Harklau, L. (1994a). Tracking and linguistic minority students: Consequences of ability grouping for second language learners. *Linguistics and Education, 6*(3), 217–244.

Harklau, L. (1994b). "Jumping Tracks": How language-minority students negotiate evaluations of ability. *Anthropology & Education Quarterly, 25*(3), 347–363.

Harklau, L., Losey, K. M, & Siegal, M. (Eds.). (1999). *Generation 1.5 meets college composition: Issues in the teaching of writing to U.S. educated learners of ESL*. Mahwah, NJ: Lawrence Erlbaum.

Keyes, J. (1999). Educators' attitudes towards language-minority education in one public school system in the southeastern United States. Unpublished dissertation, Indiana University of Pennsylvania.

Kindler, A. (2002). Survey of the States' limited English proficient students and available educational programs and services, 2000–2001 summary report. Washington, DC: NCELA. Available at: http://www.ncela.gwu.edu/policy/states/reports/seareports/0001/sea0001.pdf.

LaCelle-Peterson, M., & Rivera, C. (1994). Is it real for all kids? A framework for equitable assessment policies for English language learners. *Harvard Educational Review, 64*(1), 55–75.

Lau v. Nichols, 414 U.S. 563, 94 S.Ct. 786, 39 L.Ed.2d 1 (1974).

Lucas, T. (1997). Into, through, and beyond secondary school: Critical transitions for immigrant youth. McHenry, IL: Delta Systems Co.

Lucas, T., Henze, R., & Donato, R. (1990). Promoting the success of Latino language-minority students: An exploratory study of six high schools. *Harvard Education Review, 60*(3), 315–40.

McLaughlin, M. W. (1987). Learning from experience: Lessons from policy implementation. *Educational Evaluation and Policy Analysis, 9,* 171–178.

Mehan, H., Villanueva, I., Hubbard, L., & Lintz, A. (1996). *Constructing school success: The consequences of untracking low-achieving students.* Cambridge, England: Cambridge University Press.

Meltzer, J., & Hamann, E. T. (2004). *Meeting the needs of adolescent English language learners for literacy development and content area learning, Part one: Focus on motivation and engagement.* Providence, RI: Education Alliance at Brown University.

Meltzer, J., & Hamann, E. T. (2005). Meeting the needs of adolescent English language learners for literacy development and content area learning, Part two: Focus on classroom teaching and learning strategies. Providence, RI: Education Alliance at Brown University.

Miramontes, O. B., Nadeau, A., Commins, N. L., & Garcia, E. (1997). *Restructuring schools for linguistic diversity: Linking decision making to effective programs.* NY: Teachers College Press.

National Center for Educational Statistics. (1997). The condition of education 1997, Supplemental and Standard Error Tables: Supplemental Table 4-1. Washington, DC: U.S. Department of Education, Office of Educational Research and Improvement. Available at: http://nces.ed.gov/pubsearch/pubsinfo.asp?pubid=97988.

Northwest Regional Educational Laboratory, Center for School and District Improvement. (2004). *English language learner (ELL) programs at the secondary level in relation to student performance.* Portland, OR: Author.

Pugach, M. (1998). *On the border of opportunity: Education, community, and language at the U.S.–Mexico line.* Mahwah, NJ: Lawrence Erlbaum Association.

Romo, H. D., & Falbo, T. (1996). *Latino high school graduation: Defying the odds.* Austin: University of Texas Press.

Ruiz-de-Velasco, J., (2005). Performance-based school reforms and the federal role in helping schools that serve language-minority students. In A. Valenzuela (Ed.), *Leaving children behind: How "Texas-style" accountability fails Latino youth* (pp. 33–55). Albany: State University of New York Press.

Schecter, S. R., & Cummins, J. (Eds.). (2003). *Multilingual education in practice: Using diversity as a resource.* Portsmouth, NH: Heinemann.

Spillane, J., Reiser, B., & Reimer, T. (2002). Policy implementation and cognition: Reframing and refocusing policy implementation research. *Review of Educational Research 72*(3), 387–431.

Stritikus, T., & Garcia, E. (2003). The role of theory and policy in the educational treatment of language minority students: Competitive structures in California. *Education Policy Analysis Archive 11*(26). Available at: http://epaa.asu.edu/epaa/v11n26/.

Suárez-Orozco, C., & Suárez-Orozco, M. (2001). *Children of immigration.* Cambridge, MA: Harvard University Press.

Walqui, A. (2000). *Access and engagement: Program design and instructional approaches for immigrant students in secondary school.* McHenry, IL: Delta Systems Co.

Wortham, S., Murillo, E. & Hamann, E. T. (Eds.) (2002). *Education in the new Latino diaspora: Policy and the politics of identity.* Westport, CT: Ablex.

Zehler, A. M., Fleischman, H. L., Hopstock, P. J., Stephenson, T. G., Pendzick, M. L., & Sapru, S. (2003). Descriptive study of services to LEP students and LEP students with disabilities, volume 1A: Research report. Development Associates, Inc. Available at: http://www.devassoc.com/LEPdoclist.html.

CHAPTER 17

Inclusive Pedagogy in a Mandate-Driven Climate

NAOMI MIGLIACCI AND LORRIE STOOPS VERPLAETSE

Inclusive Pedagogy: A Review of Recommended Practices

This concluding chapter aims to accomplish two objectives. First, we acknowledge that the chapters in this volume contain a wealth of research informed recommendations for inclusive pedagogical practices for the elementary classroom, the middle and secondary classroom, community and school linkages, and school and district reform. The first part of the chapter summarizes these recommendations and accompanies them with graphic organizers. These recommendations counter many current instructional practices that were borne out of a mythology surrounding the instruction of English language learners (ELLs). These myths have been outlined in the introductory chapter of this volume.

The second of our aims is to explore the topic of how to practice these recommendations in our current mandate-driven climate. Unfortunately, many ELLs are expected to participate in standardized, mandated exams in English even before they have sufficient English-language proficiency to complete the tests. Furthermore, the pressures of this mandate-driven climate force administrators and teachers to adopt instructional practices contrary to those recommended in this book. The second part of this chapter invites the reader to consider a new set of myths that drives the current climate. Each myth is examined, and ultimately new practices are recommended to enhance the academic achievement of ELLs.

Practices in the Classroom: Elementary and Secondary

The first two sections of this book have provided us insights regarding the best instructional practices for English language learners in the elementary and the secondary classroom. Though each chapter has provided us with a unique perspective on this topic, interestingly five major tenets continue to surface. These are graphically depicted in Figure 17.1. Classroom teachers practicing effective inclusive pedagogy exhibit the following five characteristics:

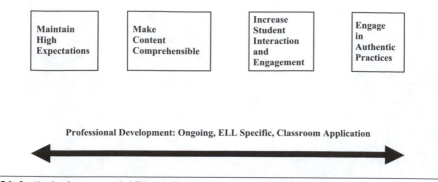

Figure 17.1 Synthesis of recommended ELL practices for elementary and secondary classrooms

- They hold high expectations for all of their students, including those with limited English proficiency.
- They consciously work to make the content comprehensible.
- They engage their students in an abundance of interaction opportunities, both written and oral.
- They create tasks, assignments, and assessments that are authentic in nature.
- They engage in professional development and thereby learn about the aforementioned strategies and perfect their abilities in these strategies. This professional development is tightly focused on ELL issues. It is ongoing, and it is directly related and explicitly applied to their on-the-job teaching.

Figures 17.2 and 17.3 provide some of the specifics as to how the elementary classroom teacher and the secondary classroom teacher manifest these five characteristics. Each of the five is discussed in the following section.

Maintain High Expectations   Probably the most important tenet of inclusive pedagogy is to hold high expectations of all students. With high expectations, it becomes the teacher's challenge and responsibility to ensure that appropriate measures are in place to realize these expectations even with the students still developing their skills or language.

Elementary Classrooms   The beginning of Yedlin's Chapter 4, a quote from the kindergarten teacher about whom she writes, captures the concept of high expectations: "I think my children can do exactly what the other children can do. However, there are ways I help them that are different." An example of how this teacher maintains high expectations is her response to lexical reductionism in the elementary classroom. Rather than simplify the word *talon*, she consciously chooses to use this term and to provide clear visuals to depict the meaning of the term so that students be exposed to rich vocabulary usage.

In Chapter 3, Willett, Harman, Hogan, Lozano, and Rubeck write about how both the second and fifth graders, buddied together in a reading and writing program, are encouraged to tap into their personal issues and cultural backgrounds in their collective reading and writing assignments. By exploring such topics as *bothersome issues* students interweave their social worlds with their academic worlds. The students assume multiple identities such as helper, tutor, sharer of feelings, and problem solver.

And in the elementary classrooms in Parker's Chapter 5, teachers integrate the targeted test tasks not just into the grade-level classrooms that matched the mandated tests but rather

Elementary Classrooms

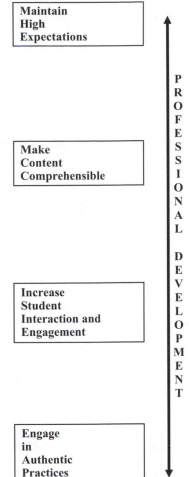

1. Use real language plentifully; do not water down language.
2. Interweave social worlds, academic worlds, and possible literate futures.
3. High expectations of those with lower skills, with appropriate scaffolding.
4. Provide ample opportunities for oral and written production.

1. Recycle and spiral content repeatedly.
2. Activate background knowledge
3. Monitor speech delivery.
4. Reinforce language and content through experiential and multimodal activities.
5. Use visuals and modeling extensively.

1. Provide ample opportunities for social interaction and multiple classroom identities.
2. Saturate the environment with oral and written language experiences.
3. Promote use of first language.
4. Select doable tasks for beginning ELLs.
5. In lieu of correcting oral talk, provide grammatically correct recasts of talk.

1. Publish student end products.
2. Infuse test tasks into instruction.
3. Use authentic texts, purposes, and audiences.
4. Explicitly teach genre and language features.

Figure 17.2 Recommended ELL practices: Elementary education

also into the classes with students of lower grades and proficiency. Similarly, though each teacher emphasizes language and learning objectives appropriate for the grade level or the students' proficiency level, they all use the same assessment administration process and set of performance rubrics.

Middle and Secondary Classrooms At the middle and secondary school level, high expectations must be appropriately accompanied by whatever instructional scaffolding is necessary to assist the learner to that higher level of achievement. Verplaetse and Migliacci, in Chapter 7, encourage teachers to maintain the same content-standard expectations but to find varying ways to differentiate how that content is presented and to assess student achievement of that content. Walqui points out in Chapter 6 that even in the ESL classes, educators must foster teaching that promotes students' conceptual and academic

<u>Secondary Classroms</u>

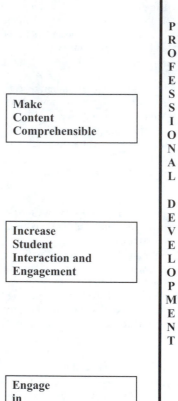

1. Differentiate instruction: maintain same content.
2. Track into college-bound classrooms.
3. Prepare students for college tasks: explicitly teach reading/writing, note-taking and test-taking strategies.
4. Foster school social development: remove barriers for extracurricular activities.

1. Create shared background; use students' experiential background as starting point.
2. Use visuals: pictures, graphic organizers, listening guides, increased experiential learning.
3. Negotiate meaning through increased Q&A, student inquiry instruction, less teacher-fronted instruction.

1. Use less teacher-fronted and more student-centered instruction; use more inquiry-based instruction.
2. Differentiate question type.
3. Challenge intermediate ELLs to produce extended text (oral and written).
4. Promote use of first language for planning and processing.
5. Use complex and flexible forms of collaboration.

1. Use relevant, meaningful, varied tasks.
2. Use authentic assessments.
3. Explicitly teach sociocultural expectations and academic norms.
4. Make a place in the school for the student's home language and culture.

Figure 17.3 Recommended ELL practices: Secondary education

development. Just as mainstream teachers are being encouraged to make their content more accessible, ESL teachers are being challenged to add more cognitively challenging content to their language instruction.

In Chapter 9, Harklau encourages secondary educators to become actively aware that many ELL students are capable and eager to attend college. To that end, she recommends that administrators assign an educator to be responsible for reviewing ELL course assignments to assure that ELL students are appropriately tracked into college-bound coursework, if so desired. Additionally she recommends that teachers explicitly teach reading and writing strategies and note- and test-taking strategies to prepare students for college-bound work. Finally, she recognizes that the social development of ELL students also determines their success; therefore, she encourages schools to remove any structural barriers that keep ELL students from fully participating in the extracurricular aspects of high school.

Make Content Comprehensible   Making course content comprehensible is the goal for any instructional process. But when language learners are part of the picture, the intent of comprehensible input becomes not only excellent instruction but also absolutely necessary instruction.

Elementary Classrooms   In the fifth-grade classroom, described by Brisk, Horan, and MacDonald in Chapter 2, the teacher incorporates scaffolding sidesteps into the rhetorical approach routine to make the lesson at that moment more meaningful to all the students. For example, the teacher inserts a word-mapping exercise into the routine so students will understand what *immigration* is. Another sidestep she adds is to model how to locate specific information in the students' research process.

In Parker's Chapter 5, teachers provide charts of the content of a task. For example, the elements of a paragraph and the strategies for reading for information are articulated on charts and referred to—and reviewed—continuously during class activities.

And in Chapter 4, Yedlin describes how kindergarten teacher Mrs. Romano reports tuning her speech in response to children's comprehension levels. For beginners she uses shorter utterances, the use of actions, and contextual cues to make the language comprehensible. Additionally, she provides children with repeated exposures to the same and similar messages. Finally, in a practice similar to that described in Parker's chapter, during the story-writing lesson, Mrs. Romano uses a piece of paper that had been prefolded into three columns, conveying tangibly the story structure concepts of beginning, middle, and end. The columns provide a concrete structural scaffold for children's writing.

Middle and Secondary Classrooms   Making comprehensible the complex and academically challenging content of middle and secondary school course work is a daunting challenge. Teachers are faced with this challenge daily—even for the students who speak their language. To attempt to make the content comprehensible for students who are still learning the language must appear to be impossible without appropriate training.

Verplaetse and Migliacci in Chapter 7 and Walqui in Chapter 6 encourage teachers to find ways to contextualize the course content, new ideas, and tasks. They recommend that teachers make extensive use of visuals, graphic organizers, and modeling. They also recommend that teachers consciously work to create shared background, using the students' experiential background as a starting point to anchor new ideas. Though Verplaetse and Migliacci advocate modifying dense reading materials for students in early language development stages as access into the authentic texts, Walqui argues that rather than simplifying a text, teachers should "amplify and enrich the linguistic and extralinguistic context that enables students to work with new concepts and relationships packaged in new language."

Harklau, in Chapter 9, echoes these recommendations by encouraging teachers to provide comprehensible and challenging instruction, particularly in the mainstream English and social studies classes. She also suggests that the college-bound preparation process is of itself a content area that teachers need to make explicitly comprehensible to ELLs in the middle and high school. One way to achieve this is to make information such as course choices and college requirements accessible to ELL students.

Increase Student Interaction and Engagement   ELL students must have plenty of opportunities to interact orally and in writing. They must constantly and repeatedly engage with each other, with the teacher, and independently with the course content.

Elementary Classrooms   As an example of increased student engagement, the teacher in Brisk et al.'s Chapter 2 assigns her students a free-writing task. The consequence of this task is twofold: (1) the students produce extended text; and (2) they activate their background knowledge on immigration. In another example, this teacher modifies a task so that all ELLs can participate despite their level of proficiency. While students are conducting reading research about immigration, ELL students with beginning-English-proficiency levels are asked to conduct interviews of recently immigrated family members.

Other examples of increased interaction and engagement are found in Yedlin's Chapter 4, where Mrs. Romano admits that there is awkwardness in interactions with language learners and that teachers are tempted to avoid embarrassment by not calling on the hard-to-understand students. However, she is adamant that it is unacceptable to avoid such students. Additionally, this same teacher speaks about the need for students to use their first language—that to hold to an "English-only" policy would be "unreasonable and counterproductive."

This teacher also speaks about the importance of saturating the environment with oral and written language. But this saturation was far from a "sink-or-swim" immersion. On the contrary, the saturated language environment is also filled with scaffolding activities and highly structured participant roles. To quote her once more, "You simply immerse them in what they need, the language, the alphabets, the stories,…hearing people speak to each other, hearing stories read on tape. And you read stories and other children read stories, talking all day long." Similarly, Chapter 3, by Willett et al., highlights the importance of ample opportunities for social interaction and emphasizes that one way to accomplish this is by encouraging activities that allow students to take up multiple identities.

Finally, in Parker's Chapter 5, one teacher reports that after a series of highly interactive instructional strategies, one particular language-learning student, who had earlier shown a low level of English proficiency, demonstrated considerable growth in writing and other skill areas. The interactive strategies included consistent and continuous practice in listening with intent, organizing content on simple graphic organizers and with drawings, producing a variety of paragraph written responses after analyzing a writing prompt, and revising and editing the responses—all tasks included in the fourth-grade state English language arts test. The teacher reports that the student "increasingly was less interested in retelling with illustrations and more interested in retelling in writing. She was able to write sentences that included more information or ideas, and the details were appropriate to the main ideas in her sentences. Her vocabulary grew as well."

Middle and Secondary Classrooms   Students in middle and secondary classrooms must have ample opportunities to produce extended talk and written text on academic topics. In Verplaetse's Chapter 8, she recommends that teachers reduce teacher-fronted classroom activities and increase student-centered activities. Additionally, strategies to increase interaction include differentiating question types for students possessing varying levels of language proficiency, providing language models for students with early proficiency levels, and promoting the students' use of the first language when planning or processing challenging materials. She also encourages teachers to consciously challenge intermediate-level students to produce extended oral and written text, recognizing that both teachers and students are conditioned to expect less. Walqui, in Chapter 6, echoes these ideas, recommending that teachers make use of complex and flexible forms of student collaboration.

Regarding writing, specifically, Harklau, in Chapter 9, emphasizes the need to practice timed essays and writing from sources, both tasks students are expected to manage when they are in college. Reviewing the recent adolescent writing research literature, Verplaetse, in Chapter 8, recommends that teachers explicitly discuss the use of varying genres and provide ELL students frequent opportunities to brainstorm, organize, plan, discuss, and peer edit texts.

Viewing interaction from its social perspective, in Chapter 9, Harklau encourages teachers to foster the participation of immigrants in the social life of the school by getting rid of institutional barriers to extracurricular activities and by fostering cohorts of college-bound English language learners.

Engage in Authentic Practices   Students who see the authentic reason or purpose of an assignment are much more likely to find themselves emotionally and cognitively engaged in the experience.

Elementary Classrooms   In both Chapter 2 by Brisk et al. and Chapter 3 by Willett et al., the students face writing assignments that have genuine purpose for them. In the case of Brisk et al.'s teacher, the students collectively decide for whom they will write the project. They choose a real audience, their past intern teacher, thus personalizing their purpose for writing. At the completion of the assignment, they hold a publishing party and present the finished product to their intended audience. Similarly, in Willett et al.'s Chapter 3, the teachers publish the students' end product and students present it to the families in a special program.

In Chapter 5, Parker introduces an important learning principle: Applying the competencies of learning-performance tasks in contexts other than test-practice materials is a more authentic experience, which leads to the ability to succeed in on-demand testing experiences. As we read about the teachers in his collaborative action research team, we see how using scoring guides to evaluate student work and sitting with students as they reflect on their own work with the use of these scoring rubrics makes the entire learning and assessment process much more real to the students. Its constructive consequence is palpable in the improved writing skills of the students.

Middle and Secondary Classrooms   Walqui (Chapter 6) and Harklau (Chapter 9) speak extensively concerning issues of authenticity. Walqui encourages educators to explicitly teach academic strategies, sociocultural expectations, and academic norms; to use tasks that are relevant, meaningful, engaging, and varied; and to view authentic assessment as an integral part of teaching and learning. She urges teachers to respond to the content of students' expressed thoughts instead of only evaluating the structure of the students' delivery.

Some of the ways in which Harklau recommends authenticity in academic practice are to help students with the authentic practices needed for college such as note-taking skills and test-taking strategies. Additionally, she encourages educators to recognize the value of the home language and home cultures and to find a place for both in the school.

Finally, in Verplaetse's review of the adolescent writing literature in Chapter 8, she reports these recommendations: the explicit attention to varying genres and the use of authentic assessments such as process writing reviews of multiple drafts in lieu of grading a single-draft assignment.

Professional Development   A less obvious, but extremely important, characteristic underlying effective inclusive pedagogy is the strong need for ongoing, ELL-specific professional development. It is unrealistic to expect that a single workshop on the issue of ELL instruction will solve the needs of today's mainstream teachers. Throughout a number of the chapters in this book, teachers have engaged in long-term professional development activities, focusing on the topic of ELLs, with the expectation that the learning will be applied back in the classroom.

Elementary Classrooms   In Parker's Chapter 5 about collaborative action research, voluntary school teams systematically examine their own classroom practices. The focus is always on making learning and teaching changes based on student performance and need and on developing coaches to this end.

In Brisk et al.'s study in Chapter 2, fourth- and fifth-grade teachers take part in eight weeks of collaborative inquiry, analyzing the language ability and challenges of bilingual students. Through this experience and because of this experience, teachers are able to determine specific steps to take to markedly increase the writing abilities of their English language learners.

Middle and Secondary Classrooms   Much of the sample work illustrated in Verplaetse and Migliacci's Chapter 7 on making content comprehensible was created because of professional development activities. For the past five years, mainstream teachers have engaged in 10-hour workshops, after which they were mentored by a graduate student pursuing a Master's degree in Teaching English as a Second Language (TESOL). The teachers then as applied their newly learned sheltered strategies back in their own classrooms. Others engaged in a full-semester course on sheltered instruction, during which they modified one of their own instructional units to make it accessible for ELLs. As a consequence of these professional development activities, teachers report that they have altered the manner in which they teach. Because of these changes some report marked improvements in the engagement and performance of their mainstreamed ELL students.

In Chapter 6, Walqui provides a detailed discussion of what it is that accomplished teachers of ELLs know and are able to do. She states that the knowledge and skills required are not just of a technical nature but also importantly include personal, social, and political aspects of a teacher's professional life. She stresses that teacher understanding and expertise is accomplished over an extended, ongoing time continuum and that certain aspects of development become more salient than others at varying times.

Community Linkages

The section on community–school linkages reveals several themes. In general, these themes are connected with issues of school reform. In other words, schools and districts have to think differently, plan differently, reorganize their schools differently, and even redefine what it means for schools to connect with community-based organizations (CBOs). In the three chapters in this section, we outline the underlying themes in terms of a set of parameters for schools and districts to form ELL-responsive environments, which ensure success for ELLs and for all students. The chapters in this section provide examples of how this was realized in several locations across the United States. The approach each author describes can be summarized as a holistic approach to working with community partners.

Table 17.1 Synthesis of Recommended ELL practices for elementary and secondary classrooms.

CELEBRATORY ATTITUDE	Start with a celebratory attitude
DEFINITION OF PARTNERSHIPS	Change the definition of community-school partnerships by changing the definition of what it means to educate ELLs
GRASSROOTS INVOLVEMENT	Promote grassroots involvement and community buy-in
SUSTAINABLE RELATIONSHIPS	Create relationships that are sustainable over time
PARENT INVOLVEMENT	Get parent involvement by working with CBOs that provide high quality, wrap-around services
NEEDS, TALENTS, INTERESTS OF ELLS	Look to accommodate the needs, talents, and interests of the ELLs and the home community they belong to
ACCESS TO AMERICAN DREAM	Provide access to the "American dream," or, create programs that realize students' future goals by creating personalized learning environments

The Holistic Approach　　Perhaps, as Colón (Chapter 10) surmises, the term *holistic* has a bad rap. Wei in Chapter 12 also feels a need to explain an approach that is not "fluffy." It really is a child-centered approach whereby educational programming revolves around the needs of the child and what is best for him or her. It includes academics, nutrition, health and well-being, physical fitness, emotional and social development, connectedness with family and community, spiritual connections, and whole-life integration with an aim for a rewarding future. The holistic approach, as we call it, has a set of guiding principles outlined that come from a synthesis of the three chapters in the community–school linkages section of this book. For a graphic representation of these principles, see Table 17.1.

Start with a Celebratory Attitude　　Rather than create programs based on problems, or challenges, think positively about what the students bring to a school, what they can and want to do, and how to best tap into their interests. In Colón's Chapter 10 and in Migliacci's Chapter 11, the community partners recognized the academic and future career potential of ELLs. In the case of the National Council of La Raza (NCLR), language and culture are to be celebrated. Similarly, the Health Professions Partnerships Initiative (HPPI) in Hartford, Connecticut, seeks to promote academic scholarship among this untapped resource. The ELLs are seen as not only potential college students but also as graduate students to medical and dental school. ELLs are not seen as problems to be fixed, as we saw in Hamann's Chapter 16 account of the attitudes in the districts he studied. In other words, community partners have the ability that sometimes public schools have lost in the large, comprehensive nature, to think and act creatively on behalf of ELLs.

Change the Definition of Community–School Partnerships by Changing the Definition of What It Means to Educate ELLs   Rather than thinking about English as a second language (ESL) versus bilingual education as the way to educate ELLs, Colón's Chapter 10 claims cause us to rethink the definition of education in terms of how it has traditionally been delivered and organized for nonnative speakers of English. Snippets of his interview bear repeating: "Education is not about the language of instruction. It's not about English; it's not about Spanish. Language is the method of instruction. … The most important part of learning is learning how to *access* the content. … The real purpose of education is to teach children how to become learners. … That's what education is about."

In a similar vein, Wei, in Chapter 12, urges us to consider who we are asking to partner with us. Traditionally, the community has only meant the local neighborhood, and though the local area might have some resources, typically they are not enough, especially in terms of funding. Migliacci in Chapter 11 lists some of the types of partnerships, services, and challenges that schools and districts can consider. NCLR, Colón's organization, is a major funding source for community–school linkages. Even though it is a national organization, it is the community of Latinos nationwide to which they belong and for which they seek to provide high-quality educational services. Therefore, they partner with schools on a national level. Wei asks us not just to think of community resources from the business community but also for more involvement at the university level. The Bulkeley–UConn partnership that Migliacci describes in Chapter 11 exemplifies a successful partnership whereby not only funding but also other resources are provided to the high school by the university. These are resources not found in the students' immediate neighborhoods, but elsewhere in the state. In addition, this partnership is all about access to content and future dreams. Finally, in all three chapters, we note that the connections are political.

Promote Grassroots Involvement and Community Buy-In   Colón in Chapter 10 starts the section on community–school linkages by claiming that the schools need to be directly tied to the students' home community's CBOs. Wei's school in Philadelphia does exactly this, as does the example Colón provides for us in Oakland, California. Although the NCLR provides funding, local personnel manage the school. In another example, Colón regales us with an example of physical brawn and sheer will on the part of the community to build a school. In Migliacci's Chapter 11 example, UConn promoted community buy-in on several levels. The university trains its faculty on diversity issues and how to work with diverse populations of students. It also trains high school science teachers. The university also provides health and education courses to community members. On the other side, the high school meets with parents and holds conferences where students and parents can join together. This partnering at every level ensures that all parties have access to knowledge and the programs available to them and that instructors, teachers, and professors are adequately trained.

Create Relationships That Are Sustainable over Time   Colón in Chapter 10 describes several programs, including his own NCLR, with numbers of years in operation because they meet the needs of the learners and the community. They are high-quality offerings that have been thoughtfully implemented. HPPI, which Migliacci describes in Chapter 11, initiated a plan whereby pieces of the program are added yearly. In addition, the roll-out plan for all the academies at the high school starts with a planning phase, implementation phase, and a sustaining phase. Wei, in Chapter 12, describes a similar roll-out plan for the school in Chinatown. A lot of planning went into the process of creating a school based on a folk-arts theme. In this way, the group was able to create a school that was realistic and rooted in values and belief systems that are vital to the community. In this case, the community buy-in was a key element to the school's success. Colón, in Chapter 10, argues that programs that have a grassroots base are sustainable over time because it is the community's desire.

Get Parent Involvement by Working with CBOs That Provide High-Quality Wraparound Services So often schools are advised to get parents involved, and too often school personnel complain that parents do not get involved and, worse, that they do not care. In all three chapters, Colón (Chapter 10), Migliacci (Chapter 11), and Wei (Chapter 12) describe relationships with schools where parents were involved and, more importantly, where the school and community partners offered more than one service, which were for the whole family. Colón claims that CBOs should provide health and education programs or advocacy work around immigration or housing rights. This critical piece allows for the cultural competence that is built into the work of the CBOs. They have the cultural and linguistic relevance and understanding of the community. Colón claims, "We also believe that the more supports, the more wraparound services you can provide to the children and to the family, the better off they're going to be, because so many issues are interconnected and are directly connected to the family." Later in the chapter, Colón describes parents with shovels, digging ditches and building a school from the ground up. Ownership is a key component in creating new school environments, but it must be done in culturally appropriate ways. Wei has a similar sentiment about the school in Philadelphia.

Colón illustrates this point further through a discussion of the Parent Institute for Quality Education (PIQE) in San Diego, California. This program helps parents understand their role as primary caregivers and the first teachers of their children. They teach parents "that nobody in this world is going to advocate for that child more than the parent." After more than 30 years in education, Colón claims it is one of the best parent-education programs in the country because it honors parents. Instructors in this program empathize with parents living in poverty; they can communicate with a poor parent who does not speak English and has little, if any, formal education.

Migliacci recounts how HPPI partner UConn provides funding, faculty resources, guest lectures, summer programs, access to facilities, and training at all levels. It is an inclusive program in terms of its services. Moreover, students learn the requirements and process by which to enter and attend the university and nationally ranked medical school. This is insider information known to the culture of colleges and universities, but not necessarily to ELLs.

In addition, Wei describes an integration of generational needs. It is not just the parents but also other members of the local community who can benefit from, and partner with, the school. In her example, both school children and the seniors need to eat lunch, so services are provided in a culturally appropriate way and both groups are served together, meeting physical, psychological, and logistical needs.

Look to Accommodate the Needs, Talents, and Interests of the ELLs and the Home Community They Belong to Migliacci (Chapter 11) includes information on how small learning communities (SLCs) are sometimes required, depending on the funding source, and are always recommended to include all students to form a diverse community of learners. Themed academies, such as Bulkeley's Health Professions Academy, do just that when they allow student interest to be one of the motivating factors for inclusion into the academy or small school. In addition, schools need to accommodate the needs of the learners, recognizing that students from different cultural background learn in different ways.

The school Wei describes in Philadelphia is a place where folkways are preserved and the artistic talents of the students are valued. Emphasis is placed on honoring local knowledge, tapping into passions, educating the whole child, connecting to all of life and becoming a good person; the focus is not on test scores. Wei also recounts her involvement with providing parents with translation services in such a way that the balance of power, or who gets to speak and when, is disrupted in favor of the students' home community.

Provide Access to the American Dream, Or Create Programs That Realize Students' Future Goals by Creating Personalized Learning Environments Although not all ELLs dream of attending college, for many who do have this dream, it cannot become a reality under the present situation. High schools are overburdened, as Migliacci points out in Chapter 11. They need the community knowledge and resources to create paths to realize their dreams. The Health Professions Academy does just this through its mentoring and job-shadowing programs, providing students with options, and forcing them to think about their postsecondary school realities. This school within a school individualizes its programming based on student interests and levels of language proficiency. It finds ways to include the ELLs and uses the resources of the larger high school.

In Chapter 10, Colón challenges us to think about the problem of the large, comprehensive high school model comprising as many as 3,000 students in the building, trying to meet the needs of all learners in a personalized way. Students eat lunch at 10:00 just to fit lunches into the students' schedules since they share the cafeteria. Large schools ensure "a loss of identity" and "anonymity" and school becomes "impersonal." Colón claims that "when the school is smaller and the school's community is smaller, it is easier to create the linkages we need with the community and allow people to become empowered." In small, personalized environments that value students' home languages and cultures, they have better access to the American dream—"to be able to graduate from high school prepared for college or career, able to get that job, able to buy that house."

School and District Reform

The chapters related to school reform really examine the deficiencies with the system, which, unfortunately, is related to an overall attitude that ELLs are "not my kids." With the increasing ELL population in the United States, and with the numbers we introduced in Chapter 1, it behooves everyone involved with public education to change (challenge?) this attitude. Though it is true that many teachers and administrators enjoy working with ELLs and see these students as good kids, so often they are still perceived as a special needs population, one in which the mainstream curriculum is not theirs. In fact, as many authors have pointed out in this book, most teachers really do not have the instructional tools they need to work effectively on the academic achievement of ELLs. School and district leaders are unsure what teachers need to accomplish this task, and they are not providing the push for teachers to get these tools and to increase their skills for working with ELLs. The students are caught in this tug of war whereby they are placed in programs that do not meet their needs. We recognize that state-level and national reforms are needed as well. We also recognize that teacher-education programs need to change and that faculty at our nation's colleges and universities need to be inclusive of the needs of ELLs in their curriculum. The section of this book on school reform offers a starting point on ways to begin to provide ELL-responsive environments in schools and districts.

Challenging Schools and Districts to Create ELL-Inclusive Environments   In Chapter 13, Coady, Hamann, Harrington, Pacheco, Pho, and Yedlin claim that the success of ELLs must be thought of in broader terms than their success at mastering the language, customs, and knowledge of the dominant culture. School success is measured in terms of the ability of students to move successfully between their multiple cultural worlds. Students should be allowed to acquire new knowledge without ignoring, displacing, deprecating, or diminishing existing linguistic and cultural knowledge. A student who becomes bilingual and biliterate is more accomplished than one who masters only one language. Creating environments like these authors describe necessitates district-wide and whole-school efforts. The authors identify the following cross-cultural differences as significant for schooling.

- How children are expected to interact with each other and adults
- How language is used by adults and children
- How knowledge is acquired and displayed
- What counts as knowledge

School practices that disregard cross-cultural differences or discount the first language, literacy, cultural identity, or self-esteem of ELLs are not likely to create effective learning environments. First-language vocabulary, oral language, and literacy skills all support successful English-literacy development. Not teaching minority students mainstream ways or academic forms of discourse is doing them a disservice. The prior knowledge and first-language proficiency of ELLs provide the foundations for achievement in U.S. schools. Success for ELLs means being able to function well in mainstream academic settings and in their home communities. Although ELLs can and should reach the same high standards as other students, they may need more time. To outline the principles of ELL-responsive learning environments, the authors include a checklist in which all members of the school community are involved in the education of ELLs.

- School leaders, administrators, and educators recognize that educating ELLs is the responsibility of the entire school staff.
- Educators recognize the heterogeneity of the student population that is collectively labeled as *ELL* and are able to vary their responses to the needs of different learners.
- The school climate and general practice reinforce the principle that students' languages and cultures are resources for further learning.
- There are strong and seamless links connecting home, school, and community.
- ELLs have equitable access to all school resources and programs.
- Teachers have high expectations for ELLs.
- Teachers are properly prepared and willing to teach ELLs.
- Language and literacy are infused throughout the educational process, including curriculum and instruction.
- Assessment is authentic and credible to learners and instructors and takes into account first- and second-language literacy development.

Challenging School and District Leaders to Provide Appropriate Professional Development

We have seen numerous times in this volume how an ELL-responsive environment uses mainstream curriculum, albeit made comprehensible, allows for interactions among peers and others in a community of learners, provides authentic tasks and assessments, and includes ELLs in the life of the school in culturally appropriate ways. As we stated previously, one of the reasons why we do not see these practices is the attitude that ELLs do not belong to, or in, the mainstream classes and that the curriculum is not for them. The idea is that ELLs should be "fixed first, by someone else," because they have "language deficiencies" or they "don't have English," which is often expressed as "they don't have language." Many in public education assume that they belong in ESL classes or special programs. In Chapter 16, Hamann acknowledges the schism between ESL and bilingual and mainstream teachers and illustrates that problem's remedy for us.

First, Hamann argues, as we do in Chapter 1, that the education of ELLs is an increasingly important issue as more students in more districts fit in that category, as they continue to fare less well than most other student populations, and as policy compliance with the No Child Left Behind Act holds schools accountable for their cumulative average yearly progress.

In both of the districts Hamann considers, neither was an exemplar of responsiveness as measured by the academic performance of ELLs. Most teachers and administrators did not see the education of ELLs as part of their own professional task. Teachers did not see a need to be trained in the areas of second-language acquisition, or content-area instruction in a second language. Leaders did not see a need to compel, enable, endorse, or prioritize that their teachers acquire such skill sets and orientations. Those credentialed teachers who worked with ELLs were not enthusiastic about collaborating with their mainstream colleagues or supporting their efforts. Special-program teachers did not want much to do with the mainstream teachers either. On the other hand, Hamann points out, in successful districts with ELLs, the intensive professional development is purposeful and coherent rather than scattershot. Hamann asks us to imagine how the two cases he presents might have differed if the following were true.

- Large portions of the faculty could claim that ELL education was also their task.
- Those with special training and credentials for working with ELLs saw their work institutionally valued and embraced, so they were not guided by a learned skepticism and skittishness in their relations with administrators and nonspecialist colleagues.
- There was less of a gap to breach between ESL programs and regular programs, which meant better coordination and alignment and less of a transition to negotiate for ELLs.
- Teacher hiring was both more purposeful in terms of the sought-after skill sets and more competent—in that those doing the hiring knew what the appropriate skill sets to be ELL responsive would look like.

Hamann concludes that the professional-development opportunities and the creation of special programs in these districts never led all or most educators to see the education of ELLs as their task too, to see that the regular curriculum aligns with the ESL curriculum that prepares ELLs for the mainstream, or to assure that professional development is consistent and coherent in regards to helping teachers understand how to meet the needs of ELLs. The districts described by Hamann needed leaders to make this happen. They needed leaders to provide professional development opportunities, such as those we saw with the collaborative action research teams in Parker's Chapter 5.

Challenging the Special-Needs Label   What happens in schools and districts unresponsive to ELLs? As Hamann and so many others point out, ELLs are not performing academically. What happens when leaders do not insist on appropriate professional development and collaborative efforts for this population? Because so many mainstream teachers and administrators are uninformed of the needs of ELLs, they are often placed into, misdiagnosed as, or overidentified as the special-needs population. In Chapter 15, De George asks us, is it language, or is it special needs? When ELLs are not successful in school, teachers, administrators, and pupil personnel need to consider what the real issues are. De George provides us with a checklist before making a diagnosis.

- Gather background information, facts about the child.
- Obtain information about the child's and family's cultural background.
- Find out about the child's parents' educational background and careers.
- Ask questions about the child's life, language development, and educational history.
- Ask questions about unusual occurrences that might have happened in the child's life.
- If the child was educated in a country other than the United States, ask questions to determine the adequacy of that education.
- If the child was previously educated in the United States, find out more about that.
- Go back to when the child first came to the school, and map out the programs and opportunities that the child has been involved with until the present, asking questions about the school's and teachers' responsiveness, training, and understanding of ELLs.
- Examine the student's progress, and determine the types of difficulties the student is experiencing and in what areas.

Challenging Schools to Use Research in Redesigning Programs for ELLs   In Chapter 14, Miranda outlines for us what schools and districts can do in general to increase their effectiveness for ELLs by examining the research—including research we have presented in this volume. Rather than seeing the ELL student as a problem to be fixed, Miranda claims that ELLs bring with them valuable resources: their languages and their cultures. We can capitalize on these resources for the success and benefit of our English monolingual students as well. This is important when schools consider the types of professional development opportunities they need that can reach all students and remain inclusive of ELL needs. Miranda postulates six principles for effective practice, much like Coady et al. in Chapter 13, which seek to translate bilingual education and second-language acquisition research into effective practice for the benefit of educating all students.

- Each second-language-learning student has his or her own individual language and content-learning profile. Therefore, schools must attain a full profile of each student's language and academic background to make the best instructional decisions for their ELLs.
- Second-language acquisition occurs in stages similar to the acquisition of the first or primary language. Therefore, effective programs for ELLs and their English-speaking peers take into consideration each stage of language acquisition when planning for instruction.
- To ensure that young second-language learners acquire language naturally, their instructional environment should be acquisition rich, that is, an environment that is comprehensible and meaningful.

- For young bilingual students, second-language literacy develops best when the child has had the opportunity to develop literacy in his or her first language; however, if the child is developing literacy in both languages simultaneously, she or he must first have oral proficiency in the new language.
- Older students, who are more cognitively mature and who have developed some level of first-language proficiency, need classroom experiences that offer a balance of language development and formal content learning.
- A thorough assessment (i.e., speaking listening, reading, and writing) of a student's language proficiency—in the student's first and second language—is essential for appropriate placement.

To achieve this, schools and districts need to reform, restructure, and redesign their programs. Miranda recommends following practical program models in providing second-language-acquisition opportunities.

- Dual-language programs
- Gradual-exit transitional bilingual education programs in combination with foreign-language programs
- In-school second-language resource centers
- After-school second-language enrichment programs

He claims that these programs produce a school environment that is a positive contributor to excellence for all students, the school staff, their parents, and the community at large. These ELL-responsive environments have the following characteristics:

- There is equity in the use of the two languages of the school.
- Cross-cultural awareness is infused within the curriculum.
- Opportunities for the integration of all students occur several times throughout the school day.

This kind of school environment is critical to the academic success of all: native speakers of English as well as ELLs.

This section summarized the findings of the chapters written on school reform issues. For a graphic representation of how we see school reform and ELLs, see Table 17.2.

Inclusive Pedagogy in Today's High-Stakes Testing Environment: A New Set of Myths

Having just reviewed a thorough account of recommended, research-informed best practices for the education of ELLs, we are left with the following challenge:

How can we achieve inclusive pedagogy when faced with the current climate of accountability and mandated standardized exams?

The movement toward stricter accountability itself is a good thing. Educators, classroom teachers, schools, and school districts should be held accountable: The end product should be the measured learning progress of each student. We believe that it is this current climate of accountability that has forced many mainstream educators to question, for the first time, their role in educating English language learners.

The problem with today's accountability movement for the measurement of academic progress for English language learners is this: Accountability is currently required to be measured strictly by standardized, quantitative assessments. As reported by the

Table 17.2 Recommended ELL practices: Elementary education

Challenges for ELLs	
THE CHALLENGES	**CHARACTERISTICS OF APPROPRIATE RESPONSIVENESS TO ENGLISH LANGUAGE LEARNERS**
Create ELL-Inclusive Environments	School leaders, administrators, and educators recognize that educating ELLs is the responsibility of the entire school staff.
	Educators recognize the heterogeneity of the student population and vary their responses to the needs of different learners.
	The school climate and general practice reinforce the principle that students' languages and cultures are resources for further learning.
	There are strong links connecting home, school, and community.
	ELLs have equitable access to all school resources and programs.
	Teachers have high expectations for ELLs.
	Language and literacy are infused throughout the educational process, including curriculum and instruction.
	Assessment is authentic, credible to learners and instructors, and takes into account first- and second-language literacy development.
Provide Appropriate Professional Development	Teachers are properly prepared and willing to teach ELLs.
	Schools value and embrace those with special training and credentials for working with ELLs.
	ESL and regular programming are coordinated and aligned.
	Schools hire teachers who can work with ELLs.

U.S. Department of Education's 2005 report on Quality Teachers, "Measurement of student progress and holding schools and teachers accountable for student achievement are fundamental concepts of the NCLB (No Child Left Behind) legislation. ... Effective teachers have been shown to raise student achievement scores on standardized tests" (p. 21).

Many educational researchers and decision makers in governmental agencies encourage the use of standardized measurements, because such measurements have passed rigorous scientific standards and are therefore reported to be the most reliable and valid means to measure student progress. In their efforts to draw attention to the numbers of students who are not receiving the education they deserve, these researchers use the measurement tools of their fields. Researchers in the fields of psychology and educational assessment, among others, tend to rely heavily on quantitative analysis, whereas researchers in anthropology and educational linguistics tend to rely heavily on qualitative analysis (e.g., observation, naturalistic studies, ethnography) for its explanatory powers.

The problem for ELL students occurs because standardized assessments use language as their vehicle for message delivery, just as teachers and classrooms use language as their

Table 17.2 (continued) Recommended ELL practices: Elementary education

Challenge the "Special Needs" Label	Appropriate information about ELLs, their families, cultures, backgrounds, and previous educational experiences is gathered for appropriate assessment.
	Programs and opportunities are mapped out since the child has been involved in the school with attention to the school's and teachers' responsiveness, training, and understanding of ELLs.
	Student progress is examined and a determination is made on the types of difficulties the student is experiencing and in what areas.
	A thorough assessment of a student's language proficiency—in the student's first and second language—is essential for appropriate placement.
Use Research in Redesigning Programs for ELLs	ELLs have individual language and content learning profiles of their language and academic backgrounds for best instructional decisions to be made.
	Effective programs for ELLs and their English speaking peers take into consideration each stage of language acquisition.
	Instructional environments for ELLs are "acquisition-rich," that is, an environment that is comprehensible and meaningful.
	ELLs need first language support.
	Older ELLs need classroom experiences that offer a balance of language development and formal content learning.

vehicle for message delivery. If ELL students do not yet have full usage of the language of delivery, then their performance on such assessments cannot possibly be a reliable or valid means to measure their learning or their progress. Yet current federal legislation requires all students, including any ELL students who have been in the school system longer than 10 months, to take part in the high-stakes standardized testing efforts.

The net result is that teachers and school administrators feel an inordinate amount of pressure to move their ELL students along at a pace that they think will allow them to pass these standardized assessments. Sadly, these pressures quite often cloud educators' judgments as to what the best practices are for the long-term academic growth of ELLs.

Curiously, then, just as we began this book with as series of myths that have often misguided important educational practices that impact ELLs, we wish to end this endeavor with a new, additional set of myths that are dangerously thriving in the current high-stakes academic environment. In the discussion of these myths, it is our hope to help dispel the power behind these mistaken beliefs.

New Myth #1

New Myth #1: Mandated, standardized tests will give us a clear, concise picture of the academic growth of a student body.

One of the problems facing ELLs is that they are often unable to demonstrate their knowledge due to their lack of English-language proficiency. A plethora of research indicates that tests are biased against the language-minority student and several options have been posited. (Butler & Stevens, 2001; Darling-Hammond, 1994; Garcia & Pearson, 1991; Gardner, 1992; Hafner & Ulanoff, 1994; Stevens et al., 2000). Some have argued that ELLs should then receive accommodations, such as more time to take tests, or that alternative assessments should be given or that the language of the tests should be modified. Some say that these testing alternatives might give us a better indicator of student performance. Although we applaud efforts to make the tests and the testing process more equitable, there are problems with this. If we are to measure ELLs on a wide scale we need to deal with issues of reliability and validity.

Others argue that tests should be translated into the students' native languages. But the research has not supported the efficacy of this practice. Furthermore, it would be a daunting task to translate tests into all the languages. Some schools have as many as 100 languages represented. Such tests would require extensive knowledge of the culture as well. Although much of the cultural bias has been attacked, though not yet successfully removed, the linguistic bias remains. For example, students coming from a particular country, say Peru, have vastly different experiences and cultures depending on where they come from. They also speak different languages. Take a native Quechua speaker who grew up rurally, speaks Spanish as her second language, and is learning English as a third language. What this student knows and how she is able to demonstrate that knowledge might be quite different from a student who grew up in an urban environment as a native Spanish speaker. Do we give all students from Peru tests in Spanish? Would we need to know a Quechua speaker's level of Spanish proficiency first? How would that test be administered?

Moreover, if the standardized tests were administered in the students' native languages, this would only be valid in situations where the students have been taught the content in their native language. In addition, standardardized tests require literacy skills, and students do not always have these skills in their native language for a variety of reasons.

Margot Gottlieb, director of assessment and evaluation for the Illinois Resource Center (Zehr, 2006) states that we do not yet have sufficient evidence as to how to best handle the problem of ELLs and standardized exams. Given the lack of resolution on this issue, government agencies and school systems should not be making high-stakes programmatic decisions based on reports of standardized test scores that include the test results of students who are ELLs. Moreover, if ELL students cannot reliably take the same standardized exams as those taken by the mainstream students, then the ELL students' progress should be measured separately with a reliable assessment tool.

New Myth #2

New Myth #2: Only instructional strategies that are supported by scientifically based research can be trusted—and fiscally supported—as effective pedagogical approaches.

The intention behind this myth suggests that educators must select educational strategies and programs that have been shown to be successful, as proven through research, which in and of itself makes perfect sense. Indeed, we should be seeking out recommended practices that are based on sound research. However, the myth lies in the fallacy of the use of the term *scientifically based*. Currently, that term is almost synonymous with *quantitative*, to include the requirement of randomized experimental pre- and posttest control-group designed studies.

Turning again to the U.S. Department of Education's most recent 2005 report on teacher quality, we can see the language used to describe the type of research currently accepted to validate educational practices. The report states,

> The Elementary and Secondary Education Act (ESEA) calls for the use of "effective scientifically based instructional strategies" (ESEA Section 1001(9) 20 ESC 6301). This means the "application of rigorous, systematic, and objective procedures to obtain reliable and valid knowledge relevant to education activities and programs" (ESEA Section 9101 (37) (A) 20 USC 7801) (p. 10).

The report continues,

> As part of the IES [Institute of Education Sciences, a division of the U.S. Dept. of Education] plan to help educators and education policymakers incorporate scientifically based research into their educational decisions, the WWC [What Works Clearinghouse, a division of the IES] can evaluate the strength of the evidence of effectiveness of various educational interventions (http://whatworks.ed.gov/) and can help educators, school districts and others identify those programs, products and practices that have demonstrated results (p. 11).

This language demonstrates how scientifically based research is considered the only valid research to identify recommended practices. The IES stipulates that scientific research measuring the success of a classroom intervention should include a randomized experimental pre- and posttreatment control-group design. We take issue with this limited definition of the term *scientifically based* because it suggests that qualitative research cannot be used to identify effective practice. Yet in the case of so many of the chapters covered in this volume, it is precisely qualitative research that has uncovered the rich findings of practices that best serve ELLs. And qualitative research can certainly be defined as the "application of rigorous, systematic, and objective procedures to obtain reliable and valid knowledge."

We present further arguments concerning Myth #2 from two perspectives:

- The disadvantages of quantitative research when dealing with ELL students
- The advantages of qualitative research

Disadvantages of Quantitative Research   Current mandates require the use of randomized, experimental control-group design and the use of standardized assessment measurements. Standardized measurements are not reliable for ELL population as discussed under Myth 1. Although quantitative research gives the clearest picture for broad generalizations concerning student learning, when ELLs are included in the student body to be measured, the reliability and validity is skewed, for ELLs do not have the language facility to manage the medium of the assessment tool.

One of the problems with quantitative research is that it often seeks to find the central tendency of a group or how students perform on average. (Someone once said that the quantitative researcher, with his feet in the freezer and his head in the oven, feels just fine on average.) Quantitative research studies, in general, do not seek to describe those outside the standard deviation curve: the outliers. Those students are often ELLs, and we need a greater understanding of what it is they do know and how they learn—what motivates them, how they make connections, and what in their backgrounds, cultures, and languages do they bring to the classroom. In other words, what is it that they know but are unable to speak or write about because of their limited skills in English?

In addition, the limited-English-proficient student comes in a variety of packages: with interrupted schooling, with high levels of literacy in the home language, as refugees with posttraumatic stress disorder, and the list goes on. The great diversity of this population can be seen across the United States and even in one school. Though it is true that some schools see more of one population than another, to randomly assign this population to a control group and an intervention group is not an easy task. In many schools, students are so transient that the attrition rate for a research study would render it useless.

Furthermore, ELLs are placed in myriad programs that seek to serve the great variety of language-minority students. The standards and instruments used to assess and place these students into the myriad programs, and the standards used to define the delivery of these programs, vary from state to state and in some cases from school to school. Researchers seek to generalize their standardized performance results, but given the variability of program types generalizability of the results is extremely challenging.

Given the extreme variability of student profiles within the ELL population and program types designed to serve this population, randomized experimental control-group design is almost unmanageable. Couple that with all the aforementioned arguments against the use of standardized assessment measures when including ELL students, and quantitative analyses do not give an accurate portrayal of the achievement of the combined group of ELLs and mainstream students, nor do they provide an accurate picture of the ELLs when disaggregated from the mainstream.

Advantages of Qualitative Research   Unlike the broad generalizations made from quantitative research, qualitative research allows us to look in detail at a particular scene, observing its finer points—points that are unobservable in a quantitative study. Because English language learners are linguistically at a disadvantage when taking standardized assessments, the results of their tests are inaccurate at best. It is observations, and the use of authentic assessments—such as rubric-based performance assessments, portfolios, and student self-assessments—that give us insight as to how an ELL is learning.

Second-language researcher Ilona Leki (1999, pp. 17–18) described at length her stand on qualitative research, in the following way:

> Qualitative research is successful to the degree that it helps us to understand ourselves and our actions. ... We try to understand the human condition by watching what humans do and trying to make sense of it. For this reason, I make no apology for the single case focus..., no caveats about this case not being generalizable to a broader sample of a population. As Stake (1995) maintained, "the real business of case study is particularization, not generalization" (p. 8). Case study research does not gain its strength from generalizability but from an experience that is unique, as all experience is, but that may also give us insights and help us understand.
>
> ... To further complicate matters is the question, "By what right do I speak for my participant?" To answer this question, I have been guided by Sullivan's (1996) argument for qualitative research as advocacy; my words speak for my participant, but "speak for" not in the sense of speaking "instead of" but in the sense of speaking in support of.

In addition to offering detailed insight, qualitative studies can also provide us with logical relationships that can help us determine recommended instructional practices. For example, if we can determine through research that certain classroom interaction promotes a sense of student identity; moreover, if research determines that a sense of student identity results in improved academic voice, then we can safely deduce that certain classroom interactions can improve a student's academic voice.

Such relationships are particularly important when we are attempting to measure something as difficult to measure as *learning*. Unlike medicine or other physical sciences, we cannot measure learning by counting numbers of cells in a petri dish. We can only measure learning by measuring behaviors. If behaviors are language mediated, and the students under measurement are still learning the language, we find ourselves, once again, in the face of dilemma. But through logical relationships that are revealed through qualitative or quantitative research, we can arrive at reasonably sound findings.

New Myth #3

New Myth #3: Scripted preparation for exam protocols will be the surest, swiftest means to achieve on mandated exams.

One of the practices we continue to observe is the requirement by certain school systems to use scripted lessons as a means to improve the high-stakes test scores. Most often, we find this practice in urban schools, with high poverty and high numbers of linguistic minority children. Naturally, schools with high numbers of ELLs will predictably score low on standardized measurements for all the reasons already discussed. It seems that teachers and administrators forget all they have learned about the value of student-centered, inquiry-based instruction when faced with low scores on state-mandated exams. The pressure to perform on these tests is so strong that administrators put aside what they know about learning and resort to practices that appear to have an immediate appeal but ultimately cannot produce the kind of learner or learning that we seek.

None of the findings or recommended practices reported in this volume argue for scripted instructional approaches. Instead, the practices recommended here argue for engaged, student-centered learning with authentic assessments, community linkages, infused instruction on test-taking skills, high expectations, extensive interaction opportunities, and an abundance of accommodations to make the content comprehensible to language learners. The findings represented in these chapters are research supported, informed by quantitative and qualitative research combined.

New Myth #4

New Myth #4: A single workshop will provide faculty with all they need to know to raise ELL achievement.

In this mandate-driven climate, educators are rushing to resolve the problem of low ELL achievement on the standardized tests. They see a solution in professional development. Often what teachers receive is a single workshop on ELL instructional strategies.

Prior to the high-stakes testing movement, few mainstream teachers received any training on instructional strategies best suited for language-minority students, even though this population has been increasing. One thing the high-stakes testing climate has accomplished is bringing to light the academic performance of ELLs and the fact that that teachers need to be trained to work with these students.

It is true that some teachers do receive some training on instructional practices that work for ELLs. Several chapters in this volume speak to the issue of professional development in detail and provide us with a framework for what professional development should include.

- There needs to be buy-in at the district level in aligning curriculum and ensuring that teacher colleagues work together to be consistent and coherent in the work they do for ELLs.
- There needs to be an understanding that teacher knowledge and expertise is accomplished over an extended continuum of time.
- Schools need to provide intensive and comprehensive professional development programs to include frequent ongoing, on-site sessions of team of teachers who share student work, read, and discuss research in the field and collaborate on instructional strategies. These sessions involve school and district administrators as instructional coaches and teachers as peer coaches.

Schmoker (1999, p. 7) amplifies the kinds of professional development activities we advocate: collaborative teamwork, goal setting, collecting and using classroom data, and effective leadership; he argues that "teachers, like other professionals, perform more effectively— even exponentially so—if they collaborate. Although true, effective collaboration represents a significant change in how most teachers work, it should become an expectation."

Schmoker (1999, p. 9) elaborates on this point saying that effective teamwork underscores the fact that "success depends on the interdependency between collaboration and goals." Teachers work in isolation, unlike true professionals, and this promotes professional insecurity. In other words, teachers are cut off from useful information, are unsure if what they are doing is best for their students, and get crushed by the myriad daily events and duties. Meetings and other gatherings that do occur are not collaborative teamwork. Instead, teachers need a common focus, and they need to build and share intellectual capital. They need to sit down and discuss with each other how they can get what they would like from their students and share their research findings.

Schmoker (1999) claims that schools lack clear, concrete goals or may have set too many unattainable goals. He says that goals need to be about whether students have learned, not about whether or not an innovation has been implemented. They are about results for students.

Another essential element to improving teaching practice is data gathering. Many teachers are afraid of collecting data because "data almost always point to action—they are the enemy of comfortable routines. By ignoring data, we promote inaction and inefficiency" (Schmoker, 1999, p. 39). Though many think that data should show results in leaps and bounds, incremental data are crucial. Data collection allows for disseminating and replicating methods in other locations. They help us communicate and substantiate our successes. Regarding teamwork, goal setting, and performance data, Schmoker (p. 55) claims that "people accomplish more together than in isolation; regular, collective dialogue about an agreed-upon focus sustains commitment and feeds purpose; effort thrives on concrete evidence of progress; and teachers learn best from other teachers. We must ensure that these three concepts operate to produce results."

Schmoker's (1999, p. 71) principles, based on research, are not enough. Research needs to be conducted on site; good research, "whether we call it best knowledge or best practice, can unleash vast, dormant forces for making every child's and teacher's life richer and more interesting."

New Myth #5

New Myth #5: Teachers trained in "differentiated instruction" already know what they need to know about the education of ELLs.

Oftentimes, after we have delivered a workshop of recommended instructional practices for ELLs (sheltered instruction), teacher participants will say that this is just good instruction. Or teacher education faculty will say that they already cover differentiated instruction in their teacher-prep course work and therefore do not need to discuss instructional strategies for ELLs as a separate issue. It is true to say that sheltered instruction is good instruction; it is also true to say that sheltered instruction is differentiated instruction. But sheltered instruction is something more and must be something more, because, unlike any other kind of instruction, sheltered instruction recognizes that the medium of instruction is language, and language is the missing element for the ELL audience.

Consequently, at every instructional moment, whether attempting to convey a new idea, to determine a student's thought, or to assess a student's learning growth, the sheltered instructor recognizes that the language requirements for each task in relationship to the language capabilities of each student can be interfering and that accommodations must be made to get around those language barriers. Sheltered instruction, therefore, is good instruction and differentiated instruction, plus the conscious application of appropriate linguistic accommodations.

Recommendations

Finally, as we come to a close, this new set of myths leads to the following set of recommendations, which we invite you to consider and practice.

- Hold fast to what we know to be true regarding inclusive pedagogy: the education of ELLs.
- Find ways to practice inclusive pedagogy amid and within the confines of the current standardized-obsessed environment. Practice subversive education. As we tell our teachers, when we close the classroom door, the classroom is ours, despite all the outside requirements, and we can still find ways to say to that marginalized ELL child, silent in the back of the room, "I see you. I know you want to learn."
- Always report truth about the myths when we are required to report standardized test results. (Remember that on average, ELLs take five to nine years to develop the language proficiency needed to perform at the 50th percentile on standardized measurements, which include the native-speaking student population.) Make clear that these mainstream, standardized measurements do not accurately reflect the measurements of ELL learning that we seek.
- Find ways for ELL students to show that they have the knowledge of the content standards, but in various ways. Remember that they can have the content knowledge but may not be able to convey it in the language-based mainstream manner because they are still developing the necessary language skills.
- Accompany quantitative reports with authentic assessment measures that do measure significant progress that is unattainable through standardized measurements. Though the standardized assessment results for an entire class may be lowered due to the scores of ELLs, disaggregate the scores, thus showing that the native-English-speaking class is progressing at a certain rate. Then show authentic assessment measures to indicate the growth of the ELL students.
- Ensure that teachers, administrators, and student service personnel take part in ongoing, ELL-specific, professional development so that all are adequately informed and prepared to successfully teach our English language learners.

- Lobby our politicians and state education specialists so that they, too, become accurately informed concerning the education of the fastest-growing minority population in America's public schools: our English language learners.

References

Butler, F. A., & Stevens, R. (October 2001). Standardized assessment of the content knowledge of English language learners K–12: Current trends and old dilemmas. *Language Testing, 18*(4), 409–427.

Darling-Hammond, L. (1994). Performance-based assessment and educational equity. *Harvard Educational Review, 64*, 5–30.

Garcia, G., & Pearson, P. (1991). The role of assessment in a diverse society. In E. Hiebert (Ed.), *Literacy for a diverse society: Perspectives, practices, and policies* (pp. 253–278). New York: Teachers College Press.

Gardner, H. (1992). Assessment in context: The alternative to standardized testing. In B. R. Gifford & M. C. O'Conner (Eds.), *Changing assessments: Alternative views of aptitude achievement and instruction* (pp. 37–76). Boston: Kluwer Academic Publishers.

Hafner, A., & Ulanoff, S. (1994). Validity issues and concerns for assessing English learners: One district's approach. *Educational and Urban Society, 26*, 367–389.

Leki, I. (1999). "Pretty much I screwed up": Ill-served needs of a permanent resident. In L. Harklau, K. Losey, & M. Siegal (Eds.), *Generation 1.5 meets college composition: Issues in the teaching of writing to US-educated learners of ESL* (pp.17–44). Mahwah, NJ: Lawrence Erlbaum.

Schmoker, M. (1999). *Results: The key to continuous school improvement* (2nd ed.). Alexandria, VA: Association for Supervision and Curriculum Development.

Stevens, R. A., Butler, F. A., & Castellon-Wellington, M. (December 2000). Academic language and content assessment: Measuring the progress of English language learners (ELLs). CSE Technical Report 552. Los Angeles: CRESST/University of California.

U.S. Department of Education. (2005). The secretary's fourth annual report on teacher quality: A highly qualified teacher in every classroom. Washington, DC: US Dept. of Education, Office of Post-secondary Education, 2005. Available at: from http://www.title2.org/TitleIIReport05.pdf.

Zehr, M. A. (2006, January 11). Scholars seek best ways to assess English-learners. *Education Week*, 10–11.

About the Authors

Editors

Naomi Migliacci currently manages the Training for All Teachers Program at Southern Connecticut State University. Her research interests include language planning and policy in various settings. Recently, she has evaluated language programs and policies in Pennsylvania, Delaware, New York, Maine, and Connecticut. Out of this work, she has developed professional development programs for school districts and universities, and has served as expert witness in diversity and discrimination cases for the U.S. Government's Civil Rights Division in Education. In addition, Naomi has conducted extensive teacher training with teachers from around the world both in the United States and in several countries including China, Iceland, Japan, Peru, Philippines, and France. In addition to long-term teaching experiences in China and Japan and teacher training in university settings, other teaching includes ELLs from K–12, ESL students in colleges and universities, and adult ESL and basic literacy. After completing a Master's degree in TESOL at Azusa Pacific University, she continued her graduate work at The Claremont Graduate School, San Diego State University, and the University of Pennsylvania.

Lorrie Stoops Verplaetse is associate professor of TESOL and Bilingual Education and coordinator of the MS/TESOL Program in the Department of Foreign Languages at Southern Connecticut State University, where she teaches courses in second language acquisition, principles of linguistics, bilingual education, and content-based ESL methods. She has authored and served as project director for two major U.S. Department of Education Title VII grants, first a Bilingual Career Ladder Grant for Salisbury State University in Maryland, and currently a Training for All Teachers Grant at Southern Connecticut State University. As a Fulbright scholar, she lived and trained EFL teachers in Plzen, Czech Republic, at the University of West Bohemia. Her research interests focus on the role of interaction in second language development, particularly in interactions between native speakers and non-native speakers, both in the classroom and in natural speech. Her work has appeared in *TESOL Journal* and *Journal of Education*. Together with Joan Kelly Hall, she edited the book entitled *Second and Foreign Language Learning Through Classroom Interaction*, published by Lawrence Erlbaum.

Chapter Authors

Maria Brisk is a professor of education at the Lynch School of Education, Boston College. She received her Ph.D. in linguistics and bilingual education at the University of New Mexico in 1972. Her research and teacher-training interests include bilingual education, bilingual language and literacy acquisition, methods of teaching literacy, and preparation of mainstream teachers to work with bilingual learners. Dr. Brisk has served as a consultant in legal matters pertaining to bilingual education, and has worked closely with regional and local groups and school systems in developing their bilingual programs, as well as mainstream programs that include bilingual learners. Dr. Brisk was the 1991 Boston University recipient of the Metcalf Cup and Metcalf Prize for excellence in teaching. She is the author of the books *Bilingual Education: From Compensatory to Quality Schooling; Literacy and Bilingualism: A Handbook for ALL Teachers;* and *Situational Context of Education: A Window into the World of Bilingual Learners.* Professor Brisk, as a native of Argentina, is a fluent speaker of Spanish.

Anthony J. Colón joined Fight For Children in February 2005 as senior manager, Education Investment Strategies. A highly regarded and nationally recognized leader in education, Mr. Colón manages Fight For Children's education investments and related education initiatives. By building coalitions and strengthening partnerships, Mr. Colón and Fight For Children are committed to increasing the number of urban youth who are prepared for post-secondary education and career opportunities. Prior to coming to Fight For Children, Mr. Colón served as vice president of education for more than five years at the National Council of La Raza, the largest national Hispanic civil rights and advocacy organization in the United States, with headquarters in Washington, DC. While at the National Council of La Raza, Mr. Colón developed and launched one of the largest nonprofit charter public school development initiatives in the nation, including one of the country's first Early College High School initiatives. Mr. Colón came to Washington, DC, from Oakland, California, where he served as the principal of the Oakland Charter Academy and a member of its Board of Directors. Prior to that he was the principal/executive director of the Beacon School, a private nonprofit, preK–12 school in Oakland. In New York City, Mr. Colón was the director of special education for Community School District Ten and served as the chairperson of the Committee on Special Education. He has served on the faculty of Lehman College at the City University of New York and at Fordham University's Department of Bilingual Services. Mr. Colón holds a Master's degree and a professional diploma in educational administration from Fordham University in New York, as well as a Bachelor's degree in sociology from St. Francis College in Brooklyn, New York.

Edmund 'Ted' Hamann, is an assistant professor in the Department of Teaching, Learning, and Teacher Education at the University of Nebraska-Lincoln and an associated researcher at the Universidad de Monterrey's (Mexico) Centro Interdisciplinario de Estudios de Educación y Superación de Pobreza. He teaches courses on educational policy implementation, high school reform, and school responses to demographic transitions. From 1999 to 2005, he was a research and evaluation specialist at the Education Alliance at Brown University and an adjunct lecturer at Brown's Center for the Study of Race and Ethnicity in America. He is the author of *The Educational Welcome of Latinos in the New South* (Praeger, 2003); coauthor of *Claiming Opportunities: A Handbook for Improving Education for English Language Learners Through Comprehensive School Reform;* and co-editor of the book *Education in the New Latino Diaspora* (Ablex Press, 2001).

Linda Harklau is an associate professor in the Teaching Additional Languages program at the University of Georgia, where she teaches courses in nonnative language literacy and research methodology. Her work on adolescent second language and academic literacy learning has appeared in publications including *TESOL Quarterly, Linguistics and Education, Educational Policy, Journal of Literacy Research,* and *Anthropology and Education Quarterly.* She was the recipient of the 1995 TESOL/Newbury House Distinguished Research Award. Her research focuses on English language and literacy learning in secondary and post-secondary classroom settings.

Tomás Z. Miranda has been a TESOL and bilingual educator for 38 years. Mr. Miranda retired as supervisor of bilingual education and ESL programs for the New Haven Public Schools, New Haven, CT. He started his career as a TESOL teacher in the Gary, Indiana Public Schools, where he was also founder of The Bilingual Education Pre-K to Third Grade Program and the Latin American Family Education Program (now known as La Casa). In 1972, he moved to Bridgeport, Connecticut, where he established and directed the Department of Bilingual Education Services, early childhood education, and founded the Multicultural Magnet School, a school focusing on Spanish, Portuguese, and English languages and cultures. He was active with the Connecticut Association for Bilingual Bicultural Education (CABBE), Connecticut Teachers of English to Speakers of Other Languages (CONNTESOL), the National Association for Bilingual Education (NABE) and National TESOL. He worked with the Connecticut state legislature and the Connecticut Department of Education in the passage of the bilingual education law and the regulations for the certification of bilingual education and TESOL educators. Mr. Miranda continues to be involved in the preparation of bilingual, TESOL, and multicultural educators and in the development of dual language programs throughout Connecticut.

Robert C. "Bob" Parker is a senior coordinator at the Education Alliance at Brown University as well as the New York City Office of the Education Alliance. Mr. Parker taught ESL for 22 years at the elementary, high school and adult levels with an emphasis on developing ESL through content area classes and courses. He has extensive experience in coaching teams conducting action research, as well as conducting training and professional development programs for education professionals, notably with a focus on sheltered English instruction for standard curriculum teachers with Limited English Proficient enrollments. His knowledge of teacher coaching and ESL methods and strategies is particularly notable, as is his expertise in performance assessment. Since the early 1980s, he has assisted city and state education departments in New England, New York, and Canada in developing bilingual and ESL programs for low-incidence numbers of English Language Learners as well as developing formative assessment plans with performance assessments to determine student readiness to participate in mandated English-language testing programs. He has provided a series of capacity-building sessions for New York City Board of Education staff on team building, action research, and performance assessment strategies. He is currently coaching teacher teams in four New York City public schools and is facilitating a Bronx-wide effort to train teams from all the Bronx High Schools in curriculum alignment and associated performance assessments in English Language Arts, ESL, Native Language, and Foreign Language courses. Mr. Parker is a co-author of the Spanish/ESL reading program *Solares,* published by Scholastic.

Aida Walquí, Director of Teacher Professional Development at WestEd, is responsible for collaborating with ongoing WestEd teacher professional development efforts and leading the evolution of an organizational commitment to supporting teachers throughout their careers from recruitment and preservice through induction and life-long learning. Previously, she taught in the Division of Education at the University of California, Santa Cruz, and the School of Education at Stanford University, where she coordinated the Cross-Cultural, Linguistic, and Academic Development emphasis in the STEP program. She has also taught in other universities in Peru, Mexico, England, and the United States. A native of Peru, she received her Licenciatura in Literature from the Universidad Nacional Mayor de San Marcos, Peru. She holds an MA in sociolinguistics from Georgetown University; and a Ph.D. in language, literacy, and culture from Stanford University.

Deborah Wei has been an educator for 25 years, and has taught in both Hong Kong and in the School District of Philadelphia. Currently, she is the lead academic coach for Asian Pacific American Studies in the School District of Philadelphia. She is a founding member and current board member of Asian Americans United, a community based organization dedicated to involving Asian Americans in Philadelphia in exercising leadership to build their communities. She is the co-chair of the board of directors of the Philadelphia Folklore Project (PFP). PFP works to preserve and strengthen the folk cultural life of communities because we believe the quality of life in urban communities is directly related to the persistence, diversity and vitality of vernacular folk cultures. She serves on the International Programs Executive Committee of the American Friends Service Committee, an international NGO committed to peace with justice in the United States and internationally, and has worked as a community organizer and activist for over 25 years. A proud beneficiary of affirmative action, she remains committed to working for peace and justice, including educational equity for all children.

Jerri Willett is a professor at the University of Massachusetts in the Language, Literacy and Culture (LLC) Program. Her research over the past 20 years has focused on the construction of language practices in classrooms and communities that include English language learners (ELL) has led to a NCLB project. Funded by a Title III professional development grant, she and her colleagues are working with 100 in-service teachers through an inquiry-based master's program to better understand and improve instructional practices for ELL students. LLC faculty and in-service teachers working on this project collaborate to document and publish what they are learning.

Jane Yedlin has been involved in the education of language minority students since 1978. She has taught English as a Second Language (ESL) and literacy to speakers of other languages, and has worked in teacher education in various New England, California, and Latin American settings. She is the author of several published ESL/Literacy texts and instructional materials. Her doctorate is in Language and Literacy from the Harvard Graduate School of Education. Yedlin works at the Education Alliance at Brown University and teaches graduate courses for ESL certification.

Index

A

AAU. *see* Asian Americans United
Abu and Bernardo summarize change of feelings in the story, 45
Abu and Bernardo's chart of anger as a theme, *46*
academic English skills, 4
academic language, 6, 64, 74, 75
    building vocabulary and, 62
    developing strategic reading skills, 167–180
    interaction and, 167–180
    secondary classroom and, 167–180
    vocabulary, 65
academic norms, explicit teaching of, 111
Academic Performance Index (API), 122
academic socialization, 49
academic strategies, 111
academic success
    BICS (basic interpersonal communication skills), 74
    CALP (cognitive academic language proficiency) and, 74
    honoring the students' identity, 209
    interaction and, 178
    parental involvement, 209
academic text, comprehensible, 139
    background knowledge, 139
    graphic organizers, 139, 145
    increased use of visuals and realia, 139
    modifying written text, 139, 145
    opportunities to negotiate meaning, 139
    timelines and summary outlines, 139, 145
academies
    Business and Finance Academy, 211
    Health Professions Academy, 211
    Technology Academy, 211

ACCELA (Access to Critical Content and English Language Acquisition), 37, 38
    alliance, 34
    courses, 36
    curriculum design, 36
    federally funded master's degree with licensure in ESL, 34
accountability, increasing, 185
Action Research Process
    collaborative analysis of student learning, 90
    data collection by CAR teams, 90
    evidence that the practice was effective, 90
    expected learning behaviors, examples of, 89
    impact on teachers as learners, 92
    impact on test performance, 93–94
    implementing action, 88
    meeting protocols and, 88
    rubrics and, 88
    selected findings, 88
    selected scoring guides, 88
    strategic learning strategies, 89
    terminology of instruction and, 88
activism, public schools and, 233
activist organizations
    Asian Americans United (AAU), 226
    Chinatown, Philadelphia, 225–242
activitist organizations, 225–244
    parental engagement and, 225–244
    Philadelphia's Chinatown and, 225–244
advanced placement classes, 121
Aetna, school reform and, 214
after–school language enrichment program model, 273
Alfie Gives a Hand (Hughes, 1985), 64
Amelia's Road, 21

American dream, 328
  bilingual education and, 206
  upward mobility, 181
American Society for Training and Development, 81
Annenberg Institute for School Reform, 3
Annenberg Research Symposium on Educating
     English Language Learners, 197, 225,
     225–244
Annie E. Casey Foundation, "Educating English
     Language Learners" (series of guides), 208
Asian Americans United (AAU), 226, 241
  activist organization, 226
  Asian American Freedom School, 238
  charter schools, CBO based, 225
  community–school linkages, 226
  meetings and, 226
Aspire Public Schools, CA, 205
Aspire Public Schools, CA, as a charter
     management organization (CMO), 205
assessment
  authentic, 116
  classroom, 117
  embedded in everyday practice, 117
  fairness and, 159–160
  language and, 247
  by learners, 116
  rubric–based, 337
  of student writing, 116
Association of American Medical Colleges'
     Project 3000 by 2000, 214
audience, sense of, 41, 45

B

background knowledge
  activating, 131
  building, 129
  shared, 130
  think-pair-share exercise, 130
bed-to-bed stories, 15
Bernardo's storybook, *43*
Betances, Samuel, 206
BICS (basic interpersonal communication skills),
     74, 263
  acquisition of, 6
  learned in one to two years, 8
bilingual education, 325–326
  academic success and, 258
  access to American dream, 206
  for all students, 257–275
  benefits of, 258
  dual-language schooling, 258
  as an educational tool, 206
  Elementary and Secondary Education Act,
     Title VII, 257

  ELLs (English Language Learners) and, 206
  foreign language skill and, 206
  late-exit transitional, 258
  Latino children, 206
  people of color as target audience, 206
  proficiency in two languages, 206
  punctuation and spelling in both languages, 90
bilingual education, models of
  after-school second-language enrichment model,
     259
  dual-language schooling, 259
  gradual-exit transitional bilingual education
     combined with foreign-language
     programs, 259
  in-school second-language resource centers, 259
bilingual education, six principles for effective
     practice, 259
  assessment of language proficiency for
     appropriate placement, 266
  each language learner has his or her own
     language and content profile, 259–260
  education programs reflect language-
     acquisition stages, 260–261
  older students require language development
     and formal content learning, 265–266
  young language learners require an
     acquisition-rich environment, 261–263
  young students and literacy development,
     263–264
bilingual learners, 29
  additional challenges of, 22
  challenges with grammar, 27
  educational issues of, 81
  individual needs of, 26
  spoken v. written language and, 29
Biology: The Living Science, 133
block scheduling, 201
Boggs, Grace Lee, 229, 233
boredom, 112
Brown University, 3, 81
Brown v. Board of Education, test scores and, 245
Buddhist economics, 240
buddy reading, 38, 48
Bulkeley High School, 212, 218, 325–326. *see also*
     Health Professions Academy
  academies and, 212
  mission statement, 215
  University of Connecticut (UConn), 212
Business and Finance Academy, 211
businesses and corporations, community
     partnerships with schools and, 218

C

California Central Valley, Hmong communities, 116–117
California Tomorrow, 236
CALP (cognitive academic language proficiency), 7, 8, 74, 263
  acquisition of, 6
  learned in five to ten years, 8
  skills in other languages and, 7
Cambridge Rindge, Health Professions Academy and, 218
CAR (Collaborative Action Research), 79
  across-districts activity, 82
  across-grade activity, 82
  across-schools project, 95
  action plan, strategic plan, 85
  activities and, 82
  collecting evidence, 86
  ELLs (English Language Learners) and, 84
  inquiry question, 84
  school teams and, 80
  strategic learning strategies, 88
  test performance and, 93–94
  uses of, 80
  using a protocol, 85
CAR (Collaborative Action Research), teachers and, 92
  better discussion during team meetings, 93
  collaboration across categories on curriculum articulation, 93
  collaboration on integration of test tasks into instruction, 93
  revision of native language and ESL syllabi to align with mandated tests and state and city content standards, 92
  variety of assessment tools, 92
CAR (Collaborative Action Research) teams, 80
  adapting the plan for their schools, 87
  coaching, 81–82
  data collection and, 90
  guiding questions for teacher inquiry and action research teams, 82
  new England and, 81
  state and city mandated tests, 99
  student growth in language proficiency, 99
  work teams and, 80
CAR (Collaborative Action Research) teams, learning principles and, 83
  applying competencies in learning-performance tasks is more authentic than test-practice materials, 83
  continuous assessment encourages teachers to diagnose student needs, 83
  discuss succeeding on mandated tests, 84

  infusing test tasks creates instruction that is more student-performance-data driven, 84
  students connect value of learning strategies with test requirements, 84
  students internalize competencies long-term through authentic learning tasks, 83
  supports students in life–long learning and on-the-job situations, 84
  test–prep made real and useful to students, 84
career goals
  ELLs (English Language Learners), 177
CBO schools, 203, 207, 208, 210
  child-centered education, 200
  community buy-in, 199
  community-run schools and, 198
  financial viability and, 199
  positive approach and, 204
  programs attended by parents, 202
  wraparound services and, 202
Center for Applied Linguistics (CAL), 163
Center for Research on Education, Diversity and Excellence (CREDE), 163
Center for the Improvement of Early Reading Achievement (CIERA), 264
Central Connecticut State University, 214
Chamot, Anna Uhl, 88
Chargaff, Erwin, 133
Chargaff's Rules, 133
charter and community based school movement, 205
  traditional public schools and, 205
charter management organization (CMO), 205
charter schools, CBO based, 197, 198, 203, 204, 207–210, 229
  Asian Americans United (AAU), 225
  children of undocumented Mexican immigrants, 202
  Chinatown, Philadelphia, 229
  community and, 228, 231
  folk art as theme, 229–230
  funding challenges, 232
  Oakland, CA, 202
  parental involvement and, 204
  Philadelphia's Chinatown, 225, 230–232
  public schools and, 204
  selection of students, 232
  size of, 204–205
  vision of society and, 234
checklist schools can use to link with community partners, 223
child-directed speech (CDS), 73
Children's Defense Fund, 238
Chinatown, Philadelphia, 225–242, 232
  activitist organization and, 225–242

charter schools, CBO based, 229, 325–328, 328
community and, 225
culture in, 226
linguistic diversity in, 226
parental engagement and, 225–242
public schools, traditional, 226
stadium issue and, 238
Church of the Advocate, 237
Cipher in the Snow (Atkinson, Mizer, & Pearson),
154
class content, 37
classes, teacher-fronted, 113
classroom culture, community of learners and, 104
classroom talk, comprehensible, 145
adjusting teacher's speech, 145–150, 157
framing main ideas, 156, 157
modeling speech, 150, 157
pausing, 148
repetition of key terms and expressions, 148–150
using graphic organizers, 157
using listening guides, 150, 157
using word walls, 150, 157
coaches of teacher inquiry or action research teams,
responsibilities of, 81–82
collaboration
comprehension and, 113
jigsaw configuration, 113–114
collaboration, school and community, 197–244
activist organization and parental engagement
in Philadelphia's Chinatown, 225–244
community based organizations as
partnerships for student success, 197–210
high school and university partnerships, 211–224
Collaborative Action Research, 80–82
Across-Grade and Across-School, 82
Activities, Products Developed, and Findings of,
82
Collaborative Action Research Teams, 79–100, 83
action plan, strategic plan, 85
adapting the plan for their schools, 87–88
applied research, 83–84
coaching, 79–100
collecting evidence, 86
description, 83
elements of the practice, 85
inquiry question, 84
Issues and Concerns, 83
protocol, using, 85
scaffolding strategies, 85–86
team language focus, 87–88
Collaborative Analysis of Student Learning, 90
college students, reading demands and, 191
Colón, Anthony, 197, 325–326, 325–327, 328
colonias, Rio Grande Valley, 209
Commission on Achieving Necessary Skills, 181

Committee on the Prevention of Reading
Difficulties in Young Children, National
Research Council, recommendations of,
264
community-based organizations (CBOs), 197,
197–210, 211
CBO based charter schools and, 207–210
charter vs. public schools and, 204–206
cultural competence and, 198, 199–202
ELLs (English Language Learners), 198
history of, 202–203
impact of community linkages for ELLs, 206
schools and, 199, 202–203
services offered by, 199–202
student success and, 197–210
community heroes, 237
community involvement, 227
academic success and, 209
student success and, 238
community members, partnerships with schools,
219
community organizations, partnerships with
schools, 219
community partnerships with schools, 236, 241
academic success and, 238
English language learners, 225
government and military, 219
parental involvement and, 226
school reform and, 222–223
types of, 219
community partnerships with schools, challenges
of, 220
assuring equal access to services of the
partners for students and families, 220
informing families about programs and
services, 220
partners must match efforts with the school's
or program's goals, 220
turf problems, 220
community partnerships with schools, outcomes of,
219
benefits to teachers of, 219
enriched curricular and extracurricular
activities, 219
exploration of careers and future educational
work, 219
positive relationships with adults, 219
sense of belonging to the community, 219
community-school linkages, 227, 325–326
establishing, 236–237
importance of community in, 234
using community in the classroom, 237–238
community, sense of, 227–228
compare and contrast matrix, 108
composition framework, 92

comprehensible course content, contextualization and, 128
comprehension, 107
    of main ideas, 90
    promoting, 63
    second-language development and, 161
conflict mediation, 201
content, teaching for language development, 36
context, teaching, 122
    collegial environments, 122
contextualization
    creating opportunities for students to negotiate meaning, 139
    new ideas and tasks, 110
    shared background, creating, 139
    sheltered instruction, 128
    using visuals, realia, and hands-on experiences, 139
conversational skills, 6
coordinated units, 50
    different grade levels and, 33–53
counselors of high school and middle school, career goals of ELLs and, 177
course placement and tracking systems, navigating
    assign an educator to review ELL course assignments, 182–183
    foster cohorts of college-bound ELLs, 184
    make information accessible on course choices and college requirements, 183–184
    talk explicitly with students about tracking, 182
Cristo Rey High School, Chicago, 218
critical literacy questions, 38
cross–cultural differences, 329
cross–cultural differences significant for schooling (listed), 247, 329, 330
    how children are expected to interact with each other and with adults, 247, 329
    how language is acquired and displayed, 247, 329
    how language is used by children and adults, 247, 329
    what counts as knowledge, 247
cross–grade dynamics, 48
Crotta, Michael, 139, 140, 150, 153
cultural and recreational organizations, community partnerships with schools and, 219
cultural capital, using, immigrant students and, 130
cultural inequity, 235
Cummins, Jim, 6, 128
curricular unit (Andrea's), 43, 44
curricular unit (Joanne's), 40
curriculum, designing, 38
    ACCELA (Access to Critical Content and English Language Acquisition) course requirements and, 39
    backward design and, 36
    city and school context, 37
    dealing with content and language, 36
    mandated standards and goals and, 36
    meaningful and comprehensible content and, 36
    powerful learning principles and strategies and, 36
    respecting and drawing on *students' funds of knowledge*, 36
    state curriculum standards and, 36
    support for ELLs through scaffolding, 37
    Teaching English to Speakers of Other Languages (TESOL), 36
curriculum, mandated, 33

D

Department of Health Career Opportunity program, 214
Dewey, John, 245–246
Dibels Reading Assessment (DRA), 38, 48
"Directions in Language Education," 264
discourse of power, teaching to minority students, 112
district assessment of Bernardo, *38*
diversity, 11
    importance of addressing, 235
Diving dolphin, 99
draft, organizing, 26
dropout rate, Latinos and, 309
dual language model, one possible way to distribute language in, 268
dual-language schooling, 190–191, 258
Dynamic Indicators of Basic Early Literacy Skills (DIBELS), 48

E

"Educating English Language Learners" (series of guides), 208
"Educating our Ells," 3
education. *see also* bilingual education
    American, 205
    child-centered, 200, 201
    diversity and, 235
    holistic approach to, 202
Education Alliance, Brown University, 3, 81, 82, 83, 245
    "Educating English Language Learners" (series of guides), 208
EFL: English as a foreign language, 12
ELA test, 96
Elementary and Secondary Education Act (ESEA)
    scientifically based instructional strategies, 335

Title VII, 257
elementary classroom, 3–102
    collaborative action research teams, 79–102
    first grade, 55–77
    first grade teaching, 55
    inclusive pedagogy, an introduction, 3–14
    integrating test tasks into everyday classroom
        activities, 79–102
    manipulatives, 131
    pedagogical thinking and teacher talk in a
        first-grade ELL classroom, 55–78
    a scaffolded approach to learning to write, 15–32
    tracking and, 48
    transforming standard practices to serve the
        social and academic learning of English
        Language learners, 15–32
elementary classrooms
    maintain high expectations, 318–319
    teaching, recommended ELL practices, 319,
        333–335
elementary classrooms, inclusive pedagogy in
    maintain high expectations, 318–319
    make content comprehensible, 321
    recommended practices, 322
ELL educational practitioners, 6
ELL practices for elementary and secondary
        classrooms, recommended, 318, 325
ELL–responsive learning environments, 248, 332
    assessment is authentic and takes into account
        first- and second-language literacy, 252
    cross-cultural awareness infused in
        curriculum, 332
    educating ELLs is the responsibility of the
        entire staff, 248
    equitable access to all school resources and
        programs, 250–251
    equity in use of two languages at school, 332
    guiding questions for, 245
    language and literacy infused throughout the
        curriculum, 251–252
    links between home, school, and community,
        250
    opportunities for integration of all students
        several times per day, 332
    recognition of heterogeneity of ELLs and vary
        responses to them, 248
    students' languages and cultures as resources
        for further learning, 249
    teachers have high expectations for ELLs, 251
    teachers prepared and willing to teach ELLs, 251
ELL–responsive learning environments, models of,
        267
    after-school second-language enrichment
        program, 271–273, 332
    dual-language programs, 267, 332
    gradual–exit transitional bilingual education
        programs combined with world
        language programs, 269–270, 332
    in-school language resource centers, 271, 332
ELL teaching strategies, reactions to, 159–160
    but how is this fair; isn't it cheating? 159–160
    but I want to give students full flavor of the
        text, 160
    but this is just good instruction, 159
    but who has time? 159
ELLs (English language learners), 11, 12, 35, 49, 83,
        168, 212, 242, 258
    academic English skills, 4
    academic needs and, 8
    academic performance and, 6, 163, 245–255
    accommodations for, 9
    autonomy and, 111
    BICS (basic interpersonal communication
        skills) and, 6
    building responsive learning environments, 245
    CALP (cognitive academic language
        proficiency) and, 6
    career goals, 177
    challenges and, 127
    college preparatory courses and, 178
    common misconceptions clarified, 4–5, 5
    community connections and partnerships, 225
    comprehensible language input and course
        content, 10
    cultural capital, using, 171–172
    decontextualized language and, 111
    demographics and, 5
    dismal success numbers and, 8
    diversity of, 4, 248, 249
    engagement, 7
    engagement and, 10, 127
    English fluency and, 6
    evaluation of success and, 247
    failure of schools to meet needs of, 103
    fairness and, 159–160
    gifted students and, 4
    grade 4 wall and, 7
    high school completion and, 4–5
    home language and, 258
    inclusive environments and, 329
    interactive strategies and, 176
    international academies and, 217
    K–12, 4
    Latino, 208
    learning ability, 10
    learning disabilities and, 4
    literacy instruction, 55–77
    mainstreaming advanced students, 71
    making course content comprehensible for, 127
    meeting the needs of ELLs, 305–317

middle school educators and, 127
numbers of, 4–5
opportunities for participation, 61
participation in themed academy, 218
performance mandated tests and, 84
personal narratives and, 30
placement decisions and, 266
preparation for culture of college work, 187–188
proficiency and, 6
proficiency in academic language, 177
public schools and, 10
reasonable accommodations and, 8, 9
recommendation for teaching writing, 177
research-informed practices and, 3
responsive learning environments and, 245–256
"rich with another language," 206
safe and stimulating environment, 10, 127
secondary educators and, 127
sheltered from interaction opportunities by
    teacher, 168
smaller learning communities (SLCs), 212
social and academic learning and, 33–52
social participation and, 59
Spanish-dominant, 4, 270, 271
spelling and, 69
standardized measurement and, 336
statistics and, 4
strengths and challenges, 211–224
student writing opportunities,
    recommendations for increasing, 178
successful schooling for, 245–256
supportive classroom environments and, 72
talk directed to, 73
teacher training and, 5
teaching of genre and, 49
transforming standard practices to serve their
    social and academic needs, 15–32
U.S. public schools and, 3, 4, 33
ELLs (English language learners), adolescent,
    103–125, 177
American schools and, 103
demographics and, 103
teacher expertise and, 103–126
teachers of, 122
writing and, 167, 177
ELLs (English language learners), language
    acquisition
early intermediate phase, 172
mid-level intermediate phase (one-to-two
    sentences, 172
one- and two-word phase, 172
pre-production phase, 172
ELLs (English language learners), misconceptions
fluency and managing mainstream classes, 6
immersion, 6–7

that earlier generations of immigrants didn't
    speak English and didn't need special
    programs, 7–8
that teachers must know home language of ELL
    to teach, 7
ELLs (English language learners), needs of
ability to engage with content and interact with
    students and teachers about that content,
    10
ability to learn, 10
comprehensible language input and course
    content, 10
safe and stimulating environment, 10
ELLs (English language learners), preparation for
    the culture of college work
instruction on test-taking strategies, 188
prepare students to work independently, 187–188
teach note-taking skills, 188
ELLs (English language learners), secondary
academic classroom talk, understanding, 139
academic texts, reading, 139
problematic aspects of course content delivery,
    139
ELLs (English language learners), special needs and,
    277–303, 300–301
achievement difficulties of ELLs, 295–296
achievement difficulties of ELLs in English
    from a language–acquisition
    perspective, 283–284
achievement difficulties of young ELLs with
    little or no education abroad, 285
acknowledging progress and assets, 289–290
the advantage for ELLs educated abroad,
    284–285, 286–288
culture and acculturation, 299–300
detecting impairments and disabilities from
    early childhood, 285–286
disabling condition, 279
education and academic background, 299
education obtained in the United States, 288
information–gathering process: child's age and
    current placement, 280–281
information–gathering process: child's life,
    language development, and educational
    history, 282–293
information-gathering process: cultural
    background of the child and family,
    281–282
information-gathering process: parents'
    educational background and careers, 282
Interview question checklist, 291–295
lack of opportunity vs. disability, 296–297
language development, 298
life history, 298
linguistic world of ELLs in the United States, 284

opportunities offered by the school district, 288–289
opportunity to learn, 297
overrepresentation of ELLs in special education due to misdiagnosis, 293–295
parental background and roles, 299
referral, common scenarios, 278
referral, drawing conclusions, 290
referral, guidelines for decisions, 277–278
referral, overall processes, 298
research and professional literature review, 292–293
special education and, 307
ELLs (English language learners), teaching of
interweaving of social and academic worlds and literate futures, 36
publication of students' work, 36
reinforcement of language and content with experiential and multimodal activities, 36
social interaction and, 36
teaching language features in a meaningful context, 36
teaching writing in different genres, 36
use of authentic contexts, texts, purposes and audiences, 36
use of everyday routines to scaffold a curricular unit, 36
ELLs (English language learners), ways of referring to
ELL: English language learner, 12
LEP: limited English proficient, 12
NNS: nonnative speaker, 12
English as a second language. see ESL
English class, sheltered, 184
English language
immersion, 6
proposed Constitutional amendment regarding U.S. official language and, 258
sound–symbol correspondence, 29
English Language Arts exam, fourth grade, 79
English language learners. see ELLs (English Language Learners)
English literacy, 8
immigrants and, 7–8
importance of first language and, 247
English-only policy, 59
English Regents exam (high-school-level), 79
ESL/Bilingual and mainstream teachers, repairing schism between, 305–316
some demographic reminders, 306–307
two cases, 307–310, 312–314
ESL (English as a second language)
myths about, 5
second language, ways of referring to, 12
ESL ghetto, 120

ESL instruction, 34, 55, 120, 127, 217, 242, 325–326
adolescents and, 106
bilingualism and, 59
effective, 106
foreign language skill and, 7, 8, 59
high school and, 177
highly controlled language, 7
highly controlled language and, 8
in-school language resource center model, 272
knowledge of home language and, 8
literacy curriculum, 59
middle school and, 177
training for in Mexico, 309
ESL Intersegmental Project (California Pathways Project), 191
ESOL: English to speakers of other languages, 11–12, 12
ethnography, 305
evaluation rubric, 98
expected learning behaviors, examples of, 89
extended discourse, literacy and, 74

F
faith-based organizations, community partnerships with schools and, 219
fine arts, 201
first language, 19
development of literacy and, 8
discounting, 329
importance of using, 8
scaffolding and, 109
successful schooling and, 246
First Steps approach to literacy and language development, 37
folk arts, 230–231
framing main ideas, 156–157
examples of (7th grade history unit), 157
Freedom Schools, 238
African American, 238
Asian American, 238
Chinatown, 238
Latino, 238

G
gated communities, 234
Gates Foundation's Early College High Schools, 184
genre, 112
identifying features of, 49
selecting, 25
Gerena Elementary School
diversity demographics of, 37

First Steps approach to literacy and language
    development, 37
    Latino population of, 37
    Springfield, MA, 37
Giuliano, Mary, 217
give one, get one activity, 132–133, *133*
government and military, community
    partnerships with schools and, 219
grade 4 wall, 7
grammar and syntax, issues of, 66
graphic organizers
    10th grade ELL history students' lesson on
        Dust Bowl, 139
    10th grade ELL history students' lesson on
        Great Depression, 140
    to accompany reading for intermediate ELLs,
        142, 142
    for beginning ELLs: Dust Bowl, *140*, 140
    course content and, 139
    created by graduate students in ESL teaching
        programs, 159
    created by mainstream classes, 159
    created through student community service
        requirements, 159
    for intermediate ELLs: Dust Bowl, *141*, 141
    lesson on Dust Bowl and, 139
    listening guides and, 150
    shared with other teachers, 159

H

*Handbook of College Reading and Study Strategy
    Research* (Flippo & Caverly), 191
hands-on experience and, 133
Hanh, Thich Nhat, 233
Harding, Vince, 233
Harman, Ruth, 34
Hartford Public Schools, 213, 214
    district mission, 213
health–care industries and organizations,
    community partnerships with schools
    and, 219
Health Professions Academy, 211, 214, 215
    Bulkeley High School, 212
    Bulkeley-UConn partnership and, 215
    educational activities and, 215
    ELLs (English Language Learners), success and,
        212
    ESL services and, 212
    field trips, 216
    flexibility of scheduling and curriculum, 212
    future projects and, 216
    Giuliano, Mary, 217
    Healthcare for Uninsured Kids and Youth
        (HUSKY) initiative, 216

nonnative English speakers and, 218
parental involvement and, 216
partnership of high school students and large
    health center, 215
service-learning activities, 216
State of Connecticut Department of Social
    Services and, 216
students to shadow doctors, 216
teleconferencing, 216
University of Connecticut and, 212, 215, 216
Health Professions Academy, goals of, 215
    aid with career choices, 215
    foster understanding of the department's role
        in the health–care profession, 215
    involve students in community service
        programs, 215
    involve students in internship programs, 215
    provide career guidance, 215
    provide experience in laboratory settings and
        scientific projects, 215
    provide exposure to the health care
        professions, 215
    provide training leading to Red Cross
        certification, 215
    stimulate independent research, 215
    student pursuit of higher postsecondary
        education, 216
Health Professions Partnerships Initiative (HPPI),
    212, 325–326, 327
    benefits to teachers and, 219
    case study, 212
    educational enrichment and support for
        minority students, 214
    increase awareness and proficiency in sciences,
        214
    increase minority students pursuing health
        professional careers, 214
*Helping English Learners Succeed: An Overview
    of the SIOP* (video, Center for Applied
    Linguistics), 131
Henry, Robert, 214
heritage language programs, 218
high–poverty neighborhoods, 221
high school and university partnerships, 211–224
    challenges of, 211
    ELLs (English Language Learners) and, 211–224
    Health Professions Academy and, 212
    Health Professions Partnerships Initiative
        (HPPI), 212
    strengths and challenges for ELLs and, 211–224
high school environment, sheltered courses, 217
high-stakes accountability, 122
highly controlled language and
    ESL teachers and, 8

Hispanic family learning institute, 208
Hispanic students, 83
    high school completion and, 4
Hmong communities, 116
    California Central Valley, 116–117
Hogan, Andrea, 33–53, 34, 37
    First Steps approach to literacy and language
        development, 37
holistic approach to education, National Council
    of La Raza (NCLR), 202
home language survey, 260
homework assignment: questions to ponder, *138*
    history class: grades 9–12, 138
Hoover Junior High, 117
humor, using in classroom, 66

I

If Your Names Were Changed at Ellis Island, 25
immersion, 62
immigrant students
    academic skills and, 110
    classes for, 113
    cultural capital and, 130–131
    English and, 206
    failure rate and, 9
    language of instruction and, 206
    social world and academic achievement, 191
    ten priorities to guide instruction design for, 104
    tracking and, 191
    training of educators and, 206
immigrant students, college bound, 181–196
    academic challenges and opportunities for,
        181–196
    beyond high school, 181–194
    college preparation, 191
    course placement and tracking systems, 181, 182
    develop strategic reading skills, 185
    discourse–level instruction on vocabulary and
        grammar, 186–187
    high school and, 181–194
    instruction on test-taking strategies, 188
    mainstream English and Social Studies classes,
        181, 184–185
    participation in school social life, 181, 189–190
    preparation to work independently, 187–188
    preparing ELLs for the culture of college work,
        181, 186–187
    teach note-taking skills, 188–189
    timed essays, 185
    writing from sources, 185–186
immigrants
    academic achievement and social world, 191

immigrants, adolescent, 107
    age-appropriate communicative competence in
        their own languages, 109
immigrants, earlier generations of, 7–8
    differences from current generation, 8
immigrants, fostering participation in school
        social life
    awareness of diversity within immigrant
        groups, 190
    awareness of popular and youth cultures in the
        school, 189–190
    make a place for home languages and cultures
        in the school, 190–191
    remove barriers to participation in
        extracurricular activities, 190
    welcome home languages and cultures, 190
immigrants, study of Mexican, 246
immigration subtopics, *24*
inclusive pedagogy, 3–14, 10, 11, 312
    common misconceptions, 4–5
    connecting with students at personal and
        instructional level, 11
    in high stakes testing environment, 332–334
    home language and, 11
    literacy acquisition as affective as well as
        cognitive, 11
    literacy experience in first-language as
        important, 11
    mandate-driven climate and, 317–342
    myth that a single workshop prepares faculty
        to raise ELL achievement, 338–339
    myth that mandated standardize tests show
        academic growth of student body,
        334–335
    myth that only instructional strategies
        supported by scientific research can be
        supported, 335
    myth that scripted preparation for exams are
        the best way to succeed on mandated
        exams, 338
    myth that teachers trained in "differentiated
        instruction" know about educating
        ELLs, 339
    parental involvement and, 11
    statistics and, 4
inclusive pedagogy, recommended practices, 317
    accommodate needs, talents, and interests of
        ELLS and their home community, 327
    appropriate professional development for
        teachers, 329
    challenge the special needs label, 331
    community linkages, 324
    create ELL-inclusive environments, 329
    create personalized learning environments, 328
    create sustainable relationships, 326

elementary classrooms, 322, 323, 324
engage in authentic practices, 323
in high stakes testing environment, 340
holistic approach, 325
increase student interaction and engagement, 321
maintain high expectations, 318–319, 319–321
make content comprehensible, 321
middle and secondary classrooms, 322–323, 323, 324
parent involvement through CBOs that provide high-quality wraparound services, 327
practices in the classroom: elementary and secondary (listed), 317–318
professional development, 324
promote grassroots involvement and community buy–in, 326
redefine community–school partnerships, 326
redefine what it means to educate ELLs, 326
school and district reform, 328–329
start with a celebratory attitude, 325
use research in redesigning ELL programs, 331
Inside High School reform: Making the Changes That Matter (Jordan Horowitz), 222
Institute for Community Research, 216
Institute of Education Sciences (IES)
U.S. Department of Education, 335
instruction
inquiry based, 15, 132
mandated techniques, 33
student-centered, 171
teacher-fronted, 171
instruction design, priorities for, 104
contextualizing new ideas and tasks, 110–111
develop a community of learners, 104–105
maximize opportunities for interaction, 113–115
promote students conceptual and academic development, 106–107
provide multiple opportunities to extend understanding and apply knowledge, 115–116
teaching academic strategies, sociocultural expectations, and academic norms, 111–112
use cyclical organization of substantive ideas, 110
using students' experiential background, 107–110
using tasks that are relevant, meaningful, engaging, and varied, 112–113
view authentic assessment as an integral part of teaching and learning, 116–117
instructional conversations (IC), 132, 169–170
intensive verbal interaction, 73
interaction
academic language and, 167–180
benefits of, 174
collaboration and, 113
linguistic, 72
maximizing, 113
native to nonnative speakers, 175
scaffolding, 109
SLA theory and, 174
studies of, 174
interaction, classroom
academic language proficiency and, 168
benefits of, 168
content learning and, 167
ELL students often sheltered from, 168
importance of, 167
social development and, 167
interaction, comprehensibility and
improved abilities to carry out academic functions, 174
improved task accomplishment, 174
increased metalinguistic awareness of grammatical structures, 174
increased vocabulary and, 174
interaction opportunities, strategies for providing, 168–172
increase student to student activities, 170
interactionally challenge the intermediate ELL student, 173–174
let ELL students use their first languages, 174
model students' responses for beginning and early-intermediate ELL students, 173
modify teacher questions, 168–169
modify teacher responses, 169
modify teacher talk in teacher-fronted classrooms, 168–169
research supporting these strategies, 174
use instructional conversations, 169
vary questioning techniques and assignments based on language-proficiency level, 172–173
international academies, as dumping grounds for ELLs, 217
international competition, 181
International High School (IHS), 107
English language learners, 105
internships, 218
Introduction to DNA structure: Chargraff's Rules, 9th grade biology, DNA unit, 135

J

jigsaw activity, 113–114, 170–171
Johnson, Mary, 145, 148
Julius Caesar by Shakespeare, rewritten text of, 145

K

K–12 administrators, 3
Keeping Track (Jeannie Oakes), 191
Kendria read her storybook to Teresa, *47*
Kendria's bothersome issue, *41*
Kendria's simile, *41*
Kendria's storybook, *43*
Kidwatching, 109
King, Dr. Martin Luther, 233, 237
knowledge, 120–121
    content, 120, 120–121
    cultural, 28
    pedagogical, 120
    self-knowledge, 120, 121
    of students, 120, 121
    subject-matter, 120
    teachers and, 120
Krashen, Stephen, 260–261
KWHL chart
    H for how I am going to learn, 130
KWL chart, 130
    KWL chart (know, want, learn), 129–130

L

LAD (language acquisition device), 9
language
    analysis, 90
    interpersonal, 128
    knowledge of, 28
    power and, 112
    primacy of English in schools, 235
language, academic
    decontextualized, 128–129
    as language of strangers, 128
language acquisition, 260
    attention to form and, 161
    brain and, 9
    comprehensible input, 9, 161
    conditions for, 161
    interaction and, 9, 167
    learner production of modified output, 161
    safe and stimulating environment, 9
language and culture division (LCD), 311, 312
language-as-resource orientation, 11
Language Assessment Battery (LAB), 90
language, decontextualized
    academic lectures, 129
    textbooks, 129
language, literacy and culture (LLC) program, 34
language of instruction, immigrant students and, 206
language proficiency profile
    interview in English and second language, 266
    norm-referenced tests in English and second language, if available, 266
    writing sample in both languages, 266
Latin School in Massachusetts
    homework help for Health Professions Academy, 218
Latino population, growth of in U.S., 206
Lau v. Nichols, 8, 307, 311
    ELLs (English Language Learners) and, 160
learning disabilities. *see also* special needs
    sheltered instruction observation protocol (SIOP) and, 163
learning, self-directed, 116
learning style
    manipulatives and, 131
learning theory, 9
lectures, 188–189
Lee y serás "Read and You Shall Be," Latino early childhood literacy initiative, 208
LEP: limited English proficient
    demographics and, 5
    English language learners, ways of referring to, 12
    statistics and, 4
lessons, contextualizing for comprehension, 128, 129
    building background knowledge,, 129
    give one, get one activity, 132, 132–133
    hands-on experience and, 131
    increased question-and-answer opportunities, 132
    inquiry-based instructional style, 132
    instructional conversations (IC), 132
    KWL chart, 129
    opportunities to negotiate meaning, 132
    think-pair-share, 130
    tickets into or out of the classroom, 132
    using realia, 131
    using the cultural capital in the room, 130–131
    visuals and, 131
Letters from Rifka, 19
Lewin, Kurt, 80
Lighthouse Community Charter school
    National Council of La Raza (NCLR), 198
    Oakland, California, 198
linguistic abundancy, 107
listening guides, 158
    10th grade ELL history students' lesson on Great Depression, 150
    7th grade history lesson and, 150
    to accompany film, 'Roots of War" for early ELLs, 154, *154*
    to accompany lecture about the Continental and British Armies, History 7th grad, 151
    for advanced ELLs and full class: Great Depression, history class 10th grade, 153

Roots of War (Vecchione, 1983), 150
literacy, 28
    first language and, 11
    interaction and, 178
    research about, 48
    standards for K–12 students at state and
        national levels, 75
    strategies for preschool-aged children, 208
literary narratives, curricular unit on, 39
Lozano, Maria Eugenia, 34
Lynn Public School, Massachusetts, 218

M

mainstream content, comprehensible, 133
    sheltered instruction and, 127–166
mainstream courses, preparation for, 106
mainstream English and Social Studies classes,
        comprehensible and challenging
        instruction in
    developing strategic reading skills, 185
    practice timed essays and writing from
        sources, 185–185
    provide discourse-level instruction on
        vocabulary and grammar, 186–187
mainstream lessons, contextualized
    examples of, 133
    in high school history lesson on colonization of
        Indochina, 133–134
    in ninth-grade biology lesson on DNA, 133–134
*Making Content Comprehensible for English
        Learners* (Echevarria, Vogt, and SHort),
        261
Malcolm X, 237
mandated tests
    English Regents exam (high-school-level), 88
    integration of into literacy and content area
        lessons, 83
    New York State, 79
    New York State English Language Arts, 88
    student readiness for, 83
Maniac Magee (Spinelli, 1990), 41
manipulatives, 131
    elementary classroom, 131
    middle school and high school, 131
Massachusetts Department of Education, 37
    curriculum standards, 37
    elimination of transitional bilingual education
        in 2002, 37
    state teacher licensure requirements to support
        ELLs in mainstream classroom, 37
material, organizing, 26
math, 85
Matthew and Tilly (Jones, Rebecca C.), 44–45

MCAS (Massachusetts Comprehensive
        Assessment System), 37
McGovern, Pat, 145, 149
McLaughlin, Barry, *Myths and Misconceptions
        about Second Language Learning:
        What Every Teacher Needs to Unlearn*, 5
metacognitive skill, 90
metalinguistic concepts and vocabulary, 65
MetLife Survey of the American Teacher, 120
Mexican university
    school partnership with, 308
middle and secondary classrooms, inclusive
        pedagogy in
    maintain high expectations, 319–321
    make content comprehensible, 321
    manipulatives, 131
    recommended practices, 322–323, 324
minilessons, 23, 30, 39, 44, 49
    genre features, 38
    scaffolding activities and, 44
minority students
    importance of comfort zone and, 236
modeled language, 154
    "Cipher in the Snow" exercise English
        literature grades 9–12, 157
    for discussion proposals: Vietnam, History
        class grades 9–12, 156
    example of, 154
    Solutions in Vietnam, History class grades
        9–12, 155
    use of for discussion proposals, *156*
morphemes, 21
motivation, 121–122
    of teachers, 121
*Multilingual Education in Practice: Using Diversity
        as a Resource (Schecter and Cummins)*,
        10–11
multiple academic registers, access to, 49
"Myths About Second Language Learning"
    ESL Standards for Pre-K-12 Students
        (TESOL, Inc.), 5

N

National Center for Family Literacy
    Hispanic Family Learning Institute, 208
    literacy in children and adult education, 208
National Clearing House for English Acquisition
        (NCELA), 305
    Language Instruction Education Programs, 264
National Coalition of Education Activists
        (NCEA), 233
National Council of La Raza (NCLR), 197–199, 202,
        325–326
    charter schools and, 209

"Educating English Language Learners" (series of guides), 208
IDEA Academy in Rio Grande Valley of Texas, 209
Latino civil rights and, 197
Lee y serás "Read and You Shall Be," 208
Parent as Partners curriculum, 208
require that their schools become a 501(c)(3), 199
National Postsecondary Education Cooperative, Working Group on Access to Postsecondary Education, 191
national service and volunteer, community partnerships with schools and, 219
negotiation of meaning, second–language development and, 161
Network of Partnership Schools, 220
New Britain School District, 214
New England school districts, 81
New England Superintendents Leadership Council, 81
New York City Board of Education, 82, 83
New York Public Schools, 79
New York State, mandated tests, 79
NNS: nonnative speaker, 12
No Child Left Behind legislation (NCLB legislation), 33, 37, 213, 228, 332
    charter schools, CBO based, 228
    underperforming schools and, 34
North Shore Community College, Massachusetts, 218
Northeast and Islands Regional Laboratory at Brown University, 3, 247
Northwestern University, 206
note–taking skills, 90
Nueva Esperanza, 199
    charter school and, 199
    education services with links to higher education, 199
    largest Latino CBO in Philadelphia, 199
    SeaMar Community Health Centers, 199

O

Office of Health Career Opportunities, 216
Office of Strategic Alliances, Connecticut, 214
on-demand performance rubric, 93
oral conversation skills
    CAR (Collaborative Action Research), 266
oral language patterns, elementary school writing and, 16
oral retell—beginner/newcomer ESL, 91
organizational structure, selecting, 25

P

paragraphs, 92, 98
    framework, 92
Parent Institute for Quality Education (PIQE), San Diego, 200, 327
Parent Teacher Association (PTA), 203
parental involvement, 45
    CBO schools and, 203
    Chinatown, Philadelphia, 225–242
    community organizations and, 225–244
    importance of, 238–240
Parents as Partners curriculum in Spanish and English, 208
partnerships, high school and university, 211–224
pedagogical thinking and teacher talk in a first–grade ELL classroom, 55–78
    academic discourse, 74
    building vocabulary and academic language, 62–66
    daily routines and modeling, 60–62
    feedback and responsiveness, 67–68
    getting and directing student's attention, 62
    grammar and syntax, 66–67
    heterogeneity: strategies that meet the needs of advanced students, 71–72
    language input, 73–74
    language, not watering down, 58
    linguistic interaction, 73
    modeling writing strategies: "When we write, we think," 69
    reflections: making connections to the research, 72–73
    shrinking the task, 72
    talk that teaches phonemic awareness, spelling, and letter recognition, 70–71
    teaching ESL without knowing another language, 59
Pérez, Angela, 109
performance assessment, 82
    strategies, 86
performance inventory
    for multiple paragraph response based on writing prompt, 97
    for note taking, 94
    for notebook, 93, 95
performance rubric for completing task without support, 96
peripheral legitimate participation, 105
Philadelphia, 225, 225–242
    Board of Education, 225
    Chinatown, 225–244
    public schools, 232
Philadelphia Folklore Project, 230
Philadelphia's Chinatown, 225–244
    charter school and, 228, 230, 231, 232

Chinese language and, 226
community meetings and, 228
folk art, 230–231
honoring local knowledge, 229
Pica, Lorraine, 140
Pol Pot regime, Cambodia, 230
policy-implementation studies, 305
poverty, 200
rates of, 208
schools and, 209
practice, 121
teachers' skills and strategies for enacting goals, 121
practices in the classroom: elementary and secondary, recommended for inclusive pedagogy, 317–318
presentation by students, 45–46
Abu and Bernardo present their chart, *46*
Preventing Reading Difficulties in Young Children (Snow, Burns, & Griffin), 264
principal, role of, 241
problem-solving, use of first language and, 174
procedural knowledge, 90
Project Advancement Via Individual Determination (AVID), high school dropout prevention and college enrollment program, 184
Project Performance Assessment Collecting Evidence (PACE), 82
prologue to "Invisible Man," grades 9–adult, 146
public schools, traditional, 203
purpose and audience, defining, 22

R

Randawa, Parminder Stevie, 142, 146, 147
Southern Connecticut State University, 144
reading instruction, components of, 265
reading texts
marginal summaries and, 134
Sample: French occupation of Indochina, history class grades 9 – 12, 135
real language, importance of using, 58–59
reasonable accommodations
ELLs (English Language Learners) and, 8
federal law and, 9
Red Cross, 216
reflection, teaching and, 122
active–interactive, 122
anticipatory (planning), 122
collaborative action research teams, 122
mindfulness, 122
professional development and, 122
recollective, 122

responsive learning environments, building, 245–255
Roll of Thunder, Hear My Cry (Taylor, 1979), 40
Romano, Eileen
approach to teaching ELLs, 55, 55–77
interview with, 55–77
social interactionist theoretical perspective, 72
Roots of War (Vecchione, 1983), 150
Rubeck, Joanne, 33–53, 34, 37
First Steps approach to literacy and language development, 37
rubrics, 100

S

Sagor, Richard, 81
scaffolding, 49, 68, 72, 106
ELLs (English Language Learners), 38
instruction and, 115
learning and teaching, 27–30
student performance and, 112
scaffolding activities, 40, 41, 44–45, 112
minilessons and, 44
scaffolding learning, 27–30, 79
creativity and, 28
rhetorical approach and, 27–30
writing process and, 28
scaffolding strategies, 86
mediating student learning and, 85
scaffolding teaching, 27–30, 30
rhetorical approach and, 30
scaffolding writing, 31
scholarships, 204
school and district reform, 245–317, 328–329
bilingual education for all students, 257–276
fixing the schism between ESL/Bilingual and mainstream teachers, 305–316
inclusive pedagogy in a mandate–driven climate, 317
language or special needs, diagnosing ELLs with achievement difficulties, 277–304
successful schooling for ELLs: building responsive learning environments, 245–256
school choice movement, 204
school lunches, 240
family style dining and, 239–249
schools
community and, 239
discriminatory patterns in, 240–241
hierarchies in, 241
purposes of, 241
toxic structures, 121
underperforming, 34
scientific writing formats and genres, 90

scoring guides
  assessment of student performance and, 88
  selected, 88, 100
SeaMar Community Health Centers
  Alzheimer's care, 199
  Latino culture in, 200
  provide health services to Latinos, 199
second-language acquisition (SLA), 5, 6, 9, 10, 84,
      161
  attention to form and, 162
  beginning speech, 261
  comprehensibility and, 161–162
  content-area proficiency and, 262
  early fluency, 261
  effective teaching of, 108
  fluency, 261
  high school foreign language requirement and,
      206
  interaction and, 167, 174, 178
  literacy development and, 28, 37
  negotiation of meaning and, 162
  pedagogy, 72
  preproduction, 261
  stages and performance expectations, 261, 262
  teacher training in, 312
  teachers' speech and, 73
  theory and, 9, 174
  writing and, 29
second language, ways of referring to
  EFL: English as a foreign language, 12
  ESL: English as a second language, 12
  ESOL: English to speakers of other languages, 12
secondary classroom, 103–196
  academic challenges and opportunities for
      college-bound immigrant youth, 181–196
  developing academic language through an
      abundance of interaction, 167–180
  development of teacher expertise to work with
      adolescent English learners, 103–126
  making mainstream content comprehensible
      through sheltered instruction, 127–166
  teaching, recommended ELL practices, 320
self-knowledge, 121
semantic contingency, 73
senior citizens, community partnerships with
      schools and, 219
sense of audience, 41, 45
sentences, 90, 98
Sesame Street, early literacy tool kit in English and
      Spanish, 208
Shalvey, Don, 205
shared background, 133
shared history, creating, 129, 131
sheltered instruction, 128, 178
  contextualizing lessons and, 133

engagement and, 128
high school and, 217
impact on student performance, 163
interaction and, 128
making content comprehensible, 127–166
research supporting, 161, 163
Training for All Teachers (TAT) program, 128
sheltered instruction observation protocol (SIOP),
      261
  building background, 163
  comprehensibility, 163
  elements of, 163
  interaction, 163
  lesson delivery, 163
  model, 128
  practice and application, 163
  preparation, 163
  review and assessment, 163
  strategies, 163
  students with learning disabilities and, 163
  studies of student performance and, 163
sheltered instruction, research supporting, 161–162
  impact on student performance, 163
  role of comprehensibility and negotiation
      of meaning on second-language
      development, 161–163
sheltered strategies to make content
      comprehensible for ELLS, 158, 158
sheltered strategies to make content
      comprehensible for ELLS, negative
      reactions to, 158–159
small groups, 170–171
smaller learning communities (SLCs), 211, 212,
      216, 218, 327
  advantages to ELLs, 218
  challenges of for ELLs, 218
  ELLs (English Language Learners), 217
  grants to establish in Hartford public high
      schools, 214
  themes and, 212, 216
social change, 229
social mobility, 181
social studies content, immigration and, 19
socialization, language and academic routine, 49
sociocultural expectations, explicit teaching of, 111
sound-symbol correspondence in English and
      Spanish, 29
South Boston High School, 221
Southern Connecticut State University, 144
  Training for All Teachers (TAT) program, 3, 128
Spanish, 107
  knowledge of, 59
  sound-symbol correspondence, 29
Spanish Speaking Unity Council, Oakland, CA, 202

special needs
  challenging the label, 331
  diagnosing ELLs with achievement difficulties, 277–304
Spellings, Margaret, 4
Spelman College, Atlanta, 233
Springfield School District, 37
  Gerena Elementary School, 37
  partnership with University of Massachusetts, 34
St. Francis Hospital and Medical Center, 216
standard practices, transforming to serve need of ELLs, 15–32, 33–52
  city and school context, 37
  finding support and opportunities for dialogue, 34
  introduction, 33
  teaching content for language development, 36
standardized testing. *see* tests, standardized
standards–based curriculum, 33
Standards for Educational and Psychological Testing, 247
State of Connecticut Department of Social Services and, 216
Stoops, Robert E., sketch, reprinted from *Thresholds in Education Journal*, 149
student growth, 90
student identity
  interaction and, 178
student portfolios, 90
student success, 197–210
  community involvement and, 209, 238
  partnerships with community-based organizations and, 197–210
  school and community collaboration and, 197–210
student work, publication of, 42
students
  addressing cultural issues of, 236
  conceptual and academic development of, 106
  experiential background, 107
  funds of knowledge, 38
  getting attention of, 62
  knowledge of, 121
subject matter, cyclical organization of, 110
subject–matter knowledge, 120
  content-area teachers of ELLs and, 120
substantive themes, 110
subtopics, 23–24
summer curriculum grants for teachers to modify units for ELLs, 159
Supreme Court, 160

T
T-list
  ELLs (English Language Learners), 134
  reading, taking notes, and organizing thoughts on, *137*
  reading, taking notes, and organizing thoughts on for history class grades 9–12, 136
teacher education
  Goodlad's national study of, 119
  preservice programs, 119
teacher expertise
  adolescent English language learners, 103–125
  development of, 103–125
teacher expertise, a model for developing, 117
  context, 122
  knowledge, 120
  motivation, 121
  optimal instruction, 119
  practice, 121
  reflection, 121
  students seen as capable individuals, 119
  unpacking the model, *118*
  vision, 119
teacher inquiry and Action Research Teams, guiding questions for, 82
teacher lectures, 188
teacher researchers, 50
teacher strategies to promote adolescent ELL student writing, 174, 175
teacher talk, 75
  mainstream teachers, 175
  native English and nonnative English speakers, 175
  science classrooms in middle and secondary school, 175
teacher training, 119
  ELLs (English Language Learners) and, 5
teacher understanding, development of, 117–118, *118*
teachers
  bilingual, 83
  bilingual education, 312
  ELLs (English Language Learners), 312
  preservice education and, 118
  professional development and, 50, 119, 122, 329
  professional growth and, 118
teachers, nonLatino
  culturally and linguistically competent in teaching Latino kids, 209
teaching assignments
  ELLs (English Language Learners), 121
teaching culturally and linguistically diverse children successfully
  explicit teaching of genre and language features, 36

interweaving of social and academic worlds and literate futures, 36
opportunities for social interaction, 36
publication of students' work, 36
reinforcement of language and content through experiential and multimodal activities, 36
use of authentic contexts, texts, purposes and audiences, 36
use of everyday routines to scaffold a curricular unit, 36
Teaching English to Speakers of Other Languages (TESOL), 324
teaching profession, 121
teaching, reciprocal, 112
teaching, recommended ELL practices, 82
elementary education, 319, 333–335
secondary education, 320
Technology Academy, 211
TESOL, Inc., 5
TESOL: teaching English to speakers of other languages, 11–12
teacher training program for ESL teachers, 12
test formats and tasks, integrating into everyday classroom activities, 84
test-taking strategies, 83–85, 90
test-taking tasks
infusing into lessons, 99
integrating into everyday classroom activities, 79–100
Testa, Immaculata, 136, 137, 138, 140, 142, 150, 154, 156
ESL teachers, 134
testing
authentic, 201
high–stakes, 33
language and, 247
tests, mandated, 79–100
bilingual learners, 79
tasks students need to do to perform on (listed), 85
tests, standardized, 201, 246, 335
modeled language and, 154
taking, 185
texts
decontextualized language and, 111
texts, modification of
highlighted sections, 142
"Invisible Man," English Literature, 11th grade, 147
The Invisible Man (Ralph Elison), 142
Julius Caesar, 144, 148
margin summaries, 142
preserving well-known lines and, 161
rewritten text, 142, 147, 148
to supplement authentic text, 142

"The Highwayman," 145, 149
The Invisible Man (Ralph Ellison), 142
theory of inquiry, 80
think-pair-share exercise, 130
Threshold Hypothesis (Cummins), 263
time lines and summary outlines, 140
The Contender (novel), 140, 143
events in Indochina, history grades 9–12, 143
TOEFL: Test of English as a Foreign Language, 11–12
test for foreign students to demonstrate competency in English, 12
"Top Ten Tips for Improving High Schools"
Inside High School reform: Making the Changes That Matter (Jordan Horowitz), 222
topic, narrowing
subtopics and, 22
vertically, 22
tracking, children of color and, 49
traditional public schools and, 209
as only charter school authorizer in the state, 205
Training for All Teachers (TAT) program
grant, 127
sheltered instruction and, 128
Southern Connecticut State University, 128
Twenty-First Century School Program Grant, 203

U

university and educational institutions, community partnerships with schools and, 211–224, 219
University of Connecticut, 325–326. see also Health Professions Academy
Bulkeley High School, 212
Health Center, 214
Mini Medical Series, 216
partnerships with Hartford high schools, 214
University of Massachusetts, partnership with Springfield School District, 34
University of Texas, 209
U.S. classrooms, First Steps approach to literacy and language development, 37
U.S. Congress, 258
U.S. Department of Education, 203
Office of English Language Acquisition, 4, 127
report on Quality teachers, 332
survey of teachers, 4
Title VII grant, 3, 128
U.S. Department of Labor, 181
U.S. Supreme Court, 307

V

Verizon, 208
Verplaetse, Lorrie, 3
Verplaetse study, 169–170
Vietnam War, 229
vision, teachers and
    ELLs (English Language Learners), 119
    optimal instruction and, 119
    of students as capable individuals, 119
    view of minority students and, 119
visuals, use of, 131, 133
vocabulary, authentic, 64
vouchers
    independent schools and, 204
    public schools and, 234

W

Warren, Justice Earl, test scores and, 245
Way Out in the Desert, 96
Wei, Deborah, 225–244
    interview with, 225–242
Wesleyan University, 214
WestEd, 122
When I Was Puerto Rican (Esmeralda Santiago), 108
White Teacher (Vivian Gussin Paley), 247
Why Are All the Black Kids Sitting Together in the Cafeteria (Beverly Tatum), 236
Willett, Jerri, 36
Wolpert, Ellen, 237
word mapping, 20
    word family map, 20, *21*
word walls, 150
    elementary classroom, 150
    secondary classrooms and, 150
wraparound services, 327
writing
    elementary classroom, 15
    formats and genres, 90
    nationwide standards and, 177
    student skill and, 83
writing competencies, 90
writing, content in
    bilingual learners and, 28
    cultural funds of knowledge and, 28
    elementary classroom and, 28
writing instruction, a scaffolded approach, 15–32
    from inquiry to practice: the rhetorical approach, 17
    language, oral-like to written-like, 16
writing instruction, recommendations for, 177
writing instruction, the rhetorical approach, 15, 17–18
    back to step 3: exploring subtopics, 24
    benefits of, 30, 31
    elementary classroom and, 31
    in a fourth-grade classroom, 18, *19*
    general steps in, 18
    good teaching habits and, 31
    improvement and, 17
    sidestep 1: concept and word mapping, 19–20
    sidestep 2: what's a subtopic, 23
    sidestep 3: how to locate specific information, 25
    sidestep 4: attending to individual needs of bilingual learners, 26–27
    step 1: explore a general topic, 19
    step 2: define purpose and audience, 22
    step 3: narrow the topic, 22–23
    step 4: select information, 25
    step 5: select genre and organizational structure, 25–26
    step 6: organize material and draft, 26
    step 7: revise, 27
    step 8: prepare a final copy, 27
    support for students learning English, 31
    teaching and, 30
    writing and, 28, 31
writing opportunities, abundance of, 177–178
    ELLs (English Language Learners), 177
writing process, 38, 42
    final copy, preparing, 27
    freewriting, 19
    revising, 27
    rhetorical approach and, 18
writing strategies, modeling, 49
written academic text, making it comprehensible, 139–145
    graphic organizers, 139
    margin summaries or highlighted sections, 142
    modification of text, 142
    rewritten text, 142–145
    timelines and summary outlines, *140*
written language, 16
    American, 112
    British, 112
    Spanish, 112

Z

zone of proximal development (ZPD), 74, 108